STRANGE FIRE

STRANGE FIRE

Reading the Bible after the Holocaust

edited by
Tod Linafelt

New York University Press
Washington Square, New York

First published in the USA in 2000 by
NEW YORK UNIVERSITY PRESS
Washington Square
New York, NY 10003

Library of Congress Cataloging-in-Publication Data
Strange fire: reading the Bible after the Holocaust / edited by Tod Linafelt.
p. cm.
Includes bibliographical references and index.
ISBN 0-8147-5165-2 (alk. paper)—ISBN 0-8147-5166-0 (pbk. : alk. paper)
1. Bible. O.T.–Criticism, interpretation, etc. 2. Holocaust, Jewish
(1939–1945)—Influence. 3. Bible. O.T.—Hermeneutics. 4. Suffering—Biblical
teaching.
I. Linafelt, Tod, 1965–
BS1171.2.S77 2000
221.6'09'045—dc21

Printed on acid-free paper in Great Britain
by Antony Rowe Ltd
Chippenham, Wiltshire

CONTENTS

Notes on Contributors   9

Acknowledgments   14

Introduction: Strange Fires, Ancient and Modern
    Tod Linafelt   15 ✓

PART I: ISSUES IN POST-HOLOCAUST INTERPRETATION

Matters of Survival: A Conversation
    Elie Wiesel and Timothy K. Beal   22 ✓

Rupture and Context: The Ethical Dimensions of a
Post-Holocaust Biblical Hermeneutics
    Chris Boesel   36 ✓

Rabbinic Bible Interpretation after the Holocaust
    B. Barry Levy   52 ✓

A Fissure Always Uncontained
    Walter Brueggemann   62 ✓

The Hebrew Bible in the Framework of Christian–Jewish
Relations in Post-Holocaust Germany
    Rolf Rendtorff   76 ✓

Of Faith and Faces: Biblical Texts, Holocaust Testimony and
German 'After Auschwitz' Theology
    Björn Krondorfer   86 ✓

Beyond Totality: The Shoah and the Biblical Ethics of
Emmanuel Levinas
    O.E. Ajzenstat   106

Edmond Jabès and the Question of Death
    Matthew del Nevo   121

PART II: ENGAGING BIBLICAL TEXTS IN LIGHT OF THE HOLOCAUST

Avraham, Emil and Andre: Re-Reading Avraham's Monologue
with the Divine in Light of Fackenheim and Neher
    Steven L. Jacobs   136

Banality and Sacrifice
    Roland Boer   146

Written in Stone: Biblical Quotation in the
United States Holocaust Memorial Museum
    Jennifer L. Koosed   161

Am I a Murderer? Judges 19–21 as a Parable of
Meaningless Suffering
    Katharina von Kellenbach   176

'Isaiah 'Twas Foretold It': Helping the Church Interpret
the Prophets
    Patricia K. Tull   192

Isaiah and Theodicy after the *Shoah*
    Marvin A. Sweeney   208

The Covenant with Death
    Francis Landy   220

Job and Auschwitz
    Richard L. Rubenstein   233

Job and Post-Holocaust Theodicy
    Stephen Kepnes 252

Zion's Cause: The Presentation of Pain in the
Book of Lamentations
    Tod Linafelt 267

Death as the Beginning of Life in the Book of Ecclesiastes
    Mark K. George 280

Suggestions for Further Reading 294
Index of Biblical References 296
Index of Authors 301

NOTES ON CONTRIBUTORS

O.E. Ajzenstat is a SSHRC Fellow in the Department of Political Science at the University of Toronto, teaching courses in modern Jewish philosophy and its relation to continental thought. Ajzenstat's dissertation, written at McMaster University, treats Emmanuel Levinas's cullings from and reflections on the Bible, the Kabbalah (Abulafia, Luria, Volozhin) and the Talmud—all from the perspective of his relation with the Holocaust.

Timothy K. Beal is Harkness Chair of Biblical Studies at Case Western Reserve University, and has been a visiting lecturer at the University of Glasgow's Centre for the Study of Literature and Theology. He is the author of *The Book of Hiding: Gender, Ethnicity, Annihilation and Esther* (Routledge, 1997) and of a commentary on the book of Esther in the Berit Olam series (Liturgical Press), co-editor of *Reading Bibles, Writing Bodies* (Routledge, 1997) and *God in the Fray* (Fortress Press, 1998), and he has published recent articles in journals such as *Semeia* and *Biblical Interpretation*.

Roland Boer completed his graduate study at McGill University and is now lecturer in Hebrew Bible and World Religions at United Theological College in Sydney, Australia. He is the author of *Jameson and Jeroboam* (1996) and *Novel Histories* (1997). Currently, he is completing a book for Routledge Press on the Hebrew Bible and Popular Culture and one for Sheffield Academic Press on postcolonialism and the Bible in Australia.

Chris Boesel is a PhD candidate at Emory University and holds a Diploma in Jewish Studies from the University of Oxford (The Centre for Hebrew and Jewish Studies). He has authored numerous papers and book reviews on philosophical theology and is currently researching the role of the Holocaust in post-structuralist thought.

Walter Brueggemann is William Marcellus McPheeters Professor of Old Testament at Columbia Theological Seminary. He is the author of dozens of books and articles on biblical interpretation and biblical theology, including most recently *Theology of the Old Testament: Testimony, Dispute, Advocacy* (Fortress Press, 1997). He is a past president of the Society of Biblical Literature.

Mark George is assistant professor of Hebrew Bible at the Iliff School of Theology. A graduate of Princeton Theological Seminary, his teaching and research interests include the narrative and wisdom texts of the Hebrew Bible, biblical theology, and the use of contemporary theoretical approaches (postmodernism, feminism, and ideological and cultural criticisms) in reading the Bible. His current research interests include constructions of identity in the Hebrew Bible, particularly as those constructions are evidenced in the Deuteronomistic History and the Priestly materials.

Steven L. Jacobs serves as the Rabbi of Temple B'nai Sholom of Huntsville, AL, and as Zimmerman Judaic Scholar in Residence at Martin Methodist College, Pulaski, TN. He received his BA (with Distinction) from the Pennsylvania State University, and his BHL, MAHL, DHL and Rabbinic Ordination from the Hebrew Union College-Jewish Institute of Religion, Cincinnati, OH. Author or more than 50 articles and reviews dealing primarily with the Shoah/ Holocaust, his books include *Shirot Bialik: A New and Annotated Translation of Chaim Nachman Bialik's Epic Poems* (1987); *Not Guilty? Raphael Lemkin's Thoughts on Nazi Genocide* (1992); *Rethinking Jewish Faith: The Child of a Survivor Responds* (1993); *Contemporary Christian and Contemporary Jewish Religious Responses to the Shoah (1994); The Holocaust Now: Contemporary Christian and Jewish Thought* (1997); and *The Meaning of Persons and Things Jewish: Contemporary Interpretations and Explorations* (1998).

Stephen Kepnes is associate professor of philosophy and religion and director of Jewish Studies at Colgate University. He earned his MA and PhD degrees at the University of Chicago. He received a Mellon post-doctoral grant from 1986 to 1988 and was a visiting scholar at the Hebrew University and at the Shalom Hartman Institute for Advanced Jewish Studies from 1993 to 1995. He is the author of *Reasoning after*

Revelation: Dialogues in Postmodern Jewish Philosophy (with Peter Ochs and Robert Gibbs); *Interpreting Judaism in a Postmodern Age*; *The Text as Thou: Martin Buber's Dialogical Hermeneutics and Narrative Theology*; and editor, with David Tracy, of *The Challenge of Psychology to Faith*. His articles on Jewish thought have appeared in such journals as *The Journal of Jewish Studies, Soundings* and *Harvard Theological Review*.

Jennifer Koosed is a PhD candidate in Hebrew Bible at Vanderbilt Divinity School, and holds a Diploma in Jewish Studies from the University of Oxford (The Centre for Hebrew and Jewish Studies). She has published articles in the journal *Semeia* and the edited volume *Imagining Otherness: Filmic Visions of Community* (Scholars Press, 1999).

Katharina von Kellenbach is assistant professor of Religious Studies at St Mary's College of Maryland, a public honors college. A native of West Germany, she studied Evangelical Theology in Berlin and Göttingen (1979–82) and received her PhD from the religion department at Temple University in Philadelphia in 1990. Her dissertation, *Anti-Judaism in Feminist Religious Writings,* was published in the Cultural Criticism Series of Scholars Press in 1994. She has since worked on reconstructing the life and work of the first ordained female rabbi, Regina Jonas (1902–44), whose papers she discovered in an archive in former East Germany. Her areas of expertise are feminist theology and Jewish–Christian relations, as well as women's history, especially during the Holocaust. She has published articles on Christian anti-Judaism, Jewish and Christian women's ordination, and women's resistance to the Holocaust.

Björn Krondorfer is assistant professor of religious studies at St Mary's College of Maryland. His field of expertise is religion and culture, with an emphasis on gender studies, cultural studies, and Holocaust studies. He is the author of *Remembrance and Reconciliation: Encounters between Young Jews and Germans* (Yale, 1995), and editor of *Men's Bodies, Men's Gods: Male Identities in a (Post-) Christian Culture* (NYU, 1996) and *Body and Bible: Interpreting and Experiencing Biblical Narratives* (Trinity, 1992). He has edited, with an afterword, Edward Gastfriend's *My Father's Testament: Memoirs of a Jewish Teenager, 1938–1945* (Temple, 2000). He has published articles in (among others) *Journal of Ritual Studies, Semeia, Journal of Men's Studies, Literature and Theology,* and *English Education.*

Francis Landy is professor of religious studies at the University of Alberta. He has published two books, one on the Song of Songs (*Paradoxes of Paradise: Identity and Difference in the Song of Songs* [Sheffield Almond Press, 1983]) and one on Hosea for the *Readings* commentary series, published by Sheffield Academic Press. He has published numerous articles, mostly on the literary interpretation of the Bible, including essays in *The Literary Guide to the Bible* (Harvard, 1987) and the *Journal of the American Academy of Religion.* He is currently at work on a book on Isaiah. Future projects include a commentary on Amos and a collection of essays.

B. Barry Levy is Dean of the Faculty of Religious Studies and Professor of Biblical and Jewish Studies at McGill University and has taught at Brown University and Yeshiva University. His publications include the two-volume *Neofiti Targum* (McGill-Queens) and *Plants, Potions and Parchments* (McGill-Queens). He translated a tractate of the Babylonian Talmud for Scholars Press and has written numerous articles on the history of Jewish biblical interpretation.

Rolf Rendtorff is professor emeritus at the University of Heidelberg (Germany). His numerous publications include *The Problem of the Process of Transmission in the Pentateuch* (1977, English Translation 1990). *The Old Testament: An Introduction* (1983, ET 1985), *Canon and Theology: Overtures to an Old Testament Theology* (1991, ET 1993), and *Theologie des Alten Testaments: Einen kanonischer Entwurf, vol. 1* (1998, ET in preparation).

Richard Rubenstein is the author of numerous books, including *After Auschwitz, Morality and Eros, The Age of Triage* and *The Cunning of History,* as well as dozens of articles in the field of Jewish Studies. He is President Emeritus of the University of Bridgeport, where he now directs the Centre for the Study of Ethics, Religion and International Affairs.

Marvin A. Sweeney is Professor of Hebrew Bible at the Claremont School of Theology and Professor of Religion at the Claremont Graduate University. He has also served as a faculty member or visiting fellow at the University of Miami, Hebrew University of Jerusalem, the W.F. Albright Institute for Archaeological Research, Hebrew Union College—Jewish Institute of Religion, Los Angeles, and the Lilly Theological Endowment. He holds the PhD from Claremont Graduate School, and he is the author of numerous books and studies in the fields of biblical and Jewish studies. His commentary on Isaiah 1–39 was published in 1996 in the Forms of the Old Testament Literature Commentary Series.

Patricia K. Tull is Associate Professor of Old Testament, Louisville Presbyterian Theological Seminary, Louisville KY. Her book *Remember the Former Things: The Recollection of Previous Texts in Second Isaiah* was published by Scholars Press in 1997. She is the author of numerous articles, chapters and book reviews on topics in biblical interpretation.

Elie Wiesel is the author of more than 30 books, including *Night*, *The Accident*, *A Beggar in Jerusalem* (winner of the Prix Medicis), *The Forgotten* and *From the Kingdom of Memory*. The first volume of his *Memoirs* appeared in English in 1995 and the second volume in 1999. He has been awarded the Presidential Medal of Freedom, the US Congressional Gold Medal, the French Legion of Honor, and, in 1986, the Nobel Peace Prize. He is Andrew W. Mellon Professor in the Humanities and University Professor at Boston University.

ACKNOWLEDGMENTS

Portions of Tod Linafelt's article, 'Zion's Cause: The Presentation of Pain in Lamentations', are reprinted from *Surviving Lamentations: Catastrophe, Lament, and Protest in the Afterlife of a Biblical Book.* Copyright © 2000 by The University of Chicago Press. All rights reserved.

An earlier version of Richard Rubenstein's article, 'Job and Auschwitz', originally appeared in *Union Seminary Quarterly Review* 25 (1970), and is reprinted in revised form here by permission of the author.

INTRODUCTION:
STRANGE FIRES, ANCIENT AND MODERN

Tod Linafelt

Into the well-ordered catalogue of sacrifices in the opening chapters of the book of Leviticus irrupts the strange story of Nadab and Abihu.

> The sons of Aaron, Nadab and Abihu, each took his pan and kindled fire in it. They placed incense on it, and they brought near to the Lord a strange fire which he had not commanded them. And fire came forth from before the Lord and it consumed them, and they died before the Lord (10.1-2).[1]

Fire, earlier a sign of God's blessing in Leviticus, here destroys the two young priests. Indeed, the fire that comes forth to incinerate the sons of Aaron is described in precisely the same terms as the fire that came forth to incinerate the burnt offering in the previous chapter.

> And fire came forth from before the Lord and it consumed the burnt offering and the fat parts on the altar. All the people watched, and they shouted and fell on their faces (9.24).

The term for 'burnt offering' in the Hebrew is *'olah*, literally 'that which goes up' (up 'in smoke' in other words). The Hebrew *'olah* becomes in Greek the adjectival form *holocaustos*, or 'wholly burnt'. Nadab and Abihu thus become in Leviticus 10—to put it bluntly— human burnt offerings, or 'holocausts'.

What could have occasioned this drastic response on the part of God? (Or as the Midrash *Leviticus Rabbah* states with incredulity: 'Even Titus, wicked as he was, could venture into the Holy of Holies, slash both veils, and go forth in peace. But Aaron's sons, who came into the tabernacle to present an offering, were taken out burnt?') The narrative refuses to yield its secrets in regard to this question. The only seeming

---

1. Translations from the Hebrew of the biblical text are my own.

clue given the reader is the enigmatic reference to a 'strange fire' (*'esh zarah* in the Hebrew) offered by Nadab and Abihu; yet as numerous interpreters have found, this phrase conceals more than it reveals. Scanning the commentaries on this passage one finds a host of speculations as to what is meant by 'strange fire', including pagan incense, fire kindled by human means rather than taken from the fire burning on the altar, a private incense offering, coals taken from an unauthorized oven, and even Zoroastrian cultic practices. The upshot of all these conjectures about the referent of 'strange fire' is that the blame for their deaths is laid upon the priests themselves. These conjectures are, in other words, thinly veiled attempts to distract the reader from the equally strange (if ultimately more destructive) fire from God. If one can solve the puzzle of what particular cultic malpractice Nadab and Abihu are guilty of, the unexpressed logic seems to be, then one need not allow God's destructive presence here to go unmotivated.

Commentators have thus worked hard to downplay or even to completely expunge the 'strangeness' of this text, rather than recognizing that such strangeness is intrinsic to the way the narrative both produces and frustrates meaning for the reader. For just as the various explanations of the strange fire fail to convince, so too does the motivation for God's burning of the two priests continue to elude us. Even the attempt by Moses, at the scene itself, to put some sort of theological spin on this horrific event falls flat.

> Then Moses said to Aaron, 'This is what the Lord meant when he said,
> "Through my near-ones I shall be holy,
> and before all the people I shall gain glory"' (10.3).

Perhaps like all theodicies, this cryptic oracle offered by Moses proves inadequate to the tragedy it addresses. How, one might ask, are we to understand God's holiness as being contingent on God's 'near-ones'? Do we follow Rashbam and Ramban who interpret this statement to mean 'I shall be *treated* as holy'? Or does the death of Nadab and Abihu somehow serve to actually sanctify God, as a more recent commentator has claimed? And in what way are we to understand God as gaining glory from the incident? Through a bullying of the witnesses? The oracle is finally unconvincing. Moreover, I do not think this is simply a case of imposing later ethical standards upon the text, nor of a 'hermeneutics of suspicion' that reads against the grain of the story, for the narrative itself works to subvert Moses' tendency toward explanation. In the first place, one notices almost immediately that Moses' attempt at explanation is met by posture of resistance on the part of Aaron—'But Aaron remained silent' (10.3). And secondly, upon looking more closely one may also notice that while Moses presents his theodicy as a quotation of God, in fact the oracle is nowhere to be found elsewhere in the canon of the Bible. The surety of Moses' tone begins to sound like a cover for uncertainty.

Questions lead to more questions in this story. The closer one reads, the more perplexing—the more 'strange'—things become. God's 'holocaust' of Nadab and Abihu continues to provoke and disturb and unsettle the reader; not because one fails to understand it properly, but rather because one understands all too well.

Attributed to God in this story, the word 'holocaust' is jarring, since in the second half of the twentieth century we have begun putting a capital letter on the word and using it to describe the attempt by Nazi Germany to annihilate European Jewry, an attempt that resulted in the actual murder of an estimated six million Jews. And so we move from holocaust to Holocaust, from the strange fire of an ancient story to the strange fire of modern genocide. As the biblical term 'holocaust' is simultaneously both appropriate and inappropriate to refer to Nazi genocide, so too does the biblical phrase 'strange fire' seem to function as a tenuous connector between ancient and modern. While it certainly is the case that not all those who perished in the Holocaust ended up in the crematoria, nor even in the death-camps (many died in front of firing squads or on forced marches; many starved to death or died from disease; many were killed as part of resistance movements), it is nevertheless the image of fire that has become the most arresting symbol of the Holocaust. The symbol no doubt owes much to the ovens of Auschwitz-Birkenau and the pits at other killing centers where the bodies of the victims were burned, yet it also derives from the figurative sense of a nearly all-consuming destruction. That is, by the time Hitler and Nazism had finally been defeated, fully two-thirds of European Jewry and one-third of world Jewry had perished, and an entire way of life (especially for Jews of Eastern Europe) had been consumed. It is certainly not too much to call this modern fire 'strange' as well. As Elie Wiesel once put it, 'I who was there still do not understand'. Neither is it necessary to engage in well-worn arguments for or against the 'uniqueness' of the Holocaust—whether in historical, philosophical, or ideological terms—in order to claim it as a datum of great significance for our present historical horizon.

The guiding conviction behind the present volume is that these two—ancient text and modern atrocity—can, and indeed must, be brought to bear on one another. The goal of this volume certainly is not to show that the Bible provides the theological or ethical resources for 'understanding' or 'explaining' the Holocaust. The Holocaust is too complex, too massive, and too much the product of the twentieth century for such an approach to have integrity. At the same time the volume is not intended to demonstrate that biblical notions of God and humanity, good and evil, or suffering and survival, are now bankrupt or irrelevant or somehow proven wrong. For as my brief comments on Leviticus 10 above are meant to show, the Bible is itself at times endlessly complex, massively disturbing, and not so far removed from the concerns of the twentieth century as one might expect of an ancient text. Rather, what all the contributors to the volume hold in common, despite a great diversity both in their approaches to understanding the Holocaust and their approaches to interpreting the Bible, is that the two can only exist in a sort of uneasy dialectical relationship (what Theodor Adorno refers to as a *negative* dialectic) in which both must be taken into account but in which neither is finally able to absorb or to nullify the other. In this way, the strangeness of each is preserved, even as we are allowed to apprehend, if not comprehend, that strangeness in a new way.

A browser in the bookstore, upon spying this book, might be forgiven for thinking, 'Not another book on the Holocaust!' Indeed, while for decades there was very little written about the subject, we have in more recent years been inundated with books dealing with seemingly every aspect of it. It is now common to find in bookstores or catalogues that a section on Holocaust studies is nearly equal in size to a more general section on Judaica that encompasses all of Jewish history and literature. Yet within either section one searches in vain for a sustained treatment of how an engagement with the Holocaust might affect the way one reads the Bible. Emil Fackenheim's brief book from 1990, *The Jewish Bible after the Holocaust,* raises the central issues in a pointed way but does not offer the sort of in-depth theoretical reflection or close attention to texts that is needed to advance the discussion. (For bibliographic information on Fackenheim's book and on the few other works that incorporate elements of post-Holocaust biblical interpretation, see the section on Suggestions for Further Reading in the present volume.)

Thus we are bold enough to imagine that *Strange Fire: Reading the*

Bible after the Holocaust offers something that is missing from the many fine books published over the years on the Holocaust—even those on religious or philosophical dimensions, which typically make little mention of the Bible—namely, a sustained consideration of how the Holocaust has affected, or should affect, the way we read the Bible. The contributors include world-renowned senior scholars in Jewish Studies and Biblical Studies (including a Nobel prize winner and a past president of the Society of Biblical Literature), as well as younger scholars on the cutting edge of new approaches in both disciplines. The result is a volume in which the nascent interdisciplinary practice of post-Holocaust biblical interpretation is not only refined and advanced, but is also made more complex and, on occasion, criticized from within. My hope is that after reading this book one's thinking about both the Bible and the Holocaust will be challenged and complicated; and one should not be surprised if the strangeness of each persists.

Part I

ISSUES IN POST-HOLOCAUST INTERPRETATION

MATTERS OF SURVIVAL: A CONVERSATION

Elie Wiesel and Timothy K. Beal

The following conversation took place on 19 March 1999, at Eckerd College in St Petersburg, Florida. The planned topic for the conversation was 'The Bible after the Holocaust'.

Tim Beal: As I read your *Memoirs* and other autobiographical writings, I am very much aware of the relationship between *remembering* and *surviving*. Surviving is, most literally, 'living over', or 'living through'. Living through is very different than living beyond. Living beyond is forgetting, living in oblivion. So survival is in some sense about not forgetting, resisting oblivion. The survivor takes something of what she or he survives into the present.

Elie Wiesel: Yes. Survival is living through. In Hebrew, the word is *sarid*. *Palit* is a refugee, or escapee. *Sarid* is one who does not escape— the battle or the slaughter, for example—but survives it, lives through it.

One never leaves the past behind. Because the past is in the present. And without the past, the present would be empty. So it is a matter of balance. Which is stronger—the past or the present? If the past overtakes the present, then the present itself becomes part of the past, and it becomes impossible to live. One carries the past. One can be carried by the past for only so long.

This is the problem with prolonged mourning, which is forbidden in the Talmud. The laws concerning mourning in Jewish tradition make it a gradual process. On the first day, the mourning is total. There is complete inaction, even non-being. All the positive *mitzvot* (commandments) are abolished on this day. Of course, the negative laws (for example, 'do not kill') are not abolished. But still it is total. You are non-being. The sages understood that in the presence of the dead, nothing can be said or done. After the first day, there is a period of seven days, during which the mourning is slightly less intense, though still the one mourning is nearly inactive. Then there is a period of thirty days, and then a whole year. After that, one is to mourn only one day each year. Thus mourning for the destruction of the Temple takes place only once each year. Likewise *Yom ha-Shoah*, the Holocaust memorial day. We are not supposed to mourn all the time. Why? Because we are told that the *Shekinah* (divine presence) does not rest in a person who is mourning. Why did prophecy stop the first time? Because of the sadness. The prophets made the people too sad. God does not want that.

Therefore, survival means what? Living over, living *through*.

Study

TB: As a survivor of the Holocaust—one who lives through but never beyond it—what has been the importance of continuing to read, teach, and write about the Tanakh, Talmud, Midrash, and other Jewish Scriptures?

EW: Really, whatever I have is from studying these texts. For me, study is a matter of survival. I study these texts in order to survive.

TB: And, I think, in order that they may survive into a new context. In your essays, especially those you've written on biblical characters such as Noah and Job, the midrashic and talmudic traditions often provide you with responses to elements in the biblical stories that you find frustrating. In particular, they allow you to open up the *silence* and what appears initially to be the passivity of many of these characters. For example, you are able to understand the silence of Job after the divine speech from the whirlwind as a defiant silence.

EW: Also the silence of Aaron, after his sons Nadab and Abihu are killed by fire from God (Lev. 10). With the sages we make it a positive silence—*wayyiddom 'aharon* ('and Aaron was silent' or 'stunned'). It is not interpreted as passive or disinterested, but as a statement in itself. What could he say? What can be said? This is what his silence says. It is a kind of advice to us: In certain situations, silence is best.

If silence occupies such an important place in my life, it is not only because of Job and Aaron but also Abraham, who was silent in the *Akedah* (the binding of Isaac, Gen. 22). His brief and cryptic response to Isaac's question, 'Where is the lamb for the burnt offering?', is the last thing he says. In fact, nothing more is said by either Abraham or

Isaac. From that point onward, Isaac has become the willing victim. In fact, the Talmud says that after Abraham lowered Isaac down on the altar, Isaac actually helped his father. He lay down on the altar and helped Abraham bind his hands. So the binding is Isaac's doing as well. What does it mean? Why doesn't Isaac shout? Why doesn't he cry out to God, 'help me! if you want to!' Abraham was told by God to sacrifice Isaac. Isaac could have said, 'Look, if it is me you want, then speak to me!' But he said nothing.

Here, moreover, we find a connection between Isaac and Job. At no point were either Isaac or Job told the truth. They are never told what God wants from them, why God is doing this to them. Elihu gives his own answer, that God is just and that one must not question God's ways. But this is unacceptable. I don't want his answer; I want to maintain the question.

So, I take a great deal from the Midrash and Talmud, but I don't take the answers so much as the questions. I draw out the answers of the sages, but in order to question them and thereby to go deeper into the biblical text. The text survives into the present situation through our attention to the questions.

TB: And the best questions will always survive—live *through*—their answers.

EW: Yes. And in that interplay of questions and answers within Scripture and interpretation, one's sense of time changes. The past is in the present. And what is the time of God? In my novels I often play with relations between past and present.

TB: In a lecture you gave at Eckerd College just before publishing the first volume of your memoirs, *All Rivers Run to the Sea*, you began with a brief meditation on Proust. Does his writing resonate with yours with regard to time and remembrance?

EW: I admire Proust's work very much, but it is very different than mine. His writing is a kind of extension. I, on the other hand, work at concentration, condensation, and contraction. Something like *tsimtsum* (contraction) in the Kabbalah.

TB: In the Kabbalistic creation story to which you refer, the *tsimtsum*, or contraction, precedes the ultimate explosion—the *shevirat ha-kelim*, or 'breaking of the vessels'. And this is creation, a story of divine creativity through a kind of contracting or condensing that ultimately breaks up.

EW: Yes. It is like the 'Big Bang', only much more poetic.

TB: Do you feel that the contraction in your writing leads ultimately to an explosion, a breaking forth?

EW: Silence is always breaking up. When you finally speak, when you open up, you break.

TB: One breaks the silence. Silence is broken. Writing attends to silence and to its breaking. So writing is a kind of contracting and exploding. This is the creative process in writing.

You mentioned the silence of Abraham and Isaac earlier, and in the opening paragraph of *Messengers of God*, you recall crying with Isaac on the altar when you were a child. Indeed, you have often recalled the prominence of biblical stories in your childhood: learning from the wandering Maggidim, laughing at Joseph as prince of Egypt, and so on. And of course you have written much about these stories in your adulthood. Yet there are few echoes to biblical texts or themes in the *univers concentrationnaire* of *Night*. Do you recall any particular biblical texts being prominent in your mind during that terrible experience?

EW: Not at the time. Really, my questions in relation to biblical texts came later. In our home, we studied *Chumash* (the books of the Torah) regularly from a very young age. Mainly, we studied Torah. I knew the prophets, but primarily from the many quoted passages in the Talmud. I did not actually sit down and study Isaiah or Jeremiah, for example, until much later.

TB: It has been suggested that *Night* is in some sense an inverted *Akedah*.

EW: What is our *Akedah*? In our *Akedah*, the father does not return. The child returns alone. This is the *Akedah* of our generation. In the camps, the children were often stronger, more resilient, than their elders. So Isaac came back, and left Abraham. Because he was old.

On Rosh Hashanah we remember the *Akedah*, and we call on God to remember the *Akedah* as well. Why? Abraham *knew* that it was a test. Otherwise he would not have agreed to it. Therefore it was a time of testing for both Abraham and God. 'You will test me, I will test you. You want me to go? I will go.' So it is God, not Abraham, who gives in. 'Do not lay your hand on the child!' Abraham was thinking, 'What did you promise me? Descendants. Whose descendants would they have been if this child had been sacrificed? I could have asked you these questions, but I did not. Now you promise me something: whenever my children remember the *Akedah*, you remember my children.' That is why on Rosh Hashanah we remember the *Akedah*, and why we call on God to remember it as well.

Storytelling

TB: Remembering and survival are of course closely related to the art of storytelling in your life and work.

EW: I believe in storytelling. The original French editions of all my books on Bible, Talmud, Midrash and Hasidism are called *celebrations*—a biblical celebration, a talmudic celebration, a midrashic celebration, a hasidic celebration. In hasidic tradition, the role of storytelling is central. It is an act of imagination. I can see Abraham and Isaac on Mt Moriah, I can see them before me. I can see Jacob mourning for his son. We do not believe in graven images, but we do believe in imaging the texts, and the texts are so rich in images.

TB: In *Messengers of God*, you write that the aim of the storyteller is to transmit what has been received, to return what has been entrusted, 'to reacquaint himself with the distant and haunting figures that molded him'. It seems to me that we could go further, and say that one's role as storyteller is also to *acquaint these ancient biblical tales* with the distant and haunting figures of their *future*, especially the Holocaust, its victims, and its survivors. When I read your 'celebrations' of the biblical figures I often have the sense that their future—our time, your time—is haunting them. In the act of storytelling, the past is always being haunted by its future, which it in no way expected or anticipated.

EW: The Midrash will often do this in the most explicit way, having earlier figures return from the dead in order to address a new historical situation. In *Lamentations Rabbah*, for example, we read of Jeremiah, despairing over the imminent demise of the country, calling out to the tombs of the patriarchs, 'wake up, wake up, wake up'. He divined them.

TB: Like the prophet, the storyteller is a kind of diviner, and the story is a kind of divination of the past into the present moment. The root sense of 'spell', as in casting a spell, is 'story'. The storyteller casts a spell between past and present, present and future. It is magical.

Teaching

TB: Your three well-known volumes of biblical and rabbinic portraits, *Messengers of God*, *Five Biblical Portraits* and *Sages and Dreamers*, are remarkable for the way in which Scripture, the history of interpretation, and personal experience intersect within the telling of the tale. I have used each of these books in college courses, and find that students respond very well to them. They provoke careful and self-critical attention to the details of the texts we are studying. They also raise powerful questions with regard to how our readings of these texts must change at the turn of the twentieth century, especially in the wake of the Holocaust. These books were published over a number of years. Where and how did they begin?

EW: They began as lectures at the YMCA in New York—the 92nd Street Y, about 35 years ago. In the beginning I committed to giving four lectures, but it became a permanent thing quickly. So each year, the first lecture would be on the Bible, the second on Talmud, the third on Hasidic tradition, and then the fourth would bring them all together and show how they influence me. And I gave four lectures per year for 25 years. Actually, I intended to stop many times. At 15 years I stopped. Then at 20, I thought that I had had enough. Then at 25 years. Now it has been over 30 years. At this point, however, I give only one or two each year. But I may start lecturing regularly again. Because I love to teach. I love to study.

Lecturing like this requires a great deal of time and focus. Before I do a lecture, I do a lot of research. I work through all the texts, all the sources. I study and study and study. I do so to this day. Then I decide on the subject of the lecture. I gather all the materials together, and try to let them speak to me.

TB: Did you write the lectures in French?

EW: Always in French, and then Marion (Wiesel) translates. I usually write out about half the lecture, and then have notes for the rest. The body is there.

TB: You and I share a love for teaching. In what sense, if at all, did you see these lectures as an opportunity, and in what sense an obligation?

EW: The opportunity became obligation, though always a pleasant obligation—to teach, and therefore to study. Of course I have always studied, but this was an opportunity and obligation to lecture to large audiences. I do not like public speaking. I like to teach in small classes. But they asked, and I said that I would try. I agreed to give four lectures over the course of a year. The first I shared with somebody else. She was the first to speak, and when she finished, everyone got up and left! Those who came for her lecture did not stay for mine.

TB: I can relate to that experience.

EW: It was a pleasant obligation, because I knew that for every year I participated, I would spend at least two years studying all the texts. Later I had a teacher, Saul Lieberman, who knew all the sources. He was a true scholar. I dedicated *Messengers of God* to him. I speak about him all the time, but *Messengers of God* is for him. He knew all the texts, and he helped me a great deal in my preparation for these lectures. Now, I am without him once again, and the research is more difficult. I have to find all the sources myself. Still, I love it. It is all about playing with the texts, in the research as in the teaching.

Those who would attend the Y lectures were also obliged to study in preparation. On the afternoon of my lecture, for two or three hours before it, a rabbi who knew the texts would prepare the audience for my lecture, so that I had some sort of common background with them, some foundation, some texts in common.

TB: So they could be prepared in some respects, having read the texts you would be working with, and yet not prepared for the way that these texts would intersect with your own experience.

EW: Yes. They would go through the texts and commentaries in preparation, then I would come and, well, make it more difficult for them. I had to do something to rend their knowledge.

TB: How do you study?

EW: All the characters I talk about, whether in the Bible or in other classical Jewish texts—I can see them. I see what they see. I can hear them speaking. And for me the words are living. What I draw from all that study and teaching is joy.

TB: In *Sages and Dreamers*, *Legends of Our Time*, and the first volume of *Memoirs*, you have written about a teacher in Paris, Harav Shushani, who was also a teacher to Emmanuel Levinas. Given the uniquely profound influence you and Emmanuel Levinas have shared on a generation of biblical scholars, theologians, philosophers and ethicists writing in the wake of the Holocaust, one must wonder about Shushani's influence on the two of you. Did you and Levinas ever study together with Shushani? What was Shushani like as a teacher? How would you describe his influence on you?

EW: Harav Shushani taught both me and Emmanuel Levinas during the same period of time, but we never met together with him. He wanted to keep us apart. It was only later, much later, that Levinas and I became close and realized this. We had known before that we were both his students, but only later did we realize that we were both his students *at the same time.*

TB: In your writings about Shushani, he appears both intriguing and disturbing.

EW: Shushani was disturbed and he taught to disturb. He was dangerous. It was after the war, and he would come to the children's home where I was staying. I am convinced now that he wanted, really, to derail me—intellectually, morally. He sought to take me away from faith.

Shushani was the opposite of Lieberman. Both were erudite, both brilliant, both knew all the texts. Lieberman was logical and methodical in his presentation. Shushani, on the other hand, was completely scattered. Yet in the end it all came together! He never looked at a book while we were studying with him. He knew all the texts. It took time for me to understand that knowledge can be dangerous.

TB: Many know your writings, but many others have known you first as a teacher. Indeed, you and I have had students in common. How often do you include biblical texts in your courses? Can you give some examples? To what extent, or in what ways, has the Holocaust figured in your teaching?

EW: I never begin a course without having the first session on the Bible. Always. Whenever I teach, it must begin with a biblical text. If I teach on suffering, we start with Job. If the subject is love, we begin with the Song of Songs; if it is despair, Ecclesiastes. Of course you know that you can use biblical literature to teach on anything. But I do this also because I want my students to know that whatever I have, I have taken it, in some sense, from that source, from studying those texts.

Although it figures into all my teaching in some way, I do not teach entire courses on the Holocaust. While at the Faculty of Jewish Studies at the City College of New York, I taught courses on the Holocaust. But after two years, slowly others took over. I don't know. It was too difficult, for me and for the students. Most of my students were children of survivors. We studied—never my books, but we studied other memoirs and studies. And together we asked, how could they? And at the end of two hours, no one wanted to get up and go. We would stay there in the classroom. But it was very, very painful. I admire deeply the hundreds of scholars today who teach courses on the Holocaust, and I am indebted to them.

To Let Suffering Speak

TB: Biblical texts, characters and themes appear not only in your lectures and essays, but also in your novels and other fiction. For example, in *Twilight*, all the inmates in Mountain Clinic except Zelig think that they are biblical characters. Most striking to me is your play, *The Trial of God*, which appears to me to involve an intersection between the books of Job and Esther. On the one hand, it is set in a small seventeenth-century town on Purim eve, after a pogrom, and they are trying to put on a purimspiel. So the play is obviously related to Esther, in these and more subtle ways. On the other hand, it seems to be very close to the book of Job. The innkeeper Berish appears to be a Joban figure—insisting, amid the gaity of the Purim players and in the wake of a deadly pogrom, to put God on trial, all the while being at least a little cynical about the outcome of such a trial. To put the judge of the universe on trial is inevitably tragic. Indeed, if you win it is most tragic. That is certainly a Joban dilemma.

EW: Absolutely. Berish is very close to Job. He has lost nearly everything. He has had enough.

TB: There are also more subtle connections between *The Trial of God* and the book of Job. The setting for *The Trial* is Shamgorod. In Hebrew, *sham* is 'there', and *garad* is a verb meaning 'scrape'. In Job

2.8, Job takes a potsherd 'to scrape' (*l^ehitgared*, a form of *garad*) himself. This is the only use of this verb in the Hebrew Bible.

EW: Yes. That's right. The name of the town is 'there he scraped'. Good for you! Nobody has noticed that.

TB: In this play, the only one who is willing to 'do theodicy', that is, to justify God, is Sam, who is revealed as Satan in the final terrible moments. So here, unlike in Job, the adversary (*satan*) is the only one willing to justify God. Does this suggest, in some sense, that to justify God in such a situation—and especially with regard to the Holocaust—is in some sense 'satanic' or evil?

EW: Satan knew the answer. He has all the answers. Actually Satan speaks like a fanatic. In this play I wanted to show the danger of fanaticism. The fanatic thinks he is justifying God. Never think that you are justifying God. To ask the questions about God's justice is alright. Moses said 'Show me your ways', and the Talmud says that what he wanted was for God to show him why the righteous suffer and the wicked prosper.

TB: There is a difference between asking questions pertaining to theodicy—questions about God's justice, or lack of justice—and answering those questions. In Christian tradition theodicy is taken to mean 'justifying God'. Milton's *Paradise Lost* was a theodicy in this sense, 'to justify the ways of God to man'. Of course, in Milton as in much of Christian theology, the answers given are less compelling than the questions that echo past them.

EW: Think of the Hebrew word for question, *she'elah*. There is *'el* (God) in *she'elah*. God is in the question. But to give the answer? Keep asking the question.

TB: This may also be a lesson in Job. Job's friends, who are trying so desperately to answer for God in the face of Job's suffering, are ultimately scolded by God, who says that they 'did not speak rightly to/about me' (42.7), in contrast to Job—the only one who has insisted on the question against all answers.

EW: God seems to be saying to the friends, 'who are you to answer for me? Who do you think you are?! Who asked you?!' And God takes the side of Job. God does not tell him the truth, but God does take Job's side over against the friends.

In a way, God at the end of Job is saying, 'look who I have to defend me!' How pathetic are these defendants! And in *The Trial of God*, it is not Beresh's friends but Satan alone who will be God's champion. Imagine, at the end of *The Trial of God*, God saying, 'look who is my defendant!' As in Job, this shows the pathos of God, the tragedy of God. And so all the questions are there—even God's.

TB: Yet in *The Trial of God*, unlike in Job, there is no voice from the whirlwind at the end. God never enters the scene, never takes a side. There is a certain silence, a theological hollowness at the end of this trial, much like the silence after a death sentence has been given.

EW: That's right. There is no voice from the whirlwind. The play was once performed at St Peter's Basilica, at the Vatican in Rome. I went to the opening performance. It was on a Sunday, and it was performed outside. At the end of the play, my stage directions call for the ringing of bells. Just as the play ended—and this was not planned—the cathedral bells began ringing!

But you see the tragedy. On the one hand, there are those who are victims of fanatics. But then the tragedy is also God's. There is another tragedy: 'Look who is my defendant!' This is the pathos of God, the tragedy of God.

TB: I am reminded of the image in Ezekiel of the divine presence leaving Jerusalem, going into exile along with the people.

EW: Exactly.

TB: In Scriptures, especially in Kings and in the some of the prophets, we find a theological argument about how to interpret the Babylonian exile that is strikingly similar to some theological arguments about the Holocaust today. On the one hand, in Jeremiah for example, Babylon is sometimes seen as God's agent, meting out God's punishment on God's people. On the other hand, there are texts such as Psalm 137 in which one gets a very different perception of Babylon. In our century, the Holocaust has led to similar theological arguments. There are some— we might call them fanatics—who see the Holocaust as parallel to Babylonian exile; that is, as a punishing of the Jewish people. I find that atrocious, personally.

EW: It is inhuman, egregious, ugly. A horrible argument. Unfortunately some who argue this are part of my own religion. This is the danger in moving beyond the question and settling on what appears to be a clear answer. I have heard this idea presented through the following story. A man who is unfamiliar with modern medicine comes to a village and is taken by accident to the hospital. He doesn't know what a hospital is. He sees people there in white suits, with masks over their faces, with knives in their hands, cutting up people. He thinks they are savages, and does not understand that their work is actually necessary for healing, for survival. This, they say, is analogous to our perception of the Holocaust. God is doing something that is necessary for healing and survival, even though it looks savage to us. My God! How can they have the arrogance, the *hutzpah* ...*They* are the savages.

I'll tell you, the problem that I have with Job is, number one, the children. The ending of Job is superficially happy. He has children again. He gets everything he used to have in excess. He is saturated. It says that he is 'saturated' ('Job died, an old man, saturated with days'; Job 42.17). I have often thought about this ending, and about the children lost at the beginning of the story. How does it speak to those of us who have experienced great loss and then find our lives again, those of us who survive? The only explanation I can find is in our generation's children. I know people who lost their children. They saw them go away, never to return. And afterwards they had other children, as in Job. Not to be the last. They do not want to be the last, to live in the past.

TB: In *Messengers of God*, you wrote that you had been preoccupied with Job, and that you are offended by Job's quick and easy surrender to God at the expense of justice for his children. Then you suggest that perhaps Job's silence is only *pretended* abdication: 'by repenting sins he did not commit, by justifying a sorrow he did not deserve, he communicates to us that he did not believe in his own confessions; they were nothing but decoys'. Interestingly, several recent interpreters have come to similar conclusions in their translations of Job's final words (42.2-6), especially his last line: *'al ken 'em'as*, 'Therefore I repudiate...'. There is no object of repudiation. Repudiate what? Whom? God? Himself? His case?

EW: He is disgusted with the process. He says I am disgusted with the process. And of course having reached this situation, I am forced to say certain things. But *'em'as*, 'I am disgusted'.

TB: Of course, Esther also figures prominently in *The Trial of God*. The lighthearted, carnival dimensions in the play are reminiscent of the carnival sense of the Esther story itself, especially as it is read in Purim festivals. Esther, like your play, is both enchanting and haunting, insofar as one cannot read it without thinking of Haman's murderous successors in the Holocaust. And so your play raises a question for me: How should we—or how do you—negotiate between the playful, carnival dimensions of Esther and Purim on the one hand, and the fact that we just cannot read Esther today without thinking of the Holocaust? How do we negotiate that tension between the carnival and the terror?

EW: It is very, very strange. There was a small theater in our town. And one of the favorite subjects for plays was Joseph being sold by his brothers into slavery. What kind of theater is this? There was carnival and joy about one of the worst days in our history. Why would we want to do that? I think that it is related to the sense of the absurd in Jewish history. So often we have nothing to do with other peoples who are struggling with one another. Think of the Christian crusades. It was a war between whom? Islam and Christianity. What did the Jews have to do with it? Nothing. But on the way to Jerusalem, there were massacres of Jews. Jewish history is filled with these stories, with names and dates. Everything is there. In Christian accounts, it is a story of glory. So idealized. In Jewish accounts: absurdity. We had nothing to do with it!

  It is this sense of absurdity that we see in Esther, which you yourself have written about in *The Book of Hiding*. The story begins with a Persian king and queen, extravagant banquets, and no mention of Jewish people whatsoever. Two chapters later and the Jews are in great danger for their lives. It is absurd! I wanted to capture this same sense of absurdity in the play. That is why I wanted to make the story itself a play, to make it a play within a play. This is the only way one can tell such a story from the point of view of the victims.

TB: Theodor Adorno wrote that 'the need to let suffering speak is the condition of all truth'. I must follow Adorno with another question: Can this condition for truth always be met? What language is capable of letting suffering speak? Is it always possible to let suffering speak?

EW: Is it possible?

TB: Is it *always* possible?

EW: Not always. But sometimes, when no words are possible, silence can be an alternative language. It is possible to transform silence into a language, to have a language of silence. It is about gestures. Take, for example, the greatest dancer in the world, and imagine that dancer on the stage, motionless. Or imagine the greatest musician, and imagine a silence. Imagine the most powerful person in the world, powerless. We must always ask ourselves what is the best language to let suffering speak. Sometimes our answer may be silence.

RUPTURE AND CONTEXT: THE ETHICAL DIMENSIONS
OF A POST-HOLOCAUST BIBLICAL HERMENEUTICS

Chris Boesel

The call for an explicit post-Holocaust biblical hermeneutics has been ethically freighted to an acute degree. This is easily shown by Tod Linafelt's recent survey of the few pioneers of this (regrettably, still nascent) field of discourse. Elie Wiesel's readings of biblical texts are, Linafelt writes, influenced by a 'commitment not to betray the memory of suffering'.[1] David Blumenthal's treatment of various Psalms are guided by a 'sensitivity to the ethical demands of the Holocaust'.[2] Emil Fackenheim's category of post-Holocaust 'mad midrash' constitutes a 'refusal to betray the memory of the dead'.[3] As an addendum to this particular survey, Linafelt announces his own proposal for a post-Holocaust biblical hermeneutics: an 'ethics of interpretation' governed by theologian Irving Greenberg's 'ethical imperative': 'No statement, theological or otherwise, should be made that would not be credible in the presence of burning children'.[4] This imperative carries with it the obligation not to interpret the Bible in such a way as to betray the memory of the dead and the reality of their suffering by dissimulating the reality of the evil under which they suffered and died. It follows that a biblical hermeneutics that would betray the memory of the victims in such a way is open to serious ethical judgment. Due to the place of the Holocaust in Western consciousness, this judgment could number among the most severe available to our contemporary moral vocabulary. Ethical freight, indeed.

---

1. Tod Linafelt, 'Mad Midrash and the Negative Dialectics of Post-Holocaust Biblical Interpretation', in Gerhard Bodendorfer and Matthias Millard (eds.), *Bibel und Midrasch* (Tübingen: J.C.B. Mohr [Paul Siebeck], 1998), pp. 263-74 (267).
2. Linafelt, 'Mad Midrash', p. 270.
3. Linafelt, 'Mad Midrash', p. 272.
4. As cited by Linafelt in 'Mad Midrash', p. 264.

While affirming Linafelt's sense of the ethical obligation under which a post-Holocaust biblical hermeneutics must labor, I nevertheless have the temerity to suggest a complication. It has to do with the relation between this ethical obligation and how the enormity of the Holocaust is specifically conceived. The call for a post-Holocaust biblical hermeneutics naturally arises from the recognition that the magnitude of the Holocaust makes it 'virtually impossible to ignore its significance for historical, philosophical, or religious studies'.[5] This is as it should be. However, I hope to demonstrate how one particular conception of the Holocaust—that of absolute rupture—can, under the force and urgency of its own ethical commitment, paradoxically create a blind spot to the general field of ethical complexity within which this specific commitment is inscribed. Given the irreducible complexity of this field, such a blind spot casts a problematic ethical shadow.

Rupture: Continuity, History, Context

Because of both the rigor of his reflection on the Holocaust and its impact upon post-Holocaust discourse, I will focus on the work of Emil Fackenheim.[6] I critique the confrontation that Fackenheim engineers between the Holocaust and the Bible through engineering a somewhat duplicitous encounter of my own. I will set Fackenheim's conception of the Holocaust as absolute rupture of context alongside Jacques Derrida's infamous formula that there is nothing (not even the Holocaust?!) outside the text, or context (which, according to Derrida, 'says exactly the same thing'[7]). By doing so I hope to accomplish the following: first, to show how Fackenheim's conception of the Holocaust as absolute rupture may itself be an ethical problem for a post-Holocaust

5.   Linafelt, 'Mad Midrash', p. 263. Linafelt points out that 'this is precisely what biblical scholars have done for over half a century' (p. 263). To amend this impoverished situation is the impetus behind his article, and, I believe, behind the present collection as well.

6.   This is no easy task. I am greatly indebted to Fackenheim's post-Holocaust thought, as well as his generous response to earlier work of mine. However, I am encouraged by the example of his own relationship to Rosenzweig and Buber, his critical readings of whom reflect no hint of diminished respect or gratitude for their work.

7.   Jacques Derrida, 'Afterword: Toward an Ethic of Discussion', in *Limited Inc* (trans. Samuel Weber; Evanston: Northwestern University Press, 1988), p. 136.

biblical hermeneutics; secondly, to suggest that questioning the conception of the Holocaust as absolute rupture is not *necessarily* a diminishment or trivialization of the enormity of the Holocaust. I do not argue that the conception of rupture is too enormous to be used appropriately in relation to the Holocaust, but that it assumes and depends upon a conception of context that is not enormous, or complex, enough; and thirdly, to suggest that such a critique is itself entailed within an 'ethics of interpretation'.

I am, in a sense, throwing down a gauntlet for biblical scholars responding to the call for an explicit post-Holocaust biblical hermeneutics—a challenge to not allow the very real enormity of the Holocaust, and the urgency of the ethical freight weighing upon our responses to it, to eclipse the full complexity of the ethical dimensions of post-Holocaust discourse in a way which can *uncritically* reverberate with ethically problematic consequences.[8]

Emil Fackenheim and the Abyss of the Holocaust

In his book *To Mend the World*, Fackenheim argues at great length that the Holocaust is a unique historical event of such radical proportions that it constitutes a rupture in history. It is an abyss which cannot be comprehended or transcended by philosophical or theological thought; a caesura against which all thought is broken and all assumptions are bankrupted. The fabric of the context of history is rent absolutely. None of its threads remain intact to span the abyss between the there and then of *before*, and the here and now of *after*.

A decade later, Fackenheim takes this same conception of the Holocaust and addresses its consequences for a biblical hermeneutics. Thus, in *The Jewish Bible after the Holocaust*, Fackenheim argues that no reading of the Bible (Jewish or Christian) can be what it was before. The Bible must be re-read as if for the first time. In confrontation with the Holocaust as rupture of history the biblical text is 'naked', bereft, as it were, of all context, denuded of all interlacing hermeneutical and contextual fabric. So also are we, the readers and interpreters of the Bible after the Holocaust (Fackenheim addresses this specifically to

8. If we take Derrida seriously, this reverberation itself is inescapable, structurally necessary. To be *self-critically* aware of it, and the ethically problematic nature of the consequences in which it endlessly embroils us, is, in a manner of speaking, the best we can do.

Jews), denuded of all lingering contextual resources.[9] There is no sliver of hermeneutical ground, no shred of hermeneutical resource from which to interpret the Bible that is not ruptured by the Holocaust.

In light of the above, Fackenheim reasons that to conceive of the Holocaust as less than absolute rupture diminishes the event to the merely penultimate. Fackenheim charges that any biblical hermeneutics grounded in such a diminishment of ultimacy reads 'seamlessly', which is to read 'as though the Holocaust had not happened'.[10] Any such hermeneutics, then, falls immediately under the shadow of Holocaust denial. It is this exhaustive stranglehold, which absolute conceptions of the enormity of the Holocaust can have upon the project of a post-Holocaust biblical hermeneutics, that I hope to bring to attention, and perhaps loosen in the process. Before turning to Derrida for the needed leverage, I want to look more closely at how Fackenheim configures the hermeneutical predicament inaugurated by the Holocaust (which, in turn, points to the corresponding requirements for a proper hermeneutical remedy).

Fackenheim argues that, to varying degrees, both traditional and modern hermeneutics assume some kind of continuity between past (the past of the written text, and the former generations of its interpreters) and present (the present of our world today). As one example of the modern version of this assumption, Fackenheim looks at the 'post-Enlightenment' hermeneutical principles proposed by Martin Buber in a 1926 essay, 'The Man of Today and the Jewish Bible'. Fackenheim shows how, despite his modern historicism, Buber's interpretive approach to the Bible still 'assumes a continuity between the "generations"' (of Jewish readers), a continuity which, Fackenheim argues, 'has been destroyed'.[11]

In *To Mend the World*, Fackenheim assesses the possibilities, yet ultimate insufficiency, of a more contemporary—what he calls 'historicist'—hermeneutics. According to Fackenheim, this hermeneutics, like Buber's, 'begins with the acceptance of historical situatedness'; this historicism, in turn, raises 'the [hermeneutical] problem of recovery of the past': 'The present interpreter of the past, like the past itself, is

9. Emil Fackenheim, *The Jewish Bible after the Holocaust: A Re-reading* (Bloomington: Indiana University Press, 1990), pp. vi-viii.

10. Emil Fackenheim, *To Mend the World: Foundations of Post-Holocaust Jewish Thought* (Bloomington: Indiana University Press, 3rd edn, 1994), p. 261.

11. Fackenheim, *Jewish Bible*, p. 16.

situated *in* history...[but they] are situated in different historical situa-tions.'[12] However, successful transmission of meaning across this gap is possible because the historicist hermeneutics assumes that the past and present historical situations are nevertheless still 'part of one continuous history'.[13] Fackenheim concludes that through the 'assertion of an unbroken historical continuity from past to present', made by both Buber and the contemporary historicists, 'so radical a gap as between past moments then and our moment now is hermeneutically bridged'.[14]

Fackenheim continues: 'That continuity is ruptured by the Holo-caust.'[15] Note that Fackenheim *affirms* both dimensions of the histori-cist hermeneutical predicament. (1) We cannot escape our (nor the text's) situatedness within history by which (2) our here and now is separated from the there and then of the text by a radical gap. Con-ceived as rupture of history, the Holocaust does not alter this fundamen-tal structure. It simply further radicalizes this gap into an absolute breach, rendering impossible any continuity between before and after, past and present. In doing so, it radicalizes—'thrusts' us into[16]—our historical situatedness: bereft of the resources of hermeneutical and contextual continuity, we cannot escape a confrontation between the Bible and the Holocaust except by an 'unauthentic' (perhaps criminal?) practice of Holocaust denial. Confrontation with the Holocaust as abso-lute rupture is the very definition of our new historical situatedness.

As Fackenheim conceives it, then, it is the impossibility of proceed-ing upon an assumption of continuity in history that lies at the heart of the hermeneutical predicament inaugurated by the Holocaust. It follows that an 'authentic' hermeneutical response to such a predicament requires a very different assumption: an assumption of rupture.

Jacques Derrida and a Hermeneutics of Rupture
Derrida's essay, 'Signature Event Context', does not advance an explicit post-Holocaust hermeneutics.[17] Nor does Derrida himself propose the

12. Fackenheim, *Mend the World*, pp. 256, 257, 259.
13. Fackenheim, *Mend the World*, p. 259.
14. Fackenheim, *Mend the World*, pp. 259, 260.
15. Fackenheim, *Mend the World*, p. 260.
16. Fackenheim, *Jewish Bible*, p. 97.
17. I anticipate that by introducing Derrida into this discourse, if I know my Derrida at all, things are likely to become rather confused. But is not the introduc-tion of confusion ethically problematic in itself? Are we not to resist all attempts to muddy the waters, muddy waters constituting an ambiguity which clouds our ability

'general field of writing' which he articulates there as a ground for one. That will be my job. I will show very briefly, as a kind of bare minimum of evidence, how the nature of this general field answers, on a certain level, Fackenheim's call for an explicit post-Holocaust biblical hermeneutics (but also how this answer bleeds back to displace the very conception of the Holocaust that raises the call; thus, the duplicity behind this encounter). This requires that we momentarily turn aside from the Holocaust and the Bible (or so it would appear—we may discover that we have not, in fact, made such a simple turning, and find ourselves wishing that we had, or more precisely, that we *could*) to risk losing our way amid a complicated, seemingly unrelated text. Bear with me, as I summarize in an admittedly too schematic fashion.

With the stroke of a 'single example', representing 'all philosophy' (Ettiene Bonnot de Condillac's *Essai sur l'origine des connaissances humaines*),[18] Derrida endeavors to show how the 'classical' concept of writing is marked by absence. He observes how this marking results in writing's subordinate position in relation to the 'classical' concepts of communication, language, and meaning in general, funded as they are, Derrida argues, by fundamental assumptions of continuity and presence. In a nutshell: when language and communication are understood as the transmission of intentional meaning, the success of this transmission presupposes a 'homogeneous space', a 'milieu that is fundamentally continuous with itself'.[19] Success is more certain the greater the proximity to the place and moment of origin, that of authorial intent. The guarantee of success is most securely insured by the intimate presence of the speaker, the greatest possible level of proximity. On the other hand, the absence (i.e. of the speaker or the addressee) implied in writing increases the possibility of the failure of the transmission of meaning.

---

to determine and make judgments concerning responsibility? Are we not obligated to deny any such shelter to the criminal, and to all complicity with the criminal? Surely the answer is yes. It is. And we are. I am therefore taking a *risk*, fully aware of the height of the stakes. I risk introducing confusion because, with a conviction similar to Fackenheim's, I believe a certain irreducible confusion —what I hope to pass off as complexity—constitutes a kind of 'historical situatedness' that we escape from, into unmuddied clarity, only through a practice of denial. Two underlying convictions: (1) risking is inescapable; (2) denial constitutes a greater risk than confusion.

18. Jacques Derrida, 'Signature Event Context', in *Margins of Philosophy* (trans. Alan Bass; Chicago: University of Chicago Press, 1986), p. 311.

19. Derrida, 'Signature', p. 311.

Writing is characterized by absence. So far, so good. However, as Derrida sees it, the subordination of writing signifies that 'the absence of which Condillac [and 'all philosophy'] speaks is determined in the most classical fashion as a continuous modification, a progressive exten-uation of presence...not...as a break in presence'.[20] For Derrida, then, the 'classical' concept of writing remains governed by a more fun-damental assumption of continuity: 'the continuity of presence to absence'.[21]

But Derrida believes this to be a cover up. He is convinced that the absence which characterizes writing is, in truth, much more radical:

> All writing...in order to be what it is, must be able to function in the radical absence of every empirically determined addressee in general. And this absence is not a continuous modification of presence; it is a break in presence...inscribed in the structure of the mark.[22]

Derrida's radicalization of absence, then, implies an assumption of break rather than of continuity to be most fundamental to the concept of writing. But Derrida will generalize this concept, which means break and rupture will be seen as fundamental to more than just writing, but to communication, language and meaning in general. Now we're getting somewhere.

The fact that this radical absence is inscribed in the very structure of the mark allows one to insist that the radicalization of absence is no mere brainchild of Derrida's own inventive reading, and that it cannot be summarily disregarded as such. Rather, it is what Derrida discovers to be inherent in the 'classical' concept of writing itself, upon rigorous examination. In this sense, Derrida does not radicalize the notion of absence at all, but merely thinks through the radical consequences implicit in the 'classical' concepts of absence, writing, language and communication. By the same logic, Derrida's articulation of a general field of writing is not 'his', not 'his doing', but is itself simply rendered necessary by a rigorous interrogation of the structure of the mark.[23]

---

20. Derrida, 'Signature', p. 313.
21. Derrida, 'Signature', p. 314.
22. Derrida, 'Signature', p. 316.
23. In this light, the assumptions (continuity, presence) funding Condillac's and 'all philosophy's' concepts of language and writing resemble a kind of repression or covering over of the radical consequences implicit in these concepts. Derrida's 'discovery' of these radical consequences carries a disturbing, threatening force (but also the opening of possibility) similar to that which often attends a psychoana-

In addition to radical absence, Derrida finds other 'nuclear traits of all writing' to be implicit within the 'classical' conception of writing: the 'disruption' of being cut off from the origin,[24] the 'force of breaking with...context', the 'force of rupture'.[25] Derrida's key move is to demonstrate how these traits—rather than characterizing writing as distinct from language and communication (as their classical conceptions would have it)—characterize in a fundamental way a general field within which 'all languages in general, but even, beyond semiolinguistic communication...the entire field of what philosophy would call experience' are inscribed.[26] This general field, then, is the text, or textuality, outside of which nothing 'is'. Consequently, Derrida argues that 'it is within the general field of writing thus defined that the effects of semantic communication [including hermeneutics] will be able to be determined as...secondary, inscribed, supplementary effects'.[27]

What does all this have to do with us? (1) Characterized as it is by the 'nuclear traits' of radical break and rupture, rather than and 'prior' to any assumptions of continuity and presence, this general field of writing constitutes a kind of general field of rupture. (2) In light of its limitless dimensions, Derrida does in fact propose this general field as a necessary condition of possibility for all language, communication and transmission of meaning in general. What does this amount to? A fundamental assumption of rupture as a kind of necessary ground for any possible hermeneutics. It is the general field of writing 'thus defined' that I suggest appears well suited to serve Fackenheim's call for a post-Holocaust hermeneutics grounded in an assumption of rupture rather than an assumption of continuity.

A general field of rupture: a gratifyingly clever and apt turn of phrase, to be sure. But only 'on a certain level'. Our sense of gratification is alarmingly short-lived. It becomes immediately apparent that, once the concept of a general field of rupture is in place, it does

lytic revelation of an unconscious, forgotten secret, or repressed memory. By this account, the violent nature of the conservative reaction to deconstruction is relatively understandable. On the other hand, anyone who claims not to be even slightly unnerved by the limitless nature of its consequences should be, in my estimation, regarded warily.

24. Derrida, 'Signature', p. 316.
25. Derrida, 'Signature', p. 317.
26. Derrida, 'Signature', p. 317.
27. Derrida, 'Signature', pp. 310-11.

not function as a ground at all, but more like the shifting sands under the current of a ceaseless undertow. In view of a *general* field of rupture, the *particular* event of the Holocaust *as* rupture is displaced: It cannot remain the *absolute* rupture of context that Fackenheim conceives it to be. For what is the possible nature of a rupture within a field fundamentally characterized by rupture—a limitless field, at that? Its ultimacy, its status as absolute, is rendered impossible.

Have we been duped? It would seem that our hermeneutical remedy has proven to be, in fact, fatally poisonous.

But hold on. Not so fast.

Before giving into a vertiginous despair, why not simply recant; confess to being fooled by appearances? Why not deliver the Holocaust from this poisonous penultimacy by simply rejecting Derrida's general field of writing as a proper ground for a post-Holocaust hermeneutics of rupture on the grounds that it has proven to be hostile, rather than filial to Fackenheim's call?

As I have already suggested, neither the general field of writing nor the effects of displacement that occur in its wake are instituted by the thought or writing of one Jacques Derrida. They are not his doing. They are nobody's doing. They are the necessary, and so inescapable (and therefore, yes, maddening) consequences found to be inherent in the structure of the mark. At the very least, this necessity prohibits the displacement of the Holocaust as absolute rupture from being dismissed on the grounds that it is solely the result of an arbitrary and rogue (and unethical?) intervention on the part of Derrida.[28] It is entailed within the concept of a general field of writing that one cannot escape its consequences by merely rejecting it as a parochial and irrelevant invention of a clever, if not fiendish imagination. Fackenheim is, as are we all, stuck with it.[29]

---

28. Although space does not allow for it, I suggest it would also be possible to show how Derrida's reading of Condillac and 'all philosophy' reveals a fault line in Fackenheim's own formulation: Fackenheim's conception of the Holocaust as a rupture which renders any assumption of continuity impossible is itself grounded in an assumption of continuity; it must assume 'one continuous history' in order to constitute a rupture of history. I would argue that Derrida reveals a necessary structural dynamic in the light of which Fackenheim's own call for a hermeneutics grounded in a conception of the Holocaust as absolute rupture has the double effect of displacing that very conception.

29. Derrida does not inflict deconstruction upon us. Rather, one might be tempted to paraphrase a favorite catch-phrase of American popular culture into the

This should not be mistaken for good news. (Beware all celebrations of deconstruction as, at long last, the true harbinger of unfettered liberation and freedom.) It constitutes a dire predicament. As such it should strike one as genuinely disconcerting. Vertiginous despair after all? Perhaps not. I would argue that the poison is not necessarily fatal. Neither, then, is the news necessarily bad.

The displacement of Fackenheim's conception of the Holocaust as absolute rupture *is* a necessary effect of a general field of writing. However, it does *not* necessarily constitute a diminishment or trivialization of the enormity of the Holocaust itself. Rather, this displacement occurs as an effect of a radicalization of the concept of context. As we have already glimpsed, the general field of writing names a kind of 'limitless context'[30] in relation to which no conception of the Holocaust could be enormous enough so as to constitute an absolute rupture.

Rupture as Determination of Context: Saturated Context or Limitless Context(s)?

There are two features of Fackenheim's conception of the Holocaust which the limitless context of a general field of writing both brings to a point of focus and limits, or renders insufficient: (1) the Holocaust as rupture of history presupposes history as a continuous context whose 'frame' or 'border'[31] is absolutely delimitable and therefore rupturable in an absolute way; (2) as absolute *rupture* of context the Holocaust simultaneously functions as absolute *determinant* of context; specifically, the context *after*ward—our context of 'today' (Buber)—'exhaustively determined' and 'saturated' as post-Holocaust. Again, I argue that as a consequence of a limitless context this limiting of the concept of absolute rupture does not necessarily constitute an ethically dubious diminishment of the enormity of the Holocaust. There can be no doubt, however, that such consequences are ethically problematic in the sense that they complicate the ethical dimensions of a post-Holocaust biblical hermeneutics.

To bring this ethical complication more fully into view we need to

---

following: 'Deconstruction Happens', or, as Derrida says explicitly, is always already happening, 'on the move in…"the things themselves"' ('Afterword', p. 147).

30. Derrida, 'Afterword', p. 136.
31. Derrida, 'Afterword', p. 152.

investigate the precise nature of this limitlessness of context a bit
further.

We have already seen the connection between the general field of
writing and a radicalized concept of context. As Derrida announces
early on in 'Signature Event Context', 'demonstrat[ing] why a context
is never absolutely determinable...or saturated' is 'the most general
question I would like to elaborate'.[32] But what does Derrida mean by an
absolutely determinable and saturated context? And why is such a thing
impossible?

Another 'nuclear trait of all writing' Derrida finds inherent in the
structure of the mark: 'Every sign, linguistic or nonlinguistic...can be
cited, put between quotation marks; thereby it can break with every
context, and engender infinitely new contexts in an absolutely nonsat-
urable fashion.'[33] An absolutely determined, saturated context, then,
would be absolutely singular. All other possible determinations of context, and so all other hermeneutical possibilities, would be squeezed
out, excluded from the 'space' of the context. It is this kind of reduction
to a single hermeneutical voice that is rendered impossible by the structure of the mark. Each context is necessarily, structurally invaded by
the possibility of an infinite number of other contexts to such an extent
that 'there are only contexts, without any center of absolute anchor-
ing'.[34] Not only is there nothing outside this limitless context, there are
only context*s*. Never just one.

The limitless context Derrida describes is not singular, but irre-
ducibly plural. The limitlessness of context, then, does not signify a
quantitative enormity (a frame or border which is simply bigger than
the dimensions of the Holocaust, such that the Holocaust cannot 'be', or
break outside of it), but an irreducible, infinite plurality. It is this
plurality, or complexity, of a limitless context which the Holocaust, and
a post-Holocaust hermeneutics, can never get 'outside' of. Consequently, the ethical obligations levied by the enormity of the Holocaust
under which a post-Holocaust hermeneutics must labor—while not
reduced, diminished, or averted—are themselves caught within this
complexity.

Here the ethical complications wrought by the consequences of the
limitlessness of context come into view. Specifically, to say that the

32. Derrida, 'Signature', p. 310.
33. Derrida, 'Signature', p. 320.
34. Derrida, 'Signature', p. 320.

Holocaust could never be enormous enough to constitute an absolute rupture of a limitless context means that it can never be made to successfully reduce contextual complexity down to an absolutely singular determination, that is, 'post-Holocaust'. In other words, the Holocaust cannot be conceived as this kind of absolute determination of context without constituting a kind of violent act of erasure: a squeezing or forcing out of a structurally necessary plurality—a plurality of possible determinations of context, and as such, a plurality of hermeneutical possibilities.

This is both complicated and disturbing. I seem to be saying that the determination of our context as post-Holocaust is itself an ethically problematic act of interpretive violence. Well, yes and no. We need to be careful here.

On the one hand, yes, our hermeneutical context of 'today' cannot be absolutely, exhaustively determined as a post-Holocaust context. But make no mistake, there is (always) an 'other hand' (but this 'always' is precisely what is disturbing us): we *are*, as Fackenheim maintains, 'situated in the post-Holocaust world'.[35] The consequences of a limitless context do not include the possibility of escaping this determination of our situatedness. Taking account of both hands, then, the complexity of a limitless context merely insists that the hermeneutical possibilities and the ethical demands which result from the post-Holocaust determination of our context are not, and cannot be, the *only* ones which come to bear in our situation 'today'. Therefore, it is the *absolute* determination of our context as post-Holocaust which constitutes an ethically problematic interpretive violence. (But on the other hand [see what I mean?], *every* particular determination of context participates in what is a fundamental, irreducible [albeit, relatively benign] level of interpretive violence,[36] and so is *always in danger of becoming* ethically problematic.)

Before I conclude, it is important that I put a face on these 'other hermeneutical possibilities' that have been hovering anonymously about this essay, and thereby breathe the life of the concrete into what has been an arid and abstract discussion. However, this transition into the concrete, necessary as it is, raises a certain danger. It may lead us to

35. Fackenheim, *Mend the World*, p. 256.

36. Derrida, 'Afterword', pp. 149-50. See also Derrida's comments in 'Remarks on Deconstruction and Pragmatism', in Chantal Mouffe (ed.), *Deconstruction and Pragmatism* (New York: Routledge, 1996), pp. 77-88 (83).

mistake the irreducible plurality of a limitless context for an *argument for* the humanism (with its own ethical codes and obligations) of a cultural pluralism or of what is nowadays celebrated as a postmodern multi-culturalism. The consequences of the general displacement put into effect by a limitless context do seem to coincide, momentarily, with the values of a cultural pluralism, and so seem to allow for a certain co-option as resource and argument. But only *momentarily*. They do not stop there. That is not their intended destination. Indeed, the effects of displacement never stop, not even for humanism.[37] They bleed back to disturb its highest, most ethical aspirations.

I suggest that feminist, womanist and post-colonial (liberation) interpretations of the Bible represent instances of 'other hermeneutical possibilities' alive and well within our post-Holocaust context. While not explicitly post-Holocaust, neither are they necessarily bereft of sensitivity to the enormity of the Holocaust and the ethical freight which it carries. However, in light of how Fackenheim's conception of the Holocaust results in an exhaustive determination of our context, what is one to make of the ethical integrity of these other interpretations? Does an acknowledgment of their validity, and the validity of what may be their own ethical demands, necessarily constitute an unethical diminishment of the enormity of the Holocaust, from ultimate to the merely penultimate, and thereby a betrayal of one's ethical obligation to its victims?

I want to be clear. I repeat, we *are* situated in a post-Holocaust context. And this *does* place us under an ethical obligation with regard to which we cannot escape the unpleasant business of making ethical judgments in relation to the infinite number of interpretations of the Bible that are, nevertheless, possible (many of which are actual). For example, in her book *Anti-Judaism in Feminist Religious Writings*, Katharina von Kellenbach shows how certain exercises in religious feminist discourse, despite their being motivated by an ethical obligation to the victims of patriarchy past and present, nevertheless involve

---

37. Deconstruction does not, cannot, limit itself to targeting only the 'bad guys' (deconstruction itself does not escape the limitless wave of its own effects; it does not control them). It is not, in itself, 'good'. Nor is it necessarily an ally of 'the good', though it can appear to be, momentarily. But, again, neither is it necessarily 'bad', nor an ally of 'the bad'—though it can appear to be. See, 'The Gift', in Geoffrey Bennington, *Jacques Derrida* (Chicago: University of Chicago Press, 1993), pp. 188-203 esp. p. 203.

themselves in an ethically problematic relation to the Holocaust and its victims.[38] Kellenbach gives examples of how Christian (and pagan) feminist rhetoric can entail (implicitly or explicitly) a supersessionist dynamic in relation to Judaism which denigrates the latter as a religion of particularism, retribution, exclusion, law and as the root of patriarchy itself. The post-Holocaust determination of our context levies an obligation to confront, perhaps harshly, the extent to which such theological and biblical interpretations might suggest an uncritical complicity with the history of Christian anti-Judaism which played so significant a role in seeding the historical soil of possibility for the event of the Holocaust itself.

However, in the same way, a post-Holocaust hermeneutics necessarily remains open and vulnerable to possible critiques by feminist and womanist interpreters—critiques of the extent to which a hermeneutics such as the one called for by Fackenheim might erase, or at least move to the periphery, the determination of our context as—*before and after* the Holocaust—one of patriarchal oppression along lines of gender, class and race. Such an erasure would involve itself in a complicitous silencing of the victims of that oppression and of the reality of their suffering.

Conclusion: Contextual Complexity, Ethical Complexity, Tragic Fabric

With the above example I am gesturing to a kind of perennial conflictual accountability between the respective ethical demands of differing hermeneutical possibilities.[39] I hope it is now clear how the contextual complexity of a limitless context gives rise to an irreducible ethical complexity which, in turn, implies this perennial conflictual

38. Katharina von Kellenbach, *Anti-Judaism in Feminist Religious Writings* (Atlanta: Scholars Press, 1994).

39. I believe I differ from Kellenbach here. While acknowledging the dicey complexity by which 'the oppressed are not exempt from responsibility for the perpetration of other forms of oppression', she nevertheless seems to suggest that the elimination of this kind of conflict is a possibility, via a 'more inclusive theory of patriarchy': 'Until all women are free, antisemitism is as much a feminist issue as racism, classism and homophobia' (*Anti-Judaism*, pp. 17-18, 31). Deconstruction foils this kind of hope for the ultimate resolution of conflict through the creation and broadening of consensus. For a related discussion of this dynamic, see Chantal Mouffe's introduction to *Deconstruction and Pragmatism*, pp. 6-11.

accountability (or at least momentarily funds an argument for such an accountability—a fine humanist value, to be sure).

In an attempt to bear witness to this chain of relations and its ethical implications for a post-Holocaust hermeneutics, I have tried to demonstrate a certain fault line in the absolute nature of those conceptions of the enormity of the Holocaust represented by Fackenheim's notion of absolute rupture: by reducing *contextual* complexity they can create a blind spot to the corresponding *ethical* complexity within which a post-Holocaust hermeneutics must labor. I suggest this blind spot can result in three levels of ethical fallout. First, it can eclipse our ethical obligation to other victims of history. Secondly, the *absolute* nature of the ethical judgments of other interpretations, and interpreters, lying implicit in absolute conceptions of the Holocaust is itself open to judgment, as an ethically problematic interpretive violence.

This suggests a tragic dimension to the ethical complexity of a limitless context. To demonstrate that an infinite number of biblical readings are structurally, necessarily possible after the Holocaust is not to argue that they are all equally ethical. Rather, it is to demonstrate the inescapable necessity of making ethical judgments with regard to them. Yet these necessary judgments are never completely immune from the possibility of becoming ethically problematic in relation to other interpreters and those other victims of history for whose memory they may be laboring. The tragic structure: necessary ethical judgments themselves (even in response to the Holocaust) cannot but open up ever new ethically problematic relations. The complexity of the hermeneutical predicament of a limitless context therefore constitutes an inescapable tragic fabric of limitless obligation.[40] This names a historical situatedness of a different stripe, one from which even the enormity of the Holocaust cannot deliver us. Neither the Holocaust, the Bible, nor ourselves are stripped of these tragic clothes.

Here we encounter a seemingly diabolical effect of displacement upon Fackenheim's concepts of absolute rupture and historical situatedness. In its light the contours of Fackenheim's formulations are thrown into menacing relief. I have shown how, conceived as absolute rupture, the Holocaust constitutes a breaking outside of the context of history. Thus, rather than 'thrusting' us into a predicament of historical

---

40. The work of philosopher Emmanuel Levinas comes into view here. See again Derrida's comments in *Deconstruction and Pragmatism*, pp. 86-87.

situatedness, it now appears to bring us, and the biblical text, along with it: we are denuded of all contextual fabric. As a result, Fackenheim's concept of inescapable historical situatedness, defined as this very contextual nakedness in confrontation with absolute rupture, is transformed into its diabolical *doppelgänger*. It takes on the appearance of a *deliverance from* the predicament of situatedness defined as the tragic fabric of limitless context and limitless obligation. The third level of ethical fallout, then: Fackenheim's own hermeneutical project takes on the hue of a kind of flight from, or immunity to historicity that he himself would judge as 'unauthentic'.

These are hard sayings. They require me to reiterate that it is not my intention to dismiss Fackenheim's call for an explicit post-Holocaust biblical hermeneutics nor his own pioneering attempt at such a hermeneutics. On the contrary, they are both necessary and invaluable. My concern has been to alert biblical scholars who take up Fackenheim's call for a post-Holocaust hermeneutics to the ethical consequences of giving the Holocaust and its determination of today's hermeneutical context absolute force. (The gauntlet: can a post-Holocaust biblical hermeneutics remain open to the possibility of other interpretations *of good faith*, without necessarily reducing them, or their practitioners, to the morally 'obscene?')[41] I have endeavored to bring out the complexities of these consequences in all their disturbing acuteness precisely because, in relation to the Holocaust, the stakes of ethical judgment are so high; and because the obligation to make (sometimes harsh) ethical judgments is inescapable, and without end.

---

41. I have in mind here the post-Holocaust theological formulations of Richard Rubenstein, see especially, *After Auschwitz: Radical Theology and Contemporary Judaism* (New York: Bobbs-Merrill, 1966), p. 153. In truth, they haunt this essay from beginning to end. The challenge simply put: can biblical scholars avoid the absolutist logic which drives Rubenstein's unquestionably powerful and important reflections to such toxically single-minded judgments?

Rabbinic Bible Interpretation after the Holocaust

B. Barry Levy

Jews who read, study, teach, preach and interpret the Bible today do so in ways that both resemble and deviate from the approaches of their forebears. In reality, many contemporary strategies to explain and to find meaning in the Bible derive from classical Jewish attempts to do the same. But should the differences be attributed merely to the fact that the modern perspectives that dominated the last half of the twentieth century see the Bible in new and original ways, or to the unfortunate historical fact that this period was ushered in by a cataclysmic upheaval in Jewish life that has yet to run its course both in terms of Jewish recovery and survival and the non-Jewish responses to it?

I

Talmudic rabbis recognized that the prophetic literature preserved in the Bible was a small sample of the revelations afforded to the ancient prophets. They understood that those few preserved prophecies differed from the many lost ones in that the former were needed by future generations while the latter possessed only ephemeral significance. Whatever historical truth may lie behind this assumption, its exegetical power has been quite substantial, because commitment to the relevance of the Bible in every generation is the primary factor in the constant return to it and the ongoing manipulation of its meanings to accommodate the needs, to answer the questions, to provide the guidance, and to anchor the teachings of every subsequent generation.

To be sure, other factors have impacted on the choice of Bible texts to which Jews are regularly exposed. The constant public reading and preaching of the Torah has kept its contents and issues before countless generations of synagogue goers, and the rabbinic requirement to review it weekly has reinforced its importance, its contents, and its perceived messages. Similar claims can be made for the five megillot (the 'five scrolls': Song of Songs, Ruth, Lamentations, Ecclesiastes and Esther) read on various holidays, for the dozens of passages from the prophets included in the supplementary haftarot readings on Sabbaths and festivals, and for the large number of psalms incorporated wholly or partly in the liturgy. *Mutatis mutandis*, the same argument applies to other biblical verses or phrases incorporated into the prayers.

By comparison, those books ignored in the liturgy have all but lost their place as objects of attention, regardless of the talmudic claims to the contrary. Compare the general levels of awareness of Hosea, Jonah and even the 21-verse book of Obadiah, which are hidden away in the Twelve Minor Prophets but called to mind at least annually in the haftarah readings, with general ignorance of Zephaniah and Haggai, which are never read in public and which many otherwise committed synagogue goers cannot even identify as biblical. Job, Proverbs, Ezra–Nehemiah and Chronicles also typify this situation. They are effectively lost books; were they removed from the Bible, most Jews would never notice. Daniel, though once popular among both Jews and Christians, seems to have lost favour with the former, perhaps because failed messianic predictions associated with its visions have dampened enthusiasm for it, perhaps because contemporary preferences for Hebrew have left the Aramaic half of the book unapproachable (a situation, however, that seems not to have hampered Talmud study), or perhaps because, like the other texts mentioned above, it lacks a liturgical context in which its contents and messages can be read, explored, taught and discussed.

As distant from the Holocaust as this may seem at first glance, it is very relevant, because the first point in understanding how Jews as a people respond to the Bible is to recognize that their reaction is dictated largely by the synagogue and its practices. Whether, for example, the plight of Job and the history of interpretation of the book that bears his name are or are not potentially relevant to the Holocaust, or whether the realities of the Holocaust can or should have any bearing on how one treats the book of Job is more or less beside the point. In fact, aside from occasional lip-service, Judaism as a public religion is barely concerned with Job. Its potential relevance to the Holocaust is moot.

II

Liturgical applications aside, other factors also influence the contemporary Jewish handling of the Bible. The Babylonian Talmud remains an important source and model for contemporary traditional approaches to the text; roughly 60 percent of its biblical citations come from the quarter of the Bible in the Torah. Statistically, Isaiah and Psalms were also important to the talmudic rabbis, but many other books seem not to have been. By way of contrast, the minimal attention given, for example, to the Former (historical) Prophets, which represent another quarter of the Bible but only some 7 percent of the talmudic attention to it, is also significant. The fact that Philo and the Dead Sea Scrolls are similarly lacking in attention to these books, as are the early patristic writers, suggests a virtually global disinterest in this material, at least in ancient times. Aside from contemporary Jewish schools that teach the Former Prophets extensively, perhaps to reinforce Jewish claims to the Land of Israel, the truth is that the Former Prophets have never really been important Jewish texts. While not totally devoid of appropriate midrashim and commentaries, their presentation to the past several generations of students has emphasized Hebrew language mastery and, to a lesser extent, history, or at least a literal reading of the narratives as if they contained history. The probing of the ethical concerns associated with war and destruction that were carried out under royal sponsorship so regularly in ancient times are often avoided. Divine directions for the ancients to commit genocide, while present in the Torah and the Former Prophets, seem to be ignored or rationalized. Again, the lack of a critical tradition of response to such behavior is exacerbated by the superficial way in which these many war-centered texts are treated. With the exception of occasional discussions of the divine commandment to annihilate Amalek, most potential links to the Holocaust are easily lost.

A spiritually sensitive friend of mine who spent years in the field of Jewish education often complained of misplaced priorities regarding these military narratives in the Historical Prophets. Without ever criticizing the Bible or its interests, he argued quite persuasively, but without much visible success, that the Later Prophets and the Psalms should replace the Former Prophets in most schools. Teaching the lessons of these books seemed to him more appropriate than those of the conquests, murders, assassinations, maimings, attacks, fights and miscellaneous immoralities so prominent in the narratives presently receiving so much class time. One may agree with him, but are his observation and suggestion motivated by the Holocaust? Knowing him, I would say it is possible; but the failure of his suggestion to have any serious impact suggests that any possible link is insignificant.

III

Other factors also influence the ways in which the Bible is handled in Jewish contexts. By the beginning of the nineteenth century, one can discern essentially three different approaches to Torah study in European Jewish contexts: Talmudic-Midrashic, Midrashic-Zoharic, and Rational-Scientific. Though medieval interpretation also exemplified different approaches to the text, there, too, one sees a series of syntheses and, by the seventeenth century, a wide range of eclectic approaches, specializations and sub-specializations had developed. Each still impacts on the contemporary handling of the Bible, though in most cases this means primarily the Torah to the exclusion of the other books.

Talmudic-Midrashic interpretation essentially derives from the Talmud and is heavily enriched by the midrashic literature. Moreover, its handling of the Bible demonstrates a profound influence from the secondary halakhic literature and the exegesis of the Talmud. This material is likely to prioritize talmudic interpretations and applications over what appears to be the Bible's own agenda and to prefer Maimonides' *Mishneh Torah*, Alfasi's condensation of talmudic law, or Rabbenu Asher's Talmud commentary to the Bible commentaries of David Kimhi and Abraham Ibn Ezra. This approach is steeped in rabbinic learning, popular in yeshivot, and dedicated to early interpretations and their latter-day developments, but not particularly based on classical Bible study or interested in non-halakhic modern applications.

The Midrashic-Zoharic approach is differentiated from the Talmudic-Midrashic approach by levels of emphasis rather than a total avoidance of the Talmud, whose contents remain important for all classes of rabbinic interpreters. Texts of this type are easily distinguished by their dominant midrashic motifs and frequent citations or jumping off points from midrashic or zoharic interpretations of the Bible. Whereas the Talmudic-Midrashic approach will often reconstruct biblical personalities or events in the light of rabbinic ideals or interpretations, the Midrashic-Zoharic one will apply the Zohar's mythological outlook and language. One simple way to differentiate between them is to examine how they treat the legal passages in Exodus 21–23. Talmudic-Midrashic interpretations will delve into the details of legal theory and application developed in the Mishnah, Talmud and halakhic midrashim; while Midrashic-Zoharic interpretations will follow the Zohar's speculations about sefirot and its kabbalistic agenda.

The Rational-Scientific School is closer to the Talmudic-Midrashic than the Midrashic-Zoharic one but differs from both in the nature of the exegetical literature it values. Unlike the other two, it derives primary sustenance from the medieval commentators and, to a lesser extent, the medieval philosophers. It is concerned much more (though not exclusively) with the literal meaning of the text, and it is attracted more by the accurate historical reconstruction of biblical events than devotion to earlier corpora of rabbinic interpretations.

These three groups are in some ways comparable to those popularly labeled Mitnagdim, Hasidim and Maskilim, though one cannot press this analogy too far, as all sorts of exceptions are easily identified. Moreover, followers of the medieval preference for allowing the best (i.e, their preferred) interpretations of all types to remain available demonstrate somewhat broader interests than those described here. This means that some writers combined two of the approaches described above as Midrashic-Zoharic and Talmudic-Midrashic or Talmudic-Midrashic and Rational-Scientific, though the percentages may have varied greatly. A few such multi-faceted writers remained true to the medieval and renaissance attitude of many kabbalists and retained an interests in science as well, and thus in some ways could be claimed to represent all three approaches, but this model has fallen from favour. Despite the exceptions and the potential for misclassification, the categories are useful at the very least as markers from which to measure various positions.

These three approaches to Bible study are still manifest in contemporary Jewish learning. The Talmudic-Midrashic approach is still popular among Orthodox rabbis, yeshivot (particularly non-hasidic ones), and preachers who identify primarily with the rabbinic texts they favor. It would be unfair to such proponents of being insensitive to the modern world and its experiences, especially the Holocaust, but truth be told their Bible interpretations are grounded mostly in ancient rabbinic texts and reflect the ancient rabbinic agenda or a modern halakhic one.

The Midrashic-Zoharic literature differs from the Talmudic one and its exegesis in important ways, but followers of it are still anchored in an essentially pre-modern mindset. Moreover, while these literatures take evil quite seriously and contain many texts that potentially can contribute to discussions of it in the contemporary world—and are often used this way by their adherents—they do not necessarily dwell on them or their biblical roots. While not closed off to the Holocaust and the indescribable levels of destruction it brought to their affiliates and institutions, distance from the Bible itself leaves the bridge between it and the Holocaust undeveloped.

While Rational-Scientific interpretation began in medieval times and maintained both religious adherents and roots in classical rabbinic philology and philosophy, for a while its nineteenth-century manifestations were closely linked to the Enlightenment. Eventually many of its adherents and defenders chose to direct their Jewish sensibilities and conduct their practice of Judaism through means other than those carefully controlled by earlier rabbinic beliefs and practices. This raised the suspicions and criticisms of many who saw themselves as highly traditional and also helped distance them from anything that sounded new and of questionable religious value. One could easily subdivide late twentieth-century Jewry into branches bearing labels like Orthodox, Conservative, Reform, Hasidic, Reconstructionist, Haredi, etc., but the dominant issue of Bible study during this century has not centered on the rabbinic flavor of one's Judaism, despite the importance this issue carries and despite the major divisions in the Jewish people it has created.

Modern Bible study is characterized primarily by devotion to determining the straightforward meaning of the text, to examining its literary qualities and their implications for understand the text's contents, and to reconstructing the Bible's historical background. In short, these may be called Text, Texture and Context, and they dominate the interests of virtually all contemporary interpreters. While such concerns also moved many medieval (and some pre-medieval) writers, the modern emphasis on this approach, largely to the exclusion of application to personal or national interests, has both rendered the talmudic observation about the Bible's eternal relevance somewhat distant and directed the major currents of interest to non-rabbinic matters. To the extent that it is valued by the rabbinic world—and that does vary greatly with the levels of dedication to rabbinic sources of the individual rabbis or their groups—it does tend to refocus interest away from the Bible's contemporary significance and toward ancient historical matters. As it succeeds, the relevance of and to the Holocaust decreases.

IV

In short, we find that several different and perhaps unrelated factors conspire to keep the Holocaust and Bible study apart. First, the traditional preferences of certain biblical texts over others has kept those perhaps most potentially relevant at a distance. In addition, the three dominant rabbinic approaches to Bible study of the last two centuries have, for different reasons, remained true to the approaches and literatures on which they are based and therefore somewhat disinterested in, if not insensitive to, Holocaust-related applications. Finally, the most powerful trend in contemporary Bible study has shifted the focus totally back to ancient times and eschewed the search for modern analogies and applications in favour of the quest for the straightforward meaning of the text, the search for the historical characters and contexts, and a fuller understanding of the Bible's literary qualities.

However, the Holocaust has not been lost to the rabbinic world; it merely has not emerged significantly from the approaches to Bible study examined above. I have labeled the textual-linguistic, literary and historical approaches as Text, Texture and Context. A fourth approach, which may be labeled Pretext, while like its fellow terms grounded to a certain extent in the text, refers to the use of the Bible for purposes assumed not to be the primary concerns of the ancient writers and texts. Pretext responds positively to the talmudic issue of perpetual relevance; it includes personal emotional and spiritual grappling with the contents of the Bible. Because of the Bible's ongoing relevance to Jews—the fulfillment of the mishnaic notion popularly associated with Ben Bag Bag's teaching that 'everything is in it'—Pretext begs to make every event in every generation a part of the biblical focus. Through the development of Pretext, the Holocaust can receive and indeed has received a voiced link with the Bible.

Such an approach is not one with which Midrashic-Zoharic or Talmudic-Midrashic interpreters can readily identify, and Rational-Scientific types find it even more distant. But without trivializing the Holocaust, one must admit that Judaism has much to say about it, and most things that Judaism has ever discussed have been expressed through biblical idioms. The notions may not deserve treatment as Bible study, but they do deserve attention.

For example, over the years the character of Haman in the book of Esther has been linked to virtually every evil person who has confronted the Jews, either locally or internationally. Indeed, the use of the book of Esther as a model for over a hundred other compositions describing miraculous acts of salvation that prevented the destruction of Jewish communities is well known. In this context, one cannot be surprised at attempts to link Haman and his intentions with the events of the Holocaust, just as earlier times had him and Ahasueros identified with royal and court figures of European countries and more recent events saw him linked with the deployers of scud missiles against Israel. These links are supported through a variety of strategies ranging from typological reading of the text to decoding names and places associated with the Holocaust from the book of Esther and the names therein. (Elsewhere I have forcefully rejected the validity of this approach to the text, but here we speak of how it is presented by and to contemporary Jews, not how it should or should not be, and it undoubtedly belongs in the discussion.)

In similar fashion, one finds Holocaust preachers and writers of different sources portraying some of the characters in Genesis as having some Holocaust-type experiences or thoughts. Abraham's near sacrifice of Isaac is one case in point, the constant wanderings of the early Hebrews is another. When Elie Wiesel presents Jacob as a successful negotiator of numerous real and potential calamities, one cannot but recognize his having reconstructed the patriarch as a Holocaust survivor. To the Bible scholar, even to the midrashist, the talmudist or the zoharist, such interpretations range from quaint to entertaining to irrelevant. But to many a contemporary Jewish reader they have a powerful ring of truth that helps deal with the tragedy and provide a new and more compelling approach to Genesis. The potential criticisms in such a reading pale into insignificance, and the relevance to non-Jews is seen, for example, in Joel Marcus's book *Jesus and the Holocaust*,[1] which reflects Christianity's long-standing interest in suffering, martyrdom and salvation. It is reflected even in the misuse of the Holocaust against Jews and Israel by Muslims who similarly value submission and martyrdom in the name of their religious ideals.

The post-Holocaust period also includes the beginnings of the postmodern one, which often is described as a philosophy that recognizes in texts only meanings that individual readers find in them. In a sense, it denies the relevance, surely the dominance, of the philological-historical approach (what I have called Text and Context) and stresses the value of Pretext and the use of intertextual strategies that allow for the comparison of virtually all things for all possible purposes. This pluralistic attitude is actually a time-honoured Jewish exegetical value

1.   New York: Doubleday, 1997.

developed by prominent kabbalists in the sixteenth century, but variants in the mishnaic presentation of Ben Bag Bag's statement (that, for instance in the Kaufmann Manuscript) suggest it is over a millennium older. For this reason, some postmodern interpreters exhibit a close affinity to midrashic interpretation, practice some of its same excesses, and defend the midrashic approach—which admittedly finds more of the reader than the biblical subject in the text—as the only reasonable one. This suggests that postmodern developments may yet contribute to heightened awareness of the need to build further links between the Bible and the Holocaust; indeed the present volume may reflect this growing trend.

The Holocaust will continue to influence many aspects of the Jewish consciousness, including its response to the Bible, but the possibility of the Holocaust's immediate impact on Bible study suggests at least one other important caveat. One must be careful to avoid the fallacy of assuming *post hoc ergo propter hoc*, and therefore attribute all contemporary reactions to the Bible—particularly the undesirable ones—to the influence of the Holocaust, though some connection can be assumed. Thus, the destruction of centers of rabbinic learning in Europe has led to many attempts to reconstruct them in other places. Many who lived in both have emphasized to me how much the reconstructions differ from the originals. The post-Holocaust rabbinic institutions have accomplished many things deemed impossible only a short time ago, but guided by the spirit of what they imagine to have existed, they have created *de novo*; they have not simply restored the pre-existing realities. The individuals and centers of learning are gone; their replacements— whether in Israel and caught between the pious, secular and nationalist forces, or in North America and working to assimilate the best of American culture or to avoid any impact from it—are different from what preceded them and focused on new and challenging tasks.

Uncharted factors in these changes include the breadth of knowledge and wealth of details about ancient texts made available to potentially everyone through modern technology; the newness and the vibrancy of these reconstructed Jewish civilizations; the intentional support of intellectual and spiritual specialization that seems to have closed off so much of the Bible-related Jewish heritage from so many contemporary Jews of such different ideological demeanor; and the general sense that the Bible is less essential to contemporary people than was often believed in previous centuries.

As well, one cannot dismiss the impact of the very existence of a Jewish state, particularly since this state is located in the biblical land of Israel, was founded closely on the heels of the Holocaust, and for decades maintained a close eye on its biblical roots through a national culture that valued and identified with the Bible. Recent surveys of Israelis call into question the extent to which different groups maintain these attitudes and allegiancies, but one has merely to walk down the streets, to listen to the inhabitants, and to examine the national consciousness in order to see the extent to which the Bible and the Holocaust have been merged into one unified whole. Has this affected deeply the ways in which the rabbinic world (or for that matter the scholarly one) presents the Bible? I think not. But it has impacted heavily and probably permanently on the Jewish national conscious. Ultimately this will become clearer, though first it must integrate with or overcome the forces of an exegetical history that has spanned three millennia.

A FISSURE ALWAYS UNCONTAINED

Walter Brueggemann

The Shoah constitutes a break in all of our certitudes to which we shall never become accustomed or jaded. The great learning of the extensive Shoah literature is that we have no categories—cultural, emotional, theological, interpretive—by which to contain, explain or understand that barbarism, let alone justify it. Our interpretive capacity is pushed to extremity, and when we reach the furthest extremity of imagination of which we are capable, we still will not have reached far enough to contain, explain or understand.

The failure of categories is expressed by two familiar aphorisms responding to the shock of the Shoah. First, from Theodor Adorno: 'To write poetry after Auschwitz is barbaric'.[1] No poetry, perhaps because poetry lives at the edge of memory and we do not know how to voice poetry that can go to the limitlessness of that death where nothing is remembered. The fact that Adorno has since qualified the claim does not change its primal power. Secondly, from Irving Greenberg: 'Let us offer, then, as a working principle the following: No statement, theological or otherwise, should be made that would not be credible in the presence of the burning children.'[2]

We are not capable of such utterances and so are reduced to silence. Because our utterances characteristically shield us from such reality, such theological utterances as we usually can muster are given the lie by the lost children, and so our usual claims end in silence.

I am not able to imagine how one from the death-camps or one linked to one in the death-camps—or any Jew—can finally respond interpre-

1. Theodore W. Adorno, *Prisms* (trans. Samuel and Shierry Weber; Cambridge, MA: MIT Press, 1981), p. 34.

2. Irving Greenberg, 'Cloud of Smoke, Pillar of Fire', in John K. Roth and Michael Berenbaum (eds.), *Holocaust: Religious and Philosophical Implications* (St Paul: Paragon House, 1989), pp. 7-55.

tively to the wretchedness that exposes all our categories. I can only respond considerably removed from the suffering; and yet as a Christian I am not completely removed, but among those included in the long-term collusion that evoked and permitted the Shoah.[3] Even at my remove as a Christian interpreter, I am not able to pretend against the fissure in any of the categories that have heretofore served me so well. As I learn, I am aware of how much unlearning I am now required to do.

I

We have for a very long time, we Western Christians, been busy establishing and maintaining hegemony, that is, the capacity to dominate by an assumed authority, without the exercise of any visible force or coercion. The tale of Western Christian hegemony is very old and very deep. It was perhaps triggered by the conversion of the empire under Constantine, then given synthetic articulation in the great medieval assemblage of empire and hierarchy. But then it came to its most dangerous form in the seventeenth and eighteenth centuries in the Enlightenment alliance between Christian power and the new science that issued in technology, largely legitimated but not critiqued by the dominant theological tradition. For all of its misgivings about Galileo, the Christian enterprise came to terms with the offer of new science and found a way to harness its vision and practice of control. The hegemony has many faces, all of which are in alliance. It is the capacity of the political domination of 'the Christian prince', not at all disrupted by the Peace of Augsburg or the Treaty of Westphalia. The assured right of political domination led to 'the age of Absolutism' and the 'divine right of kings', so that all power was legitimately held in concentrated fashion with the power to excommunicate and eliminate any variant.

Political hegemony has been matched and sustained by interpretive hegemony, so that the West proceeded with a single truth that required only assent, a single truth held by an infallible church, or a single truth held eventually by the power of reason that yielded 'assured results'. As concerns my field of study, the Hebrew Bible/Old Testament, that intellectual, interpretive hegemony has taken two forms. The more obvious

---

3. On that long-term collusion, see Steven Katz, *The Holocaust in Historical Context*. I. *The Holocaust and Mass Death before the Modern Age* (Oxford: Oxford University Press, 1994).

is the capacity of *church interpretation* to pre-empt the text and make it subservient to the dogmatic claims of the church, so that the outcome of text is largely known before reading it. But perhaps the more insidious form of interpretive hegemony has been the enterprise of the *critical tradition* that has now been shown to be profoundly anti-Semitic in its assumptions and inhospitable to Jewish alternative; thus in Solomon Schecter's famous phrase, 'higher criticism' is not far from 'higher anti-Semitism'.

The political and interpretive capacity for hegemony has characteristically been 'kicked upstairs' and expressed as an articulation of God—God of Bible, God of the Western Church—as the hegemonic force that concentrates all power and purpose. Cast in theological terms, this God has been seen to be undivided and without variation, with a monopoly of power ('omnipotence') knowledge ('omniscience'), and presence ('omnipresence'). This God has become the legitimator of the interpretive community and of its hegemonic culture.

The product of this hegemony, in all the areas of political, interpretive and theological claim, is the arrival at absolute and final truth: so absolute as to be beyond question or dissent, so final as to be beyond anxiety about any new truth that may be given as correction. That absolute and final claim seemed for so many for so long to be a given beyond question, a given without any problem. The practical and effective outcome of such absolutism and finality has been the silencing of dissent and the elimination of anyone or any claim that is different. And because the silencing and elimination came to be done with complete legitimacy, it could be done totally, shamelessly, and with a 'good conscience'.

II

For those who do interpretation—especially Christian interpretation—the Shoah stands as a dread-filled summons to unlearn a great deal. For Christians this means the unlearning of 'final readings', for 'final readings' tend, I suggest, to give ground for 'final solutions'. There can be no doubt that in Western biblical interpretation, Christian 'finality' has been intimately connected to critical 'finality'. Indeed there is some comic dimension in recent critical readings that are dead set against 'final' Christian readings, that are keen on exposing the 'ideology' of texts, but that proceed on 'critical grounds' that completely appropriate and enact the 'finality' of Enlightenment reason.[4] For all the differences, a *confessional finality* and a *critical finality* are twin operations, neither of which is open to a jarring fissure in its own 'finality'.[5]

For Christian readers who take the fissure of the Shoah as a demand and a clue for an alternative way of reading, there is much to learn against 'finality' that takes the form of 'fragmentation', that is, utterances that do not claim to be universal truth, but that are simply voices that live in the presence of many other voices, no one of which is capable of hegemony over the others. In what follows, I will consider the depriviliging of interpretive hegemony that strikes me as an urgent task for Christian, Western readers. I will mention three facets of this unlearning that occur to me.

The first, as I have indicated in my *Theology of the Old Testament*, is to recognize that the *biblical text itself* offers penetrating voices of protest and subversion that tell powerfully against 'normative claims' in the text.[6] In very much 'Church usage' that has controlled even much critical reading, these voices of protest and subversion have been marginated or excluded from the horizon of interpretation. These 'counter texts' only make sense and are understood in all their dangerous power when 'normative' texts of a 'good, faithful, reliable God' are taken seriously with their normative function and claim.

In the book of Psalms, it is the hymn of praise (and Songs of Thanksgiving) that vigorously voice YHWH as totally reliable and consistently good. It is in the face of such hymnic affirmations that the Psalms of complaint function to tell the counter-truth about YHWH,

---

4. For a typical presentation of the current consideration of 'ideology' in the text, see David Penchansky, *The Betrayal of God: Ideological Conflict in Job* (Louisville: Westminster/John Knox Press, 1990). But against such a perspective, see Stephen E. Fowl, 'Texts Don't Have Ideologies', *BibInt* 3 (1995), pp. 1-34.

5. Jon D. Levenson, *The Hebrew Bible, The Old Testament, and Historical Criticism* (Louisville: Westminster/John Knox Press, 1993) has considered the defining convergence of dominant Christian and dominant critical approaches to the Hebrew Bible. That convergence is important in the production of 'final' readings.

6. On the voices of protest and subversion, see Walter Brueggemann, *Theology of the Old Testament: Testimony, Dispute, Advocacy* (Minneapolis: Fortress Press, 1997), pp. 317-403. Behind my rubric of counter-testimony, see Emil Fackenheim, *To Mend the World: Foundations of Post-Holocaust Thought* (New York: Schocken Books, 1989), p. 11: 'The holocaust poses the most radical counter testimony to both Judaism and Christianity.' See also Greenberg, 'Cloud of Smoke', pp. 307-308.

about Israel, and about the world.[7] It is not necessary (or possible) to insist that the Psalms of complaint mark the extremity of the Shoah (which they do not), in order to see that theologically they function as challenges to normative faith and its hegemonic claims. Those Psalms of complaint assert that on the horizon of faithful Israel, there are indeed circumstances in which the affirmation of God's consistent fidelity rings false. Fidelity is permitted no 'final reading', given the presence of these texts.

A dramatic case in point is Psalm 89. In vv. 1-38 this hymn celebrates with enthusiastic repetition the faithfulness and steadfast love of God, especially toward the house of David (vv. 2, 3, 6, 9, 25, 29, 34). The hymn overflows with talk of fidelity. And then, abruptly, vv. 39-52 reverse field and acknowledge the failure of God's fidelity and the absence of God's steadfast love. While the Psalm ends with a *pro forma* doxology (v. 53), in fact the protest is left standing as the last word, completely unresolved, even unacknowledged, left there. In this Psalm as in many others, it is most often suggested that exile is the core habitat of the complaint. This may indeed be the case with reference to the sixth century. Beyond that, exile is the characteristic habitat of loss and all the negativities that go with loss. Thus it is the *utterance of complaint*, matched by *a context of displacement*, that carries Israel to rage, protest and accusation, thus departing the glad assurances of hymnic gratitude and awe.

Characteristically, as in Ps. 89.1-38 and 39-52, the core claims of faith and the characteristic utterance of protest are left to stand together, in tension, unresolved and without comment. While it is the case that in Psalm 89 the protesting prayer is last, this is not to urge that the protest is privileged or the 'final' word. It is simply there, left to have its say, subverting any easier claim. Such a juxtaposition of texts, for any who pay attention to the Hebrew Bible, is unremarkable. It is, however, most importantly remarkable in a universe of interpretation where the normative claims of power, goodness and fidelity are easily the 'final' word

---

7. On the Psalms of complaint, see Claus Westermann, 'The Role of the Lament in the Theology of the Old Testament', *Int* 28 (1974), pp. 20-38; *idem*, *The Praise of God in the Psalms* (Richmond: John Knox Press, 1965). See also Patrick D. Miller, *They Cried to the Lord: The Form and Theology of Biblical Prayer* (Minneapolis: Fortress Press, 1994), pp. 55-134, and Walter Brueggemann, *The Message of the Psalms* (Minneapolis: Augsburg Publishing House, 1984), pp. 51-121.

and never challenged or subverted. Hegemonic interpretation, both dogmatic and critical, permits texts to have only one say, a 'final' say to which all else must submit. With Psalm 89 as a particular case, the more general juxtaposition of hymn and complaint are a characteristic juxtaposition that permits no single 'final' say. Thus the interpretive situation created by the Shoah requires an unlearning of a settled, triumphant reading for a reading that attends to more texts and that reads the more texts honestly and carefully, in a way that precludes large summary conclusions to attend to the juxtapositions that permit no summary conclusions.

Secondly, unlearning of hegemonic reading is informed and instructed by characteristic Jewish ways of reading to which Western Christians have paid little attention. In dominant Western readings, texts that might protest against core claims have been quickly read over and swallowed up in a sustained act of expository denial. Confessional inclination can quickly establish the irrelevance of texts that 'do not fit', and do not serve the claims of triumphalist faith.[8] In more critical readings, 'reasonableness' cannot allow for tension or contradiction, and so such poignancies in the text are readily smoothed over by a positing of 'sources' or by editing out what is 'not credible'. The standard critical device is to make ill-fitting matters that defy the adopted 'story-line' to be 'glosses' or 'redactions'. Oddly, dogmatic over-reading and critical 'reasonable' reading can serve the same purpose, to eliminate 'trouble' in the texts so that they can be taken in one whole reading, a reading that is so clear as to be 'final'.

The text itself invites notice about how our readings have silenced enough texts to make things fit. The unlearning of a 'final' reading is given great impetus by attending to how Jews have characteristically read these texts. The entire rabbinic enterprise of midrashic reading is a cause for unlearning of hegemonic practice. Most recently, Michael

---

8.   For an example of such certitude, see Richard B. Hays, *Echoes of Scripture in the Letters of Paul* (New Haven: Yale University Press, 1989), p. 191, who makes a series of statements governed by, 'No reading of Scripture can be legitimate if...' To be sure, Hays is reporting his judgment on Paul's categories, telling enough in that way. By the time Hays's formulation is picked up by Stephen Fowl, *Engaging Scripture* (Oxford: Basil Blackwell, 1998), p. 153, the claims seem to have grown even more authoritative. I cite these statements as examples of a confessional inclination (even if it is rooted in Paul) that quickly establishes the irrelevance of texts that 'do not fit'.

Fishbane has explored the rich, generative 'exegetical imagination' of Jewish interpretation, wherein he speaks of 'the many pleasures of Midrash'.[9] I take the beginning point of Fishbane's review of interpretive method to be the insistence that 'meanings' are not given intrinsically in the texts, but are the produce of the task of interpretation.[10] This judgment means, of course, that meanings are many, that they are in part the imaginative work of the interpreter, and that they are, so to speak, done 'on the spot' as interpretation is wrought. Such an approach honestly acknowledges, even relishes, the subjective, generative, imaginative work of interpretation, thus programmatically denying any positivistic notion that meaning is given in the text 'beforehand'.

Fishbane's work in great detail exhibits the theses of Susan Handelman who has articulated the deep contrast in exegetical approaches that yield or do not yield 'final' readings: 'The infinity of meaning and plurality of interpretation are as much the cardinal virtues, even divine imperatives, for Rabbinic thought as they are the cardinal sins for Greek thought.'[11] Christians of course have been for the most part very slow in countenancing such 'plurality' and very nervous about such an option. While it is, in my judgment, a positive point to appropriate the openness of midrashic interpretation, here I wish to accent the negative of Handelman's 'cardinal sins of Greek thought'. The cardinal sin is to suggest that there is no 'final' reading, no given conclusion, no administratable truth.

It takes no great insight to see that economic-political military hegemony cannot be marked by and likely cannot survive in such fluidity of authorizing texts.[12] For that reason, the Western hegemony can engage

9.   Michael Fishbane, *The Exegetical Imagination: On Jewish Thought and Theology* (Cambridge, MA: Harvard University Press, 1998), p. 2.

10.   Fishbane, *The Exegetical Imagination*, p. 2, uses the term *poesis*: 'Every exegetical act is a conscious construction of meaning through the verbal condition of Scripture.'

11.   Susan A. Handelman, *The Slavers of Moses: The Emergence of Rabbinic Interpretation in Modern Literary Theory* (Albany: SUNY Press, 1982), p. 21.

12.   Before the fall of the apartheid regime in South Africa, a colleague there reported to me that he and others in the field were not permitted by the regime to suggest that the book of Jonah was anything except 'history'. His judgment was that to admit any playful dimension in the narrative was to hint at an instability that would contribute to the unraveling of the entire power arrangement. I cite this as an example of the way in which hegemony depends upon closed, final readings of authorizing texts.

such open exposition only if it is prepared in principle to relinquish its hegemonic grip upon meaning. Thus Joseph Dan can comment:

> The Hebrew midrash is alien to western literary, exegetical, and homiletical tradition because of the vast differences between the Jewish and Christian scriptures. Christian preachers had to rely, when interpreting scriptures and revealing their hidden meaning, mainly on the ideonic side, the implications of the content of the verse. Jewish preachers could use a total text, hermeneutically discussing not only the meaning of terms and words, but also their sound, the shape of the letters, the vocalization points and their shapes and sounds... Dogmatic thinking must rely on an unambiguous text. The Hebrew Bible does not lend itself easily to the formulation of dogma, because of the obscurities which haunt almost every verse. These two differences—the ability to use the total semiotic message of the text, and the use of an obscure, and therefore polysemous, Hebrew original—create a most significant gap between Jewish and Christian exegetes and preachers.[13]

Handelman has made clear that Freud's methods of dream interpretation and 'depth psychology' more generally are in continuity with midrashic approaches to narrative, with its endless capacity for more and other interpretation.[14] Just now I want to comment upon the remarkable ways in which the most elemental and defining insights of Freud have made a decisive difference in dominant Christian self-consciousness with an embrace by 'the pastoral care movement' and the general embrace of 'psychotherapy' in a secularized Christian culture. That remarkable embrace of 'layers of interpretive meaning' (with no particular layer of interpretive meaning privileged) that reveal the complex and convoluted reality of human life has become a truism in

---

13. Joseph Dan, 'Midrash and the Dawn of Kabbalah', in Geoffrey H. Hartman and Sanford Budick (eds.), *Midrash and Literature* (New Haven: Yale University Press, 1986), pp. 127-39 (128-29). In the same volume, Myrna Solotorevshy, 'The Model of Midrash and Borges's Interpretive Tales and Essays', pp. 253-64 (255), judges: 'The concept of the inherent polysemy of the literary text which nullifies the possibility of a univocal interpretation is one of the arch principles of Midrash.' Dan seems a bit to suggest that the difference of Christian reading and Jewish reading is largely due to the Jewish capacity to pay attention to the Hebrew text in its playfulness. That obviously is important, but the Christian propensity to universalizing closure is surely based on other power factors as well as neglect of the nuance of the Hebrew text. I note, in passing, the subversive perspective of my teacher, James Muilenburg, who with his program of 'rhetorical criticism' began to lead critical reflection in a new direction, away from hegemonic reading.

14. Handelman, *The Slayers of Moses*, pp. 129-52.

Christian culture, all the while holding to single truths and certain meanings that brook no rereading or reinterpretation at a dogmatic or critical level. I take that informal but comprehensive embrace of such interpretive methods to be the result and sign of an insatiable yearning to touch and expose and embrace precisely those elements of human life that are characteristically censored, denied, and precluded by the force of hegemonic reading life. In the actual practice of much church life, church interpretation and church reading, the reasonable 'final' reading most often is held alongside a more pastoral polyvalence without any sense of incongruity or contradiction. Moreover, as Midrash shows up in Freud, so Freud shows up in Jacques Derrida's deconstruction.[15] I have on occasion been chided for attending, as best I am able, to the density of Derrida's 'French theory'. Such chiding does not notice that in its deepest claims, Derrida's work is not only French theory but is Jewish reading as well. Of course it is endlessly satisfying for hegemonists to dismiss Derrida as a nihilist, without noticing either that his target is to a large extent logocentrism or that the targeted logocentrism is a 'final' reading upon which established power and privilege depend.

The sequence of Midrash–Freud–Derrida has been endlessly written upon, in principle needing to be 'endlessly' so. Of course the sequence, moreover, is endlessly dense and complicated. For the purposes of my theme it is enough to recognize that these characteristic Jewish ways of reading tell against every final solution and reject every final reading. This now familiar *interpretive* sequence of Midrash–Freud–Derrida has its *lived*, suffered demonstration in the Shoah that Emil Fackenheim shrewdly characterizes as 'the most radical counter testimony to both Judaism and Christianity'.[16] Of course one may not suggest that the Shoah in any necessary way is connected, from a Jewish side, with polyvalent reading. It can, however, be suggested that this barbaric act of hegemony can be connected, for Christian interpreters, to the long propensity of 'final' reading. And thus the Shoah is the *lived disruption* that parallels the *reading disruptions* that 'final' readings cannot tolerate. Every such disruption, including this lived one and every interpretive one, requires the loss of precious certitudes and the articulation of new certitudes that appropriate the new data. The new

15. Handelman, *The Slayers of Moses*, pp. 163-78.
16. See n. 6.

data, here the data of limitless brutality, may be so 'other' that the new certitude is on wholly new ground, and perhaps not certain in the ways of old certitude. Of course one may indeed say that the fissure of the Shoah is so different in *degree* as to be different in *kind* from any previous disruption, read or lived. The difference in extent or kind, however, is at last that to which one must attend in a reading trajectory of disruption, the difference that requires a radical reformulation of certitudes amid the awareness that every articulation of certitudes is provisional, an insight long known in Jewish reading that refuses 'final' reading. The dominant reading tradition in the West is so certain, so sure, and so lacking in fluidity that it can do little except engage in denial in the face of new data.

III

The deprivileging of certitude is evident *in the text* itself, especially with complaints located in a series of exiles. The deprivileging of certitude is endlessly exhibited *in the interpretive trajectory of Midrash* that in the twentieth century features, among others, Freud and Derrida. Third and finally [*sic!*], however, the issue for the Christian Western reader is not simply text or interpretive trajectory but comes down to cases, as unsettling reading comes to *unsettled God*. It follows, of course, that if these unsettled and unsettling texts concern God, then the God they yield will be deeply unsettled. It turns out, of course, that settled readings are needed for a settled God in order to root a settled economy with its arrangements of goods, power and access. The dominant Christian reading of texts—perhaps informed by the categories of Greek philosophy, perhaps propelled by the requirements of the empire of Constantine, perhaps simply in response to a felt need for coherence—has been to deliver a God in whom there is 'no variation or shadow due to change' (Jas 1.17). Specifically, Christian interpretive strategies have been in pursuit of coherence, with 'fragmentation' seen as a primal threat that, without any critical examination, is taken as 'a bad thing' in principle.[17]

17. For a positive utilization of 'fragment', see Jane Flax, *Thinking Fragments: Psychoanalysis, Feminism and Postmodernism in the Contemporary West* (Berkeley: University of California Press, 1991). 'Fragmentation' comes to be viewed very differently and very negatively in much of current theology, as in the case of Stephen Fowl. I do not contend that fragmentation carries no risks or dan-

And now, the Shoah, after which there are only fragments: traces of what was, traces of truth, traces of text, traces of God, traces of privileged established authority. The prophet Amos offers a scene of such traces:

> As the shepherd rescues from the mouth of the lion two legs, or a piece
> of an ear, so shall the people of Israel who live in Samaria be rescued,
> with the corner of a couch and part of a bed (Amos 3.12).

Two legs and the piece of an ear are not much rescue for cultural past or a claimed truth. Consequently, theology works now with fragments and traces—a disclosure here, a doxology there, occasionally a text that strikes thick with authority. The theological enterprise then 'makes' a whole that incorporates many fragments and traces, but all the while knows in doing so that it is a made whole and therefore a provisional whole that will be endlessly remade, but never 'finally' made, always provisionally, endlessly remade.[18]

I have already referred to Psalm 89 in which a deep turn occurs between v. 38 and v. 39. The turn is not marked in the poetry or even acknowledged, only inferred from what precedes and what follows. What has preceded is deeply deconstructed by what follows. The God of the Psalm, heretofore celebrated as steadfast and faithful, now becomes the absent addressee of Israel's imperative petitions, the addressee who does not show, who is silent, perhaps hearing the prayers of Israel, perhaps enjoying the doxology of v. 53, but nevertheless leaving Israel in its uttered abyss, uttered but in the abyss. Those who speak such petition and imperative can insist and wait and hope. That of course is not enough to qualify as conventional Western theology. It is, however, enough for the ones who pray and sing, who will

gers. My only insistence is that hegemonic resistance to fragmentation is equally a threat that is not much entertained by those who fear the threat of fragmentation.

18. I have referenced to 'making' as understood in Fishbane's notion of *poesis*. To deny the 'making' of theological claims is to imagine that they are objective and intrinsic and to foreclose the endless process of remaking, a deep temptation of hegemonic reading. The historical survey of confessions in the Calvinist traditions of Christianity by Jan Rohls, *Reformed Confessions: Theology from Zurich to Barmen* (Columbia Series in Reformed Theology; Louisville: Westminster/John Knox Press, 1998) suggests that in the Reformed traditions of Christianity, something like this endless 'remaking' is cherished in the tradition at its best. That same tradition, of course, also has a deep itch to give a final reading that precludes other readings.

rely upon address and not speculation, because address permits incoherence, disjunction and fragment.

This strange generativity of uttered faith leads me then to juxtapose *fragment*, *coherence* and *denial*. The Shoah evokes a redefining that permits and requires us to reread all else as fragment. It does not distort the Shoah nor does it trivialize to take the Shoah as the lens for reading the world of horror, abuse and violence everywhere all around, in forms of terrorism or in more institutionalized forms of capital punishment and welfare reform, and so on. The truth is in fragments. Those who attend to these texts (and those who do not) are endlessly [*sic*] picking up the pieces and reconfiguring them into provisional coherences. Indeed, the text in its herky-jerky, quixotic fragmentation rings so true because it is like our life, and the God given here meets fragmented life in fragmented presentation, a God who hears and does not answer, a God who loves and punishes savagely, a God of rage who forgives, a God who in devious and diverse ways meets life as lived, and authorizes durability for yet another time to come.

In the face of fragment, the empire and its theologians fling out coherence—all coherent, all reasonable, all accounted for, all understood—a plan, a creed, an organizational chart, a strategic mobilization, a budget, all accounted for. This is the way of those who manage and control. And indeed that will work for some—now and then. For most adherents of such coherence, however, the claim becomes a recipe for denial, censure and pretense, all of which issue in violence, and yet another round begins. The linkage between coherence and denial is worth more reflection. It may be that the God of Israel comes in fragments, not because of Jewish imagination, but because it is the only way to fly under the radar of denial. Fragment, traced in and through brokenness, is a way of Holiness in the world—an affirmation that Friday Christians endlessly relearn, even as we notice a yen for Sunday without Friday, a coherence without fissure, a theology of glory that deceives.

IV

The text endures such subversion. Jewish ways of reading yield fragments. The God of this tradition leaves traces. There are no texts of Pharaoh in the Bible, no texts of powerful, imperial continuity. This is a text and a God and a people and a reading habit that give their due to fissure. We do not come close in the Bible to the fissure of the Shoah; as close as we come is the fissure of exile.[19] The rich textual witness to that dislocation is sufficient evidence that Israel did not know what to say, any more than we do in our moment after fissure. As a consequence of not knowing, Israel said many things.

One of the things they say—'they' being exilic Israel—is that there will be an ending, a destruction, a dislocation. The Jeremiah tradition voices this ending most clearly and declares this ending most forcefully. And *yet*, even here the utterances of finality are not fully endings. I shall cite only two cases.[20] First in 4.23-31, the poetry vividly offers a vision of ending. But then in v. 27 this:

> For thus says the Lord: The whole land shall be a desolation;
>> yet I will not make a full end.

The same is given in 5.10:

> Go up through her vine-rows and destroy,
>> but do not make a full end;
> strip away her branches,
>> for they are not the Lord's.

The imagery powerfully bespeaks an ending. In both cases, there is the unexpected phrase, 'not a full end', so unexpected and ill-fitting that scholars pronounce 'gloss'. Such a critical judgment of course makes the text 'readable' by our rationality. But then, the occasion of the Jeremiah community is itself not 'readable'. Those in the crisis and thereafter could not see clearly, and they did not know. And so the tradition offers, a 'no, but…,' 'no future, but…' One way to make meaning (that is, a critical consensus) is to forego the 'not a full end' and let the voice give an ending. Except that they could not see and did not know. This text as divine oracle suggests that the God of Israel could not see and did not know. The same text, properly 'straightened out', is about an ending without hope. A different 'making', however, lets the odd phrase qualify the 'ending' and posits a trace of hope.

Life lived in faith is like that: unclear traces that permit but do not

19. The inadequacy of even the Joban crisis in the Hebrew Bible as an analogue for the Shoah is early and well stated by Richard L. Rubenstein, 'Job and Auschwitz', *USQR* 25 (1970), pp. 421-37; reprinted in a revised form in the present volume.

20. I have explored this problematic theme in Jeremiah more fully in 'An Ending that Does Not End' (forthcoming).

deliver hope. Such competing readings of Shoah are perhaps permitted, an ending and no hope, an ending and a trace that should not be dismissed as a loss, a hint beyond ending, a fragment. Such a trace

—might permit a poem after Adorno;
—might permit a statement even to a burning child, a small statement... beyond end.

It is the 'not clear' that requires a 'making' afresh from the text. The text is for 'making', a making in fragments; not great coherences, but not denial either. A making in fragments is all this haunted, hurting holiness requires, all that is permitted. The community around this text has regularly found such hints, haunts and hurts enough, without imagining them to be more than they are, but sometimes enough. With reference to the bloody trace of Amos 3.12 that I have cited, it is striking that after this image of remnant comes the speeches of judgment (3.13-15; 4.1-5) and a recital of curses (4.6-11), but then a strange invitation:

Prepare to meet your God, O Israel (4.12)!

And then a resilient, uncompromising doxology:

For lo, the one who forms the mountains, creates the wind,
reveals his thoughts to mortals, makes the morning darkness,
and treads on the heights of the earth—
the Lord, the God of hosts, is his name! (4.13)

We are never sure how to move from 3.12 to 4.13. We have only a text showing that the move once was made, on that pitiful occasion, by Amos. The move is a hint, not more; but likely enough.

THE HEBREW BIBLE IN THE FRAMEWORK OF CHRISTIAN–JEWISH RELATIONS IN POST-HOLOCAUST GERMANY

Rolf Rendtorff

While I am writing this essay we are preparing for the 1999 *Deutscher Evangelischer Kirchentag*, the great assembly of German Protestant Christians that is held every two years. There will be about 100,000 participants speaking, acting, listening and getting involved in an almost uncountable number of services, prayers, lectures, discussions, performances and happenings about almost as many themes, topics and agendas. Among them there will be a group of some 100 participants concentrating on problems of Christian–Jewish relations. This is, of course, a very small group related to the event as a whole; but on the other hand it is the only group that meets between the biennial assemblies, working continuously at the pending problems of Christian–Jewish relations.

Under both aspects this relation is representative for the situation within German Protestant Christianity (about Roman Catholics see below). The engagement in Christian–Jewish relations is always a matter of small groups. But these groups are working constantly, and they are very much engaged in clarifying and promoting the central topics of the agenda between Christians and Jews.[1] It took a long time for German Christians—and Germans in general as well—to genuinely confront the Holocaust. It was not earlier than 1980 that an official statement of one German regional church explicitly declared: 'We confess with dismay the co-responsibility and guilt of German Christen-

---

1. I prefer to speak about 'Christian–Jewish relations' or 'dialogue' instead of 'Jewish–Christian'. Of course, the Jews are the older ones and have to be honored as such. But the initiative for a dialogue always comes—and has to come—from the Christian side. We are glad to find Jewish partners who are willing to speak to us and even work with us on certain problems; but it is not their agenda.

dom for the Holocaust.'[2] Since then a number of German regional churches have passed similar statements and declarations. This demonstrates that among Christians in Germany there is a growing self-critical understanding of the basic impact of Christian anti-Judaism on the Holocaust.

I

To reflect on Christian co-responsibility for the Holocaust means first of all to search out what it is within Christian belief and theology that led to such strong anti-Jewish sentiment and behavior. The central point is, of course, the Christian idea of 'supersessionism', that is, of replacement of the Jewish people by the Christian church in all relevant fields. The Synod of the Church of the Rhineland calls this behavior precisely 'condemnation of the Jewish people to non-existence'.[3] Therefore the recognition of Christian involvement in the Holocaust must be accompanied by a re-thinking of the foundations of Christian self-understanding in relation to Jews and Judaism.

One of the basic points that needs re-thought is the use of Scripture. In common Christian understanding the Bible is *one* book: the 'Holy Scripture' of the Christian church. During Christian history this unity several times has been questioned by leading theologians who ascribed a lower value to the first part of the Bible, the 'Old Testament', even denying its relevance for the Christian church at all. There is a long line of such thinking: from Marcion in the Early Church, through Schleiermacher and Harnack, up to Hirsch and Bultmann in our century. Even today those voices are still to be heard. Whatever these scholars' personal attitudes to Jews and Judaism might have been, their position functioned to strengthen the anti-Jewish tradition of the Christian church and community. When the first part of the Bible was explicitly named 'Jewish', this inevitably included a devaluation compared to the second 'Christian' part, the New Testament. Even the traditional title

---

2. Statement of the Synod of the Evangelical Church of the Rhineland, 'Towards Renovation of the Relationship of Christians and Jews' (January 1980), no. 4.1. For the English text see: A. Brockway *et al.*, *The Theology of the Churches and the Jewish People: Statements by the World Council of Churches and its Member Churches* (Geneva: World Council of Churches, 1988), pp. 92-94.

3. 'Towards Renovations', no. 7; Brockway *et al.*, *The Theology of the Churches*.

'Old Testament' as such could be, and still can be, understood in such a disparaging way as to mean 'outdated' or superseded by the 'New Testament' (see below).

For German theologians during the Nazi period, these problems became even more complicated because of the fierce fight about the validity of the Old Testament within the Christian church. The contestation of its validity included the claim that, being a 'Jewish' book, the Old Testament could not be used any longer in a German Christian church. In reaction to that some of the most engaged and successful defenders of the Old Testament, as for example Wilhelm Vischer, declared the Old Testament after Jesus Christ to be a Christian book, denying any particular Jewish claim on its use.[4] As a consequence Vischer invited the Jews to realize the true meaning of the Old Testament as revealed through Jesus Christ and to join the Christian church. Thus, claiming the Old Testament exclusively for Christians meant to deprive the Jews of a central piece of their identity. Then the only way not simply to condemn the Jews to non-existence would be to exhort them to become Christians. But this is, of course, just a different way of denying their independent religious existence.

In the mainstream of German biblical scholarship before and after the Holocaust, there are to be found a great variety of approaches to the question of the relationship between the Old and New Testaments and of an adequate Christian interpretation of the Jewish Bible. One extreme position was that of Emanuel Hirsch and Rudolf Bultmann, both of whom declared the Old Testament to be necessary for Christianity, but only in order to perform the dark background for the New Testament by demonstrating the total failure (*Scheitern*) of the Jewish concept of 'law' as a way to salvation.[5] This is, of course, the most radical manner to interpret the Old Testament in a 'Christian' way.[6] Many Old

4.　W. Vischer, *Das Christuszeugnis des Alten Testaments* (2 vols.; Zürich: Evangelischer Verlag, 1934, 1942). Volume 1 translated into English as *The Witness of the Old Testament to Christ* (London, 1949).

5.　E. Hirsch, *Das Alte Testament und die Predigt des Evangeliums* (Tübingen: J.C.B. Mohr [Paul Siebeck], 1936); R. Bultmann, 'Weissagung und Erfüllung', in *idem, Glauben und Verstehen* (4 vols.; Tübingen: J.C.B.Mohr [Paul Siebeck], 1952), II, pp. 162-86. Bultmann's article has been translated into English as 'Prophecy and Fulfillment', in C. Westermann (ed.), *Essays in Old Testament Hermeneutics* (Richmond: John Knox Press, 1963), pp. 50-75.

6.　Most recently this approach has been repeated by Otto Kaiser in his book *Der Gott des Alten Testaments: Theologie des Alten Testaments* (2 vols.; Göttingen:

Testament theologians tried—and still try—to find hermeneutical methods for a particular 'Christian' interpretation of the Old Testament. All of those who are searching for this kind of method are convinced that the Old Testament is and should be an integral part of the Christian Bible, but that it has to be looked at through specific Christian glasses.

One of the most decisive positions was that of Antonius Gunneweg. He declared that only the New Testament could be the criterion for the adoption of the Old Testament as a book of the Christian church. Only where the Old Testament 'measures up' to the New Testament criteria can it be adopted in a Christian way.[7] Recently a similar voice has been heard in an article in the well-established *Jahrbuch für biblische Theologie* (1997), where the author declares: 'The basis of cognition (*Erkenntnisgrund*) of the one truth of both Testaments lies in the New Testament.'[8] Such a position continues to reproduce a Christian supersessionism in the field of biblical hermeneutics. It is particularly interesting—and rather disturbing—that here the question of the Jewish view of what Christians call the 'Old Testament', that is, of the Hebrew Bible and its function in the living religion of Judaism, is not even mentioned. But these voices are no longer characteristic for the present situation in German biblical scholarship. The just mentioned *Jahrbuch* contains a number of articles that represent a broad spectrum of hermeneutical approaches. In addition there is a growing number of books and collected essays dealing with the questions of a responsible Christian approach to the Old Testament. It would go far beyond the scope of this essay to unfold the different aspects discussed in this context. I want to summarize briefly some main points, accepting a certain simplification of theological positions and arguments.

The majority of German Christian theologians try to combine two

Vandenhoeck & Ruprecht, 1993, 1998). Kaiser refers explicitly to Bultmann and Hirsch, adopting their idea of the 'failure' of the Old Testament religion (I, pp. 86-87).

7.   A.H.J. Gunneweg, *Vom Verstehen des Alten Testaments: Eine Hermeneutik* (Göttingen: Vandenhoeck & Ruprecht, 1977); translated into English as *Understanding the Old Testament* (Philadelphia: Westminster Press, 1978); *Biblische Theologie des Alten Testaments: Eine Religionsgeschichte Israels in biblisch-theologischer Sicht* (Stuttgart: Kohlhammer, 1993), quotation from p. 36.

8.   H. Spieckermann, 'Die Verbindlichkeit des Alten Testaments: Unzeitgemäße Betrachtungen zu einem ungeliebten Thema', in *Jahrbuch für biblische Theologie 1997* (Biblische Hermeneutik, 12; Neukirchen–Vluyn: Neukirchener Verlag, 1998), pp. 25-51, quotation from p. 47.

basic aspects: to take the two-part Bible as a whole as the *Christian* Bible, and at the same time to do justice to the Old Testament as the Holy Scripture of the pre-Christian Israel. Within this framework a major difference originates from the order between these two aspects. For many theologians the Christian character of the Bible as a whole is the undisputed point of departure. But unlike the above mentioned positions, the Old Testament is admitted to have its own religious identity and message. The question is whether and in what degree this message can be relevant for the Christian community. The answer will be determined by very different hermeneutical concepts. As an example I take the traditional concept of 'promise and fulfillment', which is still in use and which can be fleshed-out in a variety of ways. In this framework it can be argued that with the fulfillment of the promise, the relevance of the Old Testament for the Christian belief came to an end. The Old Testament belongs to the pre-history of Christianity, and it is, even if venerated, now only to be read backwards from a Christian point of view.

But the concept of 'promise and fulfillment' can also be developed in quite another direction. It can be admitted that the fulfillment, while glimpsed, is not yet complete. The Messiah has come—but the kingdom of God as expected in the Old Testament did not yet come, at least not in a full and final way. Therefore Christians also are still waiting and hoping for the future. This leads to the realization that even for the Jews the promise is still open and that they are still waiting for a future fulfillment.

II

In the majority of previous concepts of the relations between the two Testaments, 'Israel' appears just as the pre-Christian people of the Old Testament, that is, as a figure of the past. In the last mentioned approach, however, Israel or the Jewish people is realized to be a figure of present reality. At the same time the two communities, the Christian and the Jewish one, can be looked at under a certain common aspect, in this case as both awaiting the future of the divine kingdom. This represents a decisive change of paradigm. Together with a new reading of the Old Testament, German Christian theologians 're-discovered' Israel/ the Jewish people. Or perhaps it was the other way around: a new awareness of the present reality of the Jewish people as the continuation of the biblical Israel led to a new realization of the Jewish view of the Old Testament.

All this happened after the Holocaust, or more precisely, after Christians in Germany began to confront Christian co-responsibility and guilt for the Holocaust. It is bad enough that only after the Holocaust, and in a sense as a result of the Holocaust, Christians began to re-discover the Jews as a religious community living at present next to them and using the 'Old Testament' as their Holy Scripture. But after this, there is no way back to any kind of Christian supersessionism or any claim to have an exclusive right to interpret the Old Testament. We began to learn that there is another religious community that has a more ancient and more original right to read and to interpret what we call Old Testament. We have to learn that the 'Old Testament' is first of all a Jewish book.

At this point the problem of the adequate naming of this book arises. It is obvious that 'Old Testament' is a purely Christian term because it includes the existence of a 'New Testament'. In addition, this term involves the danger to understand 'old' as outdated and no longer valid and therefore superseded by the 'new'. What could be the alternative(s)? For the Jewish community this problem does not exist. What for Christians is only the first part of their Bible is for Jews simply 'the Bible'. It is called *TaNaKh*, an acronym for the three parts of the Hebrew canon: *Torah*, *Nebiim* (prophets), *Ketubim* (writings). Another term for the Bible is *Miqra'* which means 'what is read (aloud)' referring to the reading of the Torah and certain passages from the prophets in the synagogue service. Yet any Christian term for the 'Old Testament' has to take into consideration the two-part character of the Christian Bible. Many Christian Bible scholars are now using the term 'Hebrew Bible'. This is fully adequate insofar as in the scholarly field the Hebrew Bible is used as the basis for exegesis and even for theological interpretation of the first part of our Bible. The term is also nice insofar as it gives us a common term to be used by Jews and Christians. But there are some problems with this designation. First, when the Christian 'Bible' came into being by adding the Christian writings, the 'New Testament', to the Jewish collection, then the whole thing was not in Hebrew but in Greek. Later the Latin translation, the 'Vulgate', was used and is still used in the Roman Catholic church. In addition to the language problem there are a number of additional writings in the Greek version—the 'Apocrypha', that are not to be found in the Hebrew Bible but, through the Vulgate, are now part of the

Roman Catholic Bible. Therefore, though the term 'Hebrew Bible' is adequate for use in scholarly and other educated circles, I do not believe that it can be used in wider Christian frameworks.

The same is true for the term 'Jewish Bible'. This will evoke the question whether 'Jewish' means 'not Christian'. Therefore in my view it is not adequate as a designation of a book that at the same time is the first part of the Christian Bible. Recently the term 'the Bible of Israel' has been proposed.[9] This expression seems to me to be more applicable.[10] The first part of the Christian Bible was, and still is, Israel's Bible. But the Christian community grew out of Israel and developed its own identity out of the confession that Jesus of Nazareth was the 'Messiah' of the Bible of Israel. So Israel's Bible became the first part of the Christian Bible, but it continued to be the Bible of Israel.

Finally, the term 'First Testament' has also come into use. The main impulse for this designation was given by Erich Zenger.[11] He argued that this term first of all avoids the traditional depreciation often connected with the term 'Old Testament'. It emphasizes the priority of the 'First' Testament to the (second) 'New' Testament, and it reminds of the first covenant God established with God's firstborn Israel. But Zenger admits that the term 'testament' as such can have certain implications such as that a 'new' testament invalidates the 'old' one.[12] Therefore the discussion remains open.

I explained all this in some detail because it is a remarkable fact that such a discussion is carried on at all. This again is a result of the re-thinking of Christian–Jewish relations after the Holocaust. Christians have come to understand that the right definition of the relations between the two parts of the Christian Bible is of crucial relevance for a renewal of Christian–Jewish relations. Interestingly enough, in this context a number of Roman Catholic biblical theologians appear in the

9.   In C. Dohmen and F. Mussner, *Nur die halbe Wahrheit? Für die Einheit der ganzen Bibel* (Freiburg: Herder, 1993), esp. p. 45; see also C. Dohmen and G. Stemberger, *Hermeneutik der jüdischen Bibel und des Alten Testaments* (Stuttgart: Kohlhammer, 1996), p. 19.

10.   See R. Rendtorff, 'Die Bibel Israels als Buch der Christen', in C. Dohmen and T. Söding (eds.), *Eine Bibel, zwei Testamente* (Paderborn: Schöningh, 1995), pp. 97-113.

11.   E. Zenger, *Das erste Testament: Die jüdische Bibel und die Christen* (Düsseldorf: Patmos, 1991).

12.   Zenger, *Das erste Testament*, p. 153.

front rank: Franz Mussner,[13] Norbert Lohfink,[14] Erich Zenger,[15] Christoph Dohmen,[16] to mention just a few.

III

Of course, the question of the right naming of the first part of the Christian Bible as such is not a central issue in Christian–Jewish relations. What counts is the realization that this book, which we might now call the 'Hebrew Bible', is (part of) the common Bible of Jews and Christians. This includes the recognition from the Christian side that this book was the Jewish Holy Scripture before Christianity came into being. Therefore the Hebrew Bible has its own message and value totally independent of the existence of Christianity. Only recently have Christians begun a serious attempt to understand this message before asking for the specific relevance of the 'Old Testament' for Christianity.

This is a very important step. In the small but active circles I mentioned above the Hebrew Bible is intensively studied under the aspects just explained. Very often Jewish Bible scholars are asked to explain certain texts or certain ideas from the Hebrew Bible to a Christian audience. This brings me back to the *Kirchentag*. In this framework we established a permanent study group which we call *Lehrhaus Judentum für Christen*.[17] In this year's program there will be at each of the three conference days three or four lectures by Jewish scholars on biblical topics. Here Jews are teaching Christians a Jewish view of the Hebrew Bible. Of course, Christian teachers are involved in this study group as well, myself included. Two years ago I gave a series of three lectures under the title 'To read the 'Old Testament' as a Christian'.[18] I tried to

13. F. Mussner, *Tractate on the Jews: The Significance of Judaism for Christian Faith* (Philadelphia: Fortress Press, 1984); cf. also n. 9.

14. N. Lohfink, *Das Jüdische am Christentum: Die verlorene Dimension* (Freiburg: Herder, 1987); N. Lohfink and E. Zenger, *Der Gott Israels und die Völker: Untersuchungen zum Jesajabuch und zu den Psalmen* (Stuttgart: Katholisches Bibelwerk, 1994).

15. See nn. 11 and 14.

16. See nn. 9 and 10.

17. The name *Lehrhaus* is taken from the usual German version of the Hebrew *bet-hamidrash* ('house of study'). But in order to make clear that we are not claiming to copy a Jewish *Lehrhaus* we added 'for Christians'. So we have Jewish and Christian teachers, but mainly Christian 'students'.

18. Now published as R. Rendtorff, 'Als Christ das "Alte Testament" lesen', in

explain (1) that we as Christians had lost the Jewish Scripture, (2) that we are now about to regain the Jewish Scripture, but (3) that we should be careful not to expropriate again the Jewish Scripture. The starting point was the almost forgotten fact that in the New Testament 'Scripture' always means the Hebrew Bible. Therefore we have to learn from anew to read the Hebrew Bible as our 'Scripture', but at the same time to be fully aware that it is first and foremost the *Jewish* Scripture. As Christians we are invited and entitled to read the Hebrew Bible as an integral part of our own Bible; but at the same time by reading the Bible we are closely linked to the Jewish people.

What happens in this central Protestant conference is to be found in a similar way in many regional and local circles. Christians are studying the Hebrew Bible, often under the guidance of Jewish teachers. But at this point I have to draw attention to a specific German problem: there are very few Jews living in our country. Of course, we are fully conscious of the fact that this is an immediate consequence of the Holocaust. Therefore we are even more grateful that there are Jewish scholars and other educated persons that are willing to come to us and to teach our Christian audiences. For years we were happy that there were certain Jews who grew up in Germany and later emigrated to other countries, but nevertheless were willing to come and help us with their teaching. But this generation is getting old, and there are less and less Jews in this field who have an original knowledge of the German language. Fortunately there is a lively Jewish community in Switzerland from where we get useful help.

IV

But it is not only because of this language problem that it remains our task as Christian theologians to lead up our congregations to a new understanding of the Hebrew Bible. This is particularly important because there is the danger of a narrowed understanding of Christian faith. Often one gets the impression that for many Christians their creed begins with the Second Article, the belief in Jesus Christ and his work. But the moment we begin with the First Article, the belief in God the Creator, we cannot give any serious answer or explication without the Hebrew Bible. This makes quite clear that to speak about 'God' is

Christen und Juden heute: Neue Einsichten und neue Aufgaben (Neukirchen–Vluyn: Neukirchener Verlag, 1998), pp. 42-87.

impossible without the Hebrew Bible. When Christians say 'God' they always speak about the one and only God who builds the fundament and the center of the Hebrew Bible.

Recently in Germany a book came out with the title *I Believe in the God of Israel*. The subtitle reads: 'Questions and Answers to a Subject that Is Missing in the Christian Creed'.[19] This book is written out of the above-mentioned insights as an attempt to bring these to the consciousness of a wider public of Christian laypeople. In a number of brief articles basic information is given about the deep rooting of Christian faith in the message of the Hebrew Bible. This is a concrete example of the growing and broadening theological endeavors in this field. Those working in this field are still a small minority. But again, they are very active and very committed because they are convinced that the recognition of the rooting of the Christian faith in the Hebrew Bible is one of the most important results of our re-thinking Christianity after the Holocaust.

19. F. Crüsemann and U. Theissmann (eds.), *Ich glaube an den Gott Israels: Fragen und Antworten zu einem Thema, das im christlichen Glaubensbekenntnis fehlt* (Gütersloh: Chr. Kaiser Verlag, 1999).

OF FAITH AND FACES:
BIBLICAL TEXTS, HOLOCAUST TESTIMONY AND
GERMAN 'AFTER AUSCHWITZ' THEOLOGY

Björn Krondorfer

> Do not fear, for I have redeemed you;
> I have called you by name, you are mine.
> When you pass through the waters, I will be with you;
> and through the rivers, they shall not overwhelm you;
> when you walk through the fire you shall not be burned,
> and the flame shall not consume you.
> For I am the Lord your God,
> the Holy One of Israel, your Savior (Isa. 43.1-3).

In the context of reflecting on the Holocaust, or Shoah, certain biblical texts lose their innocence. Passages like the prophetic words of Deutero-Isaiah quoted above have the power to evoke images which we—as a post-Holocaust generation—connect with what we know about Nazi Germany's systematic attempt to annihilate European Jews. The Shoah seems to have turned words of solace into a mockery: the fire that shall not burn has burned the innumerable.

Jews and Christians who are conscious of being a post-Holocaust generation may have difficulty affirming the vision of a protective God as spelled out in Isaiah 43. We may wonder: how was it possible to revitalize the covenantal relation between God and Israel after the unthinkable and unprecedented had happened? The temple had been destroyed, the promised land, kingdom and nation lost, and the people made homeless. How could faith in a Savior God be renewed as the people experienced the Babylonian exile? And yet, into this crisis Deutero-Isaiah spoke those words: flames shall not consume you, fire shall not burn you, rivers shall not overwhelm you, and through waters you shall move unharmed.

In a post-Holocaust world, it seems we have lost the confidence to read, speak or listen to these words in good faith. Can Jewish and Christian believers return to biblical notions of covenant, God or redemption as if nothing had happened? Or are the prophetic words irrevocably contaminated by images and stories by which we remember the Shoah? It can be argued that the Holocaust demonstrates the ultimate triumph of a secularized, technological world,[1] forcing us to reevaluate traditional religious visions of a good, just, and redemptive cosmic order.

The image of fire and flames—one of the most prevalent cultural image of the mass killings of Jews—has been seared into our collective memory. 'The past', Anton Kaes remarked in the context of postwar German film making, 'is in danger of becoming a rapidly expanding collection of images, easily retrievable but isolated from time and space.'[2] Biblical references to fire and flames recall pictures and stories of crematories, chimneys and burning pyres. After reading the accounts of Judith Sternberg Newman's arrival in Auschwitz-Birkenau ('the sky was blood red. Giant flames were rising high in the air')[3] or Elie Wiesel's words ('In front of us flames. In the air that smell of burning flesh... We had arrived at Birkenau'),[4] we must ask ourselves whether we can approach Hebrew Scriptures unchanged.

We are no longer innocent of the new terrifying dimension that is imposed on biblical texts by the reality of the ghettos and camps, the *Einsatzgruppen* and death marches. Contrary to the prophetic vision, Jews died in the flames of Auschwitz; and the God of Isaiah 43 was—according to many post-Holocaust Jewish thinkers and Christian theologians—silent, indifferent, passive, absent, in exile or dead.[5]

---

1.   See Zygmunt Bauman, *Modernity and the Holocaust* (Ithaca, NY: Cornell University Press, 1989).

2.   Anton Kaes, *From Hitler to Heimat: The Return of History as Film* (Cambridge: Harvard University Press, 1990), p. 198.

3.   Judith Sternberg Newman, *In the Hell of Auschwitz* (New York: Exposition Press, 1963), p. 16.

4.   Elie Wiesel, *Night* (trans. Stella Rodway; New York: Bantam Books, 1982), p. 26.

5.   Rather than listing the many Jewish and Christian scholars who have contributed to religious and theological inquiry regarding the Holocaust, let me point the reader to some selected books. The volumes by John K. Roth and Michael Berenbaum (eds.), *Holocaust: Religious and Philosophical Implications* (New York: Paragon House, 1989), and by Elisabeth Schüssler-Fiorenza and David Tracy (eds.), *The Holocaust as Interruption* (Edinburgh: Concilium and T. & T. Clark,

Whether we add a 614th commandment, question the traditional notion of God's chosen people, or face an abusing God, it becomes apparent that for many the Holocaust has taken on an authoritative voice equal (almost) to biblical texts.[6] More than a particularly gruesome historical event, the Holocaust is interpreted as a rupture.[7] As a negatively sacred event, or 'radical counter-testimony to both Judaism and Christianity',[8]

1984) contain selected writings of some of the important voices of the early generation. For critical summaries and discussions of Jewish and Christian thought, see Steven Katz, *Post-Holocaust Dialogues: Critical Studies in Modern Jewish Thought* (New York: New York University Press, 1983); Zachary Braiterman, *(God) After Auschwitz: Tradition and Change in Post-Holocaust Jewish Thought* (Princeton: Princeton University Press, 1998); Donald J. Dietrich, *God and Humanity in Auschwitz: Jewish-Christian Relations and Sanctioned Murder* (New Brunswick: Transaction Publishers, 1995); Eva Fleischner (ed.), *Auschwitz: Beginning of a New Era? Reflections on the Holocaust* (New York: Ktav, 1977); Ellen Z. Charry, 'Jewish Holocaust Theology: An Assessment', *Journal of Ecumenical Studies* 18.1 (1981), pp. 128-39; and Britta Jüngst, *Auf der Seite des Todes das Leben: Auf dem Weg zu einer christlich-feministischen Theologie nach der Shoah* (Gütersloh: Chr. Kaiser Verlag, 1996), pp. 136-43. A book less often discussed is Arthur A. Cohen, *The Tremendum: A Theological Interpretation of the Holocaust* (New York: Crossroad, 1981). A controversial post-Shoah Jewish theologian is Marc H. Ellis, *Ending Auschwitz: The Future of Jewish and Christian Life* (Louisville, KY: Westminster/John Knox Press, 1994); for a discussion of Ellis's work, see Richard L. Rubenstein, *After Auschwitz: History, Theology, and Contemporary Judaism* (Baltimore: The Johns Hopkins University Press, 2nd edn, 1992), pp. 266-80.

6.   The 614th commandment refers to Emil L. Fackenheim, 'Jewish Values in the Post-Holocaust Future: A Symposium', *Judaism* 16 (1967), reprinted in Roth and Berenbaum (eds.), *Holocaust*, pp. 291-95. See also Fackenheim, *God's Presence in History: Jewish Affirmations and Philosophical Reflections* (Northvale, NJ: Jason Aronson, 1997), pp. ix-xvi. The questioning of traditional Jewish notions of the covenant refers to Rubenstein, *After Auschwitz*. The notion of the abusing God refers to David R. Blumenthal, *Facing the Abusing God: A Theology of Protest* (Louisville, KY: Westminster/John Knox Press, 1993). See also Eliezer Berkovitz, *Faith after the Holocaust* (New York: Ktav, 1973), who rejects the idea of giving the Holocaust a singularly authoritative voice.

7.   Stephen R. Haynes, 'Christian Holocaust Theology: A Critical Reassessment', *JAAR* 62.2 (1994), criticizes overly dramatic terminology to describe the effects of the Shoah on Christian faith, such as 'endpoint, interruption, crisis, break, rupture, [or] paradigm shift' (p. 554).

8.   Irving Greenberg, 'Cloud of Smoke, Pillar of Fire', in Fleischner (ed.), *Auschwitz*, reprinted in Roth and Berenbaum (eds.), *Holocaust*, pp. 305-45.

the Shoah has assumed an aura of authority that calls into question the universe which the biblical texts affirm. What we remember collectively and individually as 'the Holocaust' shapes our reading of and responses to biblical notions of God, the covenant, redemption, faith, hope or justice. The image of fire in Deutero-Isaiah has turned into a strange fire indeed.

Surprisingly, among postwar German theologians it has not been self-evident to make a sincere effort of integrating the Shoah into their theological thinking. 'Beginning in the early 1970s', observes Britta Jüngst, 'an awareness for a 'theology after Auschwitz' developed among a few West German theologians, but the mainstream of established theology in Germany has continually disregarded it'.[9] But even among the few, marginalized 'after Auschwitz' theologians many are concerned more about saving the theological enterprise than understanding the history and legacy of the Shoah. 'Regrettably, in Germany we have taken the second step before the first', writes Moltmann self-critically in a recent essay. 'We have started with Jewish-Christian dialogue…and have left Holocaust conferences to the Americans, where victims speak.'[10]

When the Holocaust is not recognized as a *Zivilisationsbruch*, as radical counter-testimony, theologians do not feel compelled to discontinue with previously held doctrinal beliefs or methodological presumptions, according to a recent study by Norbert Reck, a young German Catholic scholar.[11] But shouldn't Christian theologians in general—and German theologians in particular—start with the assumption that the fire and flames of Auschwitz have the power to burn theological language itself? Or that Holocaust narratives subvert the position from which German theologians make statements about biblical notions of God and faith? How trustworthy are German theological writings that state how they have been challenged by the Holocaust but are, in the end, not willing to abandon conventional theological solutions?

---

9. Jüngst, *Auf der Seite des Todes*, p. 158.

10. Jürgen Moltmann, '"Die Grube": "Wo war Gott?" Jüdische und christliche Theologie nach Auschwitz', in Manfred Görg and Michael Langer (eds.), *Als Gott weinte: Theologie nach Auschwitz* (Reenburg: Pustet, 1997), p. 53.

11. Norbert Reck, *Im Angesicht der Zeugen: Eine Theologie nach Auschwitz* (Mainz: Grünewald, 1998), p. 14.

The Voice of Cultural Criticism

In this article, I propose to bring to bear upon Christian Holocaust theologies the voice of cultural criticism. Such a voice does not accommodate simply to the internal logic of theological reasoning but invites us to step outside in order to raise questions about the cultural location from which a particular theological position is produced. It does not treat theology solely as an independent text but considers also the particular cultural moment in which a theological work originates. This process, which interrupts the accepted structure of theological discourse (and hence may be resisted by theologians themselves), draws our attention to issues that are invisible as long as one moves within established perimeters of the theological system itself.

My interest is in viewing German 'after Auschwitz' theology from the perspective of cultural criticism. In particular, I will assess critically two short pieces on biblical theology. Doing so, I do not intend to make a judgment on the validity and sincerity of German Holocaust theology in general, which, over the years, has produced an impressive list of Catholic and Protestant authors, such as Johann Baptist Metz, Jürgen Moltmann, Dorothea Sölle, Rolf Rendtorff, Martin Stöhr, Clemens Thoma, Peter von der Osten Sacken, Friedrich-Wilhelm Marquardt, and Johanna Kohn (noteworthy also are recent responses of young, third-generation theologians, such as Norbert Reck, Britta Jüngst, Tania Oldenhage and Kirsten Holtschneider, who have taken to heart the history of the Shoah and the testimony of victims and survivors).[12] These theologies are rich in detail, elaborate and differentiated in their argumentation, and combative with each other as they try to come to terms with a difficult legacy. But I also hope to show that my criticism is relevant beyond the scope of my two examples, calling for some

---

12. Important titles can be found, among others, in the excellent bibliography of Reck, *Im Angesicht*. For the more recent work of younger scholars, see Reck, *Im Angesicht*, and 'Lernt zu lesen: es sind heilige Texte. Die Theologie nach Auschwitz und die Zeugen', in Görg and Langer (eds.), *Als Gott weinte*, pp. 129-41; Jüngst, *Auf der Seite des Todes*; Tania Oldenhage, 'Parables for Our Time? Rereading New Testament Scholarship after the Holocaust' (PhD dissertation, Temple University, 1999); and Kirsten Holtschneider, who is currently completing her PhD thesis in Birmingham, UK, on a third-generation perspective on German Protestant identity in relation to the memory of the Holocaust.

rethinking about the ways of how post-Shoah theology is done in Germany today.

The problem of German Holocaust theology, as I see it, cannot be found alone in the specifics of internal theological arguments (though one cannot, of course, ignore substantive issues). Rather, it is rooted in a fundamental blindness to one's cultural location as postwar and post-Shoah Germans. This blindness is not so much due to a lack of Christian theological sophistication but to the absence of reflecting one's German identity when writing contemporary Christian theology. In other words, the problem does not lie with the answers provided but with the questions that are *not* being asked. A shifting of perspective is required, one that foregrounds the social location of living in a (former) perpetrator culture. It is my hope that the voice of cultural criticism may help to provoke such a shift.

Since I argue here that the historical-cultural positioning of German theologians is not adequately reflected in their work, it is only fair to insert a few words about my own social location and about my motivation for writing this chapter. I was born and grew up in Germany, and I studied Protestant theology for five years in Frankfurt and Göttingen. But I no longer live in Germany, and theology is no longer my primary language with respect to my scholarly endeavors. When I came to the United States in the early 1980s, originally with the intention to stay for one year only, I switched to a doctoral program in (comparative) religious studies. With the completion of my doctoral thesis on hermeneutical issues relating to religion, art and culture, and with the eventual acceptance of a teaching position at an American college, a return to Germany became less feasible and realistic. Perhaps, I could be described as a bi-cultural religious studies scholar with a strong interest in Holocaust studies and cultural criticism.

After arriving in the United States, I met Jewish people for the first time consciously in my life (I was 24 at the time), an encounter which triggered a series of intellectual and emotional upheavals. I later learned that such personal crises are not untypical for Germans of my generation who have come in contact with the American Jewish community. In my case, these initial experiences have motivated me to become deeply involved in understanding and facilitating relations between Jews and Germans, particularly with respect to the so-called third generation.[13]

---

13. For details about my work with the 'third generation', see Björn Krondorfer,

I continue to read theological works on an occasional basis, espe-cially if they concern themselves with aspects of the Shoah. Admit-tedly, many of these works tend to put me to sleep quickly, although the topics they discuss matter to me. I usually do not take my soporific response too seriously, but the question has crossed my mind whether I am simply the wrong audience for these books (a possibility I am not discounting) or whether these Christian Holocaust theologies are less relevant than they ought to be. What would happen, I wondered, if I tried to understand what it is that tires and bothers me when reading German 'after Auschwitz' theology? The writing of this chapter, then, is also a response to this personally motivated curiosity.

I am aware that it is difficult, though not impossible, for Germans to write a persuasive post-Shoah theology today. There are many battles to be fought: with and against a Christian tradition that has instrumental-ized, marginalized, and demonized Jews long before racial anti-Semitism emerged during the nineteenth century; with and against a German history of genocidal anti-Semitism and the role of the German churches vis-à-vis the *Endlösung*; with and against a postwar society unsure of its attitude towards remembering and forgetting; with and against the specific German church–state relations that directly impact on the academic creativity of theological curricular at universities; with and against an audience of regular German churchgoers who purchase theological books; with and against colleagues who have marginalized 'after Auschwitz' theology; with and against Jewish voices inside and outside of Germany that have taken German theologians to task. Keep-ing all of these difficulties in mind, it is still important to point out that a fundamental blindness plagues German 'after Auschwitz' theologies, a blindness that is linked to the reluctance of theologians to problema-tize explicitly their cultural and national identity as Germans.

Remembrance and Reconciliation: Encounters between Young Jews and Germans (New Haven: Yale University Press, 1995); and 'Third-Generation Jews and Ger-mans: History, Memory, and Memorialization', in *Working Papers of the Volkswa-gen-Foundation Program in Post-War German History* (Washington, DC: German Historical Insitute and AICGS/The Johns Hopkins University, 1996). See also my afterword to Edward Gastfriend's, *My Father's Testament: Memoir of a Jewish Teenager, 1938–1945* (ed. with afterword by Björn Krondorfer; Philadelphia: Temple University Press, 2000).

Biblical Theology after Auschwitz: Two Examples

Two entries on biblical theology in a 1997 collection titled, *Als Gott weinte: Theologie nach Auschwitz* (When God Wept: Theologies after Auschwitz), illustrate different levels of rhetorical employment of 'after Auschwitz' discourses. According to the editors, *Als Gott weinte* is the first German volume in which Catholic and Protestant representatives of diverse disciplines address the legacy of the Holocaust: biblical theology, church history, systematic theology and pastoral/practical theology. The two contributions under the heading of biblical theology are written by Protestant theologian, Ferdinand Hahn, professor emeritus of New Testament, and Catholic theologian Manfred Görg, professor of Old Testament.[14] Whereas Hahn presents five condensed theses on the significance of a theology after Auschwitz for New Testament exegetical work, Görg reflects on his coincidental discovery of the liturgical formula 'God with you' in a prisoner's letter from Auschwitz, a formula which the author traces in the Hebrew Scriptures.

   In their 'after Auschwitz' biblical-theological studies, Hahn and Görg address the legacy of anti-Semitism and the Holocaust in different ways. Whereas Hahn employs a theological rhetoric of continuity, Görg is more attentive to the disrupting force of the Shoah. As I want to show, however, both studies misjudge the relevance of the Shoah for doing theology in Germany today, mainly due to their choice of using a Christian rhetoric that hides the authors' specific backgrounds. Hahn and Görg, like so many of their colleagues engaged in 'after Auschwitz' discourses, appropriate and handle biblical texts, Jewish traditions and narratives of victims with the confidence of professional *Christian* theologians without reflecting on their cultural, historical and moral location as post-1945 *German* theologians. They do so, I suspect, not because of individual inadequacy but because they are part of the universalizing language of Christian theology and part of a society that remains uncomfortable about the shadows that are cast upon it by its dictatorial and genocidal past. These two moments—Christianity's universalization and Germany's discomfort about remembering the

---

14. Ferdinand Hahn, 'Theologie nach Auschwitz und ihre Bedeutung für die neutestamentliche Exegese: Eine Thesenreihe', pp. 89-93, and Manfred Görg, '"Gott mit euch, meine Lieben": Die Formel vom Mitsein Gottes in, vor und nach Auschwitz', pp. 82-88, in Görg and Langer (eds.), *Als Gott weinte*.

past—are not incentives to render visible the context and descent of the individual author. However, it is precisely the disappearance of the writing subject in German 'after Auschwitz' theology that leads to a misjudging of hermeneutically relevant questions.

Example 1: Not a Different Theology

Let us turn our attention now to Ferdinand Hahn, the first case study on biblical theology. Hahn's major point is that the importance of the Shoah for Christians today is to remind them that Christianity is bound to Judaism. Hahn calls on Christians not to divorce their reading of the New Testament from its Jewish context, so as to eschew the long tradition of anti-Semitic interpretations and to be able to renew Jewish–Christian relationships. Auschwitz, he writes, made us realize the terrifying silence of God. Yet, despite God's silence, Christians can hold on to faith. This persistence in faith is possible because it is linked to 'a theology of suffering, which does not lead to passive submission or fatalism, but to responsibility for the humanness of humans'.[15] For Hahn, neither the evasive nor the cynical pathways are appropriate options for Christians because a 'correctly understood theology of the cross' prevents them from falling into cynicism in the face of God's terrifying silence in Auschwitz.[16] The cross reveals that even in moments of seemingly utter abandonment by God, faith can prevail. Christian can neither evade the cross (and, by extension, Auschwitz), nor do they turn cynical at its sight. Instead, they become responsible humans.

But we do not get the sense of existential urgency and vulnerability from Hahn's study that usually emerges out of a confrontation with Holocaust testimonies, challenging the foundation upon which faith has traditionally been built. This confrontational encounter is missing in Hahn's piece. Instead, the larger context of Hahn's theological construction reveals that he pursues a rhetoric of continuity rather than rupture. Structurally and strategically, Hahn's brief thoughts on Auschwitz are placed in between two continuities: he first shows that New Testament writings and the development of early Christianity cannot be understood outside the context of the Hebrew Scriptures and the Jewish environment (this makes up the largest part of his study), and he con-

---

15. Hahn, 'Theologie nach Auschwitz', p. 92.
16. Hahn, 'Theologie nach Auschwitz', p. 92.

cludes by saying that early Christianity has always insisted on being perceived as the continuation of Israel's *Heilsgeschichte*. In between, he inserts his thesis about the persistence of faith in light of God's terrifying silence in Auschwitz. Auschwitz, in other words, should remind Christians of the Jewish embeddedness of early Christianity (the retrospective gaze) and, progressively, of Christianity's attachment to Judaism by a *heilsgeschichtliche* continuum. The specific task of biblical theology after the Holocaust, then, is to point out that Judaism and Christianity share a 'common faith in God', a 'common faith in creation' and 'common eschatological expectations'.[17]

In the spirit of inter-religious dialogue, Hahn's focus on a shared faith in Judaism and Christianity seems praiseworthy and appropriate. Yet, by folding early Christianity into its Jewish context and simultaneously claiming that Christianity continues Israel's *Heilsgeschichte*, Hahn engages in a language of continuity that presents Judaism and Christianity as indistinguishable vis-à-vis the Holocaust. The Shoah is not perceived as having severed the ties between Jews and Christians. Instead, the Shoah has been turned into a historical event that challenges Judaism and Christianity equally. The Shoah as equal opportunity challenger? No space is left for reflecting on differences between a Christian theology that emerges from the past of a perpetrator culture and Jewish responses that are coming forth from a community severely victimized. It is not surprising, then, that Hahn can conclude that the Holocaust has not fundamentally changed theology. 'Theology after Auschwitz is not a different theology, but a correctly understood biblical theology which takes serious the challenge of the Shoah.'[18] This sentence, which opens the last paragraph of Hahn's study, is a masterpiece of theological rhetoric: Hahn simultaneously claims to take the Shoah seriously as he affirms that nothing has changed. Are we not led to conclude that the Shoah is just one historical misfortune among others rather than an event that shakes the foundations of doing theology in the land of the perpetrators?

Other questions emerge: how viable is a post-1945 German theology that speaks in the name of both Judaism and Christianity but obscures their different historical, cultural and moral locations vis-à-vis Nazi Germany's genocidal anti-Semitism? Is the lack of self-reflectivity of

---

17. Hahn, 'Theologie nach Auschwitz', pp. 92-93.
18. Hahn, 'Theologie nach Auschwitz', p. 93.

one's German identity linked to the author's desire to renew Jewish–*Christian* relations without problematizing Jewish–*German* relations? Is the claim that 'after Auschwitz' theology is 'not different' from other theology a strategy that is primarily protective of Christian theology or of German identity?

Downplaying or obliterating references to one's German identity enables 'after Auschwitz' theologians to move within the universalizing language of Christianity without grounding themselves in their own history. Such deliberate[19] social dislocation frequently results in a blend of old triumphalism, where Christians continue to speak in the name of Judaism, and of modern religious hegemony, where Christian Germans appropriate unself-critically Auschwitz as a symbol—as if this place belonged to the tradition of Christian martyrdom.

Example 2: Thanks Be to God

Manfred Görg's short and unconventional contribution to biblical theology is cognizant of the disruptive impact of the Holocaust on post-Shoah generations. But the word 'German' also does not appear as a marker for self-identification. As a result, questions about the specific burden and responsibility of doing biblical theology in Germany today remain absent.

Görg's essay opens with a detailed description of two letters he obtained at a stamp auction. These handwritten letters from Auschwitz, dated 1943, are apparently trade objects among philatelists. In the official philatelist language they belong to a genre called *Lagerpost* or *KZ- und Ghettopost*. The letters in Görg's possession are from a prisoner who pleads with his parents and sisters to send him cigarettes and bread, ending one of his penciled messages with the phrase, 'God with you, my loved ones.'[20] Görg, who is genuinely touched by the prisoner's plea, takes the concluding phrase 'God with you' (which the person had probably used out of convention rather than spiritual conviction) as an opportunity to elaborate on the apparent absurdity of writing about God's presence from the zone of death. Görg's reflections, which are more suggestive than systematically argued, raise important issues: can the old liturgical phrase 'God with you' reveal something about God's presence or absence in the death camps? Can

---

19. The term 'deliberate' is not meant here to convey intentionality on the part of the individual but to point to a strategic convention of postwar German theology.

20. Görg, 'Gott mit euch', p. 83.

theologians truly understand the reality to which documents and narratives of victims testify? Are theologians allowed to reflect on God's presence without becoming *Schreibtischchristen*,[21] that is, Christians who will not dirty their moral conscience by remaining safely behind their desks (like the infamous *Schreibtischtäter*, the masterminds of the Final Solution, who never bloodied their hands)? Can any precedence be found in the Hebrew Scriptures when contemplating God in light of such calamities?

Görg turns his attention briefly to passages in Job and Isaiah 43, wondering whether biblical faith in God has credibility in the face of crematories. Hebrew Scriptures, Görg writes, can testify to the paradoxical nature of God, as both a 'creator of light' and as 'a dark God'.[22] This apparent paradox can be understood existentially but not resolved academically. Perhaps only those who have been in the zone of death can speak with authority and understanding of God's absence or presence in the camps. To his credit, Görg allows his own reasoning to be disrupted repeatedly by questions about the futility of imposing theological meaning on the Shoah. This insight differentiates Görg's biblical theology from the rhetorics of his Protestant colleague Hahn, who, as I have shown, resorted to a language of continuity. But Görg is not free from a desire for continuity either. In the concluding paragraph, he cannot refrain from hinting at some vague cosmic order and justice. 'I am taking again the letter from Auschwitz into my hands', he writes. 'The letter has survived until today, and with it its wish to the loved ones. Thanks be to God.'[23]

Thanks be to God? After having raised profound doubts about God and questioned the comforting words of Isaiah 43, why does Görg conclude by thanking God? Is he suggesting, like his Protestant colleague, that the mysterious face of God is revealed even at Auschwitz, and hence also present in this prisoner's letter? What is he thanking God for? That the letter survived? That there is yet one more piece of historical evidence for us to contemplate? That the letter has served as a stimulant for our theological imagination? Görg does not tell us, and the reader is left to his or her own devices, perhaps puzzled like me, perhaps comforted by the enigma of an omnipresent God. Rhetorically speaking, Görg's inconclusive ending is, of course, a clever move: the

21. Görg, 'Gott mit euch', p. 85.
22. Görg, 'Gott mit euch', p. 86.
23. Görg, 'Gott mit euch', p. 87.

reader may find comfort in such vagueness, and the author is not committed to a clear position. But the inconclusiveness also reveals a weakness that runs through much of Görg's essay: the author says little about how he as a German theologian relates to the letter he had obtained at a stamp auction. We may wonder: isn't it a bit self-serving to thank God for the preservation of the letter when, in all likelihood, the prisoner who wrote it did not survive?

As readers, we learn in some descriptive detail about the letter's form and look, but we learn nothing about the person who wrote it. Selected aspects of the prisoner's background, however, must be known to Görg. For example, he mentions in passing that the address, though fading, is still legible. We can also deduce from the type of orthographic errors of the handwritten messages cited by Görg that the prisoner could not have been a native German speaker. But who was this prisoner, and where did he come from? What was his name, religion, nationality? Was he Jewish, or Polish, or Russian? To whom did he send his request? To a ghetto, the Wartheland, or another part of Nazi-occupied Europe? Do such specificities matter? They do. They would tell us, for example, whether the letter was written by a Jewish inmate from the death camp of Auschwitz-Birkenau (an unlikely scenario), or, say, from a Polish Catholic prisoner of the smaller camp Auschwitz I. The ability to ask for packages from the outside may point to a few privileges the prisoner may have enjoyed within the camp hierarchy. For all we know, the prisoner may have even survived.

Perhaps none of Görg's theological insights would have been effected by such knowledge. And still the specificities matter. Or better, it is the absence of specificity that matters. Is it a simple oversight that the prisoner remains nameless and faceless? Or is the lack of effort of identifying the prisoner a result of a hermeneutic blindness in Görg's biblical theology? After all, alternative approaches are conceivable. For example, Görg could have chosen to gather and present as much information about the prisoner as possible in order to give him back his subjectivity. Or he could have tried to find surviving relatives or other members of the prisoner's family, irregardless of how successful this search would have been (the address, as we know, is still legible). These or similar efforts would have forced the author to relate to the prisoner, to step into a personal relationship with one particular victim of the Holocaust, rather than treating the letter as an object.

Görg's study on biblical theology does not contemplate acts of relationality, and as readers we are left with the impression that the letter has served the purpose of stimulating theological thought at the neglect of the person who wrote it. Rather than lifting one person from the masses of nameless victims, what matters seems to be the preservation of the letter, now in the hands of a German, thanks be to God. Holocaust testimony as trophy? What if the theologian had tried to give the prisoner a face, or had searched and found surviving relatives? He would have become vulnerable. 'But theologians', Carol Christ once wrote, 'fear vulnerability'.[24]

Stepping to the Window

The objectifying treatment of this letter exemplifies what plagues much of German 'after Auschwitz' theology: the Holocaust remains an object. I am reminded of Zygmunt Bauman's compelling distinction between the Holocaust as 'a picture on the wall' and as 'window', with which he described his discovery of the significance of the Shoah for the discipline of sociology. To Bauman, the Shoah had always been 'like a picture on the wall: neatly framed', until he began to understand 'beyond reasonable doubt that the Holocaust was a window...[and] what I saw through this window I did not find at all pleasing'.[25] In Bauman's case, this shift of perspective led him to view the Holocaust not as marginal but central to sociological inquiry, bearing on the 'self-awareness and practice' of social theory, public institutions and contemporary society. A similar shift, I think, has not yet occurred in the field of theological inquiry. The two examples of this article—Hahn's embedding of 'Auschwitz' in a rhetoric of continuity and Görg's use of the Auschwitz letter as theological stimulant—illustrate the distance at which the Holocaust is kept. The authors have not stepped to the window to discover how perilous the history and memory of the Holocaust can be to themselves and their profession.

If Ferdinand Hahn is an example of Christian Holocaust theology (mis)appropriating Auschwitz as a place overdetermined by Christian imagery, Manfred Görg's treatment of the Auschwitz letter points to the general problematics of the Christian embrace of victim narratives—as if these narratives belonged to the Christian tradition. The danger of

24. Carol Christ, 'Whatever Happened to Theology?', *Christianity and Crisis* 35 (May 1975), p. 114.

25. Bauman, *Modernity*, pp. vii-viii.

using historical documents or accounts by survivors to illustrate theological points is that one falls easily into the trap of lamenting the absence of faith in God rather than mourning the absence of people's faces. When the writer is German, the situation is even more delicate, because it puts the difference between communities of victims and of perpetrators in even sharper contrast.

Görg, one could object, did not shy away from the Holocaust and did establish a relationship to the Auschwitz letter in his possession. But beyond this fact, we know little. Is the letter meaningful to him because he can hold it in his hands and touch it? Is it the tactile sensation of touching this document that has stimulated the theological mind? Is the theologian disturbed by it because it intrudes the tranquility of his home? Is he proud that he rescued the letter from oblivion? Is his ownership an attempt at domesticating the horrifying reality to which this letter testifies? We do not know. We are left to speculation because there is no biblical-theological reflection on what it means to have obtained the item at a stamp auction. Had the theologian stepped away from his desk and moved to the window, he might have seen what has remained invisible to him before: the prisoner, or perhaps the prisoner's relatives, may have looked back at him, questioning his motivations, attitudes, beliefs. Their questions, we can assume, would have been different from those he has brought to the letter, and, in effect, changed the power relation between the theologian as an active agent and testimony as a passive resource. Görg's question about faith in the camps would have faded in favor of recognizing the face of a single victim or survivor.

Doing theology in the face of victims and survivors is, for precisely the reason of recognition, central to the efforts of Catholic scholar Norbert Reck, who has made the encounter with survivor testimony a key to doing 'after Auschwitz' theology. Working on the (yet to be published) memoirs of a Jewish survivor residing in Munich, Reck has simultaneously developed a dogmatic/practical theology in face of witnesses, published in 1998.[26] For a theology after Auschwitz, Reck so eloquently and persuasively argues in his book, one must step to the window and wrestle with theological responses under the confronting gaze of survivors and witnesses. Once theologians relate to and respect the voices of victims, survivors and witnesses as equal others, they may

---

26. Reck, *Im Angesicht*.

discover that what they hear from the witnesses is incompatible with theological assumptions. Christian theologians, Reck asserts, cannot pick and choose from Holocaust testimony at will so as to smooth over differences. Rather, these differences are an opportunity to reflect on inadequacies of one's own theological position. 'A conversation in the face of the victims', Reck writes, 'would cause, with respect to the central event of Christianity, self-critical examinations'.[27]

When stepping to the window, we do not only see 'others' outside, and thus expose ourselves to their gaze, but we may also get a glimpse of ourselves in the reflection of the glass. In other words, 'after Auschwitz' theologians cannot have a true conversation or encounter with Holocaust testimony without having to speak about themselves. To return again to the example of Görg's biblical theology: Görg does not see the prisoner, and he does not see himself. Görg, the author, does not appear in his writing in a deliberate and conscious manner. We may wonder: what questions might emerge if some kind of self-examination had been in place? As readers, we may want to know, for example, why the theologian had obtained the prisoner's letter. Did he find it coincidentally? Does he specialize in so called *KZ- und Ghettopost*? In the case of the latter, was money exchanged to procure the item? What is its market value? And what does the owner intend to do with it? Keep it? Trade it? Donate it to a museum? Or forward it to family members in case they can be identified?

These questions are far from being irrelevant for doing a post-Shoah biblical theology. Asking them opens new dimensions for theological and ethical inquiry: the enigma of the presence of God in the camps would become less prominent than one's own position vis-à-vis appropriate forms of remembering and memorializing a nation's genocidal legacy. For instance, purchasing, possessing and trading objects that could be called Holocaust memorabilia is for many people, including survivors, an appalling idea, for it is perceived as an insult to the people who perished. It is a moral question. So we ask again: does it matter whether Görg stumbled accidentally across the letter or whether he purchased it intentionally as a stamp collector? Depending on the answer, issues of morality and relationality would come differently into focus.

Considering the issue of Holocaust memorabilia, it is obvious that

27. For the victims, Reck uses the German term *Gegenüber*, which may be best translated as 'equal other' ('die Opfer sind als *Gegenüber* zu begreifen und zu respektieren', *Im Angesicht*, p. 121).

Isaiah 43, the text that Görg had chosen to illuminate his theological queries about God's presence in the camps, cannot provide any models and insights. It is the wrong textual choice. We would have to identify different passages from the Hebrew Scriptures as counter-reading to the situation as it is now presented. Our gaze might, perhaps, fall onto Isa. 44.9: 'All who make idols are nothing and the things they delight in do not profit; their witnesses neither see nor know. And so they will be put to shame.' This passage—though not a perfect parallel (for it assumes, among other things, an intentional malice on Görg's part, which he never exhibits)—points us into a direction we must take: to abandon the objectifying treatment and appropriation of the Holocaust as idol (read 'image'), and to bear witness in such a way that we can 'see and know'.

Outlook: Doing Theology in the Face of Perpetrators

I hope that is has become apparent why resistance to making one's German identity an explicit part of one's theologizing serves a protective function: the writer removes himself from being socially, morally or biographically implicated in a culture that continually struggles with coming to terms with having perpetrated a genocide. The universalizing tendency of Christian theology is one mechanism that assists in turning a blind eye to one's own particular historical, cultural and moral situatedness. Post-Shoah German theologians seldom examine themselves over against a background of a perpetrator culture and, instead, prefer to place themselves in the context and conventions of Christian theology. Within these perimeters, they lose sight of the uniqueness and the otherness of the Jewish victims as well as of the uniqueness and sameness of the German perpetrators.

A central story that Christianity tells of itself is that it has struggled against victimization, suffered martyrdom and death, but emerged triumphant nevertheless. This story tempts Christian theologians to imagine themselves on the side of the victims of Auschwitz, even at the expense of replacing the Jewishness of the victims with Christian imagery. The Christian story does not, however, provide models for looking at oneself as a perpetrator or descendant thereof. In a perversely nostalgic and pathetic way, it is more comforting to theologize about the hanging of a Jewish boy in Birkenau than to theologize, for instance, about Rudolf Höss's confessed 'moral' dilemma of having to act against his own emotions when ordering a sergeant to tear two little, screaming children from their mother's arms and put them in the gas chamber. The mother, camp Kommandant Höss writes in his memoirs, 'was weeping in the most heart-breaking fashion. Believe me, I felt like shrinking into the ground out of pity, but I was not allowed to show the slightest emotion.'[28]

How can German 'after Auschwitz' theology respond to this scene in Höss's memoirs? What christological models ought to be employed, what biblical text quoted? How can we respond theologically to Höss's religious sentimentality that peaks occasionally through his memoirs and is, no doubt, traceable to his strict Catholic upbringing? How dangerous would it be to locate oneself as a German theologian in the cultural tradition of the Auschwitz Kommandant rather than that of the Jewish mother and her children? Would it be possible and permissible to identify, if only for a moment, with Höss's spark of 'moral' conscience, as perverted and nauseating as it may be? How could a balance be struck between recognizing one's religio-cultural roots in a tradition that led to Höss's behavior, yet keeping a critical and healthy distance to the mentality of perpetrators? The challenges that are buried in these questions may illustrate why German theologians are reluctant to acknowledge the lives and deeds of perpetrators as a ground for theologizing. Testimony and narratives of Jewish victims and survivors can be integrated into a 'Christian' story with less of an intellectual effort than the accounts of perpetrators, whether we find the latter in memoirs, interviews, trial records or archival documents.

I am not suggesting to replace Holocaust testimony of victims and survivors with testimony of perpetrators—for surely, we do not want to learn or teach how to become 'good' perpetrators. A German theological position that cuts out the victim perspective is untenable. But limiting oneself exclusively to the victim perspective raises, as I tried to show, hermeneutical dilemmas about textual choices and about one's cultural perspective, always at risk of misappropriation and false identification. Without positioning oneself as theologian consciously and explicitly in the tradition of perpetrators, German 'after Auschwitz' theology remains disingenuous and incomplete.[29]

28. Rudolf Höss, *Death Dealer: The Memoirs of the SS Kommandant at Auschwitz* (ed. Steven Paskuly; trans. Andrew Pollinger; New York: Da Capo Press, 1996), p. 162.

29. Recently, some tentative reflections on doing theology in the face of perpetrators appear in German 'after Auschwitz' theologies. See Peter von der Osten

A theology that dares to probe the limits of theologizing in the face of perpetrators will bring new insights to the often rehearsed debate over continuity and rupture. Such a theology cannot engage in a language of continuity, if by this is meant that theology after Auschwitz is 'not a different theology', or that post-Shoah Jews and Christians struggle equally with questions of faith and God. But a theology done in the face of perpetrators can also not adopt unqualifiedly the idea of the Shoah as rupture, as *Zivilisationsbruch*, because it must look for continuities in new areas: how, for example, German society has integrated perpetrators;[30] how the churches have helped to facilitate this re-integration on individual and social levels;[31] how selective stories about World War II have been transmitted within German families from generation to generation, while a partial amnesia descended upon stories about one's family's knowledge of and participation in the Shoah;[32] and how standard theological works written before and during the Nazi dictatorship have poisoned generations of postwar German theologians with their

Sacken, 'Christliche Theologie nach Auschwitz', pp. 12-29 and Moltmann, 'Die Grube: Wo war Gott', pp. 45-60 both in Görg and Langer (eds.), *Als Gott weinte*. Jüngst, *Auf der Seite des Todes*, and Reck, *Im Angesicht*, also bring awareness to this issue. But a theological perspective in light of perpetrator testimony is, to my knowledge, nowhere fully and systematically developed.

30. See Ralph Giordano, *Die zweite Schuld oder von der Last ein Deutscher zu ein* (Hamburg: Rasch und Röhring, 1998).

31. See, for example, Doris L. Bergen, *Twisted Cross: The German Christian Movement in the Third Reich* (Chapel Hill: University of North Carolina, 1996), pp. 206-30.

32. For new research on intergenerational transmission and German family history, see the work of Gabriele Rosenthal (ed.), *Der Holocaust im Leben von drei Generationen: Familien von Überlebenden der Shoah und von Nazi Tätern* (Giessen: Psychosozial Verlag, 1997); Rosenthal (ed.), *Als der Krieg kam hatte ich mit Hitler nichts mehr zu tun: Zur Gegenwärtigkeit des 'Dritten Reiches' in Biographien* (Opladen: Leske & Budrich, 1990); Dan Bar-On, *Legacy of Silence: Encounters with Children of the Third Reich* (Cambridge: Harvard University Press, 1989); Barbara Heimannsberg and Christoph J. Schmidt (eds.), *The Collective Silence: German Identity and the Legacy of Shame* (trans. Cynthia Oudejans Harris and Gordon Wheeler; San Francisco: Jossey-Bass Publishers, 1993); and Björn Krondorfer, 'Biographische Arbeit in jüdisch/deutschen Begegnungsgruppen nach der Shoah', in *Biographische Arbeit in der Erwachsenenbildung: Beispiele aus der Praxis* (Berlin: Bundesministerium für Bildung, Wissenschaft, Forschung und Technologie, 1998).

subtle or not so subtle anti-Semitism.[33] Looking through the window also means to examine such continuities. Or, as Zygmunt Bauman put it: 'The more depressing the view, the more I was convinced that if one refused to look through the window, it would be at one's peril.'[34]

As far as biblical theology is concerned, an obvious place to start implementing such a shift of perspective, as I have argued, is choosing biblical passages that speak to the issue of doing theology in the face of perpetrators. We can now, at the end of this chapter, return to Isaiah 43. We would not, however, as in the beginning, evoke the image of fire and flames, and read this image counter to narratives of victims. Rather we would turn our attention to the verses which promise that the rivers shall not overwhelm you and the waters leave you unharmed; and a passage from Höss's memoirs would serve as our counter-reading. 'When you pass through the waters, I will be with you; and through the rivers, they shall not overwhelm you' (Isa. 43.2). As we can see in the brief scene below, the waters of the river Sola—passing in front of Höss's villa and the Auschwitz *Stammlager* (main camp)—provide pleasure and do not harm. But it is the perpetrators who enjoy such protection. We would be challenged not to dismiss the bitter sarcasm of such parallel reading as a cynic's attempt to destroy theological inquiry but a critic's attempt to ground German 'after Auschwitz' theologies in their particular moment in history, and thus to make them relevant again. Höss writes:

> Yes, my family had it good in Auschwitz, every wish that my wife or my children had was fulfilled. The children could live free and easy... [They] constantly begged me for cigarettes for the prisoners... The children splashed around in the summertime in the small pool in the garden or the Sola River. Their greatest pleasure was when daddy went into the water with them. But he had only a little time to share all the joys of childhood.[35]

---

33. Charlotte Klein, *Anti-Judaism in Christian Theology* (Minneapolis: Augsburg–Fortress, 1978).

34. Bauman, *Modernity*, p. viii.

35. Höss, *Death Dealer*, p. 164.

Beyond Totality: The Shoah and the Biblical Ethics of Emmanuel Levinas

O.E. Ajzenstat

That the Shoah was a distinctly modern phenomenon does not necessarily mean that it demands exclusively new forms of response. Indeed, one of the premises of a book on post-Shoah biblical hermeneutics is that the Shoah calls in some way for a return to the past, a rethinking of what went before. This is most profoundly true for the philosopher Emmanuel Levinas, according to whom the Shoah demands a two-fold return: on the one hand, a phenomenological turn to the origin and motivation of human experience and, on the other, a textual or hermeneutical return to the Bible and the old ways of reading it, that is, to the biblical texts and their analysis in the Talmud. As Levinas sees it, these two 'movements back' provide the most adequate response to the inhumanity of the Nazis, the suffering of their victims, and indeed to all the inhumanities and sufferings of the twentieth century.

What would an adequate response to the Shoah look like? It would not explain the event. Levinas holds, like many others, that to explain the Shoah would be to explain it away, to create the illusion that we can rid ourselves of what caused it and therefore cease from lament. It would not draw a lesson or rule from it. Levinas holds, again like others, that to draw a lesson from the Shoah is to justify it, however slightly. And above all, it would not console the survivors, for, as Levinas contends, consolation in the face of the Shoah is immoral. The most adequate response, for him, is in fact precisely a critique of all these things: a critique of ultimate explanations, of positive lessons or rules, of justifications, and indeed of all intellectual and spiritual comfort. This is so for two reasons: first, because explanation, rules learned, justification and comfort were the foundations of Nazism itself, with its utopian conviction that everything could be figured out and put right, and, secondly, because the questioning of the structures by which we explain, justify or comfort ourselves is, in Levinas's understanding, the beginning of a different and more primary expression of goodness, namely, ethics or personal responsibility. Levinas's response to the Shoah, then, is a calling into question of all the grand structures that offer explanation, lesson and comfort—and a subsequent turn to responsibility for the other. The response is accomplished in the two returns, for, according to Levinas, to go back to the origins of experience is to go back to a pre-theoretical ethics of personal responsibility, and to go back to the old Jewish books is to return to ethical books, books that speak of an uncomfortable and demanding service of the other, books that are themselves our other.

The Phenomenological Return: Back to the Origins of Experience

Levinas's philosophy, broadly speaking, is governed by a single basic distinction: totality and infinity, or same and other. Totality is Levinas's word for any overarching rubric or structure, be it conceptual or practical. Ideologies, philosophies, theories, policies, explanations, ideas of a universal, systems of justice—these are all totalities. So too are the basic tools of conscious thought: languages, comparisons, juxtapositions, orders. Levinas argues that although we need various kinds of totality simply in order to live our lives, we also know that they are at bottom false since they gloss over the differences or instances of uniqueness that exist in reality; they 'make same'. And this falseness is also a moral error, for when differences are glossed over, injustice is done. According to Levinas, we come to the awareness of the falseness of totalities in face-to-face encounters with other human beings, whose glorious otherness ruptures all our pretensions to sameness.

Levinas always uses the grammatical first person to describe this experience. Whenever I meet an other, he says, I glimpse his infinite difference from me, and find, suddenly, that this difference calls into question all of my totalities. All of my certainties are shaken by the incomprehensibility of the other's gaze; my sameness is broken up by difference. Moreover, while I do not remain locked in the gaze of the other but spend most of my time employing the totalities of language, comparison, category and so on, the experience of otherness persists. The recollection of the infinity of the other's difference is maintained in totality, at best, as an openness or attention to the other's concerns (as opposed to what my preconceptions tell me those concerns should be),

and, at worst, as a scruple or twinge of remorse when I disregard otherness or subvert it by applying my preconceptions to the other.

Most readers of Levinas find his account to this point reasonable and
insightful. But here he makes a conceptual leap that many find hard to
follow or accept. The moment of rupture experienced in the encounter
with the other is Levinas's *ethical* moment, for the realization of infinite
difference which calls my conceptual structures into question is, as he
sees it, also a realization of *obligation*. Whether the totalizing conceptions with which I approached the other were malicious, or beneficent,
or neutral and innocuous, they are shattered to an equal extent, and in
their wake arises a primal desire to listen, to learn, to give, to serve. In
short, there arises an awareness of a non-transferable infinite personal
responsibility to and for the other, an awareness of the absolute ethical
necessity of allowing him to continue to be different and, to this effect,
of giving him what he needs or wants. I find myself responsible *to* him
because he knows something I cannot know and can judge me in ways I
could not judge myself. I find myself responsible *for* him because any
material needs he has are mine to fulfill. And, above all, I find myself
responsible *for* him in the sense that in order to make a space for his
difference or to make him free I must bear *his* responsibility; I must
answer for him and take his punishment. This awareness is, according
to Levinas, the only possible outcome of a face-to-face encounter in
which conceptual structures have been wiped away.

Of course Levinas understands that many or most people respond to
difference not with responsibility but with hostility, but for him this
stems from a recognition of responsibility and the desire to evade it; it
signals not only an offense taken in the face of difference but also a
recoiling from the assignation to preserve and serve that difference. As
he sees it, the very existence of murder stands as evidence for his
account, since difference would not distress us to the point of extreme
hostility unless it laid on us an extreme responsibility. So, too, the very
existence of moral behavior stands as evidence in his favor for, given
that we are all fundamentally different from one another, whence ethics
if not from the recognition of this difference? But to defend Levinas's
understanding is a great task. Here I will only sketch it out. I encounter
a uniqueness. It inspires awe. I realize that if I am to live in reality
instead of in the illusion of totalizing and same-making explanatory
rubrics, I must preserve and support the uniqueness. I recoil, and
attempt perhaps to impose a same-making explanatory rubric on the

other or even to kill him, either way ridding myself of this persecuting assignation to responsibility. I am struck by the fact that any such measures will be unsuccessful, that I cannot rid the world of his rupturing difference or rid myself of the awareness of it. And finally, I respond to his difference with responsibility, meaning that I ask him what he wants or needs and I give it.

This is not, however, the end of the story, for the other and I are not alone in the world. *In* the eyes of the other I see his difference and it calls me to infinite responsibility, but *through* his eyes I also see the eyes of his other others, and their other others, and so on, until I see the eyes of every other the whole world over. Now there arises for me the issue of competing responsibilities. I see that if I give everything to the one who stands before me, I will have nothing left for anyone else. I see that infinite responsibility is contradictory and impossible. And so, in the ethical encounter where all my totalities are ruptured, there also arises the need for certain totalities, those of the comparisons and rankings necessary to distributive justice, and the structures of thought language and politics necessary to effect them. Levinas calls this event 'the entry of the third': another other, a third person, has entered the picture, and the infinite responsibility called forth by the other gives way to a different, totalizing, kind of responsibility. But—and this is the critical point—the totalizing responsibility remains ruptured by the infinite responsibility. Though I utilize rubrics for justice, I always recall that they are at bottom inaccurate and unjust. There is an uncertainty at the bottom of all my certainties, an other at the root of all my samenesses, and if I forget it I am lost. For any justice on the level of the third to remain just, those who implement it must remember its origin in the ethics which ruptures all justices.

There we have Levinas in a nutshell. Ethical rupture is the origin of human action and experience; it leads human beings to totalize, but also to remember that their totalities are broken. The structure of this nutshell gives us the only criterion possible for a ranking of totalities. Those totalities which inscribe their own brokenness are good—for instance the 'said' of language, which, despite its nature as a static structure, exists for the purpose of dialogue, change, rupture, surprise. Those which gloss over and forget their own brokenness are bad—for instance the explanatory, regulating, consoling totalities mentioned at the beginning of this chapter, and, much more so, the structures of smug certainty we associate with Nazism and other inhuman ideologies.

For Levinas, all totalities can be referred to as politics—even language, once it becomes static, is a politics. The basic structure of his thought can thus be stated simply: politics, the mode of existence of three or more people together, must remain open to rupture by ethics, the mode of existence of two. And the hortative content of Levinas's thought can be expressed in two words: remember rupture.

Levinas's ethics is without doubt susceptible to criticism, mainly because it is unique among ethical theories. For one thing, it is unverifiable. That the other's difference lays on me a responsibility, that this responsibility is infinite, and that in the ethical encounter I not only feel the assignation but acknowledge it as my own—these things are truths which are not part of a system and thus not susceptible to systematic proof. For another thing, Levinas's ethics does not allow for any objective rankings. For him, no ethical distinction can be made between a good other and a bad other; one finds oneself in the service of any other before whom one stands. Likewise, no ethical distinction can be made between conceptual structures intended to hurt the other and those intended to help him. Levinas is well aware that it is easier to be killed by an idea of the good than by an attempt at villainy, and in this awareness arrives at the insight that all structures are called into question in the encounter. At the heart of the ethics is the rupturing encounter, where every conception, be it liberal or totalitarian, is called into question by any other, be he a Nazi or a saint. There are no guidelines here, no conception of positive virtue. Levinas ethics does not tell us what to do, for this is different in every case. Guidelines and suggestions—and rankings and rules—enter at the level of politics; they are necessary and good, but only if they remain uncertain, hesitant and aware of their own falseness.[1]

Levinas holds that people act ethically because they are struck by difference. But we know that many people are kind to others because they see them as *same,* as sister human beings, or fellows; this was certainly the case for most of the righteous Gentiles and is also the basis of

---

1. My account so far may be fleshed out with a reading of Levinas's first major work, *Totality and Infinity: An Essay on Exteriority* (trans. A. Lingis; Pittsburgh: Duquesne University Press, 1969). The remainder of this section of my article, in which I discuss the relevance of Levinas's ethics to the Shoah, is my own analysis. Levinas does not often write overtly about the Shoah; *writing as response* does not require *writing about*, and may indeed be compromised by it.

most moral philosophies. It appears that two kinds of ethical understandings are tenable, ethics of difference and ethics of commonality, and that both will foster moral action. According to Levinas, though, the ethics of difference is prior in human experience to any experience of sameness, and a moral act or theory based on commonality will thus be a moral act or theory based on a secondary and contingent phenomenon. An ethics of commonality rests on the sameness we fall back into after the rupturing ethical encounter because of the presence of the third, a sameness which can indeed be moral but which always carries the danger of injustice to the other, the danger of forgetting difference. This kind of ethical theory is tenable but flawed.

An ethics of commonality begins always from a generalized self-knowledge—the subject applying this ethics necessarily understands the other on the basis of her self-understanding. She approaches the other with the realization *he is just like me!;* continues with the correlative realization, *the matters that concern me must concern him too;* and, if she expresses her awareness with a principle, says, *do unto others as you would have them do unto you.* The first problem here is simply that the realization of commonality very seldom does become a principle, and that even as a principle it can easily be overlooked in a case where violence is deemed necessary; it may occur, for example, in the fellow feeling that arises suddenly between soldiers fighting for opposing armies, or in the empathy of the executioner for the executed. The second problem is that the whole train of thought is presumptuous, if not rude. What makes our subject think that the other is in any important way like her? What makes her think that the other wants to be done unto the way she would want to be done unto? And the third and most pertinent problem is that the whole ethics falls apart if the other is, in every visible respect and many invisible respects, fundamentally *not* the same as the subject. In this case, not even the first realization can be reached—and this *was* the case for many Nazis facing Jews, especially once the propaganda machine had more or less successfully transformed them from human beings into vermin.

An ethics of difference, in distinction, begins with the other; it is the ethics imposed upon one in an encounter. It starts with the realization, *he is not at all like me, although perhaps in certain respects I am like him;* continues with, *the matters that concern him must concern me too;* and if it is expressed as a principle takes the form given the Golden Rule by Hillel in the first century BCE, *do not do unto others as you would not have them do unto you. The rest is commentary. Go and learn.* Here we must stress the last line: go and learn. This means, first, that Hillel's initial line is only a beginning. It provides an acceptable minimum and will keep the subject out of trouble, but requires supplement from the positive laws of the Torah and the Oral Torah. But it also means, *go and learn from the other.* Don't assume what *he* wants on the basis of what *you* want. Ask him. This Levinasian ethics is not only less presumptuous, but also stronger than the ethics of commonality. The reason an ethics of commonality can be overlooked or put aside in certain cases is because it allows the subject the consoling idea that she is right on a universal scale measurable by common assumptions, or, broadly, that the other would see it her way if he were only given a chance. The ethics of difference, though, is ruthlessly demanding and carries complete authority; it is the shock of alterity, an invitation to discovery, a command which may not be overlooked. The very fact that the dehumanization of Jews in the Shoah was successful enough that fellow-feeling between them and the Nazis was at times destroyed is reason to turn in the wake of the Shoah back to the command that cannot be refused, to the conviction that what concerns the other concerns me, that I am the other's keeper, in short, to the one-for-the-other of Levinasian responsibility.

In any case, according to Levinas, the ethics that arises from difference is prior, and is the basis even for the ethics of commonality. In the moment of approach, I shoulder a responsibility for the other, a responsibility to the other, and even the responsibility of the other. The other calls out to me to fall into the pattern of realization just described, and—however I may subsequently act—some part of me responds, or begins to respond, or wishes to respond. For Levinas, this is true when a Nazi faces a Jew, and true when a Jew faces a Nazi. The Jew is not to blame for what the Nazi does, but he is responsible to and for the Nazi, and responsible for the Nazi's responsibility. To be sure, conceptions of positive virtue always intercede, and so does an ethics of commonality or a commonly shared ethics. Since I live in a world in which there are more than two people—since I live in the realm of totality—I, as a Jew, may judge and even execute the Nazi on behalf of my other others or his other others. But I remain aware that on an ethical level I am responsible for him; I refuse to judge him as he is in himself; I remain open where he is closed. To return to or recollect this pre-original ethics, this extraordinary responsibility of each-to-each-other without boundaries or conceptual structures is Levinas's response to the Shoah. Though it seems at first glance to be a lesson learned, on closer inspection it appears as an absence of lessons, a shaking of any and all foundations. It is the awareness that all lessons are at bottom false, and that conviction, especially shared conviction, is the nature of injustice.

And is this not the point of the story of the Tower of Babel, from which so much post-Shoah and postmodern reflection arises? The tower builders' sin is obviously a kind of utopianism—they have a dream of perfection and they seek to make their dream a reality. But this utopianism is surely linked to their community, their commonality. They join together to build the tower; they work as one; they speak the same language, in every sense. And when God comes down to separate them, nothing in the biblical text suggests that he sees the separation as a punishment. It is truer to the text to think of the separation as a kind of rehabilitation, a reminder of the original separations on which the world was founded in Genesis 1 and 2. Separation, difference: this is what allows there to be goodness in the world. Community, common causes: this leads to utopianism and to injustice. God's reminder of rupture which forms the culmination of the Babel story is, as Levinas has it, both a reminder of pre-original reality and also, most pertinently today, the only way to stem the enthusiasms of the totalizing society.

The Hermeneutical Return: Back to the Old Books

Whether or not Levinas draws his central ideas from the Bible is a question under debate. What is certain, though, is that he draws certain phrases, images or symbols from the Bible and uses them to express his ideas. Foremost among them are '…thou shalt not kill'; the Hebrew '*hineni*' (or 'here I am');[2] 'the widow, the orphan and the stranger'; and the 'back' of God.

Levinas often describes the moment of rupture by saying that I see in the other's face the unstated command, 'thou shalt not kill' (Exod. 20.13, Deut. 5.17). 'Killing', in this context, refers not only to mundane murder but also to any movement of thought which would rob the other of his individuality; killing is knowing, possessing, explaining or even

---

2. I include the Hebrew term because it carries nuances that are lost in the English. In the Hebrew *hineni* (as well as in the French *me voici*) the subject is in the accusative—she is *done to* rather than *doing*. In addition, there is no copula verb in the Hebrew or French, i.e., no verb of equivalence, equality or ontological structure.

cherishing the illusion that I can help the other by means of a doctrine or ideology. 'Thou shalt not kill' is the phrase which arises from the other's infinite uniqueness, the phrase which invalidates any impulse that would totalize the other by incorporating him into a pre-formed order of thought or action; the words express the way one's impulse to make the other same is invalidated by the unassailability of his difference. The unstated response to 'thou shalt not kill' is '*hineni*' or 'here I am' (Gen. 22.1, Exod. 3; 4, Isa. 6.8). These words symbolize the awareness that the other is spiritually unbridgably higher than me, that he is my judge or teacher, and at the same time economically unbridgably lower than me, that he is the one to whom I must give all I have, the widow or orphan or stranger (Deut. 27.19, Jer. 22.3). *Hineni* means that the command 'thou shalt not kill' is not only given in every face-to-face encounter but also acknowledged or accepted.

It is not surprising that the symbols 'thou shalt not kill', and 'widow, stranger or orphan' crop up in a biblically based ethics. '*Hineni*' does not initially seem to fit as well, since in the Bible *hineni* is most often (though not always) said to God. Levinas uses the term precisely to point to an ambiguity between human and divine. One of his fundamental ideas is that God enters human experience in the face-to-face, in the word or gesture or look that stands as 'thou shalt not kill' and the bending towards the widow/stranger/orphan/judge—and it is this entrance that is expressed in the word or gesture or look that stands as *hineni*. This is not to say that *hineni* is something special or mysterious. It is merely the everyday experience of opening oneself before the other or being opened by the other; it means not just 'behold me' (its literal sense), but also 'I am listening', 'my conceptions are broken', 'I am at your service'. But, according to Levinas, God enters experience precisely at this point and in this way. Whenever 'here I am' means 'I am at your service', it also means 'here I am, for you, *under God*'.

To say *hineni* is therefore to glimpse the back of God (Exod. 33.23). We do not, according to Levinas, have direct knowledge or experience of God, either in sacred text or in mystical ascent; and, indeed, those who think we do are among the most dangerous of men. Certainly not all theologians are as malignant as the Nazis, whose belt buckles were emblazoned with the words *Gott mit uns*,[3] but all of them, whether

3.   See S. Hand (ed.), *The Levinas Reader* (Oxford: Basil Blackwell, 1989), p. 291.

dogmatists or beautiful souls, are totalizers who use God as a buttress for their totalities. They think they know God, and thus are among those least likely to allow their conceptions to be ruptured, least likely to experience God as he passes in the ethical encounter. They fantasize an experience of God, but shut themselves off from the real thing, the biblical 'back', that is, God's absence or 'withdrawn-ness'. For the trace of that absence passes only in the encounter with the other, the encounter where we learn responsibility. The command 'thou shalt not kill', the response '*hineni*', and the service of the widow, orphan or stranger refer not only to the infinite otherness of the other who is present but, through that, to the infinite otherness of the absent God.[4]

Levinas is the first to admit that many different readings of biblical images or symbols are possible. But he does not believe in the viability of the standard contemporary hermeneutical paradigm; that is, he does not believe that readings must either be exegetical, and measured on their historical accuracy, or eisegetical, and measured on their ideological consistency. On the contrary, Levinas's criterion for a good reading is the same as his criterion for any good thought or act: he demands that a reading be ethical, which means responsive and responsible. This is to say that the interpreter must be responsive/ responsible to the text, willing to be ruptured by it again and again. But it is also to say that the interpreter must consider the text's *other* others: those who have previously read and written about the text, and those who will read the interpreter's commentary. Levinas thus tries to respond to a great many different human beings and a great many different human conditions in his readings. And among the people and conditions that most occupy him, the victims of the Nazis in their condition as victims are paramount. Levinas seldom writes about the Shoah, probably for fear of falling into the kind of edifying moralizing he despises, but it is nevertheless clear that he draws his ethics of difference out of the Bible, at the expense of other biblical thrusts, as part of a great mesh of response to his others—among them, the Shoah martyrs, us, and those still to be born into the post-Shoah world.

I have touched on the relevance of his ethics to the Shoah and the post-Shoah world; we can already say that he draws on the Bible the

4.   All of these images occur in *Totality and Infinity* and also in other works, notably *Otherwise than Being, or Beyond Essence* (trans. A. Lingis; The Hague: Martinus Nijhoff, 1981).

way he does, *for* the victims and *for* us. But it remains to discuss why
Levinas uses the Bible at all. It is not merely dogmatic allegiance to
Judaism that makes Levinas draw the majority of his images from that
ancient text instead of from modern literature or philosophy. Nor is it
merely the fact that the biblical images are strong, or that, for all their
familiarity, they remain in some critical sense strange and startling to
the modern reader. There are better reasons for the return, reasons
having to do with a certain stance toward the historical process, a stance
which is especially relevant to the post-Shoah world.

Levinas argues that among the more dangerous totalities—those that
subvert otherness entirely and silence speech in the conviction of their
own truth—some of the very worst are the ideological systems that
postulate a grand historical scheme or a Meaning of History. The idea
of a Meaning of History, Levinas says, occurs when *theodicy*, the
attempt to find a way to reconcile the existence of evil with the goodness of God, takes the form of an overarching scheme or a theory of
providence, the idea that every action and event is part of a great plan to
realize the good either in heaven or on earth. He contends moreover
that the idea of a Meaning of History has dominated our thinking for at
least two millennia. It began piously, as the hypothesis of a plan known
only to God; it survived the Enlightenment as a theory of evolution or
materialism in which the plan was revealed in nature and history; and it
has made its way into the canon of Western secular thought as the
source of the moral norms of contemporary society. It is there in Christian eschatology, in the Hegelian 'end of history' in the Marxist utopia,
in the liberal concept of progress, and in the Nazi dream of a Third
Kingdom which would govern men in peace forever. It is, according to
Levinas, the most dangerous of all totalizing ideas, because it subordi-
nates human suffering to a metaphysical ultimate more completely than
any other ideological system. Even at its best it allows us to ignore the
other except as a function of a plan of the whole, to close our eyes to the
other's pain and do nothing when we should be doing everything. At its
worst, it allows us actively to subjugate the other to the needs of the
plan, lending support 'to a dialectic of progress that requires war,
violence and economic depression', a dialectic in which suffering is not
merely legitimized but required by 'a teleological drama'.[5] After the

---

5. Robert Gibbs, 'Unjustifiable Suffering', a paper delivered at the 1997
annual meeting of the American Academy of Religion, San Francisco, CA.

Shoah, Levinas says, we should no longer find the idea tenable in any form.[6]

Such claims are relatively familiar. Many have argued that providence, or progress, or any similar conception of a Meaning of History is impossible after the Shoah—both because the notion of a happy ending was wiped away in the repletion of suffering in the camps and because the Nazis themselves were the quintessential representatives of historical progress and the morality it implies. What is perhaps less familiar is Levinas's claim that providential schemes are not present—or at least not paramount—in the traditional texts of Judaism. To be sure, others besides Levinas have argued that the Talmud is a fundamentally a-providential text; Jacob Neusner, for instance, has convincingly demonstrated the many times the rabbis strip biblical stories of their historical significance.[7] But Levinas goes much further, arguing that the Bible is already an ahistorical document, that it was meant to be read the way the rabbis read it. While it certainly contains evocations of hope for a better time to come and laments over the loss of past glory, these sentiments, he suggests, are not obviously wrapped up into a 'plan of the whole', and even the most apparently eschatological of them can be read as symbolizations or mythologizations of concrete existential longings.

Is Levinas right to read the Bible this way? At one point he cites a midrash on Hagar and Ishmael in which God says: 'What does the end of history matter? I judge each person for what he is, not for what he will become.'[8] These lines can be understood to express one of the tenets of his biblical hermeneutic, a hermeneutic which to this extent stands in the rabbinic tradition. He 'desacrilizes' the biblical stories and symbols, focusing on the ethical experience that underlies them rather than the position of those symbols in an ontology, an order of history or a system of law. We have seen what he does with the most sacred of the

---

6.   Levinas's analysis of the historicist totality can be found in his article 'Useless Suffering', in R. Bernasconi and D. Wood (eds.), *The Provocation of Levinas* (New York: Routledge, 1988). It is extended in critical ways in certain other essays and talmudic discussions, notably 'Between Two Worlds' and 'Messianic Texts' in *Difficult Freedom: Essays on Judaism* (trans. S. Hand; Baltimore: The Johns Hopkins University Press, 1990).

7.   Jacob Neusner, 'Paradigmatic Thinking versus Historical Thinking: The Case of Rabbinic Judaism', *History and Theory* 36.3 (1997), pp. 353-77.

8.   Levinas, *Difficult Freedom*, p. 201.

biblical rules: he draws from the proscription of murder a metaphysics of the infinite obligation to the different one; he extends the command until it brings down all certainties; he transforms it from a regulation into an existential truth. Likewise, his *creation* is the experience of not being one's own origin; his *revelation* is the experience of being called into question by the trace of God in the other; his *election* is the experience that this calling into question is not a matter of choice but rather of being chosen; and finally his *messianism* is the result of these experiences, ethical responsibility.[9] These interpretations will perhaps seem preposterous to historically minded scholars. But Levinas, in keeping with the main thrust of Jewish commentary, is not particularly interested in history; he is interested in the ethics in the text, and in his own ethical responsibility to the dead and to us. The old Jewish books, he suggests, were written before the idea of a Meaning of History became popular. And this means that a return to these books is a return to accounts of reality that looked at things in their ethical complexity without subordinating them to a plan of the whole.

Moreover, because of these books and the strange life they demand, Jews throughout the centuries have been able to escape the stranglehold of historicist totality. Other nations have seen them as standing outside the historical process. To Christians their existence was an annoyance; to Hegelians, they were an anachronism; to moderns they are an irrelevance, like all religious peoples. And, in a slightly different sense, they also see themselves as history's outsiders: they stick together; they cling to tradition; they move easily about the world; they refuse to build lasting infrastructure. In short, they deliberately take up an isolated neutral stance, watching the forces of world-historical change battle it out with the detachment of a people who can determine right from wrong without elations or enthusiasms. The tragic irony is that this position has left them open to be buffeted about by history, shuttled into ghettoes, turned out into exile, occasionally slaughtered. But they have not—at least, perhaps, until recently—slaughtered others, and this is what has saved them. Their very irrelevance makes them able to see the march of history as a dubious and dangerous phenomenon—an insight that humanity now needs desperately. As Levinas says, the famous

---

9. This is not to say that Levinas denies that God created the world in the beginning, chose the Jews, revealed the Torah at Sinai, and will send a messiah in the end. But these events, qua events, are as he sees it matters of fact (i.e., they are either true or false) and are thus outside the bounds of phenomenological discussion.

stiff-neck has turned out to be the most metaphysical part of the Jewish anatomy—and we may add that the famous shrug may be their most metaphysical gesture.[10]

This is the Judaism Levinas supports in response to the Shoah. It is a Judaism to which neither the building of the State of Israel nor the Shoah is a special revelation from God or part of a historical plan; they are merely events in the course of mundane history. Indeed, one of the few essays in which Levinas speaks at any length about the Shoah, 'Useless Suffering',[11] is a careful and respectful critique of Emil Fackenheim's notion that the Shoah is a revelation, that through the Shoah God gives us a '614th commandment', the commandment to remain Jewish. Without obviously criticizing Fackenheim, Levinas subtly suggests that this kind of theory has a number of problems. By claiming the Shoah as a message, Fackenheim twists it into a kind of good. By claiming that this message is for Jews alone, he suggests that God ignores the suffering of other peoples in the Shoah and in other similar contemporary events. By claiming that the whole meaning of the event is a message to Jews not to secularize, he relativizes the suffering of the dead, making them into a prop for a liberal Jewish ideology. And, finally, by claiming that every historical event must fit into a grand plan of revelatory dispensations, he turns away from the simple infinite personal responsibility that we should now, more than ever, be able to recollect.

For Levinas, then, it is possible to abandon all lessons and all explanations, including the idea of a Meaning of History, without abandoning Judaism and its texts—as long as we emphasize certain of the tradition's thrusts at the expense of others. But this is quite in keeping with the long Jewish tradition of commentary and interpretation. All the old books remain open; the Bible is disparate and even contradictory; the rabbinic works are comprised of argument and always preserve dissenting opinions; commentary after commentary rethinks and rewrites the founding stories and even the founding law. This arguing and rethinking has never been a free-for-all; it is dialogical response. The continuous disputes of the rabbis—followed through in countless works throughout the centuries, including the works of Levinas and those of his commentators and critics—do not occur at the expense of ethics but,

10. Levinas, *Difficult Freedom*, p. 161.
11. See n. 6.

in contradistinction, provide a paradigm for the preservation of ethics in totality. As Levinas puts it, the rabbis offer us 'decisions rather than conclusions'. Contra Levinas's critics, then, the fact that he refuses lessons—that is, refuses any fixed standard of positive virtue as well as ideological positions like historicism—does not mean that he refuses moral decision, only that he refuses moral conclusion. This is the very virtue of his position, and it is a traditional virtue.

If we abandon the Jewish tradition because we have lost our faith in the Meaning of History, it is because we assume that the tradition, being old, must advocate a version of providence. Those who argue along these lines are falling into the familiar habit of progressive thinking in which only the latest ideas are worth consideration and, insofar as they accept progress, they themselves are advocating a version of providence. But to turn back to the Bible is to move through history backwards, or, at any rate, to refuse to move through history forwards. It is already to strike a blow against the idea of a progressively unfolding historical march—even before a careful reading begins to unfold the ethical import of the texts. We do not seek to restore the past or to realize a utopian future. Instead, we serve the past and future by the ethical and hermeneutical returns, returns which open us to the trace of the past infinite, and to an unpredictable 'not yet'.

EDMOND JABÈS AND THE QUESTION OF DEATH

Matthew del Nevo

Tout commentaire est d'abord commentaire d'un silence (Edmond Jabès).

Introduction

Edmond Jabès, one of the great poets of the twentieth century, died in Paris in 1991. He was born in Cairo in 1912. In 1935 he married Arlette Cohen, also from an old Cairo family, and they had two daughters. As a result of Nasser's nationalist crackdown following the so-called Suez crisis of 1956 the Jabès family was forced to leave Cairo because they were Jews and Italian Nationals. Jabès's grandfather had become an Italian national in the 1880s as a result of political instability then and the family still held Italian passports. In 1957 they joined their eldest daughter who was then studying at university in Paris, leaving behind their property and possessions, the family library included.

Between 1963 and 1973 Jabès produced *The Book of Questions* (in seven volumes) and between 1976 and 1980 *The Book of Resemblances* (in three volumes).[1] This is Jabès's main work and is to be regarded—according to the jacketnote to the third volume of *Resemblances*, written by Jabès himself—as a single piece. *Questions* and *Resemblances* were carried out apart from the literary establishment. Jabès has said that the relationship with his wife Arlette, 'remained the core of my relationship with the world'.[2] When, in Paris in his mid-forties, Jabès's spirit was heavy with the poem that was taking shape within him, 'only Arlette shared in silence the weight of a disquieting book'.[3]

---

1. Edmond Jabès, *The Book of Questions* (2 vols.; trans. Rosmarie Waldrop; Hanover: Wesleyan University Press, 1991); *The Book of Resemblances* (3 vols.; trans. Rosmarie Waldrop; Hanover: Wesleyan University Press, 1990–92).

2. Edmond Jabès, *From the Desert to the Book: Conversations with Marcel Cohen* (trans. Pierre Joris; New York: Station Hill Press, 1990), p. 9.

3. Jabès, *From the Desert*, p. 36.

Approaching the Question of Death

The word 'Bible' is not part of Jabès's vocabulary. He speaks of 'the Book' instead, by which he means the same thing, a writing of authority; but he does not speak of those books that make up the Book, the Bible, in particular. That is because for him, after Auschwitz, the Bible no longer has the authority it had when communities could unthinkingly and trustingly believe that 'He is our God and we are His people.' This is not simply a mechanical question of a broken covenant. It is not that humans have disobeyed yet again and incurred the wrath of God, nor that God is planning something sneaky as God did behind Abraham's back (Gen. 17.18) more than once. This loss of authority is a spiritual question for Jabès and broached within terms familiar to modern French poetry. If you seek God, you will experience his absence in many quarters where he is allegedly present. Looking beyond religious convention, and especially the language of religious convention, we find God is still absent. Yet this absence *is* something, and Jabès accords religious significance to the absence of God everywhere in his writings; though what he means by 'religion' in this non-context will be, to use Rimbaud's phrase (in its proper sense) *absolument moderne*.

Furthermore, Christians—who derive their faith through Jesus from the Father of Faith, Abraham—are guided by the Bible. But what sort of guidance *is it*, Jabès wonders, when baptized and highly educated individuals (as most motivated Nazis were) could systematically, organizationally and rationally rid Europe, and possibly the world had they got the chance, of the Jewish people to whom they were related through culture and faith? Where was God for the Jews, and where for the Germans? There is something very redundant about conventional religion anyway. Modern French poetry has reflected strongly upon this redundancy, as itself a religious matter, and Jabès belongs to this creative tradition.

The Bible, as the dominant law book and spiritual guide book of both Judaic and Christian cultures, had not only failed to stop abomination by its prohibitions and teachings, but a historic culture of misinterpretation of the Bible had promoted the abomination of abominations.

The core of this culture of biblical misinterpretation is exclusivism, monoculturalism and the bigotry passing for morality that is ever the result. The Jews had historically not become a sign to the other nations, but were either inward looking or Enlightened. Catholics and Protestants were equally exclusivist, in their way, displaying increasingly sectarian characteristics, as they still do today. Exclusivism fixes on the Bible as the writing of authority for a certain group that excludes all others and legitimizes that group's power and dominion, lending it authority. After Auschwitz, Jabès believes, the authority of the Book (the Bible) has been lost. It has been lost by all those who were supposed to have kept it immemorially—the Jews and the Churches— but who continue in partisanship, exclusivism and monoculturalism. The spiritual authority of the Bible as the Book of books can become idolatrous unless one recognizes that what matters is not the power and majesty that exclusive interpretive rights and possession of this Book can command in this world, but the deep words of life that the Book is about.

The bare proverbs and superb aphorisms in which Jabès's writings excel all revolve around the deep words of life. Jabès describes the deep words of life as, 'headstrong key words for which we are veil and face, sand and horizon'.[4] These are such words as God, Jew, Law, Eye, Name, Book: 'God as extreme name of the abyss; Jew as a figure of exile, wandering, strangeness and separation, which is also the writer's condition.'[5] Death is one of Jabès's deep words of life, from which *questions* branch out and *resemblances* are made. One can never possess these words, but can only be possessed *by* them. As *authority* Jabès imagines not power in the world, such as is demonstrated by the posturing of religious institutions but *a way*. Authority is a way like a path that will lead us through the desert. If we lose the path we die, just as we would were we lost in the desert. The path will preserve us and lead us to life. For the Book, the deep words of life are like this path. When the deep words of life lose their meaning, their sense, the living are in danger of disorientation, and this will directly lead to death. It is the writers *task*, for it is a poetic task, to restore the Book's lost authority, to orient the living once again with respect to the deep words of life. This is a task that *resembles* the creation of the world.

The phrase 'after Auschwitz', famously used by philosopher Theodore Adorno, refers, for Jabès, to a state of fundamental disorientation. After Auschwitz, it is not the Book that it authoritative, but rather

---

4.   *Book of Resemblances*, II, p. 71. Jabès's sense of belonging to the Book, of the voice of ink and so on, are not merely nice metaphors of subjectivity, but have an ontological bearing, that is, a being of their own, for this poet.

5.   *Book of Resemblances*, II, p. 70.

disorientation. This is the disorientation of one lost in the desert in a sandstorm, and is Jabès's favorite metaphor for disorientated authority of the Book, and 'civilized' humanity's disorientation with respect to the deep words of life. It is not, Jabès believes, just the Jew and the writer who are disoriented after Auschwitz, to whom the deep words of life represent questions and 'torments', but even God's own self is disoriented.

Yet Jabès, unlike so many, and as befits the poet, is not completely lost. His greatness is that he takes us back to the threshold of orientation, even after Auschwitz, although without manifestly reorienting us.

> To Adorno's statement that, 'after Auschwitz one can no longer write poetry,' inviting a global questioning of our culture, I'm tempted to answer: yes, one can. And, furthermore, one has to. One has to write out of that break, out of that unceasingly revived wound.[6]

Jabès does just this: he writes out of that unceasingly revived wound. 'Mark the first page with a red marker, for in the beginning the wound is invisible', says Reb Alcé on the first page of the first volume of *Questions*. The bookmark is a metaphor for a wound which must mark every page, which must trouble our reading and infect it. At first the wound is invisible. At the threshold of the book, perhaps we hardly notice it.

Death is not merely a 'theme' of Jabès's writing with a 'meaning' that commentary seeks. Death has a voice. It is a character, a real presence in the book. As Jabès writes on the last full page of the final volume of *Resemblances*, 'O death, distinctly legible in every word.' These departing words are attributed to Reb Assin. The kind of death that gradually presents itself in the writings of Jabès is multiple: the death of humanity, the death of the Book, and the death of God. Yet death is not merely the result of mortality in these instances, but the brutal result of the inhumanities of the twentieth century. 'After Auschwitz...the thread has been cut', Jabès writes, between each person and God and between neighbors and peoples.[7] 'The rupture [between God and humanity and consequently between people] lies at the heart of my books.'[8] Jabès thinks Auschwitz is their inner landscape.[9] In this sense,

6.   *From the Desert*, p. 62.
7.   *From the Desert*, p. 61.
8.   *From the Desert*, p. 60.
9.   *From the Desert*, p. 61.

that death is their very presupposition and logic, death follows us, like our bookmark, through our reading of Jabès. And this is intended, hence Reb Alcé's words at the start.

The Death of God

Death is not merely 'deadly' for Jabès. It is not nothing, as opposed to being, as it is frequently found to be in philosophical circles (e.g., Sartre's *Le être et le néant*). If God is absent then the need for God is even greater than ever. For it means that humanity is stranded pathless in a sandy wilderness. The Book in this respect is the overarching symbol of navigation.

In *The Return to the Book*, Yukel, one of the most persistently vocal of Jabès's presences, speaks for the author. The subject is orientation and disorientation after Auschwitz. The poet wonders, how can he—the writer—question and resemble the absent Book in the books he writes? How can the word regain its primordial power as the word of God? These are the orienting and guiding questions for Jabès as a writer. In them shelters the presupposition that his words are ours, ours his, even though 'the thread has been cut' which in the past had mediated and harmonized the difference.

> At the threshold of the third *Book of Questions* I found again the granite rock on which I used to sit at nightfall, after long walks in the desert.
>
> Return to the granary, to the foot of the tallest tomb of all times. Return to mud and man.
>
> In the desert no thought takes the lead, no dream. The Void carries the Void on its shoulders as the blind man carries the lame. The abyss is the good.
>
> It is years since I left Egypt. A succession of landings marks the repose of centuries, of death.
>
> Truth is not for sale. We are our own truth: this is the solitude of God and man. It is also our common freedom.
>
> Hail to the only, the universal Truth. We try to reach it by innumerable roads whose indirection we are. Truth is in the movement toward it. It is also in the coming of a counter-truth wrapped in mystery.
>
> It depends on our progress if truth seems dark or bright, absurd or pathetic. We defend our interpretation at the crossroads. The bolder it is the more it isolates us.
>
> I am learning, in the teeth of all beliefs, to believe in the name of the Truth I invoke. My law is to read the illegible Law.

> Thus the word of truth is above all the truth of the word. That is to
> say, a word we trade in for the promised word, a word of dialogue and
> diamonds, a call to the letter through the letters we learned, to the flame
> through the fascinated facet.
>
> To lose the word means losing God in the scream of Creation.[10]

These are not new ideas. That is the whole point of them, they are
immemorial. Death cannot erase memory any more than it can erase
itself. Jabès is a poet of memory. It is in memory that Jabès seeks 'to
read the illegible Law'. That is, memory in the old sense that also
means imagination, 'magical intermediary between thought and being,
incarnation of thought in image and presence of thought in being'.[11]
Death is above all productive of memory and imagination. And Jabès
sees that death has two faces: the inhuman and the human. It is the
human face of death that has been lost, just as it is the human face of
life that has been lost. The human face (of life *and* death) that the Book
once ratified is what Jabès seeks again through his writing to question
and resemble.

The Human Face of Death

There are three particularly illuminating moments when Jabès sees the
face of death and reveals it to us. In keeping with the autobiographical
current of his writings, the first of these moments is the death of his
sister when he was twelve. She was ten years older than her brother.
The loss of his beloved sister hit him at such an emotional depth that he
describes it as a birth.[12] Her death was a spiritual experience of that
'other side' of life visible only to the eyes of the heart. In *The Book of
Questions*, written more than a quarter of a century later, Jabès writes of
death as revelation, in the profound sense of what is most revealing
about creation. In the revelation of death it is as if language—the
word—were a sign of something more primordial than death. In this
thought Jabès remembers the ancient truth that the word (*logos*) was in
the beginning with God, that, indeed, it *was God*.

> Death speaks our language. In order to be understood it comes down to
> our level—or lifts us up to the level of catastrophe, and even lends us its
> own voice. Bending over his sister's bed, he had heard her going much

10. *Book of Questions*, I, pp. 319-20.
11. Alexandre Koyré, *Mystique, spirituels, alchemistes due XVIème siècle
allemand* (Paris: Colin, 1955), p. 60.
12. *From the Desert*, p. 6.

beyond his juvenile revolt, revealing to him the far side of things, the territory of chance.

To answer the dying girl he had used, as she had, words prompted by death—the only ones which could unite them. When they fell silent, he understood that he had lost her.

Likewise with leaves and with sand. The dialogue cannot, must not be interrupted. Dialogue of the living with the leaves—dialogue of the dead with the sand.

He let go, by and by. Death had become his task.[13]

What does this mean, his *task*? It means writing, 'words prompted by death'—that is, by the revelation of death, a writing that reveals the remote sources of life and death, the dust of the well, me and you.[14] Such a vocation (as the call of death to hearken to what it has to say) puts Jabès in relation to the word as to a power over life and death. The task of the writer is Scripture: the word of God. Such writing, which is the word of God, and produces not a book, but the books that shall one day comprise the Book, is writing related to the source of life, life-giving writing, in which the word ends where it began, as the Word. This kind of truth cannot be 'spelt out', just as this kind of writing thwarts the reduction of the kind of truth it seeks (to read the illegible Law) to the literal propositions of discourse; that is why all commentary on Jabès, including this, is ultimately but obliquely a commentary on silence. Yet Jabès's silence has a personal quality that one can elicit.

The Writing on the Wall

In the second illuminating moment Jabès glimpses—by implication—the inhuman death. The inhuman death arises from the death of truth, the death of God, and the culture of death which then dominates life; this is not really death, but death (which in truth always has a human face) masked by inhumanity. Inhumanity obscures the human face of death. It is death estranged from itself, death opposed to life and to God. It is the poetics of this kind of death, above all, that Jabès is called to conjugate.

This second illuminating moment is autobiographical, although in *The Book of Questions* the moment is given to his chief 'witness', Yukel Serafi.[15]

---

13. *Book of Questions*, I, pp. 57-58.
14. *Book of Questions*, I, Dedication page.
15. *Book of Questions*, I, p. 53.

Car beams light up the front of the building. (In which street? There are
so many behind and before him that he cannot remember). He reads:

MORT AUX JUIFS
JEWS GO HOME

scrawled in white chalk, in capital letters.[16]

Jabès saw these words on a wall in the Odéon quarter where he first
lived on arrival in Paris in 1957. It was an illuminating moment because
by it he realized irrevocably that he had no home to go to and in this
new home lurked the desire for his annihilation along with his fellow
Jews. In Egypt Jabès had endeavored to be a French poet, like Max
Jacob and Paul Eluard in Paris, but in Paris he became himself: a poet
whose very substance was non-belonging.[17] Artistically, in terms of its
literary and intellectual fashions, Paris meant little or nothing to Jabès,
who had more interest in general humanitarian issues than in the various '-isms' of his day. And he never returned to Egypt, even for a
holiday. Egypt entered the book and he visited every day.

Other people in the Odéon quarter passed the writing on the wall
indifferently. It meant nothing to them. For which reason it meant, to
Jabès, all the more. Without the indifference of ordinary people passing
by, the words would not be still there. Someone would have looked,
seen, taken responsibility and washed the words from sight; but that
hadn't happened.

These words became a further source of revelation to Jabès. He was
heavy with the writing that would occupy the rest of his life. In the
writing on the wall Jabès remembered what he, and his ancestors had
more or less forgotten, that he was a stranger and pilgrim on this earth.
He had no home to go to, as the graffiti artists obviously had, as everyone, except the Jew, by definition, has; and as a living symbol of home-
lessness Jabès understands Jewishness. There was Israel of course. But
poet of memory, of the ancient of days, could hardly be ardent about
something so new, and a political entity for all that. 'Jews go home',
were to Jabès words with immense reverberation, like words of authority in a Scripture of inhumanity and exclusion that everyone took so
much for granted that the sight of the words had become invisible and
their sound inaudible.

After this revelation, the Jew for Jabès would always be a symbol of

16. *Book of Questions*, I, p. 52.
17. *From the Desert*, p. 29.

every victim of injustice.[18] The Jew, he wrote, is 'the torment of God', because there is injustice and mercilessness ruling the hearts and passions of mankind.[19] 'God is the choice of the Jew and the Jew is the choice of God.' This is the choice that leaves 'no choice except to remain true to that choice'.[20] Jabès's writing will revolve around these fundamental choices with their contemplative meaning. The meaning, after all the talk about the relation of the text to margin and periphery to center, boils down to this:

> He writes.
> He writes for the sake of his hand, his pen, to appease his eyes. For if he did not write what would become of them?[21]

Writing is Jabès's answer to indifference, for himself, for Yukel and for all the forgotten dead. Writing as a sacred, even a consecrated activity. 'The act of writing would appear to be the consecrated gesture of handing man's power over to the utterance of the book.'[22] This is the book which questions and resembles the Book of Old, the Bible, the word of God. The poet invokes such a Book 'within the same words: A divine page. A human page. And in both cases the author is God, in both cases the author is man.'

The Returned Letter

The first Jabès heard of the death of his spiritual and literary mentor, Max Jacob, was when he read the official marking 'deceased' on the envelope of a letter, which had been returned, that he had posted from Cairo to Saint Benoit-sur-Loire, where Jacob lived close to a Benedictine Church. That was in February 1944, Jacob died in a concentration camp at Drancy, near Paris. He was 68 years old. He had contracted bronchial pneumonia as a result of the harsh conditions.

In what has so far been published on Jabès, Max Jacob tends to be overlooked. He is much more important than Blanchot, who seems to be similar to Jabès on the surface, but is radically dissimilar at the philosophical level. When, after her husband's death, Arlette Jabès was called upon to give a few details about her husband as a poet, one of the

---

18. *From the Desert*, p. 42.
19. *From the Desert*, p. 57.
20. *From the Desert*, p. 57.
21. *Book Questions,* I, p. 53.
22. *Book of Resemblances*, II, p. 56.

few things she cited was the importance of Max Jacob.[23] Max Jacob had
pushed Jabès to find his own poetic voice, not to be derivative. Once he
had torn up a sheaf of Jabès's poems in front of his face, although he
said they were good, because they were not in his voice. 'He taught me
to be myself, that is, to be *different*', Jabès told Marcel Cohen.[24] Jacob's
death was the third illuminating moment for Jabès. In Max Jacob's
death the human face and inhuman anti-face of death become superim-
posed. This is how they were to remain for Jabès in the time of God's
absence—our time.

There are three things that Jabès has in common with Max Jacob and
these tie Jabès's writing to the philosophical question of death, and the
unforgettable fact of Max Jacob's death. First, both were outsiders:
Jabès from the colonies, Jacob from the provinces (the Auvergne). But
both would penetrate to the heart of contemporary French literature,
whose geographical locus is of course Paris. Jabès and Jacob were Jews
in an increasingly hostile Gentile environment. Jacob was betrayed and
murdered. His whole family died in the Holocaust. Jabès was abandoned, displaced and exiled.

Secondly, while Jabès felt a unique bond with the work and person of
Jacob, neither poet belonged to a School, nor did Jabès ever have such a
bond with another writer or artist. Jacob is often associated with the
group that formed around Apollinaire and is called a precursor of the
Surrealists. But the Surrealists did not recognize Jacob as one of them.
The association with Apollinaire had more to do with living a similar
café lifestyle in the same neighborhood. Jacob was to move in his own
direction following his conversion to Catholicism, six years after
having a vision of Christ. Both artists, Jabès and Jacob owe more to
religious sensibility and religious tradition (I am thinking only of their
mature work now) than to artistic motivations and literary tradition. It
was the dissociation from literature as a self-serving end in itself that
Jabès had in common with Jacob and which distinguishes these poets in
particular from many other modern poets.

Literature has an aim beyond itself, and this, for Jabès, we've seen, is
the question of the Book. But the Book is a metaphysical question for
Jabès, as it was for Mallarmé. For Mallarmé the Book was the dream of

23. See the supplement by Dominique Boutel and Anne Panzani to *Petites
poésies pour jours de pluie et de soleil, par Edmond Jabès* (Paris: Gallimard, 1991),
p. 30.
24. *From the Desert*, p. 10.

absolute poetic value. The poet became, in his view, like an oracle or priest of the invisible, and many modern poets were to pursue this poetic ideal in their own vocabulary. For Jabès, the Book is a *humanitarian* question. How shall mankind, which is disoriented, find its way? This dream of the Book which would show the way, as the Bible, in its present shape, has failed to do, involves writing about human concern, concrete realities of sharing (in French, *partage*), hospitality and dialogue between each person, and between each person and God. It involves questioning the Book, while at the same time, resembling it.

The third connection between Jabès and Jacob is the most important. Both writers are religious in a broad sense and neither writer is merely an ethnic author. Jacob and Jabès do not simply belong to Jewish Literature—or we lose much of the point of their work.

Jacob converted to Catholicism in 1915. For him this was a move of inner spiritual importance rather than of institutional or official affiliation. It marked a shift in the basics of his vocabulary. Jabès moved from French schooling in Cairo, which while not explicitly Catholic in a catechizing sense, was permeated with Catholic ambience merely by the fact of being a French school, in the direction of Judaism; not because he was converted but because circumstance pushed him there. The point is that both writers straddle both traditions in that both understood that religion in the proper sense has to do with what is binding about being human, what links each person with every other, and each person and God.

In Cairo, Christians and Jews are much more closely housed and historically linked than those born and bred in Northern Europe might suppose. The traditions stem from the same soil, the same forefathers, the same books. Their divergence is nowhere near as apparent as in Poland, Lithuania or Germany. Religious sensibility *which is not exclusive* is common to Jacob and Jabès. This rare sensibility was, I believe, what drew Jabès into the orbit of Max Jacob. It was not something he was consciously aware of—as we are seldom consciously aware of the forces and undercurrents that induce our most profound and lasting friendships. And just as the Holocaust divided Jacob from his Catholicism, so it united Jabès to his Judaism.

Jacob's *Méditations religieuses* were published posthumously by Gallimard in Paris in 1947. Jabès's own writing would be no less of a religious meditation in its way. His work is not as 'fragmented' and 'postmodern' as some scholars have found. Jacob is an immediate precursor, but France has a literary history of religious meditation, often very poetic and personal, dating back, at least, to Pascal. And sometimes, with Pascal's sense of the infinite Nothingness of God and the freedom of his text the *feel* (and I don't mean the sense) of Jabès is not unlike Pascal. This is no coincidence. But Jabès spills out of the critical confines of French literature, just as he does of Jewish literature; and again, in this he is akin to Jacob.

In Jacob's *Conseils à un jeune poète suivis de conseils à un étudient* (1945), we can read the sorts of things that Jacob must have said to Jabès in the 1930s. What we note with the book is the high contemplative tone, often explicitly mystical, eschewing any pretensions that do not foster the truth of the word, the truth of the writing as reflections of the soul's own culture.

> Soul cultivation. Morning Meditation is as indispensable to a pagan as it is to a Christian, without exception... Meditation does not consist in making ideas, on the contrary! It consists of making itself, of transforming sentiment and conviction. A meditation is good when it produces a YES, pronounced by the entire body, a cry of the heart: joy and sorrow! a state of tears or laughter.[25]

Religion (in the strong sense I've described) and literature are inseparable in this little work. After the death of Jacob I would hazard that this book would have assumed great importance for Jabès, and through it Jacob remained his mentor.

It is to writing—to the word—that Jabès is true, not to religion as such. Writing (poetry) is an inner vertigo of the self on the edge of the self. Religion of the inner life leads us to this vertigo of the self as well. Jabès pushes his reader toward this same point as himself: 'You are the one who writes and the one who is written', the opening line of *The Book of Questions* enigmatically states. Here at the vertiginous point the book is made to question and resemble the Book. Here at the vertiginous point also we are placed in relation with our own death—the sense that we 'are written', that when humanity fails—when love fails—and when absence rules, writing is stronger than absence and death. At the vertiginous point the language of poetry (which seems mystical only to the novice) begins—Jabès and Jacob know this equally. It is the *secret* of their collusion and their friendship.

25. Max Jacob, *Conseils à un jeune poète suivis de conseils à un étudient*, (Paris: Gallimard, 1945), p. 74.

'Lyricism is a state of thought without thinking, of feeling without feeling, to nourish an harmonious expression.'[26] Jabès has followed Jacob's advice. It is advice that can only be followed by internalizing it as one's own. While so many other modern poets and writers—especially the ideologues—have *played* with language, Jabès has 'not tried to break the meaning of the sentence, nor the metaphor, but, on the contrary, I have tried to reaffirm them.'[27] 'The word is much, but it is sentence which carries the emotion.'[28]

Jabès took Jacob's counsels very seriously, which shows how Jacob's 'manifesto' was no more governed by staunch Catholicism than Jabès's later writing by Judaism. For both, writing—allegiance to the word—comes first. As an act of meditation on the revelation of death and absence (of both God and humanity):

(In writing we wrestle with a part of death just as
we wrestle with only part of the dark.
So writing means to confront death in its fleeting
Totality, but to measure ourselves, each time, against
only one of its instants.
A trial beyond our strength, which leads us to write
Against the writing of death and to be ourselves written by it.)[29]

Three such instances in which the writer measures himself against death (and thereby is measured) have been given: the death of his sister; the writing on the wall; the death of his mentor, Max Jacob.

A Poetics of the Sacred

What Jabès, like Jacob immediately before him, discovered in writing, was the direct relation (real and poetic) between writing and death, then between death and the sacred. The sense of the sacred in Jabès's writing is to be discerned in its somewhat wayward beauty, that elusive 'something else' to which Jabès makes reference;[30] the magical quality of writing. Beautiful writing refers, yet implicitly, to a transcendence of Being present in the words, but not reducible to that presence; a quality in the words that is not merely words. The beauty is a content (what he

26. Jacob, *Conseils à un jeune poète*, p. 56.
27. *From the Desert*, p. 110.
28. Jacob, as quoted by Jabès in *The Book of Margins* (trans. Rosmarie Waldrop; Chicago and London: University of Chicago Press, 1993), p. 150.
29. *Book of Resemblances*, II, pp. 56-57.
30. *From the Desert*, p. 111.

says) and also a grace of phrasing that cannot be reduced to 'technique' without killing it. It is invoked by his many voices, especially those of his rabbis.

By the beauty of his language Jabès shows us that poetry is possible, even poetry with Auschwitz as its inner landscape. The absent are living, just as the silence of Jabès's voices, so ancient and so new, wraps and pervades their speech. His word mediates absence and presence, not allowing either to be fixed, preserving the transcendent '*essance*' of both (to use the Levinasian idiom). The presence of the dead, as present as the word on the page, and the endlessness of memory, the richness of memory beyond all price, is what is unforgettable and the great pages of Jabès are those we can scarcely read without tears.

The Book of Resemblances is less haunted than *The Book of Questions*, it is slightly removed from the inspiration of *Questions* and is more reflective, in parts more theoretical, despite Jabès's dread that his work should be connected with a *theory* of writing.[31] Theory is didactic, interpretive, subjective, dogmatic, the very opposite of being able *to divine* the transcendent qualities of truth and beauty. But only the reader with this kind of ability really enters into the reading which, here, means also the writing. To divine the sacred quality of Jabès's writing one needs to be inwardly open and receptive, as one is, Jabès reminds us, when alone in the desert, or when beside the dying.

For Jabès, as a poet, Auschwitz is not about awful statistics, the clash of impersonal forces, historical determinants, 'Germans' versus 'Jews'. It is about the human. In particular, Auschwitz is about the inhuman, which is not the opposite of the human, but the reduction of the human to what it is not and the reduction of death to what it is not, of both to the realm of godless abstraction, generality and indifference where torture, inhumanity and atrocity become the rule. But from the poet's point of view, the confrontation with the inhuman must still be human; that is to say it must always be personal and unique. It will still be found to be full of story, to feed memory, to make imaginable. The confrontation did not end with the war. For this poet there is no 'after' Auschwitz. The faceless must still be faced and given expression, at all cost, even at the cost of one's life. This was the cause Jabès gave his own life for and to which his writing is a testimony.

31. *Book of Resemblances*, I, p. 18.

Part II

ENGAGING BIBLICAL TEXTS IN LIGHT OF THE HOLOCAUST

AVRAHAM, EMIL AND ANDRE: RE-READING AVRAHAM'S MONOLOGUE WITH THE DIVINE IN LIGHT OF FACKENHEIM AND NEHER

Steven L. Jacobs

Introduction: The World of the Hebrew Bible has Changed

The events of 1933–45, specifically the years 1939–45, which saw the genocidal slaughter of almost six million Jewish men, women and children in Europe and Russia—events now known as the Holocaust, or more universally, the *Shoah* (in Hebrew: 'Devastation' or 'Destruction' and itself derived from the Torah text)—have forever and all time altered the present and future landscape of Jewish existence and with it Jewish religious tradition, *including* the reading of Judaism's most sacred text, the Torah. Simply put: Post-*Shoah* Jewish life—religious and secular, Zionist and not—can no longer proceed as if these horrendous events were akin to a distant memory, having little or no impact upon consciousness. In truth, the *Shoah* remains an unwelcome and intrusive visitor at all Jewish gatherings even now, more than half a century after the close of the Second World War.

Despite the fact that the lives of those whose personal experience of Nazi brutality are reaching their end daily, scholars and non-scholars alike are only now beginning to address the complex and problematic philosophical and theological questions of a world where the global anti-Semitic agenda of one man and one nation, along with those who rallied to their banner, was the total elimination of Jews from planet earth. Questions such as the presence or absence of God and the presence or absence of humanity continue to cause great consternation and anguish. As regards sacred scripture in particular, noted rabbi and philosopher Emil Fackenheim, now retired and living in Israel, could write in the foreword to his slender volume, *The Jewish Bible after the Holocaust: A Re-reading:*

> So enormous are the events of recent Jewish history—this is the central
> conviction informing this book's hermeneutic—that the Jewish Bible
> must be read by Jews today—read, listened to, struggled with, if neces-
> sary fought against—as though they had never read it before.[1]

The author of this essay, who has struggled with this and similar religious and theological questions and concerns all his professional and
personal life, could not agree more. And I am not alone.

For the last several years, I have participated in a public reading,
commentary and discussion of passages found both within the Torah
text and the New Testament at the Annual Scholars Conference on the
Holocaust and the Christian Churches, founded in 1970 by Franklin
Littell and Hubert Locke. My 'colleagues in dialogue' include Zev
Garber, a professor of Jewish Studies, Henry Knight, a professor of
religious studies and an ordained Methodist minister, and James Moore,
a professor of religious studies and an ordained Lutheran minister.
Together, we have both struggled and wrestled with various passages of
sacred literature, armed only with our collective conviction that their
contemporary meaning, in addition to their literal understanding, has
changed because of the historical reality of the *Shoah*. What began as
one scholarly session among many, attracting a limited number of participants, has now become, after several years, a central feature of that
conference, attracting an increasingly larger number of participants who
sense in our own struggles something akin to their own quest for meaning and sense-making. Thus far, we have published one set of our
'readings' and responses in a special issue of the journal *Shofar,* published by the Jewish Studies Program of Purdue University, Purdue, IN.
Thus, there remains precedence for the work which called these contributions into being and for which the editor of this volume merits praise.

Bereshith/*Genesis 18.16-33*:
A Text Not Yet Examined in Light of the Shoah

Approximately a third of the way into this first book of sacred scripture,
we encounter an aggressive *monologue* (often mistakenly perceived as
a dialogue) by one of God's creature-subjects over the fate of an alien
and corrupt humanity. To be sure, in all previous scripture stories—
Adam and Eve, Cain and Abel, and Noah and family—dialogue is very

---

1. Emil L. Fackenheim, *The Jewish Bible after the Holocaust: A Re-reading*
(Bloomington: Indiana University Press, 1990), p. viii.

much in evidence, but the conversation is traditionally and classically that between the master/ruler and his submissive subject(s) who demonstrate little independence of spirit and are easily cowed into submission. While all such dialogues demonstrate an intimacy with the Divine Presence quite removed from and very much foreign to Israel's neighbors and their own experience of the 'Divine-human encounter', Avraham's monologue with God over the fate of Sodom and Gomorrah stands uniquely apart. In light of the *Shoah*, it speaks volumes to us today.

Most obviously, only a people already in relationship with its God has the right to present such an aggressive and accusatory monologue without fear of arbitrary or capricious retribution on the part of the Divine Presence. Human pain and tragedy, even *in potentia*, demand of us that we challenge God to do that which only God can do: alleviate the pain and alter the course of history. In the second of these first five books, that of *Shemot*/Exodus, the people of Israel cried out to God in their distress in the hell of their Egyptian enslavement *and God heard them*:

> The Israelites were groaning under the bondage and cried out; and their cry for help from the bondage rose up to God. God heard their moaning, and God remembered His covenant with Abraham and Isaac and Jacob. God looked upon the Israelites, and God took notice of them (2.23b-25).

Thus, the conversation, the dialogue, the relationship between Divine Master and human subject exists. Humanity cries out to God and God responds. Unique to Avraham's monologue, however, as previously mentioned, is his protestation on behalf of the Sodomites and the Gomorrahites, peoples not his own and seemingly devoid of redemptive merit. Avraham struggles to find the barest minimum of 'righteous Gentiles' and thus avert the divine wrath, only to be frustrated and disappointed because they do not exist (or he is unable to find them).

Yet, during the Second World War, they *did* exist, not only in Germany but throughout Nazi-dominated Europe. In every country where Jews experienced the barbarism and brutality of the *Shoah*, 'righteous Gentiles', more often than not at risk to their own lives as well as the lives of their loved ones, came forward to save Jews. Not enough, but some. Not enough to stave off the *Götterdämmerung* brought upon Germany by its own leadership. This same intimacy which caused Avraham to speak out in protest to his God, and the Jewish collectivity in Egypt to cry out in pain to its God, enabled the Jewish people to speak out during the *Shoah* to its God, seemingly to no avail whatsoever. As Michael Berenbaum has written, 'The God who was silent then should be ashamed to act now.'[2] The God of the Bible who welcomed the challenge of words of protest at both divine and human injustice, the God who devastatingly punished Sodom and Gomorrah (*Bereshith*/Gen. 19), the God who liberated the people of Israel from Egypt and became the Hero of the *Pesach*/Passover story, evidently became the same God who stood silently by and could not or would not respond as Jewish lives were erased, despite the millions of words of address by millions of innocents. One trembles at the conclusion that such Divine–human intimacy existed and ended with the biblical text only.

Perhaps the lesson is even more troubling: that even in the deepest moments of our own personal and collective suffering, we are not to forget our common humanity but concern ourselves with the fate of all, not just some. Avraham had already experienced suffering and pain, including the pain of his wife's barrenness and advancing old age prior to Isaac's birth, and yet he still concerned himself with others. Did God truly expect of those who perished at the hands of the Nazis and their allies to feel sadness, pity or compassion for the evildoers who had willingly surrendered their humanity in exchange for the adrenaline rush of evil deeds? Is God's challenge to Jews, based on this text, to expect (even to demand) more of his Jews than is humanly possible? How, indeed, are we to read this text whereby Avraham confronts God over the fate of Sodom and Gomorrah in light of the *Shoah*? As a paradigm for our own actions or inactions during the *Shoah* and, with it, our own failure *à la* Avraham? Or as an irrelevancy? Better to focus on the intimacy of relationship, perhaps, and to conclude as Irving Greenberg has that, after the *Shoah*, the covenantal 'power positions' are reversed and Israel now assumes the voluntary role of senior rather than junior covenantal partner.[3]

Andre Neher, in his book *The Exile of the Word: From the Silence of the Bible to the Silence of Auschwitz*, makes much of the silence of God.[4] Of the *Shoah* he writes:

2. Michael Berenbaum, 'In a World without a Redeemer, Redeem!', in Steven L. Jacobs (ed.), *The Holocaust Now: Contemporary Christian and Jewish Thought* (East Rockaway, NY: Cummings and Hathaway, 1996), p. 299.

3. Irving Greenberg, 'Voluntary Covenant', in Jacobs, *The Holocaust Now*, pp. 187-215.

4. Andre Neher, *The Exile of the Word: From the Silence of the Bible to the*

That is why the Jewish experience at Auschwitz is so incapable of
appraisal... Death at Auschwitz bears comparison with no form of death
from the beginning of history until now. Until the twentieth century,
such a death was unthinkable; it will forever be irrecompensable.

Staring directly into the abyss of the *Shoah*, hearing still the anguished
groanings of its victims—Jews primarily, but non-Jews as well—we
post-*Shoah* Jews have once again become Avraham, challenging God
not only for his silence during the *Shoah* but his failure to act as well.
Our moral outrage, never allowed to become arrogant, must now trans-
late itself anew into the courage to speak out loudly against all injustice
in our world at this end of the twentieth century—'the century of genocide'—and the beginning of the twenty-first. Our failure to protest
reduces us to impotence and corrupts us in the process.

With minor variations and alternative renderings, I have heard the
following midrashic parable for many, many years: A man comes to
Sodom, enters the town square, and begins to loudly speak out against
the evils which surround him. A small boy comes up to him, asks him
what he is doing, to which he responds: 'I am speaking out against the
evils of this place.' The boy then departs. A week later, he returns, asks
the same question, receives the same answer, and leaves. Yet a week
later he returns, and, again, asks the same question. This time, the man
looks down at the small boy and says: 'When I came to this place, I
spoke out against the evils in this place in order to change the people.
Now I continue to speak out in order not to be changed by them.'

Could this not, too, have been part of Avraham's ultimate motivation
not only in attempting to save the evildoers of Sodom and Gomorrah
but in speaking out as well—not to be 'tarred with the same brush' as
part of an errant, wayward humanity? Is this not, too, a lesson of a post-
Shoah reading of this story: That we who either experienced the horrors
of the *Shoah* or inherited from our parents and grandparents the psychic
damage inflicted upon them because of the *Shoah* have the moral and
ethical responsibility to neither act nor speak with prejudice nor malice
aforethought? Must we who survived the *Shoah* not hold ourselves to a
higher standard of moral and ethical imperatives because of those who
preceded us, lest we, somehow become tainted with the evil and foul-
smelling brush of Nazism? Does not the American Jewish community

Silence of Auschwitz (trans. David Maisel; Philadelphia: Jewish Publication Society, 1981), p. 140.

in its internal dealings with itself, as well as its dealings with the larger, American, non-Jewish community, need to conduct itself above and beyond reproach? Does not the Israeli Jewish state/community need to conduct itself, most especially in its dealings with its Arab population and its Palestinian neighbor-population, above and beyond reproach? Do not the various religious streams of the Jewish people—both in the United States and in Israel—need to conduct themselves premised upon the principle of *ahavat Yisrael* ('love of Jew for Jew'), else the legacy of oppressive hatred and banal evil attributed to the Nazis continues?

The Traditional and Modern Commentators: Almost But Not Quite

Bereshith/Genesis 18.16-33 provide much food for thought for traditional and modern commentators from Rashi to Fox. What is *not* at issue, however, is the legitimation of the Divine Presence to destroy the wicked cities of Sodom and Gomorrah because of their wickedness, a precedent already having been established with the generation of the *Mabul* (the Flood) during Noah's time. Left unsaid and unwritten is the reality that the innocent, particularly the children, died along with the guilty; for the only conclusion that the commentators could countenance was the true and total lack of innocent victims in this scenario. (Thus, even the children in Sodom and Gomorrah were, somehow, 'tainted' with the sins of their own parents, and, by extension, were worthy of this punishment.)

Evidently, the original Hebrew text of verse 22, after Avraham's visitors has departed towards Sodom, read 'and the Lord remained standing before Avraham'. Such an uncomfortable anthropomorphism, coupled with an evident inequality of the master appearing before the subject, was already noted by, among others, the great commentator Rashi:

> and Abraham was still standing, etc. But is it not so that he did not go to stand before Him, but the Holy One, blessed be He, came to him and said to him (above verse 20): 'Because the cry of Sodom and Gomorrah has become great, etc.,' and it should have been written here: 'and the Lord was still standing beside Abraham?' But this is an emendation of the Scribes (*Gen. Rabbah* 49:7). (The Sages of blessed memory changed the text and wrote it in this manner) [to avoid an irreverent expression, i.e., it would be offensive to God to say that He was standing before Abraham!][5]

5. The Judaica Press, *Complete Tanach with Rashi,* CD-ROM edition (Chicago: Davka Corporation, 1999).

Far more troubling—and not found in Cohen, Fox, Hertz, Hirsch, Malbim, Plaut or Rashi[6]—is Nahum Sarna's insightful comment:

> Absent from the Sodom and Gomorrah narrative, as well as from the Flood story, is the theme of repentance. Just as Noah did not call upon his contemporaries to repair their ways, neither Abraham nor the messengers warn the people of Sodom of the impending disaster in the hope of arousing them to atonement.[7]

Among the 'bottom-line' tragedies of the *Shoah* is the simple reality that the saving of innocent Jewish lives was *not* among the Allies' highest priorities in bringing about the end of the Second World War. Knowledge of what was happening to Jews was known in the West after the German invasion of Russia in 1941, and possibly earlier. Yet the shared, all-too-often unspoken anti-Semitism of the Allies, fueled as we now know by both the reluctance to welcome Jewish refugees into the United States, Great Britain, France, Soviet Russia and British-held but Arab-dominated Palestine, and American isolationism prior to Pearl Harbor, mandated a quietus regarding future punishment of the German leadership for such genocidal atrocities. Only after the end of the war, when increasing public knowledge of these horrific events could no longer be denied, did the Allies assert their moral leadership in victory with the International Military Tribunal at Nuremberg and the new legal category of 'crimes against humanity'. Yet the call for repentance on the part of the Allies on behalf of the Jews and others to Hitler and the Nazis never came. Like Avraham and Noah before him, the Allies, too, abrogated their moral and ethical responsibilities where human lives were at stake because, evidently, those lives were not valued as highly as others.

(Parenthetically, we must not let the irony be lost upon us that, while

---

6. A. Cohen (ed.), *The Soncino Chumash: The Five Books of Moses with Haphtaroth* (London: Soncino Press, 1996 [1947]); Everett Fox, *The Five Books of Moses* (New York: Schocken Books, 1995); J.H. Hertz (ed.), *The Pentateuch and Haftorahs* (London: Soncino Press, 1961); Samson Raphael Hirsch, *T'rumath Tzvi: The Hirsch Commentary* (ed. E. Oratz; trans. G. Hirschler; New York: The Judaica Press, 1986); Malbim (Rabbenu Meir Leibush ben Yechiel Michel), *Commentary on the Torah* (trans. Zvi Faier; Jerusalem: M.P. Press, 1982); W. Gunther Plaut, *The Torah: A Modern Commentary* (New York: Union of American Hebrew Congregations, 1981).

7. Nahum M. Sarna, *The JPS Commentary: Genesis* (Philadelphia: Jewish Publication Society, 1989), p. 133.

Avraham pleaded the cause of the Sodomites and Gomorrahites before God, he failed to plead their own case directly before them. Worse, of course, was Noah, who pleaded neither before God nor before his fellow human beings. Like Noah, then, the Allies pleaded neither before God—and here we must include the silence, not only of the Roman Catholic Church under its papal leadership, but all institutionalized Christian religious traditions as well, not to mention the self-limiting public Jewish protests—nor before their enemies.)

Writing initially before the full revelatory horrors of the Holocaust/ *Shoah* became widely known, Joseph H. Hertz, late Chief Rabbi of the British Empire, senses in Avraham's question in verse 25—'shall not the Judge of the earth do justly?'—a most amazing proposition: that God, too, is ultimately bound by the dictates of justice, else the Divine–human encounter, in particular the God–Israelite/Jewish encounter, is both a sham and a fraud:

> The boldness of the Patriarch's ringing challenge, the universality of the phrase 'all the earth,' and the absolute conviction that the infinite might of God must be controlled by the decrees of Justice—that, in fact, an unjust God would be a contradiction in terms—are truly extraordinary.[8]

Thus, no matter how the need for mercy enters into the scheme of things, ultimately, the world—and God's relationship to it—functions best (and most successfully?) when justice prevails. Justice for victims of the Holocaust/*Shoah* is partial at best and not the result of the divine hand. To be sure, Germany herself has made major strides in the payment of reparations to the victims of Nazism. Switzerland has been

---

8. Hertz, *The Pentateuch and Haftorahs*, p. 66. Plaut, *The Torah*, p. 133, echoes this same sentiment thought from a more human-centered perspective when he notes: 'The important thing is that he asks altogether and that God does not reject his question out of hand. The Bible thereby makes clear that man may, with impunity, question the behavior of God. Like Abraham, man need not surrender his own sense of justice; he remains free to accept or reject the divine judgment—although he will have to submit to it in the end. Man is not reduced to a moral automaton, his spiritual freedom is preserved.'

Sarna, *Genesis*, pp. 132-33, also affirms this primary role of divine justice: 'The ensuing dialogue [*sic*] assumes that the man of faith is not expected to accept morally absurd behavior with silent resignation. God rules the pagans, judges their deeds, decides their fate, and executes His decisions. His universality finds expression, above all, in His punishment of pagans for moral corruption because He is the architect of a societal pattern that is universal in scope.'

forced to confront the shame of its bankrupt banking policies and establish a fund for victims, many of whom are no longer alive. While some, especially the 'major players' in the Nazi hierarchy were brought to trial, convicted and condemned accordingly, the overwhelming majority of those who actually perpetrated the barbarous deeds of the Holocaust/*Shoah* were never brought to trial, but, instead, were able to reintegrate themselves back into their own societies, psychologically convinced that their heinous crimes fell within the parameters of 'acts of war' for which they should not be unjustly (?) punished.

Anti-Semites, too, continue to spew forth their hate. Holocaust/*Shoah* denial continues to be an observable international networked and linked phenomenon with the likes of David Irving (England), Robert Faurisson (France), Ernest Zundel (Canada), and a whole host of lesser luminaries in this country plying their insidious craft with more and more publications, conferences and presentations. One stops short, however, of agreeing with renegade Talmudic Rabbi Elisha ben Abuyah, 'Layt din v'layt Dayyan/There is no justice; there is no Judge!'

Avraham was, according to both text and commentators, convinced that justice was of paramount importance, and, thus, drew from it the courage to confront God over the fate of Sodom and Gomorrah. He was equally convinced that his God was a just God, merciful when appropriate, but just nonetheless. Thus, knowing that he had done everything humanly possible to plead for those unworthy of pleading, he was able to return to his place (v. 33), though the text does not tell us in what frame of mind, and, ultimately, allow God to do what God needed to do: punish and destroy Sodom and Gomorrah (ch. 19).

Ere too long, the very lives of those who were Hitler's victims will collectively be at their end. To even raise the question of whether we—Jews and non-Jews alike—have done for them everything that we could have or should have is to admit that we have not, and our opportunities to correct our lapses are fast fleeing away from us. It is not only the failures of the guilty that merit condemnation; it is the failures of the innocent that will continue to haunt us long after the last victim has been laid to rest. How then can we return to our places and allow the world to continue towards whatever future is in store for it? Has our own dialogue with the Divine, our own monologue of protest at injustice come to its end in a world which countenances genocidal atrocity on a regular basis? Can one truly argue the opposite with Yehuda Bauer that 'After the Holocaust, there are three commandments: Thou shalt not be a victim. Thou shalt not be a perpetrator. Thou shalt not be a bystander.'[9]

Conclusion: And What of the Future?

The Torah remains the central sacred text of the Jewish people, at the very crossroads between itself and its God. The *Shoah* remains one of the two central realities of twentieth-century Jewish life, the other being the birth of the third Jewish Commonwealth out of its ashes. That the text can no longer be read as it was prior to 1933 is a given; that all subsequent Jewish understandings of it must now incorporate this history and this reality into this search for textual meaning poses new challenges as well as new opportunities to further come to grips with both the enduring truths of the Torah and the horrific brutalization of the Jewish people. The world of Judaism and the Jewish people has been irrevocably changed forever. One can only hope and pray that, whatever the lessons to yet be learned from both, Jewish survival may still prove to be both vibrant and vital into the twenty-first century and beyond.

9.   Yehuda Bauer, *Unpublished Speech* (Philadelphia, PA: Anne Frank House, 1986).

BANALITY AND SACRIFICE

Roland Boer

As is well known, the word 'Holocaust' means, literally, 'burnt offering'. What is rarely considered in the use of such terminology for the killing of so many Jews by the Nazis is the practice of burnt offering in the Hebrew Bible. This essay will explore some of the biblical texts, in particular the tense *Akedah* (the binding of Isaac) in Genesis 22, the banal prescriptions for sacrifice in Leviticus 1–7, and the involuted reflection on human sacrifice in Ezekiel 20. There are four moments, or layers, in this reading that connect with certain theories germane to the biblical texts: the question of ethics via Immanuel Kant's glimpse of radical evil; the logic that connects Kant with the Marquis de Sade, as announced by Jacques Lacan; the repressive hypothesis from psychoanalysis and Hannah Arendt's notion of the 'banality of evil'; and finally the return of the repressed of human sacrifice in the Christian Eucharist, the frozen moment of the perpetual, cannibalistic, eating of the sacrificial body. Behind all of this lies the question: does the Holocaust partake of the logic of sacrifice in the Hebrew Bible?

Ethics and Isaac

With the Holocaust, ethics seem to be both recovered and annulled at one stroke—the only language possible, yet grossly inadequate. Yet, as one who finds the current flood of ethical concerns a little too frenetic, I will juxtapose the enigmatic pondering over human sacrifice in Genesis 22 and Ezekiel 20 with Immanuel Kant on the question of 'radical evil'.

It has long been held, at least since Julius Wellhausen in the nineteenth century, that Genesis 22—in which God commands Abraham to sacrifice Isaac and then averts the sacrifice at the last minute in favor of a ram—functions as a signal of the abolition and rejection of human, specifically child, sacrifice among the ancient Israelites.[1] This is clearer in the earlier Elohistic account (22.1-14, 19), where what is originally a command to sacrifice Isaac (22.2) is replaced by a divine directive not to slaughter and burn him (22.12). The text then becomes one more example of a distinct Israelite identity over against its Canaanite and Palestinian environment. God, it seems, does not require human sacrifice; in the end that is elided by the ram in the bush, which is 'offered up as a burnt offering instead of his son' (22.13). It may be objected that the casting of the story as a test of faith complicates the account. Thus the story is set up as an examination (22.1) only to find its realization as the knife, about to slice the boy up, is averted: 'now I know that you fear God, since you have not withheld your son, your only son, from me' (22.12). Yet this may be seen as part of the story of the abolition of sacrifice as well: Abraham's unswerving trust sets up his unquestioned belief in the capricious change of divine direction later on.

Yet, as Jon Levenson points out, not only was Abraham never commanded to sacrifice the ram as he was his son (he is only stayed from slaughtering Isaac), but 'it is passing strange to condemn child sacrifice through a narrative in which a father is richly rewarded for his willingness to carry out that very practice.'[2] This remains the ethical problem with Genesis 22: God commands Abraham, without so much as a whiff of irony, to offer up Isaac: 'Take your son, your darling, whom you love, Isaac, and go to the land of Moriah, and burn him there as a sacrifice on one of the hills that I will show you' (22.2).[3] The ideological core of human sacrifice is found here in a most obvious place, in the divine statement: the mark of one's piety, the expectation that you would do nothing other than offer your best to God, is the theological undergirding without which sacrifice becomes callous and evil. Theologically, human sacrifice is the highest good.

All of this is reinforced by the source critical suspicion that in Genesis 22 may be found the various layers covering an initial story of human sacrifice without the final turn of the knife before it pierces

1. So, for example, Claus Westermann, *Genesis 12–36: A Commentary* (trans. John J. Scullion; London: SPCK, 1986), p. 358.

2. Jon D. Levenson, *The Death and Resurrection of the Beloved Son: The Transformation of Child Sacrifice in Judaism and Christianity* (New Haven: Yale University Press, 1993), p. 13.

3. Translation, following the Septuagint, by Stephen Mitchell, *Genesis: A New Translation of the Classic Biblical Stories* (New York: Harper Collins, 1996).

Isaac's neck, before the flame that licks the still warm body. In an inexplicable fashion that one comes to expect from the Hebrew Bible (the ideal Freudian text), traces of the earlier story remain—as in 22.19, where we read, 'so Abraham returned [singular verb] to his young men', alone and without Isaac. Only after Abraham meets the young men do the plurals return: 'and they arose and went to Beer-Sheba; and Abraham [on his own!] lived at Beer-Sheba' (22.19). As Zuckerman suggests, Gen. 22.6, 7, 12b and 16b take on a more ominous tone in the light of 22.19.[4] Thus two ascend the mountain in 22.6, but only one descends in 22.19. The 'lamb' asked about by Isaac in 22.7 becomes auto-referential, and the phrase 'you have not withheld your son, your darling son' (22.12b, with an echo in 22.16b) bears an affirmation that Abraham carried out the request of 22.2.

This argument is valid as far as it goes—there is indeed a smell of burning human flesh, a whiff of cooking protein in the soot-stained page of Genesis 22. Yet, there is something in the first position I out-lined above, not that it marks an Israelite distinctiveness, but rather, that the text also finds human sacrifice objectionable: the double layering of the objection, in the stay of Abraham's knife hand, and then the later addition in 22.15-18 that spurts forth offspring all over the page, indi-cate what is an ideological tension. Indeed, as Fredric Jameson has argued, texts function as the symbolic resolution of ideological and social contradictions.[5] Further, the papering over of such contradictions can only leave traces in the text—hence the tensions apparent in Gene-sis 22. We should be surprised *not* to find contradictions in such a cru-cial text. This means that the text, without too much arm-twisting, yields forth a tension between human sacrifice as the highest good, the purest form of devotion to God, and as something to be avoided, as evil. The alternative value to sacrifice is human life, particularly in the form of descendants. This ideological position—that offspring are of greater value alive than dead—is arrived at by a convoluted logic that betrays the tension I have traced: only absolute obedience to God, even to the point of human sacrifice, enables the perpetuation of life as a reward for such devotion. 'Now I know that you fear God' (22.12), utters the divine voice in the Elohistic version, as the knife quivers at Isaac's

---

4. Bruce Zuckerman, *Job the Silent: A Study in Historical Counterpoint* (New York: Oxford University Press, 1991), p. 19.

5. Fredric Jameson, *The Political Unconscious: Narrative as a Socially Sym-bolic Act* (Ithaca, NJ: Cornell University Press, 1981), pp. 77-80.

throat. 'By your offspring shall the nations of the earth gain blessing for themselves, because you have obeyed my voice' (22.18), utters that voice again, now as a later addition.

Genesis 22 is not the only place where the tension may be found, for in Ezek. 20.25-26 we find:

> Moreover I gave them statutes that were not good and ordinances by which they could not live. I defiled them through their very gifts, in their offering up all their first-born, in order that I might horrify them, so that they might know that I am Yahweh.

The verses come at the end of the Ezekiel-mediated word of Yahweh (20.4-26), addressed to the 'elders of Israel' (20.3), which signals tensions over the construction of the Exodus traditions within the Babylonian exile. The twist of the final verses interests me most. In his infinite mercy, his *ḥesed*, Yahweh orders Israel to carry out human sacrifice[6]— and may not Exod. 22.28-29 be read in this way?—so that 'they may know that I am Yahweh'. Rather than the law as the mark of the grace of Yahweh, it is 'the ultimate perversion'.[7] The key in Ezekiel is that the Israelites had no choice: they were doomed, in the very following of Yahweh's law, to disobey that law. Or rather, they could not live by following the law (the source of life!) given by Yahweh. While Ezekiel 20.25-26 picks up the paradox of the law—its foundation relies on a universal crime—I turn to Kant's notion of the three levels of 'radical evil' to explicate this paradox.[8] First, frailty: despite our best intentions we cannot carry out the good. Then impurity: we have strength to carry out the moral law, but do so only for personal interest. Thirdly, wickedness or radical evil: the inner sense of duty is lost, so that morality becomes a set of external rules that obstruct the pursuit of personal interests, except where these interests coincide with the law.

6. Walter Zimmerli, *Ezekiel 1: A Commentary on the Book of the Prophet Ezekiel, Chapters 1–24* (trans. Ronald E. Clements; Philadelphia: Fortress Press, 1979), pp. 411-12, is driven to theological wonder: 'Undoubtedly (!) it is the language of an age which was deeply affected by mystery and by the real possibility of the collapse of its own righteousness which dared to consider the mystery of a divine punishment, itself contained in the law, without dismissing such an idea.'

7. Slavoj Žižek, 'In his Bold Gaze my Ruin Is Writ Large', in *idem* (ed.), *Everything You Always Wanted to Know About Lacan (but Were Afraid to Ask Hitchcock)* (London: Verso, 1992), pp. 211-72 (222).

8. Immanuel Kant, *Religion within the Limits of Reason Alone* (trans. Theodore M. Greene and Hoyt H. Hudson; New York: Harper & Row, 1960).

Yet none of these options provides a plausible reading for Genesis 22, especially in light of Ezekiel 20. However, Kant suggests and then shies away from a fourth possibility—'diabolical evil', 'devilish being'[9]—that he feels does not apply to humans. This is the final logic of Kant's line of thought that requires a Hegelian completion. Here, Evil 'assumes the form of its opposite, i.e., when it is not anymore externally opposed to Good but becomes the content of the latter's form'.[10] Opposition to the moral law becomes a maxim in itself, something to be upheld even if it goes against our self interest. The problem is that raising the status of opposition to the law, of evil, to a maxim or a principle, raises it to the same status as the law. It ceases to be an opposition, but becomes the law. 'In other words, "diabolical evil" inevitably coincides with the "highest good" introduced by Kant in the *Critique of Practical Reason* as the "necessary object of the will".'[11] Indeed, Kant sets up the highest good and diabolical evil as diametrically opposed, and as beyond the human: they can only apply to God and the devil. All of this means that as an ethical act, evil *is* good, or rather, it is structurally the same as the good, opposed as superhuman principles. They are symmetrical.

This notion of evil makes most sense of human sacrifice in Genesis 22 and Ezekiel 20. For Abraham the injunction to sacrifice Isaac is the word of God, as is the injunction not to sacrifice Isaac. In terms of the later history of Genesis 22 and the shift in religious sensibilities, the former (the command of human sacrifice) is evil in itself. It can only function within this belief system as a test. Formally, however, there is no difference between the commands to sacrifice and to desist. Indeed, one can conceive a situation in which the command to sacrifice one's first-born male is the highest good, and any restriction would be evil (as for Exod. 22.28-29). However, Ezekiel 20 explicates the situation even further: God gives the people commands that were not good so that they may know the good, that is, God. The divine commands are simultaneously evil and good.

9. Kant, *Religion within the Limits of Reason Alone*, p. 32.

10. Slavoj Žižek, *Tarrying with the Negative: Kant, Hegel, and the Critique of Ideology* (Durham, NC: Duke University Press, 1993), p. 100.

11. Alenka Zupančič, 'The Subject of the Law', in Slavoj Žižek (ed.), *Cogito and the Unconscious* (Durham, NC: Duke University Press), pp. 41-73 (54).

De Sade and Sacrifice

My attention to the wrinkled figure of Kant has more than one motive: for Jacques Lacan, Kant must be read with Sade, *Kant avec Sade*,[12] and he does so in light of the burnt offering of World War II. Lacan juxtaposes the two to highlight how Sade brings out the perverse inner logic of Kant's own thought, particularly what is repressed yet everywhere evident.

> Lacan's reading of Sade as the repressed truth of Kant reveals the perverse underside of the history of Enlightenment, in which the 'pathological' object of too-much enjoyment is systematically sacrificed for the sake of the desire of a universalized Other, whether instituted as Reason, Freedom, Knowledge, or the State.[13]

The well-worn model that Lacan reinvigorates here is that of conscious and unconscious, the latter forming the seamy and bulging belly without which the former cannot exist: that is, Kant cannot be understood without Sade, particularly after the Holocaust. '*Philosophy in the Bedroom* comes eight years after the *Critique of Practical Reason*. If, after having seen that the one accords with the other, we show that it completes it, we will say that it gives the truth of the *Critique*.'[14] It turns out that Kant and Sade require a sacrifice, in the name of the other, of my neighbor. For Kant this other is the good, the law, to which obedience is signaled by pain; for Sade all is given over because of the other's right to painful pleasure, *jouissance*. This is the logic of sacrifice: the most valuable is denied, offered up, passed over, in pain, to the highest good, God.

If I connect this with Kant's radical evil and the biblical texts on human sacrifice, it seems that the designation 'Holocaust' claims, for the Jews killed, a position diametrically opposed to their depiction as a social blight in Nazi propaganda. The burnt offering to God of the 'final solution' was an offering of the precious first-born of all God's creatures, specifically for the Nazis. That is, the Nazis offered up the Jews as their most treasured thing. And yet, as with the ideological tension of both Genesis 22 and Ezekiel 20, this highest good is also the worst evil,

12. Jacques Lacan, 'Kant with Sade', *October* 51 (1990), pp. 55-104.

13. Kenneth Reinhard, 'Kant with Sade, Lacan with Levinas', *MLN* 100 (1995), pp. 785-808 (786).

14. Lacan, 'Kant with Sade', p. 55.

the result of an impossible ideological demand. Thus, in the Bible, the sacrificial victim also becomes the most abhorred: all the community's sin is placed upon the victim, whose destruction is the destruction of that sin, the appeasement of God's wrath and achievement of social harmony. Once again the dialectic of good and evil appears.

The inseparable pair of Kant and Sade appear also in the sacrificial logic of the Hebrew Bible. That is, the tension between Kant and Sade, between conscious and unconscious, reason and pleasure, mind and body, most precious sacrifice and scapegoat, good and evil, is not merely a characteristic of the Enlightenment, but also of the Bible. A simple shifting of position will open up a range of possibilities in this relation: whereas one may cast human sacrifice as the highest devotion to God, it also appears as the greatest depravity, especially when God demands it. From the other side, refusing sacrifice reads as the denial of fundamental expressions of piety, as heretical, or as the gesture of piety through the preservation of life, even if through a substitute. It all depends where one sits in the ideological/theological debate.

However, if the Nazis offered up their social and ideological firstborn with the Holocaust—as sacrifice demands—then this is also sadistic. But sadism is always, for Lacan, turned in on the subject, as the diagrams in his article *'Kant avec Sade'* outlining the twist of the Sadean fantasy suggest.[15] What begins as the sadist inflicting harm on the subject, and so finding pleasure, ends up construing the sadist as subject of that harm (for Sade this was repeated imprisonment, arranged by his mother-in-law, and commitment to an asylum by Napoleon). The ultimate destination of the sadist's infliction of pain is the sadist. So with sacrifice: it works only when our dearest is offered to the gods, for they demand nothing but our best as signs of devotion and to appease their capricious wrath. Yet, in sacrificing our best we wrench ourselves apart, we inflict the pain of sacrifice upon ourselves. It is as though we sacrifice ourselves to the gods, which is precisely what cooking the firstborn signals. Self-sacrifice is thereby continuous with animal and human sacrifice. Indeed, human sacrifice comes closest to self-sacrifice, for the human offered is but a mark of the human who makes the offering, who wants to offer himself. Sadism and sacrifice thus partake of the same logic: the pain inflicted on another is actually directed at ourselves, all for the sake of the Other's *jouissance*, God's pleasure beyond

15. Lacan, 'Kant with Sade', pp. 62-65.

pain. The Nazis, in killing the Jews, killed themselves.

Thus far I have been interested in the subject of sacrifice, the one who offers and suffers the logic of sacrifice, yet what of the other for whom the body is hacked up and burnt? It seems that the inevitable return of the sadistic act of sacrifice to the subject, as well as the need to repeat, indicate a nervousness about that other. To begin with, sacrifice fascinates (witness this volume): 'the offering to obscure gods of an object of sacrifice is something to which few subjects can resist succumbing, as if under some monstrous spell'.[16] In the face of this obscurity, the search of sacrifice is to 'find evidence for the presence of the desire of this Other that I call here *the dark God*'.[17] For Lacan, the key to desire is that it is always desire of the other for which one is searching.[18] It is an effort to answer the eternal, theological, question, *Che vuoi*? What is it that the other, God, wants from me? This is precisely what happens with sacrifice: the perpetual need to appease the unpredictable wrath of God, to entice his blessing and beneficence. For this reason the detailed ritual of sacrifice must be carried out flawlessly; the cause for any failure in the efficacy of the sacrifice can then be attributed to a flaw in the process that accounts for the inability to satisfy the desire of the other, God. Is this not a perpetual papering over for the absence, the nonexistence, of God? Sacrifice thereby serves to avoid this question.

> *Sacrifice is a guarantee that 'the other exists'*, that there *is* an other who can be appeased by means of the sacrifice. The trick of the sacrifice consists therefore in what the speech-act theorists would call its 'pragmatic presupposition': *by the very act of sacrifice, we (presup)pose the existence of its addressee* that guarantees the consistency and meaningfulness of our experience—so, even if the act fails in its proclaimed goal, this very failure can be read from within the logic of sacrifice as *our* failure to appease the other.[19]

Finally, this perpetual need to assert the existence of the other, who is then, in an inversion, the one who demands the sacrifice—this need is

---

16. Jacques Lacan, *The Four Fundamental Concepts of Psycho-Analysis* (ed. Jacques-Alain Miller; trans. Alan Sheridan; Harmondsworth: Penguin Books, 1994), p. 275.

17. Lacan, *Four Fundamental Concepts*, p. 275.

18. See further Roland Boer, 'The Second Coming: Repetition and the Insatiability of Desire in the Song of Songs', forthcoming in *Biblical Interpretation*.

19. Slavoj Žižek, *Enjoy Your Symptom!* (London: Routledge, 1992), p. 56.

also found by Lacan in Kant's moral law, the highest Good, for this Law 'is simply desire in its pure state, that very desire that culminates in the sacrifice, strictly speaking, of everything that is the object of love in one's human tenderness—I would say, not only in the rejection of the pathological object, but also in its sacrifice and murder. That is why I wrote *Kant avec Sade*.'[20]

Is it possible, then, that the Holocaust is not merely congruent with the gradual outlay of Enlightenment reason, as Lacan among others suggest, but that it is continuous with the logic of sacrifice in the Hebrew Bible as well?

Banality and Sacrifice

How might that other sacrificial text of the Hebrew Bible, Leviticus 1–7, assist in answering this question? These banal prescriptions for sacrificial procedure may be regarded as the absent text of the previous section, which may now be reread as a first commentary on precisely these chapters. The sacrifice of animals, grains and liquids, in painful and tedious detail, expresses not merely the culmination of a religious and theological system, but also nervous affirmations of God himself.

However, in Leviticus 1–7 we find a sacrificial violence so ubiquitous that it effaces itself by being everywhere. Here is an elaborate mechanism,[21] with various grades of mostly animal sacrifice linked with various types of offenses and/or festivals. Thus, in the description of the burnt offering for atonement in 1.1-17, the animal may be a bull (1.5), sheep or goat (1.10), turtle dove or pigeon (1.14). The bull is to be 'slaughtered before Yahweh', the blood splattered against the altar, the animal flayed and dissected, and then the various parts—head and fat, entrails and legs—burnt on the altar. Similarly, the sheep or goat is dismembered (1.12) and the bits and pieces—head, fat, entrails, legs and other parts—arranged and burnt. The bird, a little small for such detailed dismemberment is to be dealt with by having its head twisted off (1.15), the blood squeezed out against the altar, the crop removed and thrown away, and the body torn open by holding its wings. At the close of the description of each type of animal is intoned 'a burnt offer-

---

20. Lacan, *Four Fundamental Concepts*, pp. 275-76.

21. An elaborateness enhanced, along with illustrations of body parts and altars, by the laborious and thorough commentary of Jacob Milgrom, *Leviticus 1–16* (AB; Garden City, NY: Doubleday, 1991).

ing, an offering by fire of pleasing odour to Yahweh' (1.9, 13, 17). Yahweh is then not only butcher but also cook, a beer in one hand and skewer in the other, turning the steaks of the Lamb of God on the Barbecue.[22]

After a considerate moment for vegetarians in 2.1-6 (a tofu slab on the grill), the triple procedure repeats in Leviticus 3 for the offering of well-being, except that the animal may be male or female, and only certain body parts are to be offered—for cattle and goats the fat around the entrails, kidneys and their fat and the appendage of the liver (3.3-4, 14-15), ditto for sheep except that the tail is to be included (3.9-10).[23] And then, with some variation but an overwhelming similarity, Leviticus 4 covers sacrifice for unintentional sins for the priest (4.3-12), the whole Israelite congregation (4.13-21), the ruler (4.22-26) and the individual Israelite (4.27-35). In each case the fatty parts—entrails, kidneys and liver appendage—are sacrificed on the altar, while the rest is burnt up 'outside the camp' (4.12, 21) in the case of priest and whole people. As the litany of reasons for sacrifice progresses, the detail of each procedure diminishes, referring instead to the procedural similarity with the other offerings (4.10, 20, 26, 31, 35; 6.17; 7.7), and an increased focus on the possibilities for incurring guilt. Indeed, so banal have become the sacrificial guidelines that the narrative slides towards a battle for allocation of body parts between Yahweh and the priests. Although entitled to various portions of animal bodies and grain offerings from specific sacrifices (6.16-18; 7.6; 7.8-9, 14-18, 31-36), even those that have a contagious holiness (6.24-30), the priests are not permitted the fat or the blood: Yahweh has a fat monopoly, it seems, a liking for cholesterol that mocks the dangers for humans. 'You shall eat no fat of ox or sheep or goat... You must not eat any blood whatever' (7.23b, 26a). 'All fat is Yahweh's. It shall be a perpetual statute throughout your generations, in all your settlements: you must not eat any fat or any blood' (3.16b-17).

If the banality of sacrifice comes through in the shift in content to

---

22. Hartley is himself turning on the exegetical and theological spit, desperately denying Yahweh's desire for his flesh: '[T]his metaphor serves well to say that God himself must accept each offering in order for it to be efficacious without in any way indicating that God is dependent on these offerings for sustenance' (John Hartley, *Leviticus* [WBC; Dallas, TX: Word Books, 1992], pp. 22-23).

23. With cannibalistic fervour, Hartley, *Leviticus*, p. 40, writes: 'The ancients prized the liver and the kidneys both as centers of emotional life and as delicacies.'

arguments over food distribution, then style also plays a role. The sheer repetition of the form—with minor variations for the preparation and burning of particular animals for particular types of offering—has a deadening effect upon modern readers, an effect that has been described, after its construction in the eighteenth-century, as 'boring'.[24] The descriptions themselves are what we might term 'clinical', outlining the various procedures for killing, cutting up, skinning, giving out portions depending on the sacrifice. Yet, the stark descriptions of animal parts and the rituals guidelines are curiously soporific, their 'simple, almost monotonous sequence'[25] speaking of the everyday normality of such dismemberment.

In the end, the hegemonic violence of Leviticus 1–7 operates at a number of levels. Apart from the quotidian banality of such slaughter, dismemberment and burning, the liturgical rhythms and slaughterhouse punctuality of sacrifice move in another direction—the well-known argument of Hannah Arendt on the 'banality of evil'. Reporting on the trial of Adolf Eichmann for *The New Yorker* in 1963 (the same year that Lacan's *'Kant avec Sade'* appeared), Arendt argues that whereas the prosecutors and judges tried to portray Eichmann, one of the administrators of the 'final solution', as a liar and monster, he was in fact a middling person in every respect—in terms of his intelligence, his class, his job, his aspirations.[26] A person who lived by cliches appropriated in a somewhat unreflecting way, Eichmann's failures at school and dissatisfaction as a salesman for the Vacuum Oil Company were assuaged by the Nazis.

> From a humdrum life without significance and consequence the wind had blown him into History, as he understood it, namely, into a Movement that always kept moving and in which somebody like him—already a failure in the eyes of his social class, of his family, and hence in his own eyes as well—could start from scratch and still make a career.[27]

Arendt stresses his unexceptionalness, his terrifying normality, for to resist was abnormal in that context. Declared by psychiatrists associated

---

24. Patricia Meyer Spacks, *Boredom: The Literary History of a State of Mind* (Chicago: University of Chicago Press, 1995).

25. Martin Noth, *Leviticus: A Commentary* (OTL; London: SCM Press, 1965), p. 19—like Noth's own prose.

26. Hannah Arendt, *Eichmann in Jerusalem: A Report on the Banality of Evil* (New York: Viking, 1964).

27. Arendt, *Eichmann in Jerusalem*, p. 33.

with the trial to be 'normal', his attitude to family and friends 'most desirable',[28] Eichmann argued that his conscience would have been troubled had he not carried out his duty. In fact, he stated that he followed Kant's moral philosophy—a version 'for the household use of the little man'—specifically in regard to duty: 'the principle of my will must always be such that it can become the principle of general laws'.[29] He admitted that when entrusted with the final solution, he ceased to live by Kant's precept, although Arendt suggests that he continued to live by it, that the law was the law. 'In this household use, all that is left of Kant's spirit is the demand that a man do more than obey the law, that he go beyond the mere call of obedience and identify his own will with the principle behind the law—the source from which the law sprang'. The crux is, as Juliet MacCannell suggests,[30] that the perversion of Kant's moral law is contained within that law: 'in Kant's philosophy that source [from which the law sprang] was practical reason; in Eichmann's household use of him, it was the will of the Führer [the dark god?]'.[31] Or, to put it in terms of my earlier dicussion: the most radical evil appears as nothing but the highest good; or, Sade is the logical perversion of Kant.

Is there not a perverse correlation between the banality of sacrifice in Leviticus 1–7 and Arendt's banality of evil? After all, the final solution was also the Holocaust, which, as 'burnt offering', is the prime subject matter of Leviticus 1–7. In both cases, the hegemonic violence of

28. Arendt, *Eichmann in Jerusalem*, pp. 25-26.

29. Arendt, *Eichmann in Jerusalem*, p. 136.

30. Juliet Flower MacCannell, 'Fascism and the Voice of Conscience', in Joan Copjec (ed.), *Radical Evil* (London: Verso, 1996), pp. 46-73.

31. Arendt, *Eichmann in Jerusalem*, p. 136. Apart from becoming a crucial term of debate in Holocaust studies, Arendt's argument has drawn both elaborators and detractors. Thus, either the Nazis were passionate administrators (so M. Allen, 'The Banality of Evil Reconsidered: SS Mid-level Managers of Extermination Through Work', *Central European History* 30.2 [1997], pp. 253-94), or normal, morally numbed, bureaucrats, as the Milgram experiments suggest (see A. Miller, 'Constructions of the Obedience Experiments: A Focus upon Domains of Relevance', *Journal of Social Issues* 51.3 [1995], pp. 33-53). Even constructionist arguments about the 'Jewish problem' and the 'final solution' having their own natural history seem to support Arendt (R. Berger, 'The Banality of Evil Reframed: The Social Construction of the Final Solution to the Jewish Problem', *Sociological Quarterly* 34.4 [1993], pp. 597-618).

sacrifice is effaced through its banality. Under the ideological systems in which both Holocausts operate, such violence ceases to be such.

Eucharistic Jouissance

All the same, the objection to my argument is disarmingly simple: whereas the Jewish Holocaust involved humans, Leviticus 1–7 is happy with mere flora and fauna, particularly cows, sheep and goats. It seems to me, however, that human sacrifice in Leviticus 1–7 is everywhere apparent, yet nowhere depicted. It is time to call upon Freud's notion of repression and its return.

Basically, the return of the repressed is the process by which what is repressed in a text, dream or social formation, appears elsewhere and often in another guise; or it returns at a later stage. Freud uses the example of a girl who tries to be as different to her mother as possible, developing all those characteristics that are diametrically opposed. However, as she gets older and bears children she gradually becomes more and more like her mother, until she achieves the identity she first sought in childhood.[32] So also—and for Freudian thought more centrally—the repression of sexuality, or rather the libido, will ensure that it appears in another guise in a person with psychological symptoms or in a text, or perhaps as sexual perversity on the fringes.

> Thereupon it [the instinctual impulse] renews its demand, and, since the path to normal satisfaction remains closed to it by what we may call the scar of repression, somewhere, at a weak spot, it opens another path for itself to what is known as a substitutive satisfaction, which comes to light as a symptom, without the acquiescence of the ego, but also without its understanding. All the phenomena of the formation of symptoms may justly be described as the 'return of the repressed.'[33]

The glaring omission, the repression, in Leviticus 1–7 is human sacrifice. Human sacrifice and the complexities of its denial appear starkly in Genesis 22, as I argued above. Indeed, the *Akedah* should be read as the missing section, now as *haggadah* or midrashic commentary, of Leviticus 1–7. For Genesis 22 presents animal sacrifice as a repression of human sacrifice, as a system of sacrifice that relies on a

32. Sigmund Freud, *The Origins of Religion: Totem and Taboo, Moses and Monotheism and Other Works* (ed. Albert Dickson; Harmondsworth: Penguin Books, 1990), p. 373.
33. Freud, *The Origins of Religion*, p. 375.

missing core of human slaughter. The repression of Isaac's sacrifice, the command not to sacrifice, is the rationale for the animal substitute that Abraham finds in the bushes. And yet, as I argued, human sacrifice simultaneously appears and is elided in this text. Thus, in the later version of Genesis 22, the violence that is signified and denied (human sacrifice) in favor of that which is sanctioned (animal sacrifice) only serves to indicate the originary and enabling violence (human sacrifice) that has been concealed, forgotten and denied by naming it as something other than what *we* do. But now the relations start shifting, and one can read Leviticus 1–7 as pointing everywhere to human sacrifice through repressing precisely that dimension, while Genesis 22 treats human sacrifice as perfectly normal. If Gen. 22.2—the command from Yahweh, and Abraham's initial response—is taken as the primary text, then human sacrifice is perfectly normal, banal even. By contrast, Leviticus 1–7 becomes a text seething everywhere with the repression of a human sacrifice that it wishes to describe, but cannot.

The key in all of this is Ezek. 20.25-26, for here we find the command for human sacrifice that is repressed in its very promulgation. Yahweh gives the command, yet it is not good; it is unlivable, horrifying. The people enact it—obeying Exod. 22.28-29—only to be condemned in the act. Indeed, the text from Exodus 22 might function as an excised introduction to Leviticus 1–7—'The firstborn of your sons you shall give to me; you shall do the same with your oxen and your sheep'—to be followed immediately by Genesis 22 as the *haggadah* of the first, human, sacrifice, which is then followed in turn by the prescriptions for animals in the extant text.

However, the return of the repressed has two final trajectories, one that runs through to the Jewish Holocaust, and the other to the Christian Eucharist. For the repression of human sacrifice in the Hebrew Scriptures signals both its originary status in the theological hegemony of Judaeo-Christianity and the inevitability of its return in some other form, which is that of the Holocaust.

As for the other trajectory, the theological understanding of Christ's death, as well as the Eucharist, in terms of sacrifice has a pedigree that dates from the earliest theological reflection; although the tradition starts to sweat nervously when the relation with human sacrifice becomes clearer for a moment or two. In enabling the return of the repressed in this way, speaking everywhere in the terms of human (and divine) sacrifice, yet refusing to face its implications, transferring it into the sadistic notion of self-sacrifice, Christianity carries out its own repression.

The symptom of that repression lies in the Eucharist (from the Greek *eucharistein*, that signifies the gift and receipt of pleasure, thankfulness and so on); and the symptom is found in the little excess that has a remarkable congruence with Lacan's notion of *jouissance*, for which a shorthand may be 'painful pleasure', a transgressive pleasure that is enacted beyond the law.

When I acted as liturgist for the Eucharist at the college where I taught, I repeated the words of a textual variant, 'Take, eat; this is my body, broken for you.' And when I served the elements I said, 'The body of Christ', as the bread—torn from the loaf, dripping and bleeding—is passed from hand to hand to mouth. And soon the loaf becomes a carcass, slung over my shoulder, staining my alb with the blood and puss of some 2000 years, as I carve off yet another morsel for the waiting communicant. What is it to be this time? A piece of thigh, of the liver perhaps, or some tripe, an ear, the divine foreskin? Having dumped the carcass on the communion table, and covering it with liturgical slowness, I pick up the cup. 'The blood of Christ', I intone as I withdraw the spatula from the cup to prevent it from congealing and allow the faithful to sip the thick red blood, mingled with a little water but still remarkably well preserved.[34] My perverse pleasure in the Eucharist is found in the cannibalism it signifies. Everyone reverently lines up to gnaw away at this body and slurp the blood, one whose parts are either regrown overnight like Prometheus after the eagle's daytime assault, or whose body is so huge that even 2000 years of anthropophagy have not diminished it. For in the same way that Leviticus 1–7 stipulates what may and may not be eaten, whether by priest or people, so also human sacrifice assumes not just the slashing and burning of the victim, but also the collective consumption, the communion as Robertson Smith described it, that is central to all but few sacrifices. Not only is such cannibalism the final manifestation, the return, of the repression of human sacrifice in the Hebrew Bible, but it is also the *jouissance*, the Eucharist, demanded by the other, by God, in sacrifice itself.

34. This is obviously because it has been cooked and preserved. See my 'Graves of Craving: Fast Food, or, Manna and MacDonald's', in Roland Boer, *Knockin' on Heaven's Door* (London: Routledge, 1999).

WRITTEN IN STONE: BIBLICAL QUOTATION IN THE UNITED STATES HOLOCAUST MEMORIAL MUSEUM[*]

Jennifer L. Koosed

'You are my witnesses', proclaim the large silver letters on the black panels of the entrance hall (called the Hall of Witness) to the United States Holocaust Memorial Museum in Washington, DC. The Holocaust Museum incorporates four biblical quotations into its structure: these words from the prophet Isaiah in the Hall of Witness (Isa. 43.10), and the other three circling the Hall of Remembrance (Gen. 4.10, Deut. 4.9 and 30.19). Since the Museum is designed to move the visitor from the Hall of Witness, through the exhibitions, and into the Hall of Remembrance, these biblical verses frame the experience of the Museum. Therefore, reading and interpreting the writing on the walls also becomes part of this experience. Removed from their biblical contexts, these verses are acted upon by both the American context in which the entire Museum is embedded, as well as each visitor's personal context. And even though these quotations have been separated from the Bible, this context can enter into the interpretive equation as well. Collaborating together, these quotations interact with architectural form and display content to shape meaning for the visitor.

Reflecting the names of the halls, 'witness' and 'remembrance' are the most obvious messages the quotations embody. However, they are not the only ones contained in the words, and even these 'obvious' messages open up into a series of questions. Who is being asked to witness and remember? What is being witnessed and remembered? And who is doing the asking? The answers to these questions are neither singular nor self-evident. This article will offer a series of interpreta-

* I would like to thank the members of the graduate seminar on the Holocaust at Vanderbilt University, Spring 1999, for their contributions to this paper: Kim Baker, Heather Benko, Jarad Bingham, Finbar Curtis, Dr Jay Geller, Charles Isely, and Pamela McIntosh.

tions which explore some of the possible answers, finding that while on the surface these quotations function to command and challenge the visitor, they function in a more subtle way to connect G-d to the destruction of the Jews, and blame the very people they purport to memorialize.

I

The Holocaust Museum in Washington, DC inhabits a strange geography. It began as the President's Commission on the Holocaust, appointed by President Jimmy Carter on 1 November 1978. The task of this commission was to investigate and report on 'the establishment and maintenance of an appropriate memorial to those who perished in the Holocaust...and to recommend appropriate ways for the nation to commemorate 28 and 29 April 1979, which the Congress has resolved shall be "Days of Remembrance of Victims of the Holocaust".'[1] Approximately one year later the Commission recommended the establishment of a memorial and museum. One year after that, Congress approved the plan unanimously.

That was the last time in the history of the Museum that anything was agreed upon unanimously. Among other things, the debates have reflected the varieties of Jewish identity in the United States, as well as divergent opinions on how best to situate the Museum within the general American culture. The Museum was sanctioned and commissioned—though not funded—by the Federal government. It is situated on a priceless piece of land on the National Mall, the center of American political and civil society. Yet the Holocaust Museum is an American museum about an event that happened on European soil to (for the most part) Europeans; it is a museum that focuses on the Jewish dimension of the Holocaust in a country where Jews are a minority; it is a museum that documents racism and fascism in an area otherwise dedicated to monuments of freedom and democracy. The ways in which the founders negotiated these dichotomies are an integral part of the Museum itself.

Michael Berenbaum, the project director of the Museum during its planning, coined the phrase the 'Americanization of the Holocaust' in order to describe the ways in which the particular historical event was

---

1. As quoted in Jeshajahu Weinberg and Rina Elieli, *The Holocaust Museum in Washington* (New York: Rizzoli International Publications, 1995), p. 20.

blended with the contemporary American context in the message of the Museum. By this, Berenbaum meant that the designers strove to 'recast the story of the Holocaust to teach fundamental American values... pluralism, democracy, restraint on government, the inalienable rights of individuals, the inability of government to enter into freedom of the press, freedom of assembly, freedom of religion, and so forth'.[2] The Museum presents the racism and totalitarianism which undergirded the genocide of the Holocaust as the antithesis of the United States and American values.

In the introduction to his book, *The Texture of Memory*, James Young reminds us that 'public memory is constructed'.[3] In other words, it is constantly being formed by the political and social concerns of the people doing the remembering. As the historical event itself is not monolithic, so our understanding of it is not singular, and our memorialization of it is not static. These public debates around how best to remember 'vivify memory through the memory-work itself—whereby events, their recollection and the role monuments play in our lives remain animate, never completed'.[4] A museum is not just a building or a series of exhibits. It is also this continual process of 'memory-work'. The Holocaust Museum and all of its parts, including the biblical quotations, remain dynamically embedded in the current cultural moment in the United States.

II

The orientation film at the beginning of the exhibits at the US Holocaust Memorial Museum explains: 'This Museum is about remembering and remembering has influenced its design.' But the notion of 'remembering' manifests itself differently in different parts of the museum. Particularly distinct are the ways in which the content of the museum differs from the architectural structure. The museum was designed by Jeshajahu Weinberg as a 'narrative museum'. As such, its exhibits are based on a story—a presentation of history as a singular,

2. As quoted in Philip Gourevitch, 'Behold Now Behemoth: The Holocaust Memorial Museum: One More American Theme Park', *Harper's Magazine* (July 1993), p. 56.

3. James E. Young, *The Texture of Memory: Holocaust Memorials and Meaning* (New Haven: Yale University Press, 1993), p. 15.

4. Young, *The Texture of Memory*, p. 15.

coherent narrative. The architectural structure, however, challenges this coherence. Rather than story, the architect, James Ingo Freed, wished to embody the rupture the Holocaust caused in human culture. This is particularly true of the entrance hall, named the Hall of Witness. As aforementioned, this hall contains the first biblical quotation encountered by the visitor: 'You are my witnesses' (Isa. 43.10). The words appear about two-thirds of the way up a black paneled wall, broken with stairs, bridges and windows. The entire hall is a twisted mass of glass bridges, boarded windows and metal fences. The angles are unpredictable and jarring; the sunlight that streams through the sky lights and windows is fractured and splintered by these angles. Incorporated into the design are traces of concentration camp structures: watch towers, brick walls, the arch of an entrance way. The effect is disorientating and overwhelming, particularly when the inevitable confusion caused by large crowds of people—sitting, standing, walking in every possible direction—is added to the architectural tangle. The confluence of narrative museum and postmodern architecture asks the insistent question: how does one witness (an event with a positive predicate) a rupture (a negative space)?

To move from exhibit hall to exhibit hall once one has entered the heart of the permanent collection, the visitor must transverse glass bridges. Each of these bridges overlooks the Hall of Witness. Looking up at this quote on the wall—'You are my witnesses'—from the floor of the Hall, one sees streams of people going up the staircase next to it, going down the staircase under it, double horizontal lines of people above the quote as they move from exhibit to exhibit, and also a downward diagonal line of people moving through the permanent collection. These are the witnesses—the ones moving through the narrative of the Holocaust as told by the US Holocaust Museum. At this introduction to the museum, the one standing in the entrance hall about to embark on the story of the Holocaust is also about to become one of these witnesses him or herself.

This feeling is furthered by the historical reminiscence captured in the design of the bridges. In these bridges, Freed incorporated traces of the ghettos. Many of them had bridges crossing non-Jewish areas of town. In the Lodz ghetto, for example, a wooden bridge connected two parts of the ghetto which where severed by a non-Jewish street. These bridges allowed Jews to walk between separate parts of the ghetto without ever walking out of the ghetto. It also allowed their non-Jewish neighbors to walk their streets without obstruction. Ghettos closed in the Jews, making them all but invisible to their non-Jewish neighbors. They never needed to see the Jews in their town for they were blocked out by walls, and lifted off their streets by bridges. With each policy that separated the Jews out from general society, it became easier to forget that they were ever there, and easier to ignore their subsequent murder. If the non-Jewish people of Lodz walked keeping their eyes on the ground, if they refused to look up, then they never saw the Jews of the ghetto. In their refusal to witness, they remained bystanders. The bridges in the Hall of Witness, however, forbid the people who walk under them to remain bystanders. They are bridges that demand witness, rather than bridges that hide crime.

But this observation reveals a split in the identity of the visitors—are the people who walk through the museum witnesses or the ones being witnessed? The museum encourages those who come to identify in a variety of incompatible ways. The first impulse when standing in the entrance hall, about to embark on the story of the Holocaust, is to identity oneself with a witness. But then, when a person enters the exhibit halls, he or she is given a card with the picture and biography of a person who was a victim of Nazi persecution. As one walks through the history, one is instructed to read sections of the booklet so that as the general story unfolds, a particular story is given as an illustration. In addition to this personal identification with a victim, the structure of the exhibit enacts the movements of a person caught in the Nazi trap: one walks over ghetto bridges, through a cattle car, and under a reproduction of the famous gate of Auschwitz. The witnesses are also supposed to be victims.

Within the context of the Americanization of the museum, the addressee of the command is also identified with the American liberators of the camps. The museum chose to orient the visitor to the exhibits through the eyes of the American liberators of the camps. First, there are quotations on the wall from the Declaration of Independence and George Washington that underline America's history of tolerance and freedom. Then, the orientation film gives an overview of the liberation of the camps by US soldiers. Finally, the first picture to confront the visitor when she or he enters the exhibits is a picture of Jewish bodies taken by the army as it liberated a camp. The Americans are certainly portrayed as heroes. In this third identification, the visitor becomes the liberator.

These identifications all contribute to making the visitors separate from and superior to the events before them. But there is never any reason given for why this should be so—they are superior only by virtue of being in the museum, and, if the visitors are Americans, because they are Americans. The presumption is that simply by witnessing history, one learns from history. And the implication is that one learns to be more like Americans and less like Nazis. The visitor as witness is supposed to prevent this type of thing from ever happening again—not because they have an understanding of persecution or the ways in which a society can label others as outsiders, but by virtue of being who they are within the museum.

The addressee in the verse from Isaiah is made unclear through the multiple positioning of those who tour the museum. But, the speaker of the quote is even more ambiguous, and this same ambiguity reverberates through all of the biblical quotations used in the museum. I will return to the speaker of the commanding statements after the remaining quotes are explicated.

Freed wished to provide a space for quiet contemplation, a space that, in contradistinction to the Hall of Witness, would be full of harmonious angles and light. This space is the Hall of Remembrance. The Hall of Remembrance is the visitor's last stop in the museum and it most fully embodies the memorial function of the building. It is a large, hexagon-shaped room of cream-colored limestone. Along the outer hexagonal walls, the names of twenty concentration and death camps are written on the walls, in no discernible order, with rows of candles underneath. The visitor is encouraged to light a candle in memorial to a friend, relative, or anyone murdered during the Holocaust. The inner hexagon is ringed by benches on which to sit and rest and think. Light streams down from skylight at the top of the 70 foot dome of the Hall. There are three biblical quotations in this room. The central quote, Deut. 4.9, is written on the far outer wall opposite the entrance way:

> Only guard yourself and guard your soul carefully, lest you forget the things your eyes saw, and lest these things depart your heart all the days of your life, and you shall make them known to your children, and to your children's children.

Before it is an eternal flame, below which is written, 'Here lies earth gathered from death camps, concentration camps, sites of mass execution, and ghettos in Nazi-occupied Europe, and from cemeteries of American soldiers who fought and died to defeat Nazi Germany.' The other two quotations flank this first one on the inner walls, about one-story up. On the left is Gen. 4.10: 'What have you done? Hark, thy brother's blood cries out to me from the ground.' On the right is Deut. 30.19: 'I call heaven and earth to witness this day: I have put before you life and death, blessing and curse. Choose life—that you and your offspring shall live.'

All three passages encompass the same theme as Isa. 43.10, namely that of witnessing. One of the stated purposes of the museum is to educate visitors and protect against Holocaust denial. The museum meticulously documents the authenticity of its artifacts and documents, and its exhibit is full of eye-witness accounts. With the deaths of more and more eye-witnesses, and with the rise of Holocaust denial 'scholarship' and neo-Nazi organizations, the museum positions itself as a bulkhead against both forgetting and distorting the realities of the Holocaust. A necessary part of this project is the enlistment of the visitor. After the visitors walk through the museum, they become eye-witnesses to the events as well. As such, they can always be on guard against Holocaust denial, as well as human rights' abuses. As the museum's mission statement states, to do so is part of our 'responsibilities as citizens of democracy'.

Yet the witness is more than just one who 'sees'. The walls challenge the witness to teach—'and you shall make them known to your children, and to your children's children' (Deut. 4.9). As we move further away from the historical event, the memory of that event must be preserved from generation to generation. Witnessing also involves a choice of action, either life and blessings or death and curses. The witness in encouraged to 'choose life' (Deut. 30.19). What is life, who lives it, and how it is chosen? Within the context of the Americanization of the Holocaust, choosing life and rejecting death is part of choosing liberty and democracy, and rejecting oppression and totalitarianism. The glimpses of the Washington Monument and the Jefferson Memorial that a visitor gets through the narrow windows of the Hall of Remembrance emphasize this point. The museum galvanizes people to act against injustice—the bystander is just as responsible as the perpetrator.

This definition of 'life' is inferred from the Americanization of the museum. However, it is not the only reading. 'Life' can be defined in a variety of ways. In fact, the museum has just demonstrated this since much of Nazi ideology centered around determining whose life was valuable, and whose life was not worth living. What is the life we are supposed to choose, what life has the Museum presented before us? The last exhibit before one enters the Hall of Remembrance is the room of rescuers, followed by a movie of survivors telling their stories. The survivors are the ones who lived, though their desire for life was no more or less than the desire of the ones who died. The rescuers are the ones who choose to preserve life by saving people from the Nazi death-machine. Since there is a rescuer, particularly American-as-rescuer, orientation to the museum, this may be a further identification for the visitor with the American hero. However, there is a more general referent for life: the entire Holocaust itself. The Holocaust was an event that lies firmly within history, within human culture and capabilities, and within life itself. Without a clear referent, the reader has to decide what is meant by life, who is alive, and the appropriate way of preserving it.

Even if choosing life means choosing the (idealized) American way of life, one does not have to do anything more than affirm that it is good. The political culture of the United States is such that an event like the Holocaust could never happen here. This does not mean, however, that brutality, racism and anti-Semitism does not occur in the United States. Rather, it manifests itself differently than it did in Germany during the 1930s–40s. Thus, it is not enough to know that one should not be like a Nazi—there are many other ways of 'choosing death'. But the museum does not present any other shade—the contrast is democracy versus fascism, tolerance versus racism, United States versus Nazi Germany. To imply that all we have to do is not be like them, obscures the challenges our own culture provides in the struggle for human rights, and results in attitudes of complacency. As Philip Gourevitch states in his review of the Museum, 'as this museum becomes a major new touchstone in America's narrative of national identity...denouncing evil is a far cry from doing good'.[5] Especially if this denunciation takes place more than fifty years after the events.

We return now to the question of the speaker. As mentioned in regards to Isa. 43.10, these verses are commanding statements spoken in the first person. Who is the speaker of these verses on the walls of the museum? Who is it that commands witness? Since the museum itself is clear about its objectives concerning the effect it wants to have on visitors, in some respects it is the museum itself who is the speaker.

5.   Gourevitch, 'Behold Now Behemoth', p. 57.

And, since the museum was commissioned and authorized by the United States Federal government, the speaker behind the museum is also the government. By speaking through biblical quotation, the museum replaces the law-giver Moses (the speaker of the Deuteronomy passages), and the prophet Isaiah (the speaker in the Isaiah passages). Both of these roles are conduits of the divine word—in the Bible both Moses and Isaiah speak for G-d. In this context, the Museum acts as spokesperson for the government, and the government moves into the place of the divine.

These quotes are removed from their biblical context and asked to respond to a radically different situation at a different time. Yet their biblical context still clings to them in their present positioning on the walls. The narrative situation in Deuteronomy is the time in the wilderness between Egypt and the Promised Land. Moses is giving final instructions to his people before his death, and before they cross over into Canaan. In Deuteronomy 4, the passage quoted on the wall continues thus: 'how you once stood before the Lord your G-d at Horeb, when the Lord said to me, "Assemble the people for me, and I will let them hear my words, so that they may learn to fear me as long as they live on the earth, and may teach their children so"' (Deut. 4.10).[6] In other words, the focus in the Bible is on remembering the time when G-d revealed G-dself, when 'the Lord spoke to you out of the fire' (Deut. 4.12).

Fire is both formless, attractive and dangerous. Knowledge of G-d, too, is attractive, but the acquisition of it entails danger and the risk of death. Within the Bible and subsequent Jewish religious expression, the desire for G-d is held in tension with the ultimate unknowability of the divine. The name is unpronounceable and unable to be written. G-d appears as a voice, a cloud of smoke, a pillar of fire, an empty space contained within the tabernacle. Even attempting to approach the divine can be dangerous, for one cannot see G-d's face and live. This theological language of a G-d who defies all human attempts to describe or categorize, merges with the language used about the Holocaust. It, too, is considered something beyond our abilities to represent in either words or images. It, too, defies all past historical categories. And as one approaches closer to the center one risks being swept up in the fires

6. Biblical quotations not found in the museum but used in this paper are from the NRSV.

transforming bodies into smoke and ashes. The paradox of representing the unrepresentable is embodied by the museum as it attempts to tell a coherent story within a fragmented structure.

The biblical G-d is a G-d of history, one who is involved in historical events thus transforming them from mundane facts to happenings full of theological import. Within Judaism, one does not merely record history; rather one interprets it theologically and remembers it as part of religious ritual. The Holocaust challenged these theological notions and traditional practices. How does one integrate this event into memory, and into one's idea of the divine? Where was G-d, and what happened to G-d's covenant with the people of Israel? Post-Holocaust religious thinkers have struggled with these questions. One way of answering them builds on the confluence of divine language and Holocaust language precipitated by their common paradox of representing the unrepresentable. Since history is bound to G-d, the near-destruction of the Jews was also part of G-d's mysterious plan. Deut. 4.9 commands memory, the memory of the revelation of G-d. This quote in the Holocaust Museum subtly equates G-d's revelation in fire with the destruction of six million Jewish people, also largely by fire. To remember the Holocaust is to remember the revelation of G-d.

Deuteronomy 30 continues this insidious identification and adds another dimension to it. In the Bible, Deut. 30.19 is a warning to the people of Israel. In fact, the translation of the quote on the wall obscures a threatening note in the Hebrew. Heaven and earth are called by G-d to witness *against* the people. If they remember to keep the commandments of the Lord they shall stay in the land that G-d has given them. If they do not, they will perish. Torah is life. Idolatry is death.

> See, I have set before you today life and prosperity, death and adversity. If you obey the commandments of the Lord your G-d that I am commanding you today, by loving the Lord your G-d, walking in his ways, and observing his commandments, decrees and ordinances, then you shall live and become numerous, and the Lord your G-d will bless you in the land that you are entering to possess. But if your heart turns away and you do not hear, but are led astray to bow down to other gods and serve them, I declare to you today that you shall perish (Deut. 30.15-18).

Among other things, this passage is a clear warning against assimilation. When this verse is moved into the Holocaust context, it resonates with the theological position that G-d revealed G-dself during the Holocaust in order to punish the Jewish people for assimilation. Thus the accusation leveled against the acculturated and assimilated Jews of

Germany by some Orthodox thinkers is that they brought the Holocaust upon themselves as a result of their turning from Torah. By doing so, they chose death.

How many visitors to the Museum are well-versed enough in the Bible to sense these other meanings of the quotations is questionable. Particularly since the majority of the visitors to the museum are not even Jewish. However, parts of this verse are sure to resonate with Christian audiences, who are the majority of the museum visitors. Traditionally, Christian theology has followed Paul in viewing Jesus as a new covenant which supersedes the Torah. In his epistles, Paul contrasts this new covenant of Jesus, his Christ, to the Teachings (or Torah). Faith in Jesus brings life, whereas the Teachings lead to death: 'For through the law I died to the law... And the life I now live in the flesh I live by faith in the Son of G-d, who loved me and gave himself for me' (Gal. 2.19-20). To choose life for Paul, is to choose Jesus; to choose death is to choose the Torah. Someone from a Christian background could easily hear Deut. 30.19 through Paul, and therefore hear his rejection of Judaism in the subtext. There is a veiled Christian supersessionism lurking here.

Moving from the Deuteronomy quotations to the Genesis verse, the tone changes. On the surface, at least, the Deuteronomy quotes bring the visitor into the task of witnessing. The Genesis quote, on the other hand, is accusatory. Like the Deuteronomy quotes it is unclear who the speaker is in the context of the Hall of Remembrance. And like these verses, though in some different ways, it is also unclear who is being addressed. Several different interpretations are possible. Out of all of the quotes, this one is the most familiar to the general reader. It is from the story of the murder of Abel by his brother Cain. When questioning Cain about his brother's whereabouts, G-d speaks this sentence: 'What have you done? Hark, thy brother's blood cries out to me from the ground' (Gen. 4.10). Quoting this verse accuses the Nazis and their collaborators of murder, and guarantees that they will be held accountable for their crimes. Despite their attempts to erase the existence of the Jews, and even erase their extermination, the blood of the murdered ones will cry up from the ground. These words also gesture to the earth from the places of slaughter contained in the compartment underneath the eternal flame. As it points to this earth it is as if it were saying, 'there is the bloody earth that will speak to the crime committed upon it, there is the witness'.

The ones murdered are figured as Abel. Abel is the ultimate symbol of the murdered innocent. Abel is also the ultimate symbol of betrayal. He was killed by his own brother. Despite the Nazi propaganda which classified Jews as sub-humans who were the opposite of everything good and Aryan, these men and women were the Nazi's compatriots, their siblings even. As we are all children of Adam and Eve, we are all brothers and sisters, and the murders committed during the Holocaust were fratricides. This is how the verse reads if it is assumed it is being addressed to the perpetrators. However, how many former Nazis does the museum expect to visit? Presumably, the people standing in the Hall of Remembrance reading the quote were not in Germany and its occupied territories during the 1930s and 1940s. To whom, then, is this quotation addressed?

Although the museum is a government museum, and despite the fact that is overwhelmingly pro-American, there is some critique of the American response to the Holocaust. Anti-Semitism among the public, the people of Congress, and especially the State Department, con- tributed to the tendency toward isolationism. This prevented the United States from taking the bold and aggressive actions needed to rescue the people targeted by the Nazis for destruction. The United States was also culpable through its restrictive immigration policies, and its intentional stalling of the process for people who could legally enter the country. The refugees fleeing the Nazis had nowhere to go. Although historians debate about how much was known by whom, and how much could have been done regardless,[7] those who built the museum clearly did so believing America could have done more and will never fail in that way again. President Bill Clinton, at the opening of the Museum, stated that 'far too little was done' by the United States to stop the destruction of the Jewish people. The United States and its citizens are also culpable for the murders of its brothers and sisters abroad.

Probing this culpability further, the response of Jewish Americans during World War II was conflicted. Certainly, they were concerned about their families abroad, but there was also a reluctance to agitate too loudly. The policies of Franklin D. Roosevelt were allowing Jewish Americans to move into positions that had never welcomed them before. Many did not want to criticize the government that had done

---

7.   For an overview of the different positions, see Peter Novick, *The Holocaust in American Life* (New York: Houghton Mifflin, 1999), pp. 46-59.

them so much good, and many did not want to draw attention to themselves for fear of losing what they had so recently gained. Although there was Jewish American activism, especially as the true nature of Nazi intent became evident, feelings of guilt still plague portions of the community. The accusation from the wall perpetuates these feelings of guilt.

It needs to be stressed, however, that there was no unified and monolithic American Jewish community at this time (like there never was and never will be) and responses ranged widely. But there is at least a current popular perception that the Jewish community itself could have done more and did not do so. Elie Wiesel writes,

> The factories of Treblinka, Belzec, Maidanek and Auschwitz were operating at top capacity, while on the other side, Jewish social and intellectual life was flourishing... If our brothers had shown more compassion, more initiative, more daring...if a million Jews had demonstrated in front of the White House...if Jewish notables had started a hunger strike... Who knows, the enemy might have desisted.[8]

Whether or not this is a fair and accurate portrayal of the American Jewish communities during the war,[9] it is certainly a perception that was involved in the building of the museum.

All of these interpretations, and more, are present in the quotations around the Hall of Remembrance. What at first glance was a place for contemplation and even consolation becomes a raucous space of contradictory and accusatory voices that berate the visitor.

III

The four biblical verses inscribed on the wall of the US Holocaust Memorial Museum, in conjunction with the architectural structure, serve to encourage religious feelings in the visitor. The designers of the museum intended this experience. The Hall of Remembrance is like a synagogue or church, ringed with candles and the words of Scripture. The museum book describes the Hall of Witness thus:

8. Elie Wiesel, 'A Plea for the Survivors', in *A Jew Today* (New York: Random House, 1978), pp. 191-92, as quoted in Novick, *The Holocaust in American Life*, p. 30.

9. For an overview of the different positions see Novick, *The Holocaust in American Life*, pp. 30-46.

People speak of feelings of fear, loneliness, helplessness, almost of panic, but also of holiness... It affords visitors an experience similar to that experienced by a believer in a holy place. Like a cathedral, the Hall of Witness is awe-inspiring, overwhelming in its monumentality, making the individual feel small and insignificant.[10]

For what purpose would the designers wish to invoke the holy in an American museum dedicated to those murdered by the Nazis? What is the visitor supposed to believe in? In this context, the Holocaust is a matter of faith, and to support the American ideals of democracy and tolerance is a sacred path. Again, the historical event of the Holocaust slips into the theological realm, thereby implying that the divine was somehow involved in the near-destruction of the European Jews.

The situating of the Holocaust Museum as a holy place is partially a result of the particular complexities of American Jewish identity. In the United States, the Holocaust can become a touchstone of this identity. Generally, this is a result of the combination of little overt and violent anti-Semitism, great diversity in the American Jewish experience, and the American politics of victimization. In this environment, the Holocaust becomes a unifying force. I have found this to be true in my own life. Coming from an intermarried and largely assimilated family, learning about the Holocaust was my first impetus toward Judaism: I was Jewish because I would have been murdered had I been born in Europe during the Nazi era. Yet, I am ambivalent about the centrality of the Holocaust in the nascent stages of my identity formation. On the one hand, without a sense of community through the memory of a shared persecution, I may have never begun to explore Judaism. Without the Holocaust, the public and the government may never have been galvanized to support a Jewish presence on the Mall. On the other hand, victimhood is never a sufficient organizing principle for the self. Now, the most prominent representation of Jewish culture and experience in America is centered around persecution. When the Holocaust is the core of one's identity, and when Holocaust memorials and museums become sacred spaces, then the Holocaust becomes a strange sort of 'religion of destruction' shaped more by Hitler than by three thousand years of Jewish tradition.

Judaism is a religion that interprets historical events theologically, and incorporates their remembrance into religious ritual. Witnessing

10. Weinberg and Elieli, *The Holocaust Museum*, pp. 25-26.

and remembering can and should remain religious imperatives. However, this tendency should always be questioned and held in tension with the dangers that these theological interpretations of history entail. In this way, we should guard ourselves and guard our souls carefully against situating the murder of millions of people within the purview of G-d's plan, and against acquiescing to the complacency fostered by the Americanization of the Holocaust.

AM I A MURDERER?
JUDGES 19–21 AS A PARABLE OF MEANINGLESS SUFFERING

Katharina von Kellenbach

Traditional attempts at theodicy—often drawing on biblical stories pre-supposing that human suffering is meaningful and under divine con-trol—have maintained that individuals or communities suffer because God chastens them for their transgressions, tests them in order to strengthen their faith, or because their suffering has a redemptive func-tion in God's larger scheme. These approaches to suffering fall short when applied to the Holocaust. For instance, some religious voices maintain that the destruction of European Jewry was a punishment sent by God for Jewish violations of God's law, thereby blaming the victims and implicating God in unspeakable cruelty.[1] Theological thinkers who assert God's ultimate victory over the forces of evil search for glimpses

---

1. Few respectable academic voices argue that God acted through the Nazis in order to punish Israel for her sins. However, in some Jewish ultra-Orthodox and conservative Christian circles, this view is far from unknown. In his study of Jewish fundamentalism, David Landau cites several ultra-Orthodox rabbis who interpret the Holocaust as a punishment for Western European Jews' assimilation and for Zionism (*Piety and Power* [New York: Hill and Wang, 1993], pp. 141-44). On the Christian side, few theologians would openly affirm that God was ultimately responsible for the deaths of the Jews. However, Richard Rubenstein recounts his conversation with Dean Grüber in the early 1960s, who insisted that 'Israel as chosen people was under a special obligation to behave in ways that are spiritually consistent with Divine ordinance' (*After Auschwitz: History, Theology and Con-temporary Judaism* [Baltimore: The Johns Hopkins University Press, 2nd edn, 1992], p. 9). Although Dean Grüber does not follow this thought to its logical conclusion, Rubenstein points out that this theological position implies that Hitler acted as God's punishing arm because Jews did not live up to God's covenantal expectations. Such propositions endorse and legitimize violence against Jews by supplying divine justification for anti-Semitic violence.

of goodness but must ignore the utter physical and spiritual devastation characteristic of the Holocaust. Biblical narratives such as Jacob wrestling with God during the 'night', or Job encountering God 'out of the whirlwind' conclude with the protagonists' transformation, growth and spiritual maturity.[2] But those who survived the Holocaust did not emerge purified in their faith, blessed by insight and greater maturity like Jacob and Job.[3] Their souls remained permanently scarred despite their societal reintegration and often 'successful' lives. The model of redemptive sacrifice ascribes to the 'Holocaust' (literally, 'wholly burnt offering') a higher, transcendent purpose, thereby justifying the anti-Semitic violence unleashed by the Nazis and utilizing the victims' suffering and death as a means to an end.[4] This model misappropriates

2.   Cf. the implicit parallels in the titles of Holocaust literature: Albert Friedlander (ed.), *Out of the Whirlwind* (New York: Schocken Books, 1976); and Eli Wiesel, *Night* (New York: Avon, 1969).

3.   The book of Job rejects the 'sin-and-punishment' approach of the Deuteronomist and casts that theological position in the arguments of Job's friends. Job affirms his blamelessness and challenges God to explain his affliction. His fearless wrestling with God earns him a divine epiphany in a whirlwind and, consequently, a deeper insight into the nature of God. The story of Jacob enriches this encounter model where God tests man's physical and spiritual strength: Jacob struggles with an Angel/God throughout the night, fearful for his life, and emerges blessed and renamed. Both Jacob and Job are deeply wounded and risk their lives. But they arise renamed, blessed with insight and wellbeing. Their suffering is meaningful because they gain greater knowledge and grow in character and maturity. Suffering is seen as an educational tool in God's arsenal. This model is succinctly summarized by Tyron Inbody in *The Transforming God* (Louisville, KY: Westminster/John Knox Press, 1997), p. 61: 'Suffering purges us of our impatience, selfishness, superficiality, and egotism. It teaches such virtues as strength and endurance. It can make us noble creatures who can love and even exhibit sacrificial love for the greater good of others. Just as a parent may permit, or plan, or cause unpleasant or even potentially dangerous things to happen to a child for the child's own development into a mature adult, so God permits or causes the suffering of God's children for their own perfecting or maturing.' Dare we apply this explanation to experiences during the Holocaust?

Implicit in these biblical models is the notion that humans draw closer to God in situations of anguish and distress. But victims of (human) violence are usually not purified and ennobled but deeply shamed and stained by the experience. The humiliation and dehumanization endured by victims of violent assaults are deeply destructive of people's sense of self, their trust in the world and in God.

4.   Christianity has read the death (and resurrection) of Jesus through Isaiah's Suffering Servant (Isa. 53). After an anguished vigil in the garden of Gethsemane,

the agony and death of the victims for the spiritual benefit of survivors and bystanders.

In the following I want to consider the story of the brutal assault of the Levite and his concubine in Judges 19–21 as a story of meaningless suffering. God neither ordains their brutalization nor does it serve any higher purpose. The cruelty of the text shocks and forces the reader to confront the absurd destructiveness of violence. By critically engaging Phyllis Trible's feminist exegesis of Judges 19–21 and rereading the narrative in light of Calel Perechodnik's memoir, *Am I a Murderer: Memoir of a Jewish Ghetto Policeman*,[5] we may come to a distinct post-Holocaust interpretation of this unsettling story, one that avoids the pitfalls of theodicy.

Gender, Ethnicity and Violence

The story in Judges 19–21 describes an attack by 'base fellows' (Judg. 19.22)[6] on a Levite and his concubine in the Benjamite town of Gibeah. It is a highly disturbing text, which enjoys some notoriety among feminist exegetes and theologians because it dramatically depicts the sexual victimization of women. Violence against women is, according to

---

Jesus accepts God's will and submits to his sacrifice. Jesus' death on the cross atones for the sins of mankind; his suffering brings about redemption. Although this understanding of suffering as redemptive is predominantly Christian, the Jewish thinker Ignaz Maybaum, in *The Face of God after Auschwitz* (Amsterdam: Polak & Van Gennep, 1965), p. 103, has framed the Holocaust along similar lines, in terms of redemptive sacrifice: 'The death of martyrdom, the death of the six million, has vicariously worked salvation for you.' He continues: 'The innocent who died in Auschwitz, not for the sake of their own sins, but because of the sins of others, atone for evil and are the sacrifice which is brought to the altar and which God acknowledges favorably... Their death purged Western civilization so that it can again become a place where man can live, do justly, love mercy, and walk humbly with God' (p. 84).

This interpretation harmonizes the horrors of the Holocaust with traditional religious vocabulary of 'atonement', 'sacrifice', 'martyrdom' and 'purgation'. The notion that God might approve of the 'burnt offering' of six million people seems preposterous. Can we tolerate the image of the Lord who approves of Noah's sacrifice after the flood and who 'smelled the pleasing offerings of the altar', this time coming from the ovens at Auschwitz?

    5.   Calel Perechodnik, *Am I a Murderer: Testament of a Jewish Ghetto Police-man* (ed. and trans. Frank Fox; Boulder, CO: Westview, 1996).

    6.   All biblical quotes are taken from the RSV.

Trible, the text's implicit and explicit message.

The Levite has reclaimed his concubine from her father's home in Bethlehem where she escaped after 'she became angry with him' (Judg. 19.2). The pair and their servant are traveling home when they are offered hospitality for the night by an old man in the town of Gibeah. There the 'men of the city' beat on the host's door demanding the Levite's eviction so that 'they may know him'. His host instead offers his two virgin daughters and the man's concubine in order to spare the male guest.

> But the men would not listen to him. So the man seized his concubine, and put her out to them; and they knew her, and abused her all night until morning. And as the dawn began to break, they let her go. And as morning appeared, the woman came and fell down at the door of the man's house where her master was, till it was light (Judg. 19.25-26).

The concubine remains silent throughout the text. When her master orders her to get up, she does not. Incredibly, he loads her onto his donkey without attending to her injuries and leaves for home. There he divides her (dead or alive?) into twelve pieces and sends her to the twelve tribes of Israel. 'Is the cowardly betrayer also her murderer?' asks Trible.[7] And she adds: 'Neither the other characters nor the narrator recognize her humanity. She is property, object, tool, and literary device. Without name, speech, or power, she has no friends to aid her in life or mourn her in death.'[8]

The concubine's ordeal remains shrouded and overshadowed by the political uses to which her murder is put. Alice Keefe calls her gang rape and subsequent dismemberment a 'gruesome ritual act' and 'anti-sacrifice'[9] which symbolizes the fragmentation of Israel into warring factions. Her 'tortured and broken body...becomes the interpretive key for assessing the meaning of Israel's internecine violence'.[10] Far from being redemptive, her 'anti-sacrifice' leads to a retributive civil war, which nearly wipes out the men and women of the tribe of Benjamin. Her torment during the night does not lead to divine blessing or transformation but to retribution, more death, rape and abduction. As Trible points out:

7. Phyllis Trible, *Texts of Terror* (Philadelphia: Fortress Press, 1984), p. 80.
8. Trible, *Texts of Terror*, pp. 80-81.
9. Alice Keefe, 'Rapes of Women/Wars of Men', *Semeia* 61 (1993), p. 87.
10. Keefe, 'Rapes of Women', p. 86.

> The story of the concubine justifies the expansion of violence against women. What these men claim to abhor, they have re-enacted with vengeance. They have captured, betrayed, raped and scattered four hundred virgins of Jabesh-Gilead and two hundred daughters of Shiloh. Furthermore, they have tortured and murdered all the women of Benjamin and all the married women of Jabesh-Gilead.[11]

Trible focuses on the violence against women and their silenced suffering. Her exegesis emphasizes that the violence moves along gender lines, that 'it depicts the horror of male power, brutality, and triumphalism; of female helplessness, abuse, and annihilation'.[12] The exclusive focus on gender violence, however, neglects and conceals the racialized context of the violence portrayed in the text.

Recent critics have raised objections from various perspectives.[13] In particular, German Christian feminist Ilse Müllner raises concerns about anti-Jewish overtones in feminist interpretations such as Trible's.[14] She notes that this text often serves to bolster anti-Jewish notions of the 'Old Testament' as the epitome of a brutalizing patriarchy where men appear to freely offer their virgin daughters and coldly sacrifice their concubines in order to save abstract principles of hospitality and their own hides. Müllner points out that these readings, which cast all men in the role of perpetrator and all women in the role of victims, conveniently disguise the actual power differences among the characters. Some men (e.g. the Benjamites) have more power than others (e.g. the Levite and his host). The lack of a deeper power analysis creates a caricature of Old Testament culture, Judaism and Jewish men as callous misogynists and hardened male supremacists who renounce women without a second thought.

Müllner rightly emphasizes the need to combat such anti-Jewish parodies in feminist Christian exegetical texts by fusing gender analysis with an awareness of race and difference.

---

11. Trible, *Texts of Terror*, p. 83.

12. Trible, *Texts of Terror*, p. 65.

13. For example, African-American scholar Koala Jones-Warsaw examines Trible's interpretation from a 'womanist biblical hermeneutic' which takes seriously the "tridimensional reality" of racism, sexism and classism'. See Koala Jones-Warsaw, 'Toward a Womanist Hermeneutic: A Reading of Judges 19–21', in Athalya Brenner (ed.), *A Feminist Companion to Judges* (Sheffield: Sheffield Academic Press, 1993), pp. 172-86.

14. Katharina von Kellenbach, *Anti-Judaism in Feminist Religious Writings* (Atlanta: Scholars Press, 1994), pp. 91-96.

This story knows no heroes. It presents no unambiguous perpetrators and no unambiguous victims. The graphic violence moves along boundaries and differences. Violence is sexualized and even as sexual [violence] it is not restricted to men as perpetrators and women as victims. The demand of the Gibeonites is first directed at the Levite as object of sexualized violence... Feminizing him averts the threat, which emanates from the foreign man. The foreign-ness is transformed into another form of Other-ness, which can be appropriated by means of sexual violence. The foreign man is forced into a double liminality, into complete placeless-ness, which is characterized by foreign-ness and femininity.[15]

Müllner brings into focus the fact that the Levite is also the survivor of a violent crime. As contemptible as his decision to sacrifice his concu-bine might have been, it was a choice made *in extremis*—not unlike the inhuman choices forced upon many Jewish men and women during the Holocaust. By directing feminist outrage toward the Levite and the host for their abandonment of the concubine and the virgin daughters one loses sight of the real perpetrators: the Benjamite thugs who are out to brutalize foreigners. Both the Levite and his concubine, Müllner insists, are assaulted as foreigners and become victims of xenophobia. Judges 19–21 then moves beyond its use as a proof text of Hebrew misogyny and becomes an instructive account of gendered and sexualized deploy-ment of racial and xenophobic violence.

Racial hatred is often acted out in gendered and sexually charged ways, as we have been reminded recently in Rwanda, Bosnia and Kosovo. Initially the Gibeonites' animosity focuses on the Levite. They demand his violation. But his concubine serves as his surrogate. Through her, they attack him. Her rape and defilement brings the added pleasure of demoralizing him. The Gibeonites succeed in dehumanizing the Levite by forcing him into what Lawrence Langer has called a 'choiceless choice'.[16] The moment the Levite abandons her, his attack-ers have achieved their goal of humiliating and dehumanizing him. His act breaks his dignity and self-respect as a man. His inability to protect

15. Ilse Müllner, 'Tödliche Differenzen: Sexuelle Gewalt gegen Andere in Ri 19', in Luise Schottroff and Marie-Theres Wacker (eds.), *Von der Wurzel getragen: Christlich-feministische Exegese in Auseinandersetzung mit Antijudaismus* (New York: E.J. Brill, 1996), pp. 94-95.

16. Lawrence Langer, 'The Dilemma of Choice in the Deathcamps', in John K. Roth and Michael Berenbaum (eds.), *Holocaust: Religious and Philosophical Implications* (New York: Paragon House, 1989), pp. 222-32.

his wife 'feminizes' him (almost) as effectively as if they had raped him.

The ghettos and concentration camps of Nazi Germany were testing grounds for 'choiceless choices, where critical decisions did not reflect options between life and death, but between one form of "abnormal" response and another, both imposed by a situation that was in no way of the victims own choosing'.[17] In countless situations, parents were forced to choose between their own lives and that of their children.[18] One's own survival often entailed the death of someone else. Every time the *Judenräte* (local Jewish councils) were required to send a specific number of people on transports, they had to make choices over who would live and who would die. Whatever criteria were used, whether the *Judenräte* based their decisions on skill, age, class, gender, health, religion or political affiliation, they were drawn into profoundly immoral dilemmas. Similar to the Levite, they sometimes made fatefully wrong decisions based upon gender assumptions. For too long, they believed that the threat to men was greater than the threat to women.

In the case of the German Jewish community, men were sent more often and earlier to safety abroad because it seemed that they would be at greater risk in Nazi Germany than would Jewish women. In the end, 'the Nazis, whose propaganda trumpeted the threat of Jewish men as rapists, thieves, and crooks, murdered a high percentage of elderly Jewish women'.[19] The situation for Jews was, of course, quite different in Eastern Europe. Nevertheless, 'the population and deportation records of certain ghettos offer evidence that more Jewish women were deported than men and may have been murdered in greater numbers than Jewish men in the killing centers'.[20] It appears that Jewish women were selected earlier and sent more frequently on transports in a

17. Langer, 'The Dilemma of Choice', p. 224.
18. The Holocaust perverted and turned the *Akedah* into a gruesome reality. Some women 'chose' to abort or kill their newborn children in order to avoid their own death (Katharina von Kellenbach, 'Reproduction and Resistance during the Holocaust', in Esther Fuchs [ed.], *Women and the Holocaust: Narrative and Representation* [Lanham: University Press of America, 1999], pp. 19-32). See the account of Ruth Elias, *Die Hoffnung erhielt mich am Leben* (Munich: Piper, 1990).
19. Marion Kaplan, 'Jewish Women in Nazi Germany: Daily Life, Daily Struggles, 1933–1939', in Carol Rittner and John K. Roth (eds.), *Different Voices: Women and the Holocaust* (New York: Paragon House, 1993), p. 204.
20. Joan Ringelheim, 'Women and the Holocaust: A Reconsideration of Research', in Rittner and Roth (eds.), *Different Voices*, pp. 373-419.

desperate effort on the part of families and the Jewish ghetto leadership to save able-bodied men with marketable skills in order to prove the usefulness of the ghetto to the German economy. Although the Nazis' goal of exterminating all European Jews was gender-neutral, gender nevertheless impacted *how* people lived, worked, resisted, collaborated, fought, died or survived.

Am I a Murderer?

A memoir written by Calel Perechodnik during 1943 while in hiding, titled *Am I a Murderer?: Testament of a Jewish Ghetto Policeman,* eerily echoes the Levite's story. I want to read Judges 19–21 through Perechodnik's account and explore the intricate interaction of gender and power, responsibility for self and for the other, victimization and collaboration, which entrapped Holocaust victims in 'choiceless choices'. This chronicle which Perechodnik calls his 'deathbed confession' records his role as a Jewish ghetto policeman who was eventually forced to load his wife and two-year-old daughter onto a train, which transported them to their deaths in Treblinka. He had ignored his wife's earlier pleas to go into hiding and to procure a false Gentile identity card (*Kennkarte*), because he believed himself and his family safe on account of his privileged position as a Jewish ghetto policeman. He was only partially right: he was safe (for the moment), but his wife and daughter were not. On the day of the transports out of the ghetto, he was required to guard, assemble and load the Jews of his hometown Otwock onto the train. Only towards the end of the day did he realize that the families of the Jewish ghetto police would not be spared. He and the other policemen were required to load their own wives and children into the cattlecars as well. Like the Levite, he confronts his powerlessness and fear. 'You [his daughter] stretch out your hands to me, but I have no right to take you, if I do that, I will immediately get a bullet in my head... Ach, that fear, the panicky fear of slaves.'[21]

His 'choice' to stand back haunts him for the rest of his life. His impotence and inability to intervene, to help and protect his wife and two-year-old daughter tortures him. He is tormented by his sense of guilt. His 'choice' to save his own self by abandoning the other has two destructive consequences: First, it destroys his ability to relate to his

21. Perechodnik, *Am I a Murderer*, pp. 36-37.

wife. He can no longer bear to look at her and turns away in shame: 'Anka [his wife] is looking at me; she says nothing, doesn't even reproach me for not getting her a *Kennkarte*. God in heaven! Am I guilty? I turn away, am silent. What can I say? Explain myself or ask for forgiveness? Can one really say anything in the face of death?'[22] Secondly, he loses his self-respect and dignity as a man. Throughout the book, his agonized self-loathing is expressed in sentences like the following: 'We Jewish men are not worthy of being avenged! We were killed through our fault and not on a field of glory.'[23] After the trains leave, he imagines the journey of his wife and daughter moment by moment, 'in the fourth car from the locomotive, a car that is almost completely filled with women and children. In the whole car there are only two men—are these your protectors?'[24] But even these two men abandon the cattlecar and jump to safety. The women and children remain without male protection and are abandoned by their husbands who remain alive in the ghetto for a little while longer.

The abandonment of the other has irrevocable and shattering effects on the self. Can we detect similar destructive outcomes in the life of the Levite in Judges? Like Perechodnik, the Levite secures his own survival ('they meant to kill me' as he reports later in Judg. 20.5) by handing over his concubine to be 'ravished' (Judg. 20.5), thus abandoning her. But he is forced to listen to her violation throughout the night, unable to intervene, powerless to protect her. In the morning, like Perechodnik at the station, the Levite cannot look at his concubine. The striking absence of empathy the morning after the deadly rape should perhaps not be attributed to the Levite's patriarchal attitudes or to feelings of male supremacy but rather to his victimization and powerlessness. How could the Levite inquire how she is feeling? His shame and guilt, one may presume, go too deep. Her agony is forever tied to his cowardice and emasculation. Could the Levite and the concubine have forgiven each other?[25] The Levite turns away, unable to relate emotionally to this dying or dead woman. Trible comments that 'no

22. Perechodnik, *Am I a Murderer*, pp. 36-37.
23. Perechodnik, *Am I a Murderer*, p. xxi.
24. Perechodnik, *Am I a Murderer*, pp. 45-46.
25. See the recent report on victims of rape in Kosovo, where a husband acknowledged that if his wife admitted to him that she had been raped, he would divorce her (Elisabeth Bumiller, 'Deny Rape or Be Hated: Kosovo Victim's Choice', *New York Times*, 22 June 1999, p. A1).

mourning becomes the man; no burial attends the woman'.[26] The Levite cannot mourn the concubine's death without admitting his guilt and igniting his self-contempt.

Perechodnik describes the emotional condition of the surviving Jewish ghetto policemen: 'the majority of those who lost their wives lost their energy and the will to live. They didn't have the courage to kill themselves. They existed rather than lived, not caring about anything; they surrendered passively to their fate.'[27] What kept them going was their 'animal...instinct for self-preservation' and their 'fear of death',[28] two powerful forces to which Nazi terror and dehumanization had reduced them. They act automatically and cannot afford to feel their desolation. One may presume that the Levite has similarly lost his ability to feel. There seems to be only one way to face his shame: revenge. Subsequently he acts out of blind rage and deep humiliation.

> And when he entered the house, he took a knife, and laying hold of his concubine he divided her limb by limb, into twelve pieces, and sent her throughout all the territory of Israel (Judg. 19.29).

Perechodnik's impotent rage also expresses itself in dreams of vengeance. In his own self-hatred, he demands the total annihilation of those responsible. Perechodnik cannot imagine a life for himself after the war. 'After this that I have lived through, I cannot live a normal life...I will never be a useful member of society. So what can happen to me? Neither a Jew, nor a Catholic, nor a decent man, not even a thief— simply a nobody.'[29] His own sense of 'nobodiness', of being a ravished wreck, fuels his desire for revenge. He dreams of the creation of a 'war volunteer battalions made up of such wrecks as myself' who can 'deport the Germans to the same Treblinka—precisely there and not elsewhere'.[30]

> In my whole life I never raised my hand against a fellow creature, but I feel that I would cease drinking, that my thirst would be quenched with German blood, especially that of small children. For my daughter, for all the Jewish children, I would take hundredfold revenge. My heart is already pounding with joy; my pale cheeks are glowing with the thought

---

26. Trible, *Texts of Terror,* p. 80.
27. Perechodnik, *Am I a Murderer,* p. 69.
28. Perechodnik, *Am I a Murderer,* p. 73.
29. Perechodnik, *Am I a Murderer,* p. 173.
30. Perechodnik, *Am I a Murderer,* p. 173.

of the physical and psychological tortures I would inflict on the Germans
before their final deaths. And then satiated with blood and revenge, I
could perish together with my enemies.[31]

A caveat is in order: Perechodnik wrote these words in the middle of
1943, indulging in violent revenge fantasies while in hiding. Most
Jewish survivors who did live to see the end of the war did not engage
in acts of vengeance and were able to lead 'normal lives' and to become
'useful members of society'.[32] But in the context of Judges, Perechodnik's words are accurate predictions of the unfolding of the story.
Blinded by his own victimization, the Levite does not think about what
might be best for his concubine, namely proper burial and mourning,
but what he needs to restore his sense of manhood and self-respect:
revenge and justice!

Blood flows freely in the aftermath. The men of Benjamin are killed
by the tens of thousands and 'the women are destroyed out of
Benjamin' (Judg. 21.16). Having vowed not to give their daughters as
wives to the male Benjamite survivors, the tribes authorize a raid on the
inhabitants of Ja'besh-gil'ead, who are smitten 'with the edge of the
sword'. Four hundred virgins are abducted and forcibly wed to the male
survivors of Benjamin (Judg. 21.12), as are the daughters of Shiloh,
who are kidnapped as they dance in the vineyards (Judg. 21.20-23). The
initial rape is multiplied in the process of securing a future for the tribe
of Benjamin. Here again, this violence should not be evaluated exclusively from the perspective of gender and sexual violence, but also with
respect to 'attempting to regenerate the nearly lost tribe of Benjamin,
and to restore their inheritance'[33] as Jones-Warsaw points out. 'The
Israelite chose the lesser of evils—between allowing marriage through
capture or the death of the Benjamite tribe.'[34] This ending of the narrative in Judges raises the ethically ambiguous questions of punishment
and forgiveness, retribution and reconciliation.

My reading of Judges 19–21 may provide a biblical starting point to
'invent a vocabulary of annihilation appropriate to the deathcamp
experience'.[35] It defies theological attempts at making sense and forces

31. Perechodnik, *Am I a Murderer*, p. 173.
32. William Helmreich, *Against all Odds: Holocaust Survivors and the Successful Lives They Made in America* (New York: Simon and Schuster, 1992).
33. Jones-Warsaw, 'Toward a Womanist Hermeneutic', p. 181.
34. Jones-Warsaw, 'Toward a Womanist Hermeneutic', p. 181.
35. Langer, 'The Dilemma of Choice', p. 231.

us to 'redefine the terminology of transcendence—"dignity", "choice", "suffering" and "spirit"'[36]—as Langer challenges us to do. Although the night of terror, that befell the couple in Gibeah is worlds apart from the grinding death machines of European ghettos and death camps, Judges illustrates the devastating effects of 'choiceless choices' in situations where people are forced to choose between their own and the survival of an other. I do not wish to suggest a moral analogy between the Levite's choice and the choices confronting European Jews during the Holocaust, since the range of choices available to the Levite were vastly different from those confronting Jews living in ghettos and concentration camps. Langer's 'choiceless choices' refer to the complete

> absence of humanly significant alternatives—that is, alternatives enabling an individual to make a decision, act on it and accept the consequences, all within a framework that supports personal integrity and self-esteem— one is plunged into a moral turmoil that may silence judgment...but cannot paralyze all action, if one wishes to remain alive.[37]

The Levite did not choose between death and death, since the concubine's life was not even at stake until her husband threw her out of the house. In contrast, during the Holocaust, all paths led to extermination and the 'choices' available to the victims of the Holocaust affected, sometimes, the when, where and how of death.

It is not so much the moral analogy that makes this biblical narrative interesting for post-Shoah readings of the Bible but the absence of theodicy. God remains absent from this text until the matter of justice is debated. No prior sins are cited as possible reasons for the calamity that happens to the concubine and the Levite. The crime against them was not intended as a test. Neither victim nor perpetrator grew from this experience psychologically, spiritually or ethically. The concubine's death served no redemptive purpose: 'Her body has been broken and given to many', quotes Trible, but her 'anti-sacrifice' promotes no release and no deliverance. Nothing good comes of it. There are no heroes or heroines and no role models emerge from this narrative. Judges 19–21 portrays morally ambiguous decisions for survival and muddled pathways into the future.

---

36. Langer, 'The Dilemma of Choice', p. 231.
37. Langer, 'The Dilemma of Choice', p. 226.

An 'Interhuman Perspective' on Theodicy

The philosophical project of Emmanuel Levinas is helpful to probe the spiritual devastation brought about by the involuntary abandonment of the other, routinely enforced during the Holocaust. Levinas rejects traditional theodicy and argues that the suffering of the Holocaust should be acknowledged as 'meaningless'. For Levinas, the Holocaust exposes 'the blatant disparity between suffering and any theodicy'[38] and he asserts that 'the justification of the pain of the Other is with certainty the origin of all immorality'.[39] He criticizes the traditional human-divine perspective of theodicy because it abstracts from the reality and 'immanent and wild concreteness' of the pain of the neighbor.[40] Instead, we should approach 'suffering from an interhuman perspective',[41] which remains embedded in our relationship and 'interestedness'[42] in the other. For Levinas the self's responsibility for the other is grounded in timeless transcendence. 'The responsibility for the other (*autrui*) cannot have begun in my commitment, in my decision.'[43] Rather it precedes the self and is rooted in the Infinite. For Levinas, 'the positivity of the Infinite is the conversion into responsibility, into approach of the other (*autrui*)'.[44]

> What is exceptional in this way of being signaled is that I am ordered toward the face of the other. In this order, which is an ordination, the nonpresence of the infinite is not a figure of negative theology. All the negative attributes, which state the beyond of essence, become positive in responsibility, a response answering to a nonthematizable provocation and thus a nonvocation, a trauma. This response answers before any consciousness and any present, but it does answer, as though the invisible that can do without the present left a trace by the very fact of doing without the present. That trace lights up in the face of a neighbor in the

38. Emmanuel Levinas, 'Sinnloses Leiden', *Sinn und Form* 47.1 (1995), p. 23, my translation. For a complete English translation, see Richard Cohen (trans.) 'Useless Suffering', in R. Bernasconi and D. Wood (eds.), *The Provocation of Levinas* (London: Routledge, 1988), pp. 156-67.

39. Levinas, 'Sinnloses Leiden', p. 25.

40. Levinas, 'Sinnloses Leiden', p. 29.

41. Levinas, 'Sinnloses Leiden', p. 27.

42. Emmanuel Levinas, *Basic Philosophical Writings* (ed. and trans. Adriaan T. Peperzak; Bloomington, IN: Indiana University Press, 1996), p. 10.

43. Levinas, *Basic Philosophical Writings*, p. 117.

44. Levinas, *Basic Philosophical Writings*, p. 119.

ambiguity of the one *before whom* (or *to whom*, without any paternalism)
and *for whom* I answer. For such is the enigma or ex-ception of a face,
judge and accused.[45]

The Other anchors the self in the infinite and responsibility for the other
is the place where the trace of God is revealed and becomes present.
This explains the spiritually devastating effects of 'choiceless choices'
where people were forced to 'choose' between their own lives and that
of the other. In so doing, they were forced to eclipse 'the trace' of God,
to deny their connection with the Infinite. More than ethical devastation, 'choiceless choices' create spiritual desolation.

During the Holocaust, the destruction and betrayal of the other
brought about the effacement of the 'trace' of the Infinite. Instead of
explaining the suffering of the Holocaust with reference to a higher
divine plan or purpose, Levinas's interhuman perspective forces us to
accept the utter devastation of the Holocaust. If the face of God is
revealed in the face of the other, then 'ethics [becomes]...the spiritual
optics'[46] and ethical concerns become the starting points of any God-
talk. How we fail the other is intrinsically bound to how we fail God.
After Auschwitz, theodicy must account for the mechanisms that
dehumanize the neighbor and analyze the power dynamics that 'de-
face' the other on the basis of ethnicity, gender, race and religion. The
question 'where was God in Auschwitz?' must be rephrased into 'where
was the neighbor?' Theodicy after Auschwitz must, therefore, confront
the structures of domination that enable the obliteration of the other and
must clarify the intricate chains of violence, their movement from
ideology to politics, from religion to education, from technology to the
administration, from military annihilation to personal betrayal of the
other.

Search for Justice

'The first question in the interhuman', writes Levinas, 'is the question
of justice.'[47] In Judges, the question of justice looms large. Twelve gory
body parts cry out for justice and retribution. The bloody war against
the tribe of Benjamin (especially the women!) strikes modern readers as

45. Levinas, *Basic Philosophical Writings*, p. 119.
46. Quoted in Colin Davies, *Levinas: An Introduction* (South Bend, IN: Notre
Dame University Press, 1997), p. 36.
47. Levinas, *Basic Philosophical Writings*, p. 168.

highly problematic. It seems self-evident to reject the quasi-genocidal warfare that ensues in response to the Benjamite men's violence. But current forms of punishment in response to genocidal mass violence remain troubling and unsatisfying. The grisly remains of genocide in the twentieth century have not occasioned much more sophisticated or creative responses. Then as now, we respond with violence and war: the Second World War, the failed attempts at UN peacekeeping (cf. Rwanda, Bosnia) and the recent aerial bombing campaign against Yugoslavia. Judicial prosecution, which might have been the better way in the context of Judges, where a few Benjamite men could have been isolated and prosecuted individually, works less well in the context of the Holocaust and other instances of genocide. Tens of thousands of German perpetrators and collaborators from various European nationalities were implicated. Some were tried before the Nuremberg Tribunal and before allied military courts, several thousand more stood trial before German and other national civilian criminal courts. But these trials touched only the tip of the iceberg. When it seems impossible to prosecute and punish individual perpetrators adequately, how do we deal with the communal responsibility for the victimization and wholesale slaughter of others? Were the Benjamite women innocent victims of retributive bloodshed or were they rightly punished for their entanglement in the crime of their husbands? What was their responsibility towards the concubine and for the prevention and punishment of their husbands' violence? Koala Jones-Warsaw rightly points out that 'like the Benjamites, we must distinguish whether it is better to stand in solidarity with our brothers or not, and at what cost. By refusing to surrender the guilty individuals, the entire Benjamite tribe was nearly destroyed, all the women were destroyed.'[48]

While the guilt of the Benjamite and Nazi perpetrators seems clear cut, the responsibility of the Levite and of Perechodnik for their involvement in the betrayal of the other is more complex. How do we assess moral responsibility as distinct from legal culpability? What is revealed in the faces of the perpetrators, 'for whom', according to Levinas, we must also answer? How do we punish those who commit crimes without denying their humanity and the fact, that they, too, are our neighbors? The philosopher Levinas does not provide specific ethical and political answers to these questions, but his insistence on

---

48. Jones-Warsaw, 'Toward a Womanist Hermeneutic', p. 184.

our absolute obligation towards the other implies that we will have to accept some moral ambiguity as we negotiate the twin poles of *Vengeance and Forgiveness*,[49] of war and remarriage. In Judges 19–21 a bewildering and contradictory path emerges between punishing the perpetrators (involving more violence) and accepting their reintegration and future (victimizing more women).

Lamentation

What appropriate responses are left to religious communities if Levinas is right that 'the Holocaust of the Jewish people under Hitler's domin-ion seems to be the paradigm of senseless human suffering?'[50] By insisting that their suffering was 'senseless', Levinas challenges us to resist the temptation to digest the experience of the Holocaust by distill-ing moral lessons or extracting theological interpretations. Instead, the meaninglessness of the suffering during the Holocaust makes this event undigestable. The raw agony of Perechodnik's 'deathbed confession' refuses to be absorbed into ethical-theological formulas. It cannot be 'put to rest' by incorporating it into an overarching theological or moral discourse but must be appreciated in its particularity. By calling for the acceptance of suffering as meaningless and non-redemptive, one keeps the chilling voices of individual sufferers alive and raw. The refusal to provide a (happy) ending to meaningless suffering by integrating it into grand theological narratives of redemption, forces us to respond spon-taneously to the suffering of the other as our neighbor. As their neigh-bor, we are required to answer for their violation by testifying against the perpetrators and grieving the victims. Their betrayal and senseless anguish compels us to engage in protest, lamentation and mourning. In this way, the end of theodicy creates new solidarity.

49. Martha Minnow, *Between Vengeance and Forgiveness* (Boston: Beacon Press, 1998).
50. Levinas, 'Sinnloses Leiden', p. 24.

'ISAIAH 'TWAS FORETOLD IT':
HELPING THE CHURCH INTERPRET THE PROPHETS

Patricia K. Tull

For many years John Pawlikowski has been an outspoken advocate of reform in the Christian church vis-à-vis Judaism. Recently he outlined three major phases in the progress of changes in Christian discourse about Judaism.[1] The first phase, the removal of anti-Jewish material from educational curricula, he considered mostly complete. The second, major revisions in biblical scholarship, he saw as well underway. But the third, changes in Christian theological discourse, and with it, the language of worship and liturgy, is a phase he said had barely begun.

For Scripture scholars involved in post-Shoah studies, this time of transition is both exhilarating and frustrating. The vast paradigmatic changes emerging within biblical scholarship from a deepened appreciation for Judaism certainly evoke Isaiah's image of blind eyes opening and deaf ears unstopping. At the same time, those of us who work with church institutions experience a double reality: insights that now seem obvious within the guild have not touched the consciousness of most lay people, or even of most church professionals. Ecclesial statements made directly in relation to Judaism often fail to influence what the church says in other contexts, conveying the distinct impression that 'these are statements the churches make only when speaking with Jews and not when engaged in self reflection and internal education'.[2] Consequently, the church continues to carry forward structures and messages that stand at odds with interfaith understanding.

Some time lag is always inevitable with such issues. Many of today's

---

1. John Pawlikowski, 'Accomplishments and Challenges in the Contemporary Jewish-Christian Encounter', in Howard Clark Kee and Irvin J. Borowsky (eds.), *Removing Anti-Judaism from the Pulpit* (Philadelphia: American Interfaith Institute, 1996), pp. 29-35.
2. Pawlikowski, 'Accomplishments and Challenges', p. 34.

churchgoers listen to preachers who were educated in the 1970s by lecturers who graduated in the 50s and 60s during the heyday of the 'biblical theology' movement. John Bright's *History of Israel*, with its final paragraphs describing Jesus as the 'destination of Old Testament history and theology, the sufficient fulfillment of Israel's hope', still lingers on many a pastoral bookshelf.[3] The slow pace of change is indeed understandable. Yet biblical scholars committed to the church's moral healing have many opportunities to engender conceptual changes that will help the church abide more consistently by its own self-image of love and charity.

I

Though there are numerous topics in biblical interpretation worth examining, in this chapter I will focus primarily on the notion of messianic prophecy. The age-old hermeneutic of 'the Old Testament as prophecy of Christ', though long recognized among scholars as historically and theologically problematic, continues to thrive in the Christian church. Though it is only one of many possible conceptions of the relationship between the Hebrew Scriptures and the church, it enjoys disproportionate institutional support through lectionary readings, preaching guides, hymns and prayers, even in denominations which have for the past thirty years engaged actively in Christian–Jewish reconciliation. Conceptual tools are available for reframing the relationships between the Hebrew Scriptures and the church in such a way that the Christian tradition can be affirmed without devaluing Judaism. Scholars wishing to help the church use these tools must both broaden our own knowledge base and re-examine the ways in which Scripture is taught. Two recent experiences prompt my reflections. The first was an assignment I

---

3.   John Bright, *A History of Israel* (Philadelphia: Westminster Press, 3rd edn, 1981), p. 464. Ronald Clements has outlined the way in which scholars of the past two centuries abandoned the notion that specific prophetic words were meant to refer to Jesus, yet substituted a historicized accounting in which the church became the fulfillment of a vaguely defined 'prophetic hope'. Clements cites Bright's final chapter, 'Towards the Fullness of Time', as an example of such confusion between historical and theological discourse, 'present[ing] the history of Old Testament times as though it moved in a natural and necessary course towards a fulfillment in the New'. (Ronald Clements, 'Messianic Prophecy or Messianic History?', *HBT* 1 [1979], p. 96).

gave to a first-semester seminary class. The second was an invitation to teach an advent Bible study in a local Presbyterian church.

For the class assignment, each student interviewed three other churchgoers, asking them what they knew about the Old Testament. The ignorance they discovered was only occasionally downright shocking, such as when one person said his favorite Old Testament stories were the Good Samaritan, the woman at the well, and the birth of Christ. Another churchgoer opined that the Old Testament 'was written more than a million years ago by two or three rabbis in order to teach morals to children'. More interesting than ignorance was the range in significance seen in the Hebrew Scriptures. A few respondents found in them guidance, wisdom and comfort, as well as a welcome link between their own faith and that of their Jewish friends. But by far the majority of responses were limited to pat formulas such as 'part one of a two-part saga', the incomplete promise fulfilled in the New Testament, or the record of Israel's longing for Jesus Christ. Advocates of the 'Biblical Theology' movement would have been proud to see their impact on a whole generation of mainline Protestants. Other answers would have delighted the Church Fathers and even Marcion: the record of Israelite failure, legalism and obstinacy, an obscure and violent Jewish book, too hard to understand and really quite superfluous anyway.

Certain themes emerged from these conversations. First, almost nobody, even those familiar with the New Testament, believed they knew these Scriptures well. Secondly, what they did know they attributed to the teaching of pastors, usually in the context of Sunday worship. Thirdly, those who viewed the Hebrew Bible as antithesis to or precursor of the New Testament derived little benefit from it, but would rather bypass these Scriptures in favor of the gospels and Paul. But those who had learned appreciation for the Hebrew Scriptures in their own right read them both more often and with more comprehension. Fourthly, students discovered that views of the Hebrew Scriptures went hand-in-glove with attitudes toward Jews, both ancient and modern.

The second event that prompted my thinking had to do with the weekly lectionary. Many mainline Protestant pastors choose their sermon texts from the Revised Common Lectionary, an ecumenical effort based on the 1969 Roman Catholic Lectionary. Largely because of the time period of its formation, the Catholic lectionary owes tremendous hermeneutical debts to the biblical theology movement and its promise-and-fulfillment theme. Readings are organized around the Christian year, giving primacy to the synoptic gospels, with additional readings each week from the epistles, Psalms and, usually, the Hebrew Scriptures. From Advent to Easter, Old Testament selections are controlled by the liturgical seasons and the corresponding gospel readings. From Easter to Pentecost they are superseded by the book of Acts.

Both the Catholic lectionary and its Protestant derivative have been roundly criticized for the paucity of Hebrew Scriptures, for their antiquated selection principles, and for their lack of continuity and context.[4] Recent revisions address some of these problems, but many still debate whether the present lectionary offers any improvement over older Protestant practices of continuous week-by-week reading of canonical books.

Teaching from the advent lectionary brought me face to face with problematic messages emerging from its text choices during this important season. During the four Sundays immediately before Christmas in 1996 (Year B, which recurred in December of 1999), the sequence of readings developed a story line that is not only unfortunate for Christian–Jewish relations, but unbiblical as well. The first three readings are from Second and Third Isaiah, while the fourth reading jumps to 2 Samuel. They are ordered by no discernible sequence either canonical or historical.

The first reading, Isaiah 64.1-9, excerpts nine verses from a much longer collective lament over Jerusalem's destruction by Babylon in the sixth century BCE (Isa. 63.7–64.12). The lament begins with the recollection of past divine deeds on Israel's behalf (63.7-9) and of Israel's past rebellion, followed by their remembrance of God's favor in the exodus from Egypt (vv. 10-14). On the basis of this grace/rebellion/remembrance story, the lamenters plead that God 'look down from heaven and see', reminding God that even though they seem forgotten, God is still their father (vv. 15-19).

This reflection is followed by the section employed by the lectionary: 'O that you would tear open the heavens and come down, so that the

---

4. Articles on this subject are too numerous to mention, and may be easily sought out. The fullest treatment I am aware of are three volumes by Shelley Cochran, entitled *The Pastor's Underground Guide to the Revised Common Lectionary, Year A* (St Louis: Chalice Press, 1995); *Year B* (1996), and *Year C* (1997). She offers helpful discussions of the assumptions behind text selection and arrangement, and suggests principles for pastors wishing to steer a course through the lectionary.

mountains would quake at your presence.' In its original context this image is not about God becoming flesh according to Christian understanding, but rather it echoes a widely shared biblical motif of God as divine warrior.[5] The reading goes on to confess that when God was angry, the people became 'like one who is unclean, and all our righteous deeds are like a filthy cloth...' (Isa. 64.6). A clear description in vv. 10-11 of the lament's context—the desolation of Jerusalem and the burning of the temple—is omitted from the lectionary reading.

Torn from its sixth-century setting, recontextualized in Christian advent, shorn of the remembrance of God's deeds in the past, and truncated until all that remains is the wish for God to descend from heaven combined with the confession of Israel's sin, the reading presents itself rather imperiously as Israel's depressed, repentant wish for Jesus to come and save them. These two themes, Israel's sin and God's descent, are buttressed by the New Testament readings: 1 Cor. 1.3-9, in which Christians are praised by Paul in language that contrasts sharply with the confession of Israel's perfidy, and Mk 13.24-37, on the coming of the Son of Man. In many churches, this radical cut and paste of Isaiah 64 is driven home by hymns that, while lovely, present a historically false picture of first-century Israel: 'O come, O come, Emmanuel, and ransom captive Israel, that mourns in lonely exile here until the Son of God appear.'[6]

On the following Sunday, Isa. 40.1-11 is read: 'Comfort, O comfort my people.' This passage, originally the opening of 'Deutero-Isaiah' with its theme of redemption and return from exile, includes verses that are most familiar to Christians in the context of the gospel presentation of John the Baptist. Enforcing this interpretation, Mk 1.1-8 is read, with its significant misquotations that are well known to scholars but not necessarily obvious to clergy or laity: 'As it is written in the prophet Isaiah, "See, I am sending my messenger ahead of you, who will prepare your way; the voice of one crying out in the wilderness: 'Prepare

5.   See for instance Hab. 3.1-15; Nah. 1.2-8; Ps. 29.

6.   Warren Carter, 'The Gospel Lections for Advent: Some Unseasonal Thoughts,' *Quarterly Review* 16 (Fall 1996), pp. 283-90 (286-87), comments that the advent lectionary's themes of 'waiting expectantly for God to fulfil God's promises and send the eagerly and widely awaited Messiah', and of 'God's absence before the gift of God's presence', are inaccurate historically and contribute to 'profoundly unhelpful Christian attitudes and actions towards Jewish traditions and people'.

the way of the Lord, make his paths straight'," John the baptizer appeared in the wilderness...' In this context, Isaiah 40 seems to offer as an answer to the previous week's lament the comforting announcement of John the Baptist, preparing the way for Jesus Christ.

The third Sunday jumps forward again to Isa. 61.1-4, 8-11. Like the second week's reading, this passage is most familiar to Christians through its association with the gospels, since it appears in Jesus' own mouth in Lk. 4.18-19: 'The spirit of the Lord God is upon me, because the Lord has anointed me; he has sent me to bring good news to the oppressed...' Even though Luke's story is not read, many will remember (or the preacher will remind them) that this passage ends badly for Jews: 'all in the synagogue' attempt to murder Jesus after his homily. The week's gospel reading is Jn 1.6-8, 19-28, in which John the Baptist announces the presence of one 'whom you do not know'.

The last Sunday before Christmas leaps to another book of another genre set in an entirely different historical period, five hundred years previous to the readings of the first three weeks: 2 Sam. 7.1-11, 16, in which God instructs his messenger Nathan to promise King David: 'Your house and your kingdom will be made sure forever before me; your throne will be established forever.' The gospel reading is Lk. 1.26-38, in which another messenger from God, the angel Gabriel, announces to Mary concerning her unborn son that 'the Lord God will give to him the throne of his ancestor David. He will reign over the house of Jacob forever, and of his kingdom there will be no end'. These paired readings leave the almost inevitable impression that, anticipating Gabriel by a thousand years, the prophet Nathan predicted Jesus to his ancestor King David.

To summarize, the four Old Testament advent readings in Year B, wrenched from both canonical and historical context and set in the season of Christ's coming, seem designed to tell the following story: In answer to Jewish sin and misery (Isa. 64), the prophet Isaiah/John the Baptist heralds the coming of Jesus Christ (Isa. 40), upon whom the spirit of the Lord rests to preach and heal (Isa. 61), and who is destined from all time to reign as King over Israel (2 Sam. 7). Such a narrative is found neither in the Hebrew Scriptures nor in the New Testament. Rather it is created in the lectionary from decontextualized segments, like a ransom note assembled from magazine clippings. Certainly it is not the only reading that can be derived from these texts, but centuries of repetition have predisposed Christians to read them in this way. In fact, despite my historical-critical labors, participants in the Bible study had no trouble following the lectionary's path to the well-trodden question: 'So why didn't the Jews recognize their Messiah when he came?'

These advent readings indeed combine two critically and inter-religiously problematic claims, claims that are reflected in the church's interpretation of the Hebrew Scriptures from its early days till now: first, that Jesus the Messiah came in response to Jewish failure as the people of God and, secondly, that the prophets, who pointed out this failure, foretold his coming. Other lectionary sequences employ one or the other of these motifs. For instance, during Lent of the same year, the Pentateuch and prophets are used to construct a 'covenant/fall/new covenant' *Heilsgeschichte*, or 'salvation history' (Gen. 9.8-17; Gen. 17.1-7, 15-16; Exod. 20.1-17; Num. 21.4-9; Jer. 31.31-34; and on Passion Sunday, Isa. 50.4-9a). Similarly, the advent readings for both Years A and C, like Year B, present a synthesis of stock messianic prooftexts. In Year A, First Isaiah is employed (Isa. 2.1-5; 11.1-10; 35.1-10; 7.10-16), and in Year C, a more miscellaneous collection is gathered (Jer. 33.14-16; Mal. 3.1-4; Zeph. 3.14-20; and Mic. 5.2-5a). Consequently, the only relationship between the testaments ever presented by the advent lectionary is one of prophecy-fulfillment, leading Christians to believe that 'the prophets clearly foresaw the details of Jesus' birth and that their words were primarily directed to this event'.[7]

Although few academics exercise direct influence on the lectionary itself, ecclesiastical publishing companies regularly turn to biblical scholars for lectionary commentaries. These guides offer silver-platter opportunities to address the significance of prophetic texts in Christian worship and the relations between the two faith communities who share them. The task of interpreting texts from a foreign culture thousands of years ago, for the benefit of people here and now, in relation to events from yet a third era in between the two, is fraught with historical and hermeneutical complexity. Yet all too often these guides, perhaps too hastily written, blur crucial theological and historical tensions. Some writers, faithful to historical criticism, present a decent overview of the text in its setting, but ignore its subsequent use as a Christian text. Thus they leave to the preacher's imagination the older text's relevance to modern people preoccupied with the savior's birth. Others, faithful to

---

7.   John Pawlikowski, 'Preaching in Advent: Rethinking the Fulfillment Theme', *Christian Jewish Relations* 15.4 (1982), pp. 12-16 (15).

themes of advent and Christian theology, ignore the text's own setting, leaving the deceptive impression that the writer intended to discuss the coming of Christ. Thus they forbid the text to speak in its own right.[8]

When the creative tension between distinct times and communities is blurred, the message becomes garbled and superficial. The many pastors who respect critical scholarship and honor interfaith dialogue are left confused, and the many pastors who reject critical scholarship and have never heard of interfaith dialogue are authorized to continue proclaiming that Isaiah saw Jesus across the centuries and spent his life waiting for Christmas. Congregations are left to view Isaiah as a kind of proto-Christian, and his listeners—and their descendents, up to this day—as having completely missed the point. Jews become at best (in the tongue-in-cheek words of David H.C. Read) 'a wonderful people who "missed the boat" when Jesus came',[9] and at worst (in the painfully earnest words of John Calvin) folks who 'by much caviling, have laboured, as far as lay in their power, to pervert the true exposition' and instead, having 'laboured, by all means possible, to torture the Prophet's meaning to another sense'.[10]

Problems of tension between the Hebrew Scriptures and their Christian use need not be ignored. Arthur Dewey's work on the same lectionary selections demonstrates that historical accuracy and theological

---

8.   The following are two examples among many possible. Thomas Dozeman, in *Preaching the Revised Common Lectionary, Year B, Advent/Christmas/Epiphany* (Nashville: Abingdon Press, 1993) tends to follow a historical-critical agenda. His discussion of Isaiah 40, for instance, focuses on its exilic setting, without mentioning either advent or the text's reappearance in the gospel reading from Mark. He sometimes makes a leaps to include advent, such as: 'Isaiah 61 provides detailed guidelines concerning how we live the life of faith during Advent' (p. 42). Walter Brueggemann, in *Texts for Preaching: A Lectionary Commentary Based on the NRSV—Year B* (Louisville, KY: Westminster/John Knox, 1993), on the other hand, omits all reference to the setting of Isa. 64.1-9 and even to the larger poem of which it is a part, and refers to the speaker in Isaiah 61 as the 'Anointed', the 'One powered by God's own resolve', whose 'work is to bring the gospel' (capitalizations his).

9.   'Reflections of an Imported WASP', in Kee and Borowsky (eds.), *Removing Anti-Judaism*, p. 63.

10.   John Calvin, *Commentary on the Book of the Prophet Isaiah* (5 vols.; Grand Rapids: Eerdmans, 1958), I, p. 244, commenting on the phrase 'behold, a virgin shall conceive' in Isa. 7.14. Ironically, his rejected 'other sense', that Isaiah's prophecy does indeed relate to his own day, has been commonly accepted by Christian and Jewish scholars alike for many generations now.

prudence can greatly enrich interpretation. Writing about Isaiah 40, he
draws attention not only to its reuse in Mark 1, but to the changes that
the gospel writer introduces, saying, 'What is going on here? Is it
merely a word game? On the contrary, the passage is the result of serious scribal sifting of Scripture based upon the assumption that God's
word will come to pass.'[11] Commenting on Isaiah 61, he notes its use in
Luke 4, but cautions against drawing hasty conclusions, since 'despite
the Christian appropriation of these verses, this utterance is still unful-
filled in the modern world', and he invites readers to consider, 'Dare we
celebrate this vision with anticipatory thanksgiving?'[12] Finally, in dealing with 2 Samuel 7, Dewey explicates the passage's continuing, and
contested, significance. Pointing out that the Jewish wars of independence and the reading from Luke 1 represent two different communities'
ways of keeping the Davidic dream alive, he comments, 'We may even
understand the subsequent disputes among the "peoples of the Book" as
dynastic struggles, arising from disparate (and sometimes tragic) interpretations of such ancient material.'[13] By distinguishing between the
texts themselves and their subsequent Christian use, and by attending
sympathetically to both of them, Dewey creates a much more complex,
accurate and informative picture.

Dewey's work reflects a concern that biblical scholars working in
interfaith relations are finding increasingly important to explore: the
clash of interpretive worlds, both over the course of time and among
concurrent, diverse communities. In the remainder of this article I will
outline some conceptual approaches to that clash in both research and
teaching, approaches that I believe affirm the Christian tradition while
maintaining respect for the integrity of the Hebrew Scriptures and for
the interpretations of Judaism.

II

My thoughts begin with Daniel Patte's recent book, *Ethics of Biblical
Interpretation: A Re-evaluation.* There he heuristically distinguishes

---

11. Arthur Dewey, Advent/Christmas volume for *Proclamation 6, Series B:
Interpreting the Lessons of the Church Year* (Minneapolis: Fortress Press, 1996),
pp. 22-23.

12. Dewey, *Interpreting the Lessons of the Church*, p. 26.

13. Dewey, *Interpreting the Lessons of the Church*, p. 32.

three 'levels' of interpretive reading.[14] The first level is an ordinary, personal reading, an intuitive interaction between text and situated reader with no claim to authority or exegetical rigor. Out of the plethora of potential significations in the interaction between a text and its readers, one in particular is actualized. Such a reading is not yet a critical interpretation, and whether it will enlighten other people is yet to be seen, but still it remains a fruitful, valid insight for the interpreter.

Second-level reading, according to Patte, involves exegetical exploration of a text to elaborate a first-level reading, to refine the original insight and articulate it in a compelling way. Naturally, what kind of exegesis is chosen to inform a preferred reading depends upon the hermeneutical norms of the interpreter's community. Laity, seminary students, and clergy do not necessarily interpret according to the norms of critical scholars, nor do critical scholars from different eras, different continents, or even different sections at the annual meeting of the Society of Biblical Literature interpret similarly. Nevertheless, Patte suggests that even at this point diverse readings, even mutually exclusive readings, need not surprise or alarm those who understand that texts can be, and always have been, activated in multiple ways.

It is in what Patte calls the third level of reading that interpretive conflicts lie.[15] This is when, having worked out a system that accounts satisfactorily for the elements of the text that seem significant (and in the process suppressing—usually unconsciously—elements deemed superfluous, even though these may be the very building blocks of someone else's reading), an interpreter makes a dogmatic and patently impossible claim: 'I have exhausted this text; I have interpreted it correctly.' Patte comments that 'any theological exegetical interpretation that diverges from this fundamental truth is excluded as illegitimate and invalid, whatever the accuracy and consistency of its representation of the text might be'.[16] In Patte's view, any reading born of dogmatic exclusivity is invalid by definition, not only because it absolutizes the claims of one interpreter, but also because it precludes accounting for the entire text in its polysemic, multi-dimensional nature.

---

14. Daniel Patte, *Ethics of Biblical Interpretation: A Re-evaluation* (Louisville, KY: Westminster/John Knox Press, 1995).

15. It has been pointed out that this is not technically a 'level' of reading analogous to the other two, but rather a reading assumption. I agree, but will continue to use Patte's own language.

16. Patte, *Ethics of Biblical Interpretation*, p. 90.

Patte's categories suggest a recasting of the issue: the greatest danger presented by Christian messianic interpretation of Scripture, or for that matter by any dogmatic interpretation, is not really critical inadequacy, historical inaccuracy, apologetic conditioning, or methodological obsolescence. No matter how thin the hermeneutic used to get from Isaiah to Jesus may sometimes seem by modern standards, the root of the problem is not, in itself, the insistence that Isaiah is about Jesus. The danger lies rather in the insistence that Isaiah is *only* about Jesus, that such a christological reading exhausts the text, that there is no other valid way to understand the Hebrew Scriptures, and therefore that the Jews are simply wrong.

Patte's model illuminates a historic progression from first- to third-level reading practices that can be discerned in the early church. As several studies of the New Testament's use of Scripture have shown, earliest Christian writers display much variety in their appropriations of Scripture, often revealing more interest in explaining the Christian community in terms of Scripture than in explaining Scripture in terms of the Christian community. Though descriptions of Jewish contemporaries by Jesus and the apostles may appear jaded or dismissive, and though the writings indeed bear seeds of discord that will grow in time, it is possible to view many, if not most, of the early New Testament readings of the Hebrew Scriptures as forms of first- and second-level reading.

Before long, however, decided rhetorical differences appear. In his apologetic discourse, *Dialogue with Trypho*,[17] composed in the mid-second century, Justin Martyr not only offers Trypho the Jew lengthy christological interpretations of the prophets but, and more importantly, accuses him of 'perverting and misinterpreting' the Scriptures:

> You do not tremble at God's threats, for you are a people foolish and hard-hearted. 'Therefore, behold, I will proceed to remove this people,' saith the Lord; 'and I will remove them, and destroy the wisdom of the wise, and hide the understanding of the prudent.' Deservedly too: for you

17. 'Dialogue of Justin, Philosopher and Martyr, with Trypho, a Jew', in Alexander Roberts and James Donaldson (eds.), *The Ante-Nicene Fathers: Translations of the Writings of the Fathers down to AD 325*. I. *The Apostolic Fathers: Justin Martyr and Irenaeus* (Grand Rapids, MI: Eerdmans, 1981), pp. 194-270. For a very helpful contextualization of Justin in the larger world of Christian–Jewish debate of the early centuries, see G.N. Stanton, 'Aspects of Early Christian-Jewish Polemic and Apologetic', *NTS* 31 (1985), pp. 377-92.

are neither wise nor prudent, but crafty and unscrupulous; wise only to do evil, but utterly incompetent to know the hidden counsel of God, or the faithful covenant of the Lord, or to find out the everlasting paths.[18]

Trypho's only foolishness, if it could be called that, consists in offering alternative readings of Scripture and pointing out what is contrived or debatable in Justin's christological readings.[19] Such strong words as Justin's may be viewed as mere rhetoric, but his main argument is that the legitimacy of his reading proves the illegitimacy of Trypho's. When alternative readings cannot coexist, third-level, dogmatic reading has clearly set in, with all the social problems that follow in its wake.

Justin's *Dialogue with Trypho* marks only a beginning. After such oppositional discourse appears, it is simply a matter of time before the conversation partner disappears. Justin has the genial but unconverted Trypho saying in the end, 'I have been particularly pleased with the conference' and openmindedly wishing to continue this interfaith Bible study.[20] Apologetic dialogues from later periods ended instead in the Jews seeing the light and converting, and still later, as Frank Manuel points out, 'the Jewish protagonist was often eliminated and the Christian held forth without the impediment of contradiction'.[21] It was not in carrying out a Christian reading of Scripture, but in denying the validity of other readings, that calumny and disdain have expressed themselves. As Nancy Fuchs-Kreimer has noted, what began as rhetoric came to be viewed as if it were incontrovertible fact.[22] The more familiar we become with interpretive history of this sort, the better equipped we are to understand its residue in today's church. Exegesis of the interpretations of influential scholars such as Justin Martyr, John Calvin and Julius Wellhausen can shed at least as much light on what is happening in the advent lectionary, and in the minds of Christians, as exegesis of the prophets themselves. Similarly, familiarity with other texts that

18. 'Dialogue', ch. 123, p. 261.

19. See for instance chs. 51 (pp. 220-21); 79 (p. 238).

20. Ch. 142 (p. 270).

21. Frank Manuel, *The Broken Staff: Judaism through Christian Eyes* (Cambridge: Harvard University Press, 1992), p. 14.

22. Nancy Fuchs-Kreimer, 'Christian Old Testament Theology: A Time for New Beginnings', *JES* 18 (1981), pp. 76-93. In a section entitled, 'From polemic to history', she discusses the unfortunate use of New Testament depictions of Jews and Judaism as the source for historical facts in such widely read works as the *Interpreter's Dictionary of the Bible*.

have for a variety of reasons resisted or ignored messianic interpretations can throw light on the prophets in invigorating new ways. To be
sure, such breadth of reading defies the common categories of specialization to which we have grown accustomed. Yet a cross-disciplinary
approach to Scripture study, in which we collaborate with, learn from,
and share our insights with those who specialize in the documents of
interpretive history, cannot help but enrich not only our understanding
but that of our colleagues as well.[23]

Patte's heuristic categories suggest not only new areas for study, but
a shift in our approach to the teaching of Scripture. The dominant
strategy of Scripture scholars when dealing with students' pre-critical
dogmas has been to fight third-level readings with third-level readings.
We often teach that Scripture ought correctly to be interpreted in terms
of its own time and context, *rather than* christologically, or ecclesiologi-
cally, or typologically, or any other way that is deemed less than
scholarly. To be sure, attention to the originating setting enables readers
to approximate more closely the impact of a text on its first audience, to
understand better the issues the text was made to address, and to avoid
anachronism. Yet the insistence that the text be read *only* in terms of its
original context easily falls prey to the very same fallacy that Justin
Martyr did with Trypho: the assumption that there is only one 'best'
interpretation of a biblical text, that the validity of one reading strategy
necessarily cancels out the validity of all others. In that sense, those
who discredit Jewish interpretation because it does not see Jesus in the
Hebrew Scriptures, and those who discredit christological interpretation
because it does, have more in common with one another than one might
at first think, since both fail to take seriously, on their own terms, competing interpretations. Especially in light of the many ways scholars
have read Scripture over time, a statement that boils down to 'You can't

23. An excellent example of such cross-disciplinary study occurred in the Formation of the Book of Isaiah Group at the 1998 annual meeting of the Society of
Biblical Literature, where Richard Hays investigated the use of Isaiah in Paul's
Romans and Elsie Stern studied its reception in the Haftarah readings of early
Judaism. Both interpretive texts partake generously of the same prior text, Isaiah
49–55. Yet by creative highlighting and shifting, the two interpretations create
completely different characterizations of Israel, depending upon the apologetic
needs of the two communities. See Richard Hays, '"Who Has Believed our
Message?": Paul's Reading of Isaiah', *SBLSP* 37 (1998), pp. 205-25; and Elsie
Stern, 'Beyond *Nahamu*: Strategies of Consolation in the Jewish Lectionary Cycle
for the Ninth of Av Season', *SBLSP* 37 (1998), pp. 180-204.

read that way, because I read this way' is as problematic in a modern classroom as it was in Justin's conversations. Students who agree with the notion that a text can only be interpreted in one way, but who happen to prefer a christological reading, will simply reject the methods and results of modern critical exegesis.

But the fact that critical interpretations fail to convince all listeners is not their only problem. By dwelling only on authorial setting, histori-cal-critical exegesis skirts the crucial question of how messianic readings arose in the first place. However it came about that early Christians began to see Jesus whenever they gazed upon Scripture, their doing so reflects a reality that historical critics often overlook: that is, that if Isaiah could only be profitably heard in terms of his own times, then the very next generation would not have bothered to read him. The interpretive impulse of reactivating scriptural words in ways unantici-pated by the original writers did not begin with early Christians, but is, as redaction critics have been claiming for years, inherent in the com-position of the prophetic books themselves.[24]

The very property of Scripture that has enabled it to adapt with suppleness to successive generations—its inexhaustible plethora of potential readings—also insures that diverse interpretations will arise simultaneously. Only on the third level of reading do these become mutually exclusive. Just as theorists of Christian–Jewish relations envision Judaism and Christianity as sibling descendents of the same parent religion, so also the Scriptures themselves have spawned multi-ple, sibling interpretations. As emerging Judaism and emerging Christianity defined themselves, each sought guidance in Scripture, one community finding in the Torah a paradigm for religious devotion, and the other finding in the same Torah warrant to reshape its message for Gentiles. Those of us who wish to open the minds of Christians to the

24. Michael Fishbane's work on inner-biblical exegesis provides helpful con-ceptual tools for comprehending the contours of the interpretive process. See especially his *Biblical Interpretation in Ancient Israel* (Oxford: Clarendon Press, 1985). Grounding in intertextual theory as it relates to the reading and misreading of authoritative texts can be instructive both for understanding inner-biblical exegesis and for reading post-biblical interpretive texts. On intertexual theory as an exegetical tool, see my *Remember the Former Things: The Recollection of Previous Texts in Second Isaiah* (SBLDS, 161; Atlanta: Scholars Press, 1997), esp. ch. 2, and 'Rhetorical Criticism and Intertextuality', in S. McKenzie and S. Haynes (eds.), *To Each its Own Meaning* (Louisville, KY: Westminster/John Knox Press, rev. edn, 1999), pp. 156-80.

richness of scriptural interpretation in the two traditions must mold our own teaching to make room for such richness in the classroom itself, to live graciously even with readings that threaten our own, and thus to create a microcosm of interpretive tolerance. By acceptance rather than rejection, we can teach students in the seminary and church to explore their own interpretations, raise them from first to second-level readings, refine them, inquire into the exegetical, theological and philosophical assumptions that contribute to them, project the ethical implications of claiming them, and compare them with other readings.

To summarize, the more we know the journeys that Scripture has taken over time, the better equipped we are to help heal the damage done by our forebears. If we can draw distinctions between the original desire to view the church in continuity with the prophets and the more exclusive claim that the prophets were somehow proto-Christians, we may be able to help the church work backward through its interpretive levels, to appreciate reinterpretation, its richness and its dangers. If we ourselves can model respect for multiplicity in interpretation, we may well be able to introduce other readings of the prophets *alongside of* messianic readings. Not by taking away readings, but by adding to them, we would invite Christians to explore other streams of interpretation, and help worship leaders imagine alternatives to the prophecy-fulfillment model, alternatives that could even influence lectionary and liturgical materials for the next generation of Christians.

III

One evening not long ago, at a conference for Christian–Jewish dialogue in Connecticut, a gospel choir sang the hallelujah chorus from Handel's Messiah: 'Hallelujah! For the Lord God omnipotent reigneth!' As an onlooker who habitually brought to such events a hermeneutics of nervousness, I couldn't believe it was happening. What I further couldn't believe was that the huge auditorium of Jews and Christians began singing along: 'And he shall reign forever and ever!' The rabbi in front of me was nearly standing on his chair in enthusiasm: 'The kingdom of this world is become the kingdom of our Lord, and of his Christ, and of his Christ!'

I would have given anything to have been authorized to stand at the door afterward and conduct exit interviews to find out what that song meant to the various people singing it. At the very least I thought that

Jews who come to such conferences are prepared to be as forgiving toward good musicians as Trypho was toward enthusiastic rhetoricians. But if anyone had asked me, I would have had to conclude that the moment seemed like an eschatological foretaste of a day when the many symbols that the two religions share, such as the messiah and the reign of God, are no longer hotspots of interpretive strife but instead many colored, many textured, many layered symbols of our deepest shared hopes.

ISAIAH AND THEODICY AFTER THE *SHOAH**

Marvin A. Sweeney

Isaiah is generally recognized as one of the most progressive books of
the prophetic corpus. It portrays YHWH's world-wide sovereignty, and
calls upon the nations to join Israel at Zion in order to inaugurate an age
of universal peace in which YHWH's Torah would be taught to all.[1]
Both Judaism and Christianity see in Isaiah an affirmation of some of
the most positive and cherished aspects of their respective world views.
Christianity sees in Isaiah a prophet who points to an age when all the
world will recognize Jesus Christ as the suffering servant who brings
about an age of universal salvation.[2] Judaism views Isaiah as a book of
comfort that points to the centrality of Jerusalem and Torah as the basis
for cosmic order and peace.[3] Both traditions clearly view Isaiah as a
representation of an ideal world.

Nevertheless, Isaiah presents some very troubling aspects of divine
sovereignty that challenge fundamental notions of YHWH's righteousness, particularly in the aftermath of the Shoah. The book presents a

*   Various versions of this article were read at the Claremont Colloquium on
Philosophy of Religion and Theology (October, 1997), the Annual Meeting of the
National Association of Professors of Hebrew, San Francisco (November, 1997),
the Annual Meeting of the Association for Jewish Studies, Boston (December,
1997), and Temple Beth Israel, Pomona, California (October, 1998). I would like to
express my appreciation to Professors Anselm Min (Claremont Graduate
University), Zev Garber (Los Angeles Valley College), and Jon D. Levenson
(Harvard Divinity School), as well as the Adult Education Committee of Temple
Beth Israel for their invitations to present these papers.

1.   For a full analysis of the book of Isaiah, see my *Isaiah 1–39, with an Introduction to Prophetic Literature* (FOTL, 16; Grand Rapids, MI: Eerdmans, 1996).

2.   For example, James A. Sanders, 'Isaiah in Luke', *Int* 36 (1982), pp. 144-55.

3.   Thus the Babylonian Talmud, *B. Bat.* 14b, which states that Isaiah speaks
entirely of comfort. See further, Marvin A. Sweeney, 'The Book of Isaiah as
Prophetic Torah', in Roy F. Melugin and Marvin A. Sweeney (eds.), *New Visions of
Isaiah* (Sheffield: Sheffield Academic Press, 1996), pp. 50-67.

scenario of judgment against Israel in which YHWH calls upon nations to act as agents of divine punishment. Although the punishment is presented as a corrective measure intended to lead to the universal peace presented at the beginning of the book, Isaiah makes it very clear that YHWH allows no repentance for those who are to be punished. Throughout the book, YHWH identifies with the imperial conqueror, and consigns Israel to a punishment from which it is unable to escape. By identifying Israel's sin as a refusal to recognize YHWH, Isaiah blames the victims of conquest for their suffering. Even at the end of the book, the inaugural vision is not realized as YHWH continues to call for punishment of the wicked.

This issue is particularly important in light of recent critical discussion that calls for a unified reading of the final form of Isaiah.[4] Whereas past scholarship could ignore or overlook this issue by arguing that selected texts need not be considered as they were later additions, a unified reading of the book places the question of theodicy at the forefront. Indeed, the final form of Isaiah must be considered as a deliberate presentation of the issue. This article therefore treats three major dimensions of the question of theodicy in Isaiah: YHWH's identification with the conqueror, YHWH's decree of judgment against Israel without the possibility of repentance, and the failure of YHWH's program to be realized by the end of the book. I argue that Isaiah does indeed recognize the problem of theodicy, and offers a critique of YHWH's sovereignty that calls upon the reader to challenge both YHWH and her/himself to take responsibility for doing justice.

I

The book of Isaiah consistently identifies YHWH with the nations that conquered Israel throughout the eighth–sixth centuries BCE, that is, Assyria, Babylonia and Persia. YHWH's identification with the imperial conqueror is especially clear in Isaiah 40–55, in which Deutero-Isaiah names Cyrus as YHWH's anointed monarch or messiah:

> Thus says YHWH to his anointed, to Cyrus, whose right hand I have grasped,
> to subdue nations before him and ungird the loins of kings,

4. For a survey of recent critical discussion on Isaiah, see my 'The Book of Isaiah in Recent Research', *Currents in Research: Biblical Studies* 1 (1993), pp. 141-62.

to open doors before him that gates may not be closed:
'I will go before you and level the mountains,
I will break in pieces the doors of bronze and cut asunder the bars of
    iron,
I will give you the treasures of darkness and hoards in secret places,
that you may know that it is I, YHWH, the G-d of Israel,
who call you by your name' (Isa. 45.1-3).

Cyrus is well known as the king of Persia (ruling 550–530 BCE), who conquered Babylon peacefully in 539 BCE after securing the support of the priests of Marduk.[5] He is likewise known as the benevolent ruler who decreed that Jews be allowed to return to their homeland from Babylonian exile and to rebuild the Temple in Jerusalem. Cyrus was recognized as king of Babylonia when he participated in the Babylonian Akitu or New Year Festival in which the gods of the cities and nations that comprise the Babylonian empire and the king processed around the city to the ziggurat Etamenanki to recognize Marduk's sovereignty over creation and the nations of the world and to reaffirm the king's right to rule as the human agent of Marduk's will.[6] During the ceremony, the king 'seized the hand of Marduk' as a sign of his submission to the deity and received a royal oracle and the 'tablets of destiny', which enabled him to rule. Indeed, these features appear in Deutero-Isaiah's oracles, which refer to Cyrus as YHWH's 'shepherd' and 'anointed', YHWH's grasping the hand of Cyrus to subdue nations, and the granting of the 'treasures of darkness'.

It is clear that the Babylonian Akitu festival has greatly influenced Deutero-Isaiah's presentation of YHWH, and that the prophet has melded motifs from the Akitu festival with those drawn from Israelite tradition.[7] Deutero-Isaiah clearly articulates YHWH's role as the creator who puts the world in order by defeating the sea dragon Rahab, much as the Babylonian epic Enuma Elish portrays Marduk as the creator who slays Tiamat, the chaos dragon of the sea.[8] Deutero-Isaiah

---

5. For discussion of Cyrus and the Persian empire, see Pierre Briant, 'Persian Empire', *ABD* 5, pp. 236-44.

6. See Jacob Klein, 'Akitu', *ABD* 1, pp. 138-40.

7. For Deutero-Isaiah's use of motifs from the Akitu festival see, e.g., Isaiah 46, and the comments by R.N. Whybray, *Isaiah 40–66* (NCB; Grand Rapids, MI: Eerdmans, 1975), pp. 113-18.

8. See Isa. 51. For a translation of the Enuma Elish, see James B. Pritchard (ed.), *Ancient Near Eastern Texts Relating to the Old Testament* (3rd edn with supplement; Princeton: Princeton University Press, 1969), pp. 60-72.

portrays the submission of the nations to YHWH as they come in sup-
plication to Israel and await YHWH's justice and law, much as the gods
in the Akitu festival acknowledge Marduk and accept the sovereignty of
the Babylonian king. The polemical aspects are clear as the Babylonian
gods are portrayed in procession, bowing under the weight of their bur-
dens, in contrast to YHWH who calls upon Cyrus to rule them.[9]
Throughout Deutero-Isaiah, YHWH announces the coming of Cyrus
and the restoration of Jerusalem as divine acts that demonstrate
YHWH's sovereignty over all creation. In short, Deutero-Isaiah identifies YHWH with the imperial power of Persia.

Until recently, Deutero-Isaiah has been read by critical scholars in
isolation from the rest of the book as they correctly claim that Isaiah
40–55 represent the distinctive work of an anonymous exilic prophet.[10]
Deutero-Isaiah's portrayal of YHWH's sovereignty and Israel's redemption is generally understood as the triumph of good over evil as the
oppression of Babylon comes to an end. Although Isaiah 1–39 and 56–
66 appear to derive largely from the eighth-century prophet Isaiah ben
Amoz and the anonymous sixth- and fifth-century writings referred to
as Trito-Isaiah, they, too, presuppose the identification of YHWH with
the Persian empire in their present form. Both Isa. 2.2-4 and 60-62
portray the nations streaming to Zion in order to recognize YHWH's
sovereignty and to receive YHWH's justice and law, and correspond
well to the identification of YHWH's sovereignty with the rise of the
Persian empire.

The oracles concerning the nations in Isaiah 13–23 likewise point to
the identification of YHWH's sovereignty with the Persian empire.[11]
Many interpreters mistakenly identify the prophetic oracles concerning
the nations with an eschatological portrayal of worldwide judgment, but
the nations represented in Isaiah 13–23 do not constitute a universal
portrayal of all the nations of the world. Persia is notably missing, and
the nations that are represented—Babylon, Assyria, Philistia, Moab,
Aram and Israel, Ethiopia and Egypt, the Wilderness of the Sea (i.e.
Babylon), Dumah (Edom), Arabia, the Valley of Vision (Jerusalem),
and Tyre—are all nations or territories that were conquered and incorporated into the Persian empire. Indeed, Isa. 21.2 presents Elam and
Media, two components of the larger Persian empire, as the nations that

9.   Contrast Isa. 46 with Isa. 44–45.
10.   For discussion, see Sweeney, *Isaiah 1–39*, pp. 31-62.
11.   Sweeney, *Isaiah 1–39*, pp. 212-17.

lay siege to Babylon. YHWH's treatment of the nations constitutes a fundamental theme of the book that must be considered together with YHWH's treatment of Israel. Both constitute aspects of YHWH's identification with the imperial power of Persia.

II

The second major dimension of theodicy in Isaiah, YHWH's decree of judgment against Israel without any possibility of repentance, is a key element in the first half of the book, whereas the second half of Isaiah presupposes that the punishment has been realized and the time of restoration is at hand. The grounds for judgment are clearly articulated throughout chs. 1–33: Israel and Judah have arrogantly failed to recognize YHWH as the sovereign who determines world events, have abused the rights of the poor, have turned to foreign gods and nations for assistance in times of crisis, and so on.

The key text concerning the theme of YHWH's judgment is Isaiah 6, in which the prophet sees a vision of YHWH enthroned in the Temple and surrounded by Seraphim who announce YHWH's holy presence throughout the world.[12] The setting is the Holy of Holies in the Jerusalem Temple where the ark of the covenant resides under the protection of the Cherubim as a symbol of YHWH's sovereignty. The imagery is clearly royal. The Seraphim, a representation of the Cherubim in the Holy of Holies, constitute the royal entourage. Indeed, the ark is conceived as the throne of YHWH or the footstool of the throne (Ps. 99.1; 1 Sam. 4.4; 2 Sam. 6.2; 2 Kgs 19.15; Isa. 37.16; 1 Chron. 13.6; cf. Ps. 132.7; Isa. 66.1). The theme of judgment suggests that the occasion for the passage is the observance of Yom Kippur, the Day of Atonement, when the high priest appears before YHWH in the Holy of Holies to atone for the sins of the people (Lev. 16). Overall, the presentation of YHWH is modeled on that of the Davidic king seated on his throne passing judgment on his subjects (1 Kgs 3.16-28; cf. 2 Sam. 12.1-15).

When the Deity asks, 'Whom shall I send, and who will go for us?' Isaiah responds that he will go. YHWH commissions him to speak a message of irrevocable judgment:

---

12. For discussion, see Sweeney, *Isaiah 1–39*, pp. 132-42.

Go and say to this people:
'Hear and hear, but do not understand; see and see but do not perceive.'
Make the heart of this people fat, and their ears heavy, and shut their
  eyes;
lest they see with their eyes, and hear with their ears, and understand
  with their hearts,
and turn and be healed.

When Isaiah asks how long this situation will last, YHWH responds:

Until cities lie waste without inhabitant, and houses without people,
and the land is utterly desolate, and YHWH removes people far away,
and the forsaken places are many in the midst of the land.
And though a tenth remain in it, it will be burned again, like a terebinth
  or an oak,
whose stump remains standing when it is felled.
The holy seed is its stump.

Perhaps the most striking feature of the message is YHWH's pro-
nouncement that the prophet is to make sure that they do not understand
the message so that they will not repent and thereby avoid the punishment. This stands in stunning contrast to other passages which call upon
the people to change their ways (e.g. Isa. 1.10-17); indeed, a major
thrust of Isaiah's message is to make known YHWH's intention to
bring punishment. One would have to conclude that Isaiah either
deliberately refused to carry out his commission, or that he tried to do
so and failed. Scholars generally maintain that the passage is a later
composition, either by the prophet or by a later writer, that reflects upon
the significance of Israel's experience in light of the prophet's message.

It is instructive in this regard to examine Isaiah 7, the narrative concerning Isaiah's confrontation with King Ahaz at the time of the Syro-
Ephraimitic War, as this chapter constitutes a primary illustration in
Isaiah as to why this decree of punishment must take place.[13] The
historical setting of this encounter is 'in the days of Ahaz' when Aram
and Israel attacked Judah for its refusal to join the Syro-Ephraimitic
coalition against Assyria. The chapter notes Ahaz's fear in this situation—he has no allies to turn to for protection—and portrays him
inspecting his water system, the key to the defenses of Jerusalem, when
Isaiah meets him together with his son Shear-Yashub, that is, 'a remnant shall return'. The boy's name symbolizes the survival of a portion
of the people in the face of the Syro-Ephraimitic attack, and underlies

13. Sweeney, *Isaiah 1–39*, pp. 143-64.

the prophet's message that Ahaz should rely solely on YHWH to deliver him in this time of crisis. The prophet concludes his remarks with the statement, 'If you do not believe, surely you will not be established,' which conveys the ideology of YHWH's faithful promise of security to the faithful David.

Apparently, the young king has some doubts about a promise of protection that requires him to do nothing while his people are decimated. The prophet calls upon Ahaz to 'ask a sign of YHWH your G-d; let it be as deep as Sheol or high as heaven'. Ahaz declines to test YHWH, and responds, 'I will not ask, and I will not put YHWH to the test'. Interpreters tend to understand Ahaz's response to Isaiah as an indication of his lack of faith in YHWH's promise of protection.[14] This understanding is reinforced not only by the prophet's reaction in the Isaiah narrative, but by the account of Ahaz's reign in 2 Kings 16 which relates his request for assistance to Tiglath Pileser III and his forced submission to Assyria after the Assyrians rescued Judah by defeating Israel and Aram. Ahaz's actions stand in contrast to those of his son Hezekiah later in the book: whereas Ahaz refused YHWH's protection and saw his country punished by the Assyrians as a result, Hezekiah turns to YHWH in Isaiah 36–37 at the time of Sennacherib's invasion and sees YHWH's miraculous deliverance of Jerusalem. Hezekiah is the model of piety in Isaiah, but Ahaz is the faithless goat who richly deserves his punishment.[15]

Nevertheless, several aspects of this presentation are quite disturbing in relation to the issue of theodicy. First is the prophet's proposal that Ahaz should accept the decimation of his people. Why should Ahaz's faith in YHWH require that his people die?

Secondly, Ahaz's response to Isaiah actually is a model of piety, 'I will not ask, and I will not put YHWH to the test.' Ahaz refuses to question YHWH, and thereby to express doubts about his G-d. In all fairness to Ahaz, he probably considered his strategy of appealing to Assyria for assistance as consistent with his faith in YHWH's protec-

14. See, for example, the discussion by Hans Wildberger, *Isaiah 1–12* (Continental Commentaries; trans. Thomas H. Trapp; Minneapolis: Fortress Press, 1991), pp. 302-18.

15. For an insightful comparison and contrast between the presentations of the two kings in Isaiah, see especially, Peter Ackroyd, 'Isaiah 36–39: Structure and Function', in *Studies in the Religious Tradition of the Old Testament* (London: SCM Press, 1987), pp. 105-20, 274-78.

tion. Ahaz's assessment would turn out to be wrong, but there is no evidence that Ahaz intended to do evil or lacked faith in YHWH; he simply understood it differently than did Isaiah.

Finally, the presentation of Hezekiah in Isaiah 36–39 raises serious questions. In contrast to Ahaz, Hezekiah is generally understood to present a model of piety in the book of Isaiah that aids in introducing the message of salvation in the second part of the book.[16] Like Ahaz, Hezekiah suffers the invasion of his own country and the siege of Jerusalem resulting in the loss of many thousands of Judean lives. But unlike Ahaz, Hezekiah recognizes his error in trying to oppose the Assyrians, and turns to YHWH for help. He receives YHWH's response through the prophet Isaiah that YHWH will defeat the Assyrians for their arrogance and deliver Hezekiah and Jerusalem. It would seem that Hezekiah's repentance constitutes what YHWH requires in the book of Isaiah, but Hezekiah is ultimately unable to deliver his people as well. The narrative concerning Sennacherib's siege in Isaiah 36–37 is part of a larger block in Isaiah 36–39 which relates two other events that took place prior to the siege: Hezekiah's sickness in Isaiah 38 and the Babylonian embassy to Jerusalem in Isaiah 39. Hezekiah demonstrates his faith in YHWH in Isaiah 38, but in Isaiah 39 Hezekiah receives the ambassadors of the Babylonian prince, Merodach Baladan, who is apparently his ally in revolt against Sennacherib. When Isaiah hears that Hezekiah has received the Babylonians and shown them his storehouses, he condemns Hezekiah and tells him that his wealth and his sons will some day be carried off to Babylon, an apparent reference to future Babylonian exile. Isaiah 39 indicates that Judah and Hezekiah are already condemned. Although Hezekiah wins respite for the surviving remnant of Sennacherib's siege, his people will ultimately suffer the Babylonian exile. Hezekiah's piety does not deliver Israel from punishment.[17]

In sum, Isaiah makes it very clear that YHWH's judgment against

16. See Peter Ackroyd, 'An Interpretation of the Babylonian Exile: A Study of II Kings 20 and Isaiah 38–39', in *Studies in the Religious Tradition of the Old Testament*, pp. 152-71, 282-85; Christopher R. Seitz, 'The Divine Council: Temporal Transition and New Prophecy in the Book of Isaiah', *JBL* 109 (1990), pp. 229-47.

17. According to the Babylonian Talmud, *Sanh.* 94a, G-d wished to appoint Hezekiah as the Messiah, but the Attribute of Justice protested that David was more entitled.

Israel is irrevocable. Israel is set up to fail so that its experience may demonstrate YHWH's sovereignty.

III

The third major aspect of theodicy in Isaiah, the failure to realize the initial portrayal of world peace, once again raises questions concerning YHWH's sovereignty, power and righteousness. The problem is signaled at the outset of Deutero-Isaiah's writings:

> Comfort, comfort my people, says your G-d. Speak tenderly to Jerusalem,
> and cry to her that her warfare is ended, that her iniquity is pardoned,
> that she has received from YHWH's hand double for all her sins (Isa. 40.1-2).

This statement indicates that the punishment of Jerusalem's sin is complete. Indeed, the reference to receiving double for all her sins recalls the punishment for theft in Exod. 21.37, that is, a thief is required to pay double for what is stolen. The writings of Deutero-Isaiah presuppose throughout that the punishment of Israel is over. As a result, Israel is to be restored to Jerusalem and the nations will recognize YHWH's sovereignty. Isaiah 55 applies the eternal covenant of David to Israel at large, and commissions Israel to serve as a witness to YHWH's sovereignty:

> Incline your ear and come to me; hear that your soul may live;
> and I will make with you an everlasting covenant, my steadfast, sure love for David.
> Behold, I made him a witness to the peoples, a leader and commander to the peoples.
> Behold, you shall call nations that you know not,
> and nations that knew you not shall run to you
> because of YHWH your G-d, and the Holy One of Israel,
> for he has glorified you (Isa. 55.3-5).

The balance of the passage calls upon the reader to seek YHWH, and the material in Trito-Isaiah defines the means by which foreigners may join YHWH prior to the presentation of the nations streaming to Zion to restore the exiles in Isaiah 60–62. Obviously, this material functions in the present form of the book to point to the realization of the initial vision of world peace.

But as the reader moves through Isaiah 56–66, it becomes increasingly evident that there are obstacles to this realization. These chapters portray the righteous who perish and the frustration of YHWH's intentions to forgive as the wicked continue in their sins. They announce the transgression of the people, and portray YHWH preparing to slaughter the wicked among both the nations and Israel. By the end of the book, YHWH impotently states,

> I was ready to be sought by those who did not ask for me;
> I was ready to be found by those who did not seek me.
> I said, 'Here I am, here I am,' to a nation that did not call on my name
> (Isa. 65.1).

The concluding verse of the book makes it clear that the punishment is not yet complete:

> And they shall go forth and look on the dead bodies
> of the men that have rebelled against me;
> for their worm shall not die, their fire shall not be quenched,
> and they shall be an abhorrence to all flesh (Isa. 66.24).

One may legitimately ask, 'What happened?' The end of the Babylonian exile and the accession of Cyrus to the Babylonian throne was supposed to signal YHWH's sovereignty. Historically, one might cite the turmoil of the Persian empire during the late sixth and fifth centuries, when Darius I and later monarchs were faced with continued warfare that belied the expectations of world peace during the reign of Cyrus.[18] Just as YHWH is identified with the successes and downfalls of previous conquerors, so YHWH is identified with the difficulties faced by the Persians during these years. It is the price of linking YHWH too closely to the vagaries of world empires and events. When the empire fails, so does YHWH. One might argue theologically that in fact Israel's sin and that of the nations was not complete, and that further punishment was necessary to purify the world for the manifestation of YHWH's sovereignty.[19] But this requires the conclusion that YHWH was mistaken in the statements of Deutero-Isaiah.

These considerations reveal a disturbing facit of YHWH's sovereignty in Isaiah, namely, YHWH failed to achieve the aims set out at the

18. See Briant, 'Persian Empire'.

19. See, for example, Paul Hanson, *The Dawn of Apocalyptic: The Historical and Sociological Roots of Jewish Apocalyptic Eschatology* (Philadelphia: Fortress Press, 1975), pp. 161-86, who reads this passage in relation to a larger conflict between hypothesized visionary and priestly parties who charged each other with evil as they attempted to control postexilic Judaism.

beginning of the book. YHWH's identification with the imperial power
of the conqueror is too constraining. It limits YHWH to the success or
failure of empire, and renders YHWH wrong when the empire fails.
The book attempts to meet this challenge by pointing to the future
realization of the promise, but it can only do so by positing the
continuous sin of the people. In the end, Isaiah blames the victims for
their victimization.[20]

IV

One might conclude from this discussion that Isaiah's presentation of
YHWH's interaction with Israel is a theology of failure, but this leads
us to a further aspect of the book's theology, namely that the success of
the program outlined in the book of Isaiah requires that human beings
serve as responsible partners with YHWH. From the perspective of
Isaiah, human beings did not accept that responsibility.[21]

At the outset, one might claim that this failure is evident in the
refusal to recognize YHWH's sovereignty; after all, this is a constant
theme of the book. But one must ask why Israel does not recognize
YHWH. The answer seems clear: YHWH is identified with the imperial
conqueror throughout the book, and as each empire fails, so does
YHWH. This might suggest a great deal of frustration on the part of
Isaiah's various writers as they point to the continued rejection of
YHWH, but perhaps they or we misconstrue an essential aspect of the
book. What does constitute responsible human action in the book of
Isaiah?

Ahaz and Isaiah present two very instructive cases. As noted above,
Ahaz responds to Isaiah's demand that he test YHWH with the statement, 'I will not ask, and I will not put YHWH to the test.' Ahaz
appears to know full well that Isaiah's or YHWH's proposal will cost
many Judean lives. It is striking, however, that Ahaz does not challenge

---

20. Cf. Richard Rubenstein, *After Auschwitz: Radical Theology and Contemporary Judaism* (Indianapolis: Bobbs-Merrill, 1966), who argues that traditional
Jewish and Christian concepts of a moral G-d must be abandoned in the aftermath
of the Shoah in part because such theologies lead to the conclusion that suffering is
caused by moral failing.

21. For discussion of the notion that the Shoah was the result of the failure by
human beings to exercise full responsibility for the world of creation, see Eliezer
Berkovitz, *Faith after the Holocaust* (New York: Ktav, 1973).

Isaiah or protest, but simply mouths empty piety. Other figures in the Bible do not seem to have this problem. Amos asks that YHWH spare Jacob (Amos 7.1-3, 4-6), Job challenges YHWH when injustice is visited upon him (Job 31), Moses challenges G-d when G-d proposes to destroy Israel in the wilderness (Exod. 33; Num. 14), and Abraham demands that the judge of all the earth do justice when he thinks that YHWH is willing to kill righteous and wicked alike (Gen. 18). Not only was Ahaz wrong because his course of action led to Assyrian hegemony over Judah, he was wrong because he failed to confront blatant injustice. The reader of Isaiah will never know what might have happened if Ahaz said no, but it is very clear what happened when he declined to do so.

Much the same may be said of Isaiah. When he stood before YHWH and heard YHWH's decree that he was to prevent the people from understanding their sin and repenting, his only response was 'How long?' He does not protest YHWH's decision or ask that YHWH change it. Again, Abraham, Amos and Job challenged YHWH when they thought that YHWH was wrong, and each received what they sought: reprieve for the righteous, respite for Jacob, and YHWH's response. The results for Isaiah are not so promising; by the end of the book, YHWH's program of judgment still has not succeeded in attaining its goals. One may only speculate as to what the outcome of a challenge might have been.

In conclusion, it appears that the book of Isaiah deliberately posits the problem of theodicy in order to elicit a human response. It presents YHWH as an imperial monarch who unjustly decrees judgment without the possibility of repentance, and who subsequently fails to realize the goals for world peace and absolute sovereignty set out at the beginning of the book. By presenting major figures whose piety prevents them from challenging YHWH's decree, the book of Isaiah presents a critique of the conception of YHWH as absolute monarch and the uncritical acceptance of divine (or human) royal authority. YHWH's demands for justice throughout the book of Isaiah include the obligation to demand justice, like Abraham in Genesis 18, from YHWH.[22]

---

22. Cf. David Blumenthal, *Facing the Abusing G-d: A Theology of Protest* (Louisville: Westminster/John Knox Press, 1993), who argues that G-d must be viewed as an abusive parent whom the victims of abuse must learn to confront and ultimately to forgive.

THE COVENANT WITH DEATH

Francis Landy

For we have made a covenant with Death...and in Falsehood we have concealed ourselves (Isa. 28.15).

I once knew a madman who thought the end of the world had come. He was a painter—and engraver. I had a great fondness for him. I used to go and see him, in the asylum. I'd take him by the hand and drag him to the window. Look! There! All that rising corn! And there! Look! The sails of herring fleet! All that loveliness! (*Pause*). He'd snatch away his hand and go back into his corner. Appalled. All he had seen was ashes (Samuel Beckett, *Endgame*).

To ride on a bay trotting horse over four-inched bridges (Shakespeare, *King Lear* III.iv.55).

To make, literally in Hebrew to 'cut', a covenant with Death, to seal and demarcate a haven of immunity, immortality, 'the surging scourge when it passes through will not reach us' (Isa. 28.15), while at the same time to commit oneself to Death, the master, 'the Master from Germany',[1] that is our dearest bliss and profoundest irony. For no one can make a covenant with Death, which is nonetheless our most intimate companion, and the transactions and deferments with which are the condition for our lives, always temporary, always on credit.

We incorporate our deaths, make sense of them and thus ourselves, talk to them and humanize them. Death is that which makes one human, according to Hegel. And this is our greatest illusion. For death is that which does not speak, at least to us, which can only be incorporated, as a silent companion, object of fear, fantasy, decomposition, as a dead weight.[2] Death also as unspeakable, as a transcendent of language, and

---

1. The phrase is from Paul Celan's poem, 'Todesfuge'. In the background of Celan's phrase is Hegel's account of death as the 'sovereign Master'.

2. Julia Kristeva, *Black Sun: Depression and Melancholia* (trans. L.S. Roudiez; New York: Columbia University Press, 1989), p. 4, describes death as 'the inner threshold' of depression, identified with the original mother from whom the infant must separate to survive.

humanity. Which turns our life into death.[3] 'Death strolls between letters', says Jacques Derrida in one of his early essays. Death is that which cannot be written, which intervenes in the gaps, the silences, between words and letters, attests to the discontinuity in Being and in God. Every writer, in passing from one letter to the next, from one thought and metaphor to the next, risks the encounter with death. 'To write…assumes an access to the mind through having the courage to lose one's life, to die away from nature.'[4]

And poetry? Poetry that speaks the truth? What interests me here is poetry that breaks with the conventions of poetic language, the weight of what is known and expected, to speak for that which is unknown and unrepresented and to listen, as Heidegger puts it, to the rift in being,[5] a civilization or person, to that place where death enters. The entirely new, unaccommodated and terrifying. 'Desist from human being, in whose nostril is breath, for in what is it thought?' (Isa. 2.22).

Mass death, the death of a culture, a people, of humanity, differs from our personal death, not in the obvious ways—the impersonality, the loss of continuity, the destruction of the community in which death is understood and ritualized as part of life—but in its inversion of all human values. Edith Wyschogrod, in her remarkable book *Spirit in Ashes*, says that in the death world all language has the significance of death. 'On the one hand, all the patterns of the life-world as we understand them persist… *But at the same time the signifier is also and always death.*'[6] Language speaks for and of death, is only a translation, a metaphor, of the language of death. 'Names which…seem the traces, each one, of another language, at once disappeared and never pronounced, which we cannot restore without reintroducing them into the

3. D.W. Winnicott, *Playing and Reality* (London: Tavistock/Routledge, 1991), p. 65, writes about the kind of person for whom the environment is so unsupportive that he or she is unable to live creatively. For such a person it does not matter if they are alive or dead (p. 69).

4. Jacques Derrida, *Writing and Difference* (trans. Alan Bass; London: Routledge & Kegan Paul, 1978), p. 71. Likewise, Kristeva, *Black Sun*, p. 26, sees the impress of the death drive and the lost, maternal object in the 'blanks of discourse' characteristic especially of depressed speech.

5. Being, for Heidegger, is an abyss, at least in this age which Heidegger regards as destitute (*Poetry, Language, Thought* [trans. Albert Hofstadter; New York: Harper Collins, 1975], pp. 91, 97). Only song reaches into the abyss.

6. Edith Wyschogrod, *Spirit in Ashes: Hegel, Heidegger, and Man-Made Mass Death* (New Haven: Yale University Press, 1985), p. 31. Italics in original.

world.'[7] A poet's words are haunted by what they cannot say, by the echo of the mirror in which language dissolves. From this side Paul Celan writes 'es sind/noch Lieder zu singen jenseits/der Menschen' ('there are/still songs to sing on the other side/of humanity').[8] Every word is negated, canceled, in the language of death. But the poem also speaks in and across the disaster, the chasm in world and self, between the thought and what cannot be, or has not yet been, thought. Between the exhausted, corrupt debris of the world, and the unimagined. Hélène Cixous writes that the poets she loves are those who 'look straight at the face of God',[9] which is to die, or at least to face death. Such a poet, of course, is Isaiah. Let us quote Cixous again: 'All great texts begin in this manner that *breaks*. They break with our thought habits, with the world around us, in an extreme violence that is due to rapidity. They hurl us off to foreign countries.'[10] Celan writes that the poem speaks in the inmost concern of an other, the Other. The other who may be God, or (as Celan says) the infinite, or death. In any case, the poem imparts estrangement, self-estrangement. There is a null point at its centre, which may be death, or the interface between life and death.

In Celan's celebrated poem, 'Psalm', death—the death of holocaust victims, but also of all of us, the death of the death-event—is uncreation. It returns us to that which precedes creation:

> Niemand knetet uns wieder aus Erde und Lehm,
> niemand bespricht unsern Staub.
> Niemand.
> (No one moulds us again from earth and clay,/no one conjures up our
> dust/No one.)

We are created by no one, spoken by no one into existence, the union of dust and breath of God with which creation began is now that of dust, and nothing, absence. The dust (*Staub*) is also the filament (*Staubfaden*) with which we pollinate, in the language of poetry, in the waste of heaven (*Himmelswüst*),[11] the reflex of primordial chaos. We are

7. Maurice Blanchot, *The Writing of the Disaster* (trans. Ann Smock; Lincoln: University of Nebraska Press, 1986), pp. 95-96.

8. From 'Faddensonnen'.

9. Hélène Cixous, *Three Steps on the Ladder of Writing* (trans. Sarah Cornell and Susan Sellers; Ithaca: Cornell University Press, 1993), p. 63.

10. Cixous, *Three Steps*, p. 59.

11. The allusions to Genesis throughout the poem suggest a reversion to the 'waste and void' (in German, *wüst und leer*) of Gen. 1.2. The resurrection of the dead

nothing ('A nothing/ we were, are shall/remain'), nothing and no one speaks through us, the 'Nothing and/No-one's rose' ('die Nichts, die/ Niemandsrose').

Of nothing one can say nothing, 'Nothing will come of nothing.' Celan's poetry is characterized not only by progressive ellipsis and constriction, the breach in self and world,

> Die Posaunenstelle
> tief im glühende
> Leertext,
> in Fackelhöhe,
> im Zeitloch:
> (The trumpet part/deep in the glowing/lacuna/at lamp height/in the time
> hole)

but also by iteration of words signifying nothing:

> In der Mandel—was steht in der Mandel?
> Das Nichts.
> Es steht das Nichts in der Mandel.
> Da steht es und steht[12]
> ('Mandorla')
> (In the almond—what dwells in the almond?/ Nothing./ What dwells in
> the almond is Nothing/ There it dwells and dwells).

Language disintegrates ('*Pallaksch. Pallaksch*')[13] and is inverted. In the conversation with Nelly Sachs, ascension ('*Himmelfahrt*') is also Treblinka.[14]

To go back to 'Psalm'. The psalm, the language of praise ('Praised be you/No one') of the 'No one's rose' is the crown of the King[15] who,

through the prophetic/poetic word may recall also Ezekiel's Vision of Dry Bones.

12. John Felstiner, 'Paul Celan: The Strain of Jewishness,' *Commentary* 79 (1985), pp. 44-54 (48), writes that the almond is a symbol for Jewishness throughout Celan's work. It may also have kabbalistic connotations, especially given the kabbalistic influence on the collection in which it appears, *Das Niemandsrose*.

13. From 'Tübingen, Jänner' ('Tubingen, January').

14. From 'Zürich, Zum Storchen' ('Zürich, The Stork Inn'). Both poets experienced their meeting as an epiphany (Felstiner, 'The Strain of Jewishness', p. 53). The image of the ascension, used in the poem, may reverberate with its ironic usage in Treblinka.

15. '*Der Krone rot/vom Purpurwort*' ('our corolla red/with the crimson word'). The rose is a kabbalistic symbol for Israel (see the Zohar 1a); the king in the centre of the rose is God, as the Infinite or as the Nothing from which everything emerges. On the symbolism of the rose, see also Shimon Sandbank, 'The Sign of the Rose:

according to the poem 'Mandorla', dwells in nothing', at the centre, perhaps, of the rose. The petals are words (*'Purpurwort'*), rich and royal, but also blood: 'das wir sangen/über, o über/dem Dorn' ('that we sang/over, o over/the thorn').[16] The thorn over which we sang the purple word—at the moment of death? the unreachable date from which, according to Celan's essay 'The Meridian', the poem emanates?—pierces, or perhaps *is*, the nothingness and no one.[17] Nothing speaks to nothing, but through pain, sharpness, the point (*'A la pointe acérée'*)[18] round which the poem turns, the one metaphor not subject to negation.

'What are poets for in a destitute time?' Heidegger asks, in the name of Hölderlin,[19] the precursor of this age when the gods depart, and we can only follow their traces. Traces into the abyss, the *Abgrund*, where they are fled, and there is only absence, only groundlessness.[20] Elsewhere, the abyss is the rift (*Riss*) between World and thing, between Being and beings, which is also intimacy, dif-ference as that which separates and transfers, the diaphora between one and the other.[21] The threshold, according to Heidegger in a commentary on a poem by Georg Trakl, is pain,[22] the conjunction between inside and outside, the

Vaughan, Rilke, Celan,' *Comparative Literature* 49 (1997), pp. 196-208.

16. Sandbank, 'The Sign of the Rose', p. 209, holds that there is a clear reference here to the Crucifixion of Jesus, which is identified with the death of Jews in the Holocaust.

17. Paul Celan, 'The Meridian', in *Collected Prose* (trans. Rosmarie Waldrop; Manchester: Carcanet Press, 1986), pp. 37-57. See Jacques Derrida's powerful essay on dates in Celan, with its extended discussion of 'Meridian' ('Shibboleth', in G. Hartman and S. Budick [eds.], *Midrash and Literature* [New Haven: Yale University Press, 1986], pp. 307-47 [309-14]).

18. See Derrida, 'Shibboleth', pp. 308-309. The *'pointe acérée'* is the 'unrepeatable', the date, the ash, from which the poem emanates.

19. Quoted from his elegy 'Bread and Wine', in Heidegger, *Poetry, Language, Thought*, p. 91.

20. The *Abgrund* is 'the complete absence of the ground', which Heidegger thinks characterizes the modern age (*Poetry, Language, Thought*, p. 92). But it is also 'the abyss that underlies all beings' (p. 117).

21. The 'dif-ference' (*Unter-schied*) differs from difference as ordinarily conceived, as a generic term for distinctions, in that it is the difference between world and things whereby they are both held apart and become one (Heidegger, *Poetry, Language, Thought*, p. 202).

22. Heidegger describes the pain as the rending which is simultaneously a joining, a gathering to itself in the intimacy of the dif-ference (*Poetry, Language, Thought*, p. 204).

house of being and language and that which surpasses it, is unsaid and unthought in it. The poet listens to the chasm, the stillness, which opens the 'clearing'[23] in which death—the downward 'draft' or 'relation' in which all is gathered[24]—is no longer evaded, but is given voice and becomes human (i.e. linguistic). In this chasm humans are unprotected; and this is their security.

Pain as the joining, as the threshold: what has this to do with real pain?[25] With the pain and abyss in Celan (and in Isaiah) at the destruction of their worlds. As Derrida says, for Heidegger death is always 'my death', the object of my intimate concern, the nothingness in which my life shelters. For Celan, however, death is always the other, the infinite, from which his life is barred, as a survivor, even perhaps if he takes it. What he hears is not the calling into the stillness where the world elements meet, but an absolute rupture, a language of chaos ('nur lallen und lallen...Pallaksch. Pallaksch') and of horrified witness. The gods for Celan are not fugitive; they are not, indeed, gods. God, 'the winter creature', 'who washes the world nightlong', ('Eins') is the familiar presence, the '*du*' (in one of the forms manifested by the '*du*'), to whom the poems are agonizingly, inaccessibly addressed. One of Celan's images is the crevasse in the temporal glacier.[26] Heidegger entitles his meditations on poetry and language '*Holzwege*', 'paths in the wood', a metaphor, by implication, for the philosophic enterprise.[27] For Celan, especially in his long poem 'Engführung' ('The Straightening'), the paths in the woods are the railway tracks that lead, ever narrowing, to the camps, and the letters of the text, torn asunder, reveal that which one cannot look at, that to which one cannot go.

Death is inscribed in many ways in the book of Isaiah, explicitly and implicitly, by name or through attribute and metaphor. Death is the unseen, perhaps silent, dialogue partner, towards which all the words of the book are cast, as propitiation, negation or solicitation, and in which they are swallowed: 'Therefore Sheol has stretched its throat, and gaped

23. Heidegger, *Poetry, Language, Thought*, pp. 53-55.

24. Heidegger, *Poetry, Language, Thought*, pp. 124-26.

25. Wyschogrod, *Spirit in Ashes*, p. 203, notes that for Heidegger the destruction of persons is always secondary to the destruction of things.

26. 'Weggebezeit' ('Etched Away').

27. See the discussion in Mark C. Taylor, *Altarity* (Chicago: University of Chicago Press, 1987), p. 48; also David Krell's introduction to Martin Heidegger, *Basic Writings* (San Francisco: Harper, 1993), p. 34.

its mouth without limit' (5.14). Death is the player in this game we cannot win, by which the play space we inhabit is shaped, with which it is in permanent altercation. According to Winnicott, the 'play space' is that which grows between mother and child, and is the foundation of all psychic reality, culture and religion.[28] In the play space, the child acquires a sense of reality, what Jacques Lacan might call the symbolic order. The mother is displaced by, and conceals, death, as the ultimate container, that from which we come and to which we return. The mother as death is a familiar figure, biblically and cross-culturally. According to Kristeva, matricide is our vital necessity, since the mother is the undifferentiated totality from which we have to separate ourselves (in Kristeva's term, to 'abject') in order to live.[29] Winnicott holds that the absence of the mother is the first premonition of death; thought is founded on an initial threshold of terror. The mother, as the psychopomp, enables the child to enter the play space safely. Gradually she withdraws, dissimulating herself.[30]

In Isaiah, the circularity of death is disrupted by God. The poet speaks in the name of an Other, the Other, as well as himself; his voice is split. God is both that which speaks death, the purveyor of the death that pervades the book in all its disguises, and profoundly antonymic to death. The prophet's words are both words of death, and words that speak against death, the 'absolute master'.

There are others, however, for whom the bond with death is primary:

> Therefore hear the word of YHWH, O men of scoffing, rulers of this
> people who are in Jerusalem. For you have said, 'We have made a
> covenant with Death, with Sheol we have framed a compact, the surging
> scourge when it passes by will not reach us, for we have set up Lie as our
> refuge, and in Falsehood we have concealed ourselves (Isa. 28.14-15).

The covenant with Death, together with all the other terms in this passage, inverts proper values: one who owes allegiance to Death is already under its sway. Similarly, one who seeks asylum in Lie and hides in Falsehood is liable to be self-deceived; Lie and Falsehood are untrustworthy allies. As Wildberger shows, the speech mimics liturgical

---

28. Winnicott, *Playing and Reality*, p. 22. See also the chapter entitled 'The Location of Cultural Experience' (pp. 95-103).

29. Kristeva, *Black Sun*, p. 27.

30. Winnicott, *Playing and Reality*, p. 10, stresses that what he calls the 'good-enough' mother is one who is becomes gradually less available to the immediate satisfaction of the child's needs, and thus introduces it to a sense of reality.

language: YHWH is the familiar refuge, dwelling in supernal concealment.[31] The covenant with Death is the opposite of a covenant with Life
and with YHWH, and hence of the fundamental premise of the relationship between Israel and God in the Hebrew Bible. Finally, the word for
'compact' (חזה), which occurs only here in the Hebrew Bible, is a pun
on that for 'vision', such as that which introduces the book.[32] In the
place of the 'vision'—in which the prophet sees beyond the appearances of things, sees, in a sense, with God's eyes—the wise men[33] of
Jerusalem have an agreement, perhaps a 'vision', with Death and Sheol.
They have substituted Death, self-concealment and mystification for
God, prophecy, truth and mystery.

Some see the covenant with Death as a metaphor for political
alliances, such as with Egypt (probably the dominant hypothesis),
others as a cult of the dead or necromancy; still others posit the worship
of gods of death, such as Mot and Osiris. In 8.19, the dead are
described, in a quotation attributed to the people, as deities: 'Should not
a people inquire of its gods, on behalf of the living to the dead?' However, hypothesizing a particular reference reverses the metaphorical
relationship. The dead signify death, as do personifications of death,
like Mot, and fatal alliances. The covenant with death is *the* alternative,
throughout Isaiah, to the covenant with YHWH, and to the poetic con-
tract, or vision, between prophet and God.

Death, Lie, Falsehood offer security, shelter, concealment, from the
'surging scourge'. One escapes from disaster into lies—the only alternative to the refuge in YHWH—just as one hides oneself in delusions

---

31. Hans Wildberger, *Jesaja* (BKAT, 10; Neukirchen: Neukirchener Verlag,
1980–89), p. 1073. See also Jörg Barthel, *Prophetenwort und Geschichte: Die
Jesajaüberlieferung in Jes 6-8 und 28-31* (Tübingen: Mohr Siebeck, 1997), p. 319.

32. For the pun, see J. Cheryl Exum, 'Whom Will He Teach Knowledge?: A
Literary Approach to Isaiah 28', in D.J.A. Clines, David M. Gunn and Alan J.
Hauser (eds.), *Art and Meaning: Rhetoric in Biblical Literature* (JSOTSup, 19;
Sheffield: JSOT Press, 1982), pp. 108-39 (137-38 n. 31); and Peter Miscall, *Isaiah*
(Readings; Sheffield: Sheffield Academic Press, 1993), p. 74. Barthel, *Propheten-
wort und Geschichte*, p. 307, proposes an etymological link between the two
usages, adducing Exod. 18.21.

33. משלים may mean either 'rulers' or 'aphorists'. Those exegetes who are
allergic to ambiguity in the prophetic texts opt for one meaning or the other (e.g.
Wildberger, *Jesaja*, pp. 1064, 1072). William H. Irwin, *Isaiah 28–33: Translation
with Philological Notes* (Rome: Biblical Institute, 1977), p. 2, cleverly translates as
'reigning wits'.

and false hopes. Death may provide the rulers/aphorists with a 'crypt', a zone of immunity, a pre-emptive death that will inoculate them against ultimate death. Kristeva describes patients who entomb themselves, so as not to separate from the death-bearing mother and risk the passage into life and death.[34] In 8.19, and elsewhere, the dead are the ghosts, who 'chirp and coo' from the ground. The people who turn from the living to the deified dead, to the ancestral spirits, affirm dependence on, as well as responsibility for, the past. The dead and the living implicitly inhabit the same world, above and below ground, a continuum in which the living become the venerated dead, and are generated from them; the relationship with death is comforting, circular and maternal.

However, reliance on ancestral piety will not survive the irruption of death that will destroy the continuum of life and death, the meaning of death. If the ancestors signify the past, and hence a culture, mass-death threatens that culture and robs us of the capacity to make sense of death ritually, imaginatively, and hence culturally. Further, God is both unremittingly hostile to ancestral cults, outside every natural continuum, and the author of, implicitly the one who endorses, that continuum. God is both the matrix of life and death and the paternal judge, whose attributes (name, invisibility, and so on) testify to the disjunction between himself and the natural order.

The ancestral cult is characterized throughout by anxiety. The people inquire of the dead in desperation, just as for the rulers/aphorists the covenant with death is a stratagem to outwit the invader. The dead are the 'chirpers and cooers' (8.19), whose voices express their faintness and estrangement from human reality.[35] The ghostliness of the dead turns them into parodies of maternal presence. The cult of death is accordingly uncanny, in the Freudian sense, a discordant and impossible reiteration of the past. The mother's voice is heard only through

34. For the concept of the crypt in which patients entomb themselves, see Kristeva, *Black Sun*, pp. 53, 79, 89, and 266 n. 13. The description is, however, all-pervasive in her illustrations of feminine depression (pp. 69-94). Baruch Halpern, '"The Excremental Vision": The Doomed Priests of Doom in Isaiah 28', *HAR* 10 (1986), pp. 109-21 (117), thinks that the rulers/aphorists literally imagined themselves as being concealed in a crypt from the invader.

35. Karel van der Toorn, 'Echoes of Judean Necromancy in Isaiah 28:7-22', *ZAW* 100 (1988), pp. 199-217 (210-12), understands these as the sounds made by mediums to represent the voices of the dead, who were assimilated to birds. See also the lengthy comment in Wildberger, *Jesaja*, pp. 349-52.

distorted and dispersed traces. The solace of the continuum of life and death is then dislocated by the irretrievability of death, the recovery only of absence.

The opposition of the two voices and covenants—God and Death, prophet and people—is replicated by the divisions in each, in God as antonymic to death and the one who brings death, as maternal and paternal, in the dual allegiance of the prophet and the double origin of his voice, in the nostalgic solace of death and death as that from which there is no return. The covenant with death is founded on nothing, on death as that which annuls all covenants, all discourse, on a perception of death as that which exposes the lack of foundation in all being— Heidegger's abyss, perhaps. It is the antithesis of the covenant with God, but also of all covenants, and in particular, the 'cosmic covenant', since it sunders all ties. The covenant with death, that confident assertion, is hollowed out, anxious, displaces other voices, but it is also implicated in the poetic anxiety of the poem, the intolerable paradoxes from which its voice emanates, and which it imparts.

It is claimed by the 'men of scoffing, rulers/aphorists of this people who are in Jerusalem'. Once again, we have an inversion of proper values, emphasized through word-play. 'Men of scoffing' (לָצוֹן) is a distortion of 'men of Zion';[36] the last three consonants of 'Jerusalem' (יְרוּשָׁלִַם) are identical to those of 'rulers' (מֹשְׁלֵי). Those who rule in Jerusalem are scoffers, who mock at all sacred institutions. They are also 'aphorists', inventors of parables, similitudes, ballads. The Hebrew word used here, *mashal*, whatever its meaning, may be the stock in trade of scoffers, satirists, those outside the establishment. It is, however, identified with sacred and political order. The aphorist *par excellence* in the Hebrew Bible is Solomon, who is said to have composed three thousand (1 Kgs 5.12). The 'men of Hezekiah', perhaps the very rulers/aphorists of our verse, were responsible for an edition of Solomonic proverbs, according to Prov. 25.1. Wisdom literature throughout the ancient Near East is aphoristic; the political and social order on which it comments, from the point of view of the ideal sage, is mimicked in a literary language of the utmost economy and parallelistic symmetry. Wisdom literature is politically conservative, representing itself as ancestral wisdom, and as a manifestation of the order of

36. As noted by Exum, 'Whom Will He Teach Knowledge?', p. 124.

creation.[37] The sage may be in league with death, with the collective wisdom of the past. The authority of the aphorism is anonymous, omniscient, and detached, demarcating a zone of linguistic perfection and intellectual equanimity from which to observe the affairs of the world. The punning word, מֹשְׁלֵי, 'rulers/aphorists', indicates the convergence of political and poetic agendas, the synthesis of the wisdom tradition and the political establishment. At the same time, it implies an antinomy of two kinds of poetry: that of the sage, with its complacent reliance on received wisdom, and that of the prophet, whose poetic voice signifies that which will destroy political and poetic order.

The wisdom tradition is turned against itself, is parodied here. One could imagine the quotation, attributed to the sages, as a typical satiric comment, just as the wisdom tradition is generally devoted to the exposure of falsehood, not its perpetuation. Isaiah may then speak for the wisdom tradition against its representatives; similarly, he promotes a political vision antithetical to that of the powers that be. The perversion of politics, its failure to conform to 'justice' and 'righteousness' (28.17), is concomitantly a failure of poetry.[38]

Poetry and politics are seemingly incompatible enterprises; the pun is accordingly oxymoronic. They juxtapose the real and the imaginary, the administration of state with the deployment of words and ideas. The intersection of the two realms suggests a metaphorical transfer. Politics colludes with poetry, as an instrument of power, but also as seduction, self-delusion. For instance, the politically fostered belief in the invulnerability of Zion, impervious to time and chance, corresponds to the linguistic enclave represented by the aphorism.[39] The phrase שׁוֹט שׁוֹטֵף, 'the surging scourge',[40] at the centre of the aphorism, with its repeated

---

37. James G. Williams, *Those Who Ponder Proverbs: Aphoristic Thinking and Biblical Literature* (Sheffield: Almond Press, 1981), pp. 35-46.

38. Barthel, *Prophetenwort und Geschichte*, p. 319, notes the antithesis between Lie and Falsehood in v. 15 and Justice and Righteousness in v. 17.

39. Williams, *Those Who Ponder Proverbs*, p. 1, cites Pascal that aphorism is his only means for expressing 'true order' in a disordered world. For a discussion of Gerhard Neuman's view that aphorism represents a 'paradise of ideas', see Williams (pp. 72-75).

40. There is much scholarly debate whether to adopt the qeri, שׁוֹט or the ketib שִׁיט, 'oar'. שׁוֹט is supported by IQIa and generally seems much the stronger reading, especially given the parallel in v. 18. See Barthel, *Prophetenwort und Geschichte*, p. 307. Hartmut Gese, 'Die Strömende Geissel des Hadad und Jes. 28:15 und 18', in *Archäologie und Altes Testament: Festschrift K. Galling* (Tübingen: Mohr, 1970),

syllables, overlays and compresses two opposing metaphors and metonymies for the disaster: the whip, inadequate as it might be as a metaphor for death, but which is nonetheless a powerful metonymy for oppression and captivity, and the flood, which has been used as a metaphor for invasion in 28.2 and 8.7-8. Behind the Assyrians is death. The concatenation, 'the surging scourge', is repeated in 28.18, and augmented by an evocation of marching: 'the surging scourge when it passes through, you shall be for it as a trampling'. The compound elements—whip, flood, feet—juxtapose and implicitly collapse into each other the motif of sudden violence with that of inundation.

Repeating syllables and words—as with שׁוט שׁוטף, 'the surging scourge'—are characteristic of the passage. Just before, God's stuttering nonsense language is conveyed by צו לצו קו לקו, to the delight and perplexity of commentators (vv. 11, 13).[41] In the next verse, the divine edifice is invested with magniloquent grandeur through the repetition of terms: אבן אבן מוסד מוסד.[42] Stone is added to stone; the foundation is more deeply founded. 'The surging scourge' (שׁוט שׁוטף), in the middle of the verse, suggests a caesura, bordered by a symmetrical, and symmetrically opposed, figure for dissolution, disfigurement and rupture. The whip cuts through flesh, history and language, on the other side of which is the *longue durée*, the infinite extension of the flood, marked by

pp. 127-34, provides interesting iconographic illustration.

41. Critics are divided as to whether these words are a quotation of the prophet's antagonists, mocking the prophet's speech. Those who disagree attribute them to YHWH, to the priests and prophets Isaiah is satirising, or to the Ephraimite leaders and the invader. Willem Beuken, 'Is it Only Schismatics Who Drink Heavily?: Beyond the Synchronic versus Diachronic Controversy', in J. C. de Moor (ed.), *Synchrony or Diachrony: A Debate on Method in Old Testament Exegesis* (Leiden: E.J. Brill, 1995), pp. 15-38 (31-38), holds that there is a deliberate blurring of the actants. It is evident that there are many crossovers and variants on these models. Critics are also divided as to whether the words are simply babble or have import. A widely-adopted hypothesis is that they are part of the Hebrew abecediary. Others suggest that they echo the vomit and excrement in 28.8, the ventriloquist speech of spirit mediums, or the Assyrian order for deportation. My own view is that the words are those of YHWH, as in v. 13, corresponding to his strange commission in 6.9-10. Their primary significance is babble, illustrating the 'stuttering speech' (בלעגי לשׁון) of v.11, which is, however, dense in implication, as the aforementioned critics have abundantly demonstrated.

42. Exum, 'Whom Will He Teach Knowledge?', p. 126, notes that 'piling up of phrases is itself a building process'.

the protracted second syllable of שׁוֹטֵף, 'surging'. In the rest of the line, כִּי[43]יַעֲבֹר לֹא יְבוֹאֵנוּ, 'when it passes through will not reach us', the advent of the disaster coincides with its non-arrival. The caesura is projected into the sequence, becomes interminable.

The disaster is that which never appears.[44] It is the gap, the annihilation, between two words, two nominations that can never reach it.[45] The rulers/proverb-makers hide themselves in their lies, their illusions and language. But what is the lie and illusion exactly? Is it Death and Sheol, as the artful, symmetrical parallelism suggests, or is Death the Truth, as well as that which swallows up the Truth? And what is our responsibility, our covenant, with the dead and with Death? To work over their traces, to exclaim '*Pallaksch. Pallaksch.*' צַו לָצָו קַו לָקָו: there is something comforting in the repeated syllables, the debris of language signifying nothing. Cluck, cluck, tss, tsss…coo and chirr. Language becomes solely emotive, phatic, signifying presence. Stone on stone. The accumulation of divine language.

The trap: לְמַעַן יֵלְכוּ וְכָשְׁלוּ אָחוֹר וְנִשְׁבְּרוּ וְנוֹקְשׁוּ וְנִלְכָּדוּ, 'that they should go and stumble backwards and be broken and trapped and taken' (28.13). What is the word of YHWH to which the rulers/proverb makers of Jerusalem should listen? וְהָיָה רַק זְוָעָה הָבִין שְׁמוּעָה, 'and it shall be just horror to understand that which is heard',…כִּי כָלָה וְנֶחֱרָצָה שְׁמַעְתִּי מֵאֵת אֲדֹנָי ה' צְבָאוֹת עַל כָּל הָאָרֶץ 'For annihilation and doom I have heard from my Lord, YHWH of Hosts, over all the earth' (28.22).[46]

---

43. Reading with the qeri, rather than the ketib עבר.

44. The non-arrival and ever-imminence of the disaster pervades Blanchot's *Writing of the Disaster*. 'We are on the edge of disaster without being able to situate it in the future: it is rather always already past, and yet we are on the edge or under the threat…if the disaster were not that which does not come, which has put a stop to every arrival' (p. 1). See also Wyschogrod, *An Ethics of Remembering: History, Heterology, and the Nameless Others* (Chicago: University of Chicago Press, 1998), p. 140: 'Properly speaking, there is no experience of the disaster, not only because the I that undergoes experience is carried away, but because…the disaster recurs in perpetuity…as a "non-event".'

45. Wyschogrod, *Ethics of Remembering*, pp. 17-18, argues that the cataclysm is a nihil that resists nomination, yet demands to be spoken of, to be given a name. Arthur A. Cohen, *The Tremendum: A Theological Interpretation of the Holocaust* (New York: Crossroad, 1988), has notably promoted the view of the Shoah as a caesura in Jewish theological consciousness.

46. For the connections between these terms and the transformation of the incomprehensible speech of vv. 10-13 to YHWH's 'wondrous plan', see Barthel, *Prophetenwort und Geschichte*, pp. 327-28.

JOB AND AUSCHWITZ

Richard L. Rubenstein

For more than two millennia the figure of Job, the righteous sufferer, has served as an image that enabled people to speak truthfully about their destiny without compromising their faith in the biblical God. Trust and skepticism are wonderfully balanced in the Job tradition. Whenever it seemed impossible to reconcile the existence of a just and omnipotent God with unmerited suffering, the example of Job helped to preserve faith. The image of Job assured the relatively innocent sufferer that his was a shared destiny that was not without its special dignity. If the Job tradition could not fathom the religious meaning of gratuitous suffering, it could at least give men a model of how to respond with great nobility. Unfortunately, even in their most demonic fantasies the biblical writers could not have anticipated the radically novel experiences of the twentieth century. Job does not provide a helpful image for comprehending Auschwitz.

Job's Challenge to Tradition

Although human beings are in no sense exempt from the vicissitudes of biological existence, they alone possess the illusion of a world potentially devoid of suffering, pain and death. This fantasy has been especially potent among those who believe that the world has come into being through the will of an omnipotent Creator. If those aspects of existence that men and women find hard to bear are ultimately the expression of the Creator's power, one can always hope that an omnipotent God might somehow change things. The belief that things are the way they are because of the will of God and the hope that they could be different were God, so to speak, to change his mind underlies the world view of the Bible, in both its Jewish and Christian forms. The hope for salvation follows from the biblical belief in creation as an act of divine will.

Biblical man was convinced that God ruled the world in justice. Given this conviction, as well as the fact that few men or women can accept their inexorable path to decay and annihilation, it is not surprising that biblical man came to regard biological limitations of existence such as sickness and death as inherently punitive. Both classical Jewish and Christian interpreters of the biblical tradition agree that had Adam remained without sin, God would not have inflicted suffering and death upon humanity. Thus, the rabbis assert, 'There is no death without sin'.[1] Paul of Tarsus echoes the same conviction in his crucial myth of the Last Adam: 'Then as one man's trespass led to condemnation for all men, so one man's act of righteousness led to acquittal and life for all men.'[2] Common to both traditions is the hope that there is a way out of mortality, and that it cannot be said of the human condition that it has no exit.

Biblical man paid a high price for such hope. At one level, the price was paid in the conflict he was compelled to endure between his ordinary powers of observation and his yearning for salvation. That tension has been reflected in the conflict between faith and reason. When common sense found itself in opposition to religious belief, the victory usually went to faith. Perhaps Søren Kierkegaard's greatest contribution to modern theology may have been the lucidity with which he depicted what is required to affirm biblical faith against common sense. Kierkegaard rejects all attempts to harmonize the conflict between our knowledge of the indifferent givenness of things and belief in a God who could, if he but chose, so alter the human condition that our yearnings for immortality and eternal felicity might be fulfilled.

Kierkegaard's insistence upon the absolute chasm between human understanding and the ways of God is strangely echoed in the works of the contemporary novelist and death-camp survivor, Elie Wiesel. In spite of the unspeakable existence into which he was thrown at Auschwitz, Wiesel has never been able to deny God. Nevertheless, he could only make sense of his relationship to God in terms of the image of Job. Thus, Wiesel writes:

1.   *Šab.* 55a. See the discussion of this issue in Richard L Rubenstein, *The Religious Imagination* (Indianapolis: Bobbs-Merrill, 1968), pp. 46ff.
    2.   Rom. 5.18.

> I prefer to take my place on the side of Job, who chose questions and not answers, silence and not speeches. Job never understood his own tragedy which, after all, was only that of an individual betrayed by God.[3]

Elsewhere, Wiesel is prepared to see God as a madman, but he is not prepared to deny him.[4]

The book of Job would never have been written were it not for this agonizing conflict between religious belief and common sense. Had men in biblical times been convinced that they dwelt in a cosmos entirely indifferent to human categories of good and evil, the problem of the innocent sufferer would have been meaningless. Suffering and death would simply have been regarded as inevitable. If conflict was present in the experience of the relatively innocent sufferer, it would have been portrayed as the conflict between the sufferer's actual experience of misfortune and his yearnings for safety and security. Similarly, had men in biblical times been wholly convinced that, despite all appearances, an omnipotent and just divinity is the ultimate author of all events, there would have been no problem of the innocent sufferer. It is only because an influential group of men stood in a kind of religious border-country, unable either to reject God or to regard all human misfortune simply as punitive, that the book of Job became a permanent part of the religious heritage of the Judeo-Christian world.

Loss and Infanticide

The book's prologue divides Job's calamities into two categories, the loss of children and possessions and the afflictions visited upon his person. As grievous a calamity as was the loss of offspring, there may have been latent factors in Job's acceptance that had little to do with religious trust. David Bakan has pointed out that coping with the infanticidal impulse looms large in biblical religion. Bakan has cogently argued against Freud that the experience of biblical man witnessed few

---

3. Elie Wiesel, *Legends of our Time* (New York: Holt, Rinehart and Winston, 1968), p. 181.

4. Wiesel, *Legends of our Time*, p. 6. See also Maurice Friedman, *To Deny our Nothingness* (New York: Delacorte, 1967), pp. 348-54. Friedman has described Wiesel as an exemplification of 'the modern Job'. By describing the predicament of contemporary man in terms of Job, Friedman has been especially helpful in formulating the issue under discussion in this paper. Cf. Maurice Friedman, *Problematic Rebel* (New York: Random House, 1963).

instances of parricide but many of infanticide.[5] If Bakan's analysis is correct, Job's response to the death of his children is more complicated than would initially appear from his overly brief and apparently pious affirmation: 'The Lord gave, the Lord took away. Blessed be the Lord's name' (1.21).[6] If there was any residue of the infanticidal impulse in Job, the pain he experienced could be seen as the pain of his conflicting feelings. The protecting father within Job was aggrieved; the latent infanticide was not entirely displeased. One need not agree with Bakan's contention that the book's latent content deals with Job as infanticide to recognize that Job was not exempt from the impulse as it manifested itself in his time. There is even a suggestion of a similar impulse in God, who is depicted as entirely willing to do away with Job's children in order to prove a point to Satan. Throughout the book there is much discussion of Job's misfortune, but not a word about the sons and daughters who perish simply because God wishes to win an argument. Nor ought we to ascribe this omission to the 'lower' moral sensitivity of an earlier age. On the contrary, what was involved was biblical man's fortunate capacity to objectify his conflicting impulses in the image of a Father-God. By so doing, biblical man was able to cope constructively with some of his most disturbing inner conflicts. Both the Akedah story (the binding of Isaac) and the tradition of the atoning crucifixion of Jesus contain similar intuitions of the infanticidal impulse projected upon the Father-God. One of biblical man's most precious resources in dealing with such conflicting impulses was his image of God, and so, I might add, is ours. Part of the religio-moral crisis of our age derives from the fact that many of us are no longer able to project conflicting human impulses onto credible contemporary images of God.

Satan wisely rejects the loss of children as a test of Job's righteousness. He maintains that Job can hardly be seen as a victim until his own person is directly affected:

> Skin after skin.
> All that a man has
> He will give for his life.

---

5.   David Bakan, *The Duality of Human Existence* (New York: Random House, 1966), pp. 197ff; *Disease, Pain and Sacrifice* (Chicago: University of Chicago Press, 1968), pp. 96ff.

6.   All translations from the book of Job are taken from Marvin H. Pope, *Job: Translated with an Introduction and Notes* (AB; Garden City, NY: Doubleday, 1965). However, where Pope uses the term 'Yahweh' I substitute 'the Lord'.

Reach out and strike him,
Touch his bone and flesh,
And he will curse you to your face (2.4-5).

Satan in effect demands that God change Job's position from that of Abraham, who is called upon to offer up his own offspring, to that of Isaac, who must accept the victim's hazards. Satan is confident that Job will not exhibit Isaac's unfaltering devotion or trust. That is a wager God is willing to make.

Attack upon the Ego

Job is then visited with an affliction so drastic that his only response is to curse the day of his birth and wish for a speedy end to his miserable existence. The Hebrew term used for Job's affliction is *Shêhîn*, a skin disease. In all probability Job was afflicted with an advanced case of leprosy so that his entire body was covered by burning, pussy, ulcerous boils that left him prostrate.[7] Looking and smelling like human refuse, he could find no more suitable place of habitation than the village dunghill. It is small wonder that death became for Job a longed-for release. The skin constitutes the border between the organism and its environment. Initially, the ego is a body-ego and remains so throughout life.[8] A total attack on the skin is a drastic attack on the ego as such. Everything that lent stability, continuity and integrity to Job's ego was decisively threatened by the leprous attack on his skin. Quite incidentally, his ego ceased to have any sense of masculine competence. As a result of his affliction, he was functionally castrated even if his sexual urge remained somewhat intact. Job asserts: 'My flesh is clad with worms and dust; my skin cracks and oozes.' Even sleep offers no escape to Job:

If I say, 'My couch will comfort me,
My bed will ease my complaint,'
Then You dismay me with dreams,
Terrify me with nightmares,
Till my soul would choose strangling
Death rather than my loathsome pains (7.13-15).

Nevertheless, Job's ego retains its integrity. Whatever may have been the ambiguities of his response to the loss of children and property, the

7. Cf. Pope, *Job*, p. 21 n. 7.
8. Otto Fenichel, *The Psychoanalytic Theory of Neurosis* (New York: Norton, 1945), pp. 34ff.

violent attack on his ego does not produce a breakdown. Job never asks for a restoration of his former prosperity and health. In his reply to Eliphaz (6.22-23) he demands: 'Have I said... "Rescue me from an enemy?" "Redeem me from brigands?"' Job seeks insight, not escape: 'Teach me, and I will be quiet; show me where I have erred' (6.24).

Erik Erikson has described the possessor of ego integrity as 'ready to defend the dignity of his own life style against all physical and economic threats.'[9] That description certainly applies to Job. The psychological importance of the book rests in large measure upon the fact that it describes in greater detail than elsewhere in the Bible a personality with an authentically integrated ego. Job faces a catastrophic crisis in the second half of life. He retains his dignity, his clarity and his honor. He does so without falsifying his own insights or his culture's canons of behavioral appropriateness. He challenges some widely accepted opinions of his time, but does so in such a way that his religious life is deepened rather than perverted. The rabbis maintained that Job never in fact existed. The purpose of the tale was to serve as an example.[10] This would suggest that the fiction we have inherited represents the objectification of a new level of consciousness by the book's author(s) and redactor(s). The men who gave us this book intuitively understood the phenomenon of ego integrity.

Job neither breaks nor does he become rigid. His friends are convinced that misfortune is ultimately punitive in character. They believe Job must be guilty simply because of what has happened to him. In their eyes, the fact of gross misfortune alone is sufficient evidence of Job's guilt before God. Nor ought we to denounce in haste the rigidity of the friends' worldview. Their refusal to alter their inherited beliefs in the light of convincing evidence to the contrary involves a fundamental issue. The friends of Job and their traditionalist successors to this day cannot face existence as a wasteland ultimately indifferent in its givenness to all human aspiration and yearning. If Job is really innocent, one must draw conclusions even more drastic than those drawn by Job when he cries out:

> Guiltless as well as wicked He destroys.
> When the scourge slays suddenly,
> He mocks the despair of the innocent.

9.   Erik Erikson, *Identity Youth and Crisis* (New York: Norton, 1968), p. 140.
10.   *B. Bat.* 15a. Cf. Bakan, *Disease, Pain and Sacrifice*, pp. 100ff.

Earth is given to the control of the wicked.
The faces of her judges He covers—
If not He, then who? (9.22-24).

Accusing God

Job accuses God. He never faces the possibility that the God whom he accuses does not exist, that earth is merely the dumb witness to the succession of amoral passion, power and violence that we call the human adventure. Perhaps the author(s) and redactor(s) of the book had yet to conclude that it was at least thinkable that Job's sufferings, if unmerited, could mean that God is neither madman nor infanticide, that the biblical God is nothing and of no account save as an objectification of biblical man's conflicted self-image. In rabbinic times, confronted by the gratuitous suffering of the innocent, Elisha ben Abuya was compelled to conclude '*Leth din v'leth dyan*' ('There is no judgment and there is no Judge').[11] Since there is nothing to indicate that biblical man was less intelligent or less insightful than men and women in our generation, we have no reason to believe that biblical man was incapable of drawing conclusions similar to those drawn by Elisha ben Abuya. In all likelihood, the author(s) repressed their insights because they were fearful of the price to be paid for living in a spiritual and metaphysical wasteland. To this day traditionalists, who echo the friends of Job in their insistence that misfortune is evidence of estrangement from God, have at least the indirect justification that few men can really live in the wasteland. By taking his stand for a world that is meaningful in terms of God's justice and human sin, the traditionalist asks sufferers like Job to become a new kind of Isaac: for the sake of a coherent religious world, without which the generality of mankind could not survive, the traditionalist asks the sufferer to regard his pain as a sign of divine punishment.

If I may suggest a fantasy of what such a traditionalist might say to a Job-like sufferer, I would imagine him as saying:

> I know your sufferings are extraordinarily painful. I would alleviate them
> if I could, but I cannot. I know that the worst anguish you experience is
> your fear that God has inexplicably become your enemy, that you have
> been accounted as one guilty and deserving of misfortune. Nevertheless,
> I implore you to confess a guilt you cannot understand and to beg God's
> forgiveness and mercy. Your sacrifice is greater than Isaac's. Isaac was

11. *Qid.* 39b.

only asked to submit to his father's violence without being accounted guilty. You are asked both to submit and to confess your guilt even though you regard yourself as innocent.

I ask you to reflect deeply before you question God's justice. If you are really innocent, God may very well be a demon. If he is a demon, all of our efforts to create a decent world in the face of human cupidity and lust will collapse. Was it not difficult enough for us to control man's worst impulses when we were really convinced of God's power and justice? We imagined that the Creator was our ally. We had a chance. If God is the demonic power who smites the innocent and allies himself to the wicked, we have no chance. We might as well satisfy our worst lusts until we are overcome by someone more powerful or by the demon-Creator Himself.

The traditionalist would continue:

> There is even a more terrifying possibility: if you are innocent, there may be no Creator. Even a demon-God offers men the hope that they are not nakedly alone in the cosmos, that they may find at least some twisted hope in serving the Satanic Creator. If there is no God, we are of no greater significance than any insect, and, like the most repugnant organism, we have nothing to hope for but everlasting oblivion.
>
> Even if you are absolutely convinced of your own innocence, even if you honestly believe that the Creator is nothing and of no account, *lie* for the sake of humanity. Men cannot bear to live in the world you, and perhaps we, know to be the real one. Confess your sin; bow before a God who may not exist. Perhaps we must deceive each other, pretending that God rules the universe in justice. Nevertheless, it is better thus. We shall never know death. We shall assuredly know the terrors of a godless world if men cease to hope and to believe.

My fantasy is not entirely original. After all, there are only a limited number of theological options available to human credulity. In the nineteenth century Dostoevsky offered a somewhat similar tale in his 'Legend of the Grand Inquisitor'. We must not quickly dismiss the friends of Job or their contemporary heirs. More can be said in their defense than is usually suggested. Nevertheless, we can surmise what the Job-like sufferers reply might be:

> You ask me to offer myself up as a sacrifice. I would gladly offer my body for the sake of mankind, but you ask more of me than your God asked even of Jesus. Jesus willingly gave himself for the salvation of mankind, but he expired as an innocent. He died for other men's sins. Nowhere do we find even a hint that he was compelled to see himself as

a sinner. I can sacrifice my own life; I cannot sacrifice my integrity. Let the demons of heaven and hell do their worst. I cannot do this for God or for man.

The book reports that Job was not required to sacrifice his integrity. Job is overwhelmed by the sheer presence of God at the end of his trial. He recognizes the limits of his strength and understanding. He chooses silence. He remains no closer to understanding than before, but he now has the implicit understanding that the mysterious God is not his enemy. Above all, he has the very great satisfaction of knowing that he has not caved in, that he has taken the worst and remained his own man. There is no surrender even in the presence of God. There is great dignity in both of Job's replies to God:

> Lo, I am small, how can I answer you?
> My hand I lay on my mouth; I have spoken once, I will not reply;
> Twice, but I will say no more (39.4-5).

and

> I know you can do all things;
> No purpose of yours can be thwarted...
> I talked of things I did not know,
> Wonders beyond my ken...
> I have heard of you by hearsay,
> But now my own eyes have seen you;
> So I recant and repent in dust and ashes (42.2-6).

At the end of his trial, Job finds himself beyond resentment. He recants before the presence of God. Nevertheless, had God not revealed himself, there is little doubt that Job's protest would have remained essentially unchanged. Job has demonstrated that maintaining one's own integrity constitutes a greater righteousness than obedient acceptance of traditional norms that do violence to one's deepest self-perceptions.

Job and Auschwitz

We have already noted that one contemporary sufferer has seen Job as the most appropriate model for a religious response to the death camps. Elie Wiesel's Job-like affirmation of trust in God after Auschwitz has been met with almost universal respect among those who have encountered his writings. I concur in the personal appropriateness of Wiesel's use of the example of Job in order to comprehend his own situation. Nevertheless, I believe that the use of Job as a metaphor for the experi-

ence of the Jewish people and as a means of reconciling Auschwitz
with the existence of the biblical God of history has at best a questionable validity.

At Auschwitz, because of the selection process the vast majority of
Jews had no opportunity to be likened to Job. As new inmates entered
the camp, they were divided into two groups, one marked for immediate
death, the other for some form of slave labor. Most were marked for
immediate extermination. Such victims cannot be likened to Job who
survives his trial. In the aftermath, Job sits on his dung heap and challenges both God and man. The vast majority of Europe's Jews vanished
through the smokestacks of the crematoria. Wiesel can regard Job as a
model for his anguish, because he survived and his sufferings were in
truth a test for him. Moreover, he survived his ordeal with his faith
somehow deepened. To repeat, one cannot liken those who were killed
immediately to Job. They had neither time nor opportunity to come to
terms with their experience. Even if in some way they knew that the
death camps awaited them once incarcerated, the knowledge that certain death lay ahead was almost universally repressed.[12] Somehow the
facts were known yet not known. Those who went to their death
immediately can be likened to Job's children but not to Job.

Nor can the Jewish people as a whole be likened to Job, who, incidentally, was often regarded as a righteous Gentile by both classical
Jewish and Christian interpreters.[13] There is nothing in the relative
comfort and safety that was common among the Jews of the Western
hemisphere that could justify regarding their World War II experience
as Job-like. *After* the event, non-European Jews experienced an
unprecedented trauma from which, I believe, they have yet to recover.
Nevertheless, there was little that was Job-like in their experience at the
time of Auschwitz.

Psychological Reaction
Those Jews compelled to adapt to the death camps as, so to speak, their
'normal' way of life constitute the group most likely to be regarded as

12. Elie Cohen, *Human Behavior in the Concentration Camp* (trans. M.H.
Braaksma; New York: Grosset and Dunlap, 1953).
13. See the introduction to Nahum N. Glatzer (ed.), *The Dimensions of Job: A
Study and Selected Readings* (New York: Schocken Books, 1969), pp. 16-17, 24-
34; also Jean Daniélou, 'The Mystery of Man and God', in Glatzer (ed.), *The
Dimensions of Job*, p. 101.

Job-like. There was an adaptive process that made it possible for some people to survive for relatively long periods in the camps. To my mind, Primo Levi has given us the best description of how a few survived. Levi describes his entry into Auschwitz after having been transported from Italy to Poland in mid-winter in an unheated, overcrowded boxcar with no provision for food, water, waste elimination or protection from the bitter cold. Arrival at Auschwitz was followed without pause by the infamous selection process in which those judged fit for slave labor were separated out from the majority sent to their death immediately. Levi describes his own reaction:

> Imagine now a man who is deprived of everyone he loves, and at the same time of his house, his habits, his clothes, in short, of everything he possesses: he will be a hollow man, reduced to suffering and needs, forgetful of dignity and restraint, for he who loses all often easily loses himself. He will be a man whose life and death can be lightly decided with no sense of human affinity, in the most fortunate cases on the basis of a pure judgment of utility. It is in this way that one can understand the double sense of the term 'extermination camp,' and it is now clear what we seek to express with the phrase: 'to lie on the bottom'.[14]

The psychological reactions of the prisoners at Auschwitz have been studied extensively by a number of psychiatrists who were themselves inmates. Elie Cohen and Viktor Frankl, are among the best-known former inmates who have undertaken psychiatric studies of what happened to individuals under camp conditions.[15] Elie Cohen has observed that survival in the camps depended upon the way in which the inmate passed through three psychological stages: initial reaction, adaptation and resignation.[16] It must be remembered that the majority of the prisoners had neither the luck nor the inner resources to pass through all three stages. Anarchic misfortune could and usually did fall upon most inmates from the minute they arrived.

The prisoner who survived the 'ceremony of reception' as he entered Auschwitz experienced an *acute depersonalization*. Cohen and others testify to the prevalence of the reaction. In the condition of acute depersonalization the individual does not believe that what is happening is

14. Primo Levi, *Survival in Auschwitz: The Nazi Assault on Humanity* (trans. Stuart Woolf; New York: Collier MacMillan, 1978), p. 23.

15. See Cohen, *Human Behavior*; and Viktor Frankl, *From Death Camp to Existentialism* (Boston: Beacon Press, 1959).

16. Cohen, *Human Behavior*, pp. 115-20.

really happening to him. This reaction was defensive and permitted the prisoner's ego to function at some level without breakdown. Cohen tells us: 'I felt I did not belong, as if the business did not concern me; as if I were looking at things tbrough a peephole.'[17]

After a month or two in the camp, most prisoners understood that what was happening to them was real indeed. They had arrived at the second stage, *adaptation*. Success in remaining alive now depended upon how well the prisoners adapted to the routine of the camp-universe. Stripped of every shred of human dignity, their names never used, in the eyes of their captors they were mere numbers. Their previous identities were of no consequence. Many no longer bore much resemblance to the human beings they once were. They were addressed by the SS with the familiar *du* but were compelled always to address the SS as *Sie*. Rigidly controlled, they could perform no bodily function without permission. They were compelled to sleep with little cover in bunks with several mates so that, as with Job, even sleep was no escape. Their food largely consisted of watery soup served in bowls used by several inmates without cleaning. Bed-wetting and diarrhea were common. Unable to attend to elementary requirements of bodily cleanliness, the inmates were in a constant state of hunger. In a word, the camps were deliberately arranged to destroy any remnant of human dignity in the victims. Primo Levi offers a harrowing description of the end product of the system, the *Musselmänner*:

> To sink is the easiest of matters; it is enough to carry out all the orders one receives, to eat only the ration, to observe the discipline of the work and the camp. Experience showed that only exceptionally could one survive more than three months in this way. All the musselmans [*sic*] who finished in the gas chambers have the same story, or more exactly, have no story; they follow the same slope down to the bottom, like streams that run down to the sea. On their entry into the camp, through basic incapacity, or by misfortune, or through some banal incident, they are overcome before they can adapt themselves; they are beaten by time, they do not begin to learn German, to disentangle the infernal knot of laws and prohibitions until their body is already in decay, and nothing can save them from selections or from death by exhaustion. Their life is short, but their number is endless: they, the *Musselmänner*, the drowned, form the backbone of the camp, an anonymous mass, continually renewed and always identical, of non-men who march and labour in silence, the divine spark dead within them, already too empty to really

---

17. Cohen, *Human Behavior*, p. 116.

suffer. One hesitates to call them living: one hesitates to call their death death, in the face of which they have no fear, as they are too tired to understand…if I could enclose all the evil of our time in one image, I would choose this image which is familiar to me: an emaciated man, with head dropped and shoulders curved, on whose face and in whose eyes not a trace of a thought is to be seen.[18]

Among the reactions of those who managed, often by sheer chance, to stay alive were *regression* and *identification with the aggressor*. To repeat, for some these defensive reactions made survival possible. By regression, I mean 'reversion from a higher to a lower stage of development'.[19] The psychological relationship of these inmates to the SS was somewhat like that of very small children to parents. Survival depended upon the arbitrary and unpredictable will of the SS. Aggression was deflected away from the enemy back to the safe target, the self. For such victims, hatred toward the SS was largely absent. With a godlike power of life and death, the SS could and did compel compliance with even the most arbitrary commands. In many instances, traces of the inmate's adult status had been obliterated.

Anna Freud has observed that children often protect themselves from fear of attack by a mechanism of defense she calls *identification with the aggressor*. She writes, 'By impersonating the aggressor, assuming his attributes or imitating his aggression, the child transforms himself into the person making the threat.'[20]

Reduced to what the psychoanalysts characterize as an infantile level of emotional response, many camp inmates could only ward off anxiety by some measure of identification with those who were dedicated to degrading and annihilating them. The degree of identification varied. The sadistic Kapos identified most completely with the SS. Apparently, most prisoners identified to some degree with their tormentors.

Resignation
The final stage was reached when the prisoner resigned himself to camp life and death. Few of the prisoners reached that stage completely.

18. Levi, *Survival in Auschwitz*, p. 82.

19. Sigmund Freud, *Introductory Lectures on Psychoanalysis* (London: Allen and Unwin, 1949), p. 287.

20. Anna Freud, *The Ego and the Mechanisms of Defense* (London: International Universities Press, 1946), pp. 118ff.

Those who did were usually Kapos or criminals. Some Jewish Kapos exhibited anti-Semitism too thoroughly imitative of the German model. H.O. Bluhm concluded that in the camps identification with the aggressor 'was a means of defense of a rather paradoxical nature: survival through surrender; protection against the fear of the enemy—by becoming part of him; overcoming helplessness—by regressing to childish dependence'.[21] Unhappily, in the camps the majority of inmates, with the exception of believing, religious Jews and those with unshakeable political or religious commitments, were so totally degraded that little of what Erik Erikson identified as ego integrity remained intact. This is an important reason why Job fails as a model for understanding the camps theologically. Admittedly, there were Job-like survivors like Elie Wiesel, but psychiatrists who have studied behavior in the camps and who possess first-hand knowledge of the subject have concluded that most inmates were so assaulted both emotionally and physically that they were incapable of maintaining a sense of their own ego-integrity and dignity. It is precisely this capacity that distinguishes Job in his trial before God and man. The Germans not only deprived their victims of their lives but sought to strip them of their dignity before administering the final blow. This was a deliberate policy toward men and women who were first dehumanized, then murdered with an insecticide, and finally disposed of through incineration as if they were so much refuse.

Job may have sat on a dung heap but he was not transformed into dung. The biblical authors of the book of Job portrayed the experience of radical misfortune as understood in their own time. In their worst nightmares they could not have imagined a descent into hell so total yet so rationalized and bureaucratic as the twentieth-century extermination camp. The experience of our times has exploded our ancient categories of the meaning and our understanding of both human suffering and human evil. The biblical authors do not fail to offer a meaningful model through lack of wisdom. They were incapable of anticipating the technological revolution of the twentieth century. They were unable to foresee that one of technological civilization's supreme 'achievements' in its pre-computer stage would be a heightened capacity to degrade and dispose efficiently of mega-quantities of human beings with no

---

21. H.O. Bluhm, 'How Did They Survive?', *American Journal of Psychotherapy* 11.1 (1948).

significant reactions on the part of most camp personnel, save the satisfaction of a job well done. To compare the extermination-camp experience with that of Job is understandable only as a defensive oversimplification. Unfortunately, such oversimplifications compromise our capacity realistically to cope with the demonic potentialities of contemporary technological civilization. Moreover, World War II technology anticipates only crudely the material and psychological capabilities available to would-be contemporary perpetrators of mass destruction. The technology of human waste disposal has more than kept pace with the production of superfluous human beings we call 'overpopulation'. The Germans have successfully demonstrated that mass human waste disposal is entirely practical and need have few adverse long-term reactions on its perpetrators. Incidentally, I see no evidence of a distinctive German proclivity to evil that sets them apart from the rest of humanity. Their distinction was that they were able to apply the fruits of technological civilization in this area more effectively than any other national community. As we have seen, in the Balkans and in Rwanda, neither the victims nor the perpetrators were the same as in World War II. The most terrifying thing about the Germans is not how different but how very much like the rest of us they are. Humanity in the twentieth century crossed a radically new moral threshold that biblical man in his simpler wisdom never anticipated.

Inutility of the Image of Job

I have suggested that biblical man objectified his conflicting feelings of intergenerational love and hostility in his images of God. Elsewhere I have sadly and reluctantly offered my reasons for arguing that biblical man's objectifications, though profoundly rooted in human psychology, can no longer be valid for us.[22] Biblical man could envisage God as the divine Father because he regarded the cosmos, for all of its hazards, as a place in which man could ultimately be at home. The family in biblical times was ultimately envisaged as cosmic in scope. Beyond earthly patriarchs, biblical man envisaged an Arch-Patriarch whose love, power and concern prevented any aspect of experience from being devoid of some measure of meaning. Even God's punitive anger had elements of consolation. An angry God remained a caring and a concerned God.

22. Richard L. Rubenstein, *After Auschwitz* (Indianapolis: Bobbs Merrill, 1st edn, 1966).

Moreover, the problem of reconciling the biblical God with Auschwitz is not a contemporary expression of the perennial problem of God and radical human evil. Would that it were that simple. The very idea of a fixed, unchanging category of evil is problematic in dealing with Auschwitz. As Peter Haas has argued, far from being contemptuous of ethical norms, both the perpetrators and the complicit bystanders acted in strict conformity with their ethic, the Nazi ethic, that held that, however dirty, difficult and unpleasant the task might be, mass extermination of the Jews and Gypsies was entirely justified. Haas argues that the Holocaust as a sustained effort was only possible because 'a new ethic was in place that did not define the arrest and deportation of Jews as wrong and in fact defined it as ethically tolerable and even good'.[23] I would add that an ancient theodicy was in place that regarded the extermination of the Jews as compatible with the benevolence of an all-powerful God and made possible the new ethic.

According to Haas, the Nazis offered the Germans a new definition of good and evil. He argues that the Holocaust was not an example of Hannah Arendt's 'banality of evil' but of the human capacity to redefine good and evil and act accordingly. This is because an ethic is a 'complete and coherent system of convictions, values and ideas that provides a grid within which some sorts of actions can be classified as evil, and so to be avoided, while other sorts of actions can be classified as good, and so to be tolerated or even pursued'.[24] Thus, any formal system that permits human beings to make such judgments, irrespective of the system's contents, is an ethic. The power of an ethic 'ultimately resides in the fact that it provides a system for judging every action in a coherent, non-self-contradictory and intuitively correct way'.[25]

We need not follow Haas in dismissing Hannah Arendt. I believe that Haas is on target in asserting that most Germans believed that they were carrying on a 'just war' against the Jews during World War II.[26] Never-

---

23. Peter Haas, *Morality after Auschwitz: The Radical Challenge of the Nazi Ethic* (Philadelphia: Fortress Press, 1988), p. 7.

24. Haas, *Morality after Auschwitz*, p. 3.

25. Haas, *Morality after Auschwitz*, p. 4.

26. Although I find simplistic Daniel Jonah Goldhagen's thesis that the central causal agent in Hitler's decision to annihilate European Jewry was *German* anti-Semitic beliefs about Jews, I nevertheless concur that there was widespread, if not

theless, as Arendt and others have pointed out, the kind of bureaucratic decisions that made Auschwitz possible had far more in common with the day-to-day decisions of normal banks, corporations, and government bureaus than with the great satanic personalities of the past.[27] People followed orders and did their job. The web of complicity involved all of Germany and almost all of the Germans. Was the old-school German general, of which there were a few, guiltless? His conquests made ever more Jews available to the SS, the *Ordnungspolizei* and the *Einsatzgruppen* for slaughter. Was the postman guilty for delivering government forms that made classification of the victims possible? Was the Reichsbank clerk guilty who recorded the influx of newly acquired assets? Was the railroad employee guilty who facilitated the transport of the victims? All were doing their job for their country in wartime. Who was not doing his job? Is there such a thing as guilt in a rationalized bureaucracy?

Auschwitz must be seen as one of the many potentialities of contemporary technological civilization. The real question is whether any inherited image of a providential God continues to make sense in the world of computers, the Internet, media manipulation, rationalized bureaucracy, organ transplants, interplanetary exploration and environmental spoliation. The art of the late twentieth century is largely the art of the technological world. One has only to compare its representative creators with those of earlier centuries to become aware of the extraordinary transformation in cultural and religious sensibility that has taken place. God is absent from contemporary art; not surprisingly, so too is man. I do not say this to fault the artist. The poet and the artist cannot help themselves. They must speak the truth as they find it. The world they describe is a world without God.

In conclusion, I would like to express very briefly some elements of

almost universal, support of the regime's exterminationist policies. Nevertheless, by stressing the *unique* character of German anti-Semitism, Goldhagen passes over the breadth of support the destruction of Europe's Jews had among political and religious elites throughout Europe and beyond. See Daniel Jonah Goldhagen, *Hitler's Willing Executioners: Ordinary Germans and the Holocaust* (New York: Vintage Books, 1997).

27. See Raul Hilberg, *The Destruction of the European Jews* (Chicago: Quadrangle Press, 1961); Richard L. Rubenstein, *The Cunning of History* (New York: Harper & Row, 1975); Hannah Arendt, *Eichmann in Jerusalem: A Report on the Banality of Evil* (New York: Viking Press, 1963).

my personal faith: 1 do not believe the world will long remain godless. Gods die; other gods arise to take their place. Already a rumor is heard that an old-new God is making his way among us. He cannot be found beyond the stars. He does not stand above the human drama in a mysterious righteousness that forever humbles men, as did the awesome God of Job. He does not annul suffering; he shares it. He is incarnate in human life, passion, bliss and forgetfulness. He participates in both the agonies and the ecstasies of men more completely than did the Christian Savior, who knew men's sufferings but not their joys. He has devotees among those who call themselves Jews and those who call themselves Christians. They require but a glance for mutual recognition. He has slumbered for centuries among the peoples of the Western world. Dionysus is reborn among us. He cannot reign alone. He requires the balancing presence of his brother Apollo. Together they offer men something infinitely more precious than the illusory promise of salvation and the reality of Auschwitz; they offer men the certitudes of mortality, the delights and the searing pains of human abundance. Given the institutional structure and history of the Western religions, Dionysus and Apollo will take upon themselves Jewish and Christian guises. Nevertheless, they will outlast both the God of Moses and the God of Jesus.

Author's Note
This essay was revised for inclusion in the present volume in July of 1999. Although I have changed much in this essay—originally written in 1969 and published in the *Union Seminary Quarterly Review* in 1970—I have left the last sentence intact as a record of where I stood 30 years ago, even though it expresses a radicalism that I no longer hold. I do not recant my insights concerning Dionysus and Apollo. I do, however, find them one-sided. There is a vast difference between the experience and understanding of a 45-year-old academic and a 75-year-old Chief Executive Officer of a complex university. If nothing else, a person in the latter position has a far greater understanding of the need for order, structure and continuity than did the younger theologian-intellectual. I most emphatically no longer believe that Dionysus and Apollo 'will outlast both the God of Moses and the God of Jesus'. Neither do I believe they will ever be brought low by the God of Moses, Jesus or Mohammed. Both the God of the Abrahamitic tradition and Dionysus/Apollo constitute legitimate objectifications of abiding

dimensions of the human condition. They survive because they continue to be relevant to human experience in depth.

Moreover, over the years I have come to stress the maternal element in divinity which in my case derives from insights to be found in the mystical tradition. The most succinct expression of this view is 'Everything proceeds from the One; everything returns to the One.'[28]

28. A more current expression of my views on the subject is to be found in the chapter entitled 'God after the Death of God' in Richard L. Rubenstein, *After Auschwitz* (Baltimore: The The Johns Hopkins University Press, 2nd edn, 1992), pp. 293-306.

JOB AND POST-HOLOCAUST THEODICY

Steven Kepnes

Earth do not cover my blood;
Let there be no resting place for my outcry (Job 16.18).[1]

The above words of Job resonate deeply with those who suffered during the Shoah. That the blood of innocent victims should not be covered, that the voices of outcry should be heard and the event of destruction not forgotten, these are the central requests of Holocaust dead and survivor alike. But these words that we quote are from an ancient text. The book of Job was probably written sometime in the sixth century BCE at the time of the Babylonian exile. This, of course, was an entirely different world than the world of twentieth-century Europe. Thus, from the outset, we must recognize the vast differences between the two worlds and the fundamental incommensurability between the Holocaust experience and the experience of Job (who may or may not have been an actual historical figure). Recognizing this fundamental difference should also make us aware that when we use Job as a resource to respond for those who suffered during the Shoah and for those who came after, we necessarily are forced to stress elements of the story that traditional interpretation may have ignored. In fact, contemporary interpreters who have created Joban responses to the Shoah have had to push the story in radically new ways. One could even say they have had to deconstruct the story in order to make it serviceable to their understanding of the proper theological response to the Shoah. Yet at the same time the best interpreters, like Martin Buber and Elie Wiesel, have followed in the tradition of their rabbinical forebears by always basing their interpretation on the language and symbols inherent in the text

---

1. Quotations from the book of Job are taken from the *Tanakh*, the Jewish Publication Society Version of the Hebrew Bible, unless preceded by 1955 to refer to the 1955 Jewish Publication Society Version.

itself. Thus, even though the content of what is said by post-Holocaust theologians is often so radical as to contradict traditional Judaism, the hermeneutic method conforms to traditional rabbinic interpretive practices and in this way must be seen in continuity with Judaism. Indeed, given that the Shoah represents a radical challenge to Jewish continuity both in physical demographic terms and theological terms, I would suggest that one reason Buber and Wiesel use the biblical text of Job to respond to the Shoah is to reassert Jewish continuity in the face of the radical challenge that the Shoah represents.

But why Job? What is it about the text of Job that makes it so serviceable for post-Holocaust theology? The power of the book of Job lies first in the depth, breadth and honesty of expression of human suffering. The first sentence of the book tells us that Job is *tam*. This is a Hebrew word which means both innocent and complete, simple and whole. In the case of Job it conveys the sense that Job is above all honest and direct and this means that he tells it like he sees it. And he sees it all: evil, injustice, the cruelty of human beings and the apathy of God. What we need first after the Shoah is honesty. And Job, the *'ish tam* ('simple/innocent man'), gives us honesty. But honesty, though it may require simplicity and innocence to relate does not come out simple. Job's simple honest outcry is expressed in a complex array of thoughts, emotions and vivid descriptions which require nothing less than poetry to be expressed. Thus we can call the book of Job 'the poetry of suffering' and as such it remains a resource not only for Holocaust sufferers but for other innocent victims as well.

Saying that Job presents the poetry of suffering is certainly saying a great deal yet still not enough. For as well as giving honest expression to his suffering Job reflects on his suffering and seeks reasons for it and understanding of it. In this sense the book of Job also presents a philosophy of suffering. Beyond this, Job thinks of his suffering in specific relationship to God. Indeed, though there are friends about him attempting to justify his suffering and console him, the real object of his words is God. Job is thus a theological work as well. Because he attempts to understand his suffering in the context of God's goodness we can properly call Job a work in 'theodicy', an attempt to justify the goodness of God in the face of unjust human suffering. As a work in theodicy the book of Job has, finally, a healing, life affirming and redemptive purpose. This goal, which is represented in the ending and its restoration of Job's family, wealth and social status, has been most controversial when the text is used to respond to the Holocaust. Indeed, because of the 'happy ending' many who have used Job in post-Holocaust theology end before the end with Job in God's presence but not yet restored to his former status. But I will argue that even the redemptive ending can and should be appropriated for post-Holocaust theodicy. For this ending contains the message of healing, affirmation of life, and the necessity to continue to fight for justice which must be the final legacy of the Holocaust in a yet unredeemed world.

The Prologue and its Questions

The Lord has given and the Lord has taken away;
Blessed be the name of the Lord (Job 1.21).

The Prologue of the book of Job sets up many of the most perplexing questions raised by the text. After establishing the simple purity and goodness of Job we see God allowing Satan to manipulate him into the cruelest of wagers. 'Lay your hand on all that he has…and on his bones and his flesh and he will blaspheme you to your face' (1.11, 2.5). Why does God allow himself to get so easily manipulated by Satan? Is God, in fact, manipulated by Satan or is the test really his own idea from the beginning? If we look at the text we see that it is, in fact, God who begins the discussion: 'Have you noticed my servant Job?' (1.8). Therefore, it could be said that God, who knows how Satan will respond, is the one who instigates the wager. This raises the big question of the book. Why does God want to make the innocent and good Job suffer? This question has clearly resonated with Jews who suffered in the Shoah. Like Job, they lost their possessions, social status, families and friends and suffered hunger and vast physical pain. Perhaps they were not as good and righteous as Job, but whatever their sins they could not warrant the senseless cruelty which they suffered. And how do they understand their suffering? Was Hitler, like Satan, manipulating God and world alike? Or worse, was God himself behind Hitler forcing his hand in the destruction of European Jewry? Richard Rubenstein, one of the most radical of post-Holocaust Jewish theologians, has suggested that the implications of the last two questions are so harsh and difficult to fathom, God causing the Holocaust, that they forced him to abandon a belief in God 'as the omnipotent author of the historical drama'.[2] Yet

2. Richard Rubenstein, *After Auschwitz* (Indianapolis: Bobbs Merrill, 1966), p. 46.

Job does not take this radical step; he accepts his fate and refuses to take the advice of his wife and 'curse God and die'. Instead, Job 'said nothing sinful' (1.10) and remained loyal to God. And perhaps it is because of this that he has been so important for Holocaust survivors and post-Holocaust theological reflection. Because Job's loyalty to God initiates a further question, a question of perhaps even deeper significance than the first theological question, and that is the human question. How could Job, who suffered so much, remain loyal to God and to life? How did Job muster the personal strength to go on after the tragedies he experienced? What strategies did he employ? Can we learn them, can we learn from Job how to not only survive but live after destruction?

In addition to these theological and human questions, the prologue raises issues of a stylistic nature which serve to complicate the book. The Hebrew of the prologue is simple prose and distinct from the complex poetry of the bulk of the text. We are introduced to timeless, mythic, almost fairy tale scenarios. 'There was a man in the land of Uz...'; 'One day the divine beings presented themselves before God'. God, Satan, Job—all are simply drawn one-dimensional characters. God is regal, distant and dispassionate; Job is saintly, emotionless and largely silent. The stylistic use of simple, formulaic descriptions and repetitions of scenes (compare 1.6-22 and 2.1-10) suggest that we are being presented not with real-life events and characters but, as the text itself suggests, with a parable designed to deliver a message. The contrast between the styles of the prologue and the poetic section of the text (chs. 3–41) has led some to suggest dual authorship and allowed others to take the interpretive path that I suggested earlier, to end before the ending when Job is restored. Yet others like Martin Buber[3] and Nahum Glatzer[4] have chosen to see the text as a whole and to use the stylistic differences to complicate and multiply the hermeneutical possibilities in interpreting the text. For if the prologue is stylistically simple the book as a whole becomes so much more complex when the prologue is placed alongside the body of the text. It allows us to ask the question, for example, why is Job so quiet in the prologue and at the

3.   Buber's writings on Job are found in two places: *The Prophetic Faith* (New York: Harper & Row, 1966 [1942]), pp. 188-202; and 'The Dialogue between Heaven and Earth', in N. Glatzer (ed.), *On Judaism* (New York: Schocken Books, 1967), pp. 214-27.

4.   Nahum Glatzer, *The Dimensions of Job* (New York: Schocken Books, 1969), p. 4.

epilogue (ch. 42) and so loquacious in the middle of the text? Why are the friends so compassionate in the prologue yet so cruel and insensitive later? Buber suggests that the prologue allows for not one or two but four different views of God and correspondingly four different answers to Job's questions.[5] The prologue, I would suggest, gives the text its massive scope, its epic quality. The prologue suggests that the questions that the text will address are the great questions, the timeless questions, which even with Job's answers will continue to be asked. Indeed, I would further offer that it is the genius of the text of Job to bring us to a particular moment of human suffering, which, as we see in chs. 3–41, is time and locale bound and, at the same time, universal to all human beings.

The Poetry of Suffering

Perish the day on which I was born (Job 3.1).

Jewish interpreters of the Bible learned early that they could unlock the meaning of biblical texts by attending to repetitions in language.[6] I have already noted the contrast between the silent Job of the prologue and the talkative Job of chs. 3–41. This contrast is hinted at in the text itself as ch. 3 begins. 'Job began to *speak* and *cursed* the day of his birth, Job *spoke* up and *said...*' (emphasis added). The Hebrew uses four different verbs of speech and thus is suggestive of what Job himself tells us, 'I will not speak with restraint' (7.11). Indeed, as I remarked in the opening of this essay, Job's power and the strength of the book as a resource to address human suffering lies in Job's decision to throw off restraint and give voice to his suffering. Thus he begins.

> Perish the day on which I was born,
> And the night it was announced...
> May obscurity carry off that night
> May it not be counted among the days of the year...
> Why did I not die at birth,
> Expire as I came forth from the womb?...
> Why does he give light to the sufferer
> And life to the bitter in spirit?
> My groaning serves as my bread;
> My roaring pours forth as water (3.1-24).

5.   Buber, *Prophetic Faith*, p. 189.
6.   Meir Weiss, *The Bible from Within* (Jerusalem: Magnes, 1984).

Here the dispassionate, silent and saintly Job of the prologue opens up to his own human suffering and bears witness to it for himself and others. One hesitates to use the expression 'the poetry of suffering' for fear of rendering Job's suffering beautiful. But as Buber has said, we would have to search long and far in world literature to find human suffering expressed so simply and profoundly.[7] Job does not 'curse God' (2.9) but, instead, he takes his clear and honest anger and curses the day of his birth and the very fact of his birth. The desire to be rid of life, to be rendered into oblivion and no longer to feel the physical and emotional pain is palpable. Job's very continued existence is suffering to him. His food is his own groaning, his outcry water which cannot quench his desire to be drowned: 'would that God consented to crush me' (6.8). Thus Job gives voice to his pain, his despair and his anger in speech after speech which are truly unique in biblical literature and in sacred literature in general. No wonder that his friends grew tired and moved from their respectful and compassionate silence in the prologue to arguing with Job and making apologies for God. Imagine your own reaction if you were actually faced with a Job speaking those words! The melancholy is difficult enough to hear by added to it is Job's rage. First toward the day of his birth, then toward his friends, then toward God, Job expresses the 'bitterness of his soul' (10.1). But it is obvious that this expression has a cathartic and curative dimension to it.

Unfortunately Job's friends are 'physicians of no value' (13.4) and 'sorry comforters' (16.2). Instead of listening to Job they spout platitudes, lecture at him, grow tired of his anger and protestations and, finally, condemn him. In fact, we can learn a great deal about how not to react to human suffering from Job's friends. Where the friends believe that Job's anger will 'tear him to pieces' (18.4) and seek to silence it. The expression of Job's anger is actually a key to allowing him to cope with his suffering.

Job's description of himself—'The neck of my tunic fits my waist' (30.18), 'My flesh is covered with maggots and clods of earth, my skin is rotten and festering' (7.5)—has an eerie resonance with descriptions of emaciated concentration camp inmates who were covered with mud, excrement and lice. Terrence des Pres has labeled the camp process of reducing inmates to mud and shit as an 'excremental assault'.[8] He

7.   Buber, *Prophetic Faith*, p. 188.
8.   Terrence Des Pres, *The Survivor* (New York: Oxford University Press, 1976).

identified its objective as depriving inmates of human dignity and increasing their sense of shame.

Job's poetry of his suffering chronicles the cruel social consequences of his tragedy and sickness. His friends read his sickness as a sign of sin, his relatives abandon him, his former servants ignore him, he is even 'repulsive' to his wife (19.17). These people follow the basic principle of retributive justice in the Torah (Deut. 11). God punishes the sinful and rewards the good. As Elihu puts it, God 'pays a man according to his actions' (Job 34.11). But one does not have to adhere to biblical notions of retributive justice to judge people according to their appearance and fate. It seems that there is always the hidden assumption that the misfortunate did something to deserve their fate. Certainly the victims of the Holocaust suffered from these assumptions which were rampant at the time of the Holocaust and persist until today. Thus one can still hear people say 'the Jews must have done something to warrant such hatred and murderous intentions'.

Job cannot help but contrast the reaction of young and old to him with his current state of affliction. Formerly, 'young men saw me and hid, elders rose and stood; nobles held back their words...and waited for my counsel' (29.9, 21). Now, his friends regard his words as 'idle prattle' (11.3); the elders ignore him and the young mock him and spit on him; he is the 'butt of their gibes' (30.9). Job's dignity has 'vanished like a cloud' (30.15), he is filled with shame (10.15). The condemnation of 'the people' (12.2) and the assault on his sense of dignity and pride compound Job's physical maladies with more suffering. But the immense strength of Job is seen in his ability to preserve his integrity despite his appearance, his pain, his shame and the universal disgust he evokes in the world. It is clear to Job, if to no one else, that he is the same person now as he was before and he clings to that self-perception despite the change which others perceive. Thus Job stands alone, by himself, still the honest and righteous *'ish tam* supported by himself and his thoughts alone as his only advocates (16.20; JPSV, 1955). And these thoughts still sing clear as the courageous voice of the innocent victim.

> Until I die I will maintain my integrity.
> I persist in my righteousness and will not yield;
> I shall be free of reproach as long as I live (27.5-6).

Job and God

Indeed, I would speak to the Almighty
I insist on arguing with God (Job 13.3).

And what of God with whom Job insists on arguing? What does Job want from God? Despite his ignorance of the wager which God makes with Satan Job clearly places the blame on God for his fate. 'The arrows of the almighty are in me; My spirit absorbs their poison' (6.4). Job's attitude toward God is complex and contradictory. He feels alternatively harassed and suffocated by God's wrath (30.21) and utterly abandoned, distanced and hidden from him (30.20; 23.6). At first Job responds with bitter anger at God but then slowly his emotional response turns more intellectual. For it is not only the loss of his family and friends, and wealth, health and social standing he loses, Job has lost his intellectual bearings. His worldview has been shattered, the center of his universe, God, no longer appears trustworthy. This is another form of suffering for Job, a deep philosophical suffering. Job knows that he is not only innocent but that he has done everything that his ethical traditions have asked of him. He has fed the hungry, clothed the poor, supported the orphan and lodged the wayfarer (ch. 31). Why must he suffer like a scoundrel? Job's actions invite comparison to the actions of God who comes out lacking. Why does not God act toward Job as he, Job, has acted toward the innocent sufferer? Nothing makes sense any longer to Job. As he looks at the world he sees that it is not only he that has been abandoned but so have other innocent victims. Thus in a very profound way Job questions God.

Why are times for judgment not reserved by the [Almighty] Shaddai.
Even those close to him cannot foresee His actions.
People remove boundary stones;
They carry off flocks and pasture them;
They lead away the donkeys of the fatherless…
They chase the needy off the roads…
They snatch the fatherless infant from the breast…
The souls of the dying cry out
Yet God does not regard it as a reproach.
…For all of them morning is darkness (24.1-17).

Life has become chaotic, wrong has become right, day night, injustice justice. And where is God, why does he not act? This litany of offenses against justice, this world turned upside-down, a world of no boundaries where everything is permissible, a Kingdom of 'endless night' is again evocative of the Holocaust. And Job's profound thinking through this situation has sparked some of the most trenchant post-Holocaust theology.

Job seeks a hearing before God, a moment in God's court, where he can plead his case, prove his innocence and be acquitted. He simultaneously knows that he cannot win his suit (9.2) yet insists on articulating it and thus shows that he never gives up on God and his justice. Job stands confronted by what Buber calls the 'rent at the heart of the world'[9] and a host of contradictions which he has no choice but to embrace.

Job continues to believe in justice in spite of an unjust God. And he believes in God in spite of his belief in justice. Thus Job can no longer have a 'single faith' and asserts instead what we could call a 'rent' theology. This is a theology of contradiction summarized by Job's immortalized words: 'Thou he slay me, yet will I trust in him' (13.15; JPSV, 1955). It is a theology 'in spite of' God for the sake of God, a theology of justice and right in spite of the fact that God has taken away what is just and right. Buber suggests that Job develops a theology 'in spite of'[10] logic, which is nevertheless true. It is true because it comes from the 'reality' of the 'living God'. And because of its reality Job cannot deny it. This theology is said as only the sufferer become poet or the poet giving voice to the sufferer could.

> As God lives who has taken away my right
> And the Almighty who has dealt bitterly with me,
> All the while my breath is in me,
> And the spirit of God is in my nostrils,
> Surely my lips shall not speak unrighteousness...
> Till I die I will not put away my integrity from me...
> For what is the hope of the godless
> Though he get him gain,
> When God takes away his soul
> Will God hear his cry? (27.1-9).

What a host of contradictions. A living God who 'takes away what is right'. An Almighty who 'deals bitterly' with a good man who declares that the spirit of this same God of unrighteousness is within him and therefore this man surely can only speak righteously! So that he then

---

9. Buber, *Prophetic Faith*, p. 192.
10. Buber, *Prophetic Faith*, p. 192.

declares that God only abandons the unrighteous and does not abandon the righteous. Even though the righteous man himself has been abandoned by God he hopes in God's righteousness. 'He believes now in justice in spite of believing in God, and he believes in God in spite of believing in justice. But he cannot forego his claim that they will again be united somewhere, sometime, although he has no idea in his mind how this will be achieved.'[11]

At this point Job has clearly arrived at a different understanding of God, justice and the role of humans in bringing justice to the world. Although he still voices nostalgia for his former simple faith in a God who 'watched over' (29.2) him and guided his way like a light shining over his head (29.3), his bitter experience has educated him with a more mature and sophisticated wisdom and 'source of understanding' (28.12). Job realizes that it is all far more complicated than he had originally thought. For Job, too, had naively assumed, like his friends, that the good are rewarded and the evil are punished. His experience brought him to contemplate the reverse that the evil are rewarded and the good punished but as an *'ish tam* he could not hold to that nihilistic proposition. Job readily sees that to give up hope, to declare the wicked the victor, to renounce God's power is, indeed, 'nonsense' (27.12). Job knows that 'the evil man's portion from God' (27.13) is, finally, 'a plague' but when and how his recompense is received is a mystery beyond him and can not be predicted by him. Similarly, the righteous will 'share the silver' (27.17) reward but how and when they receive it is also a mystery. Thus, the central issue of the text moves from Job's despair at the conquest of evil in the present moment to the issue of hope and the possibility of a future that is redeemable.

The basis for hope, and the ground for a redemption is, of course, contact with God. So that whereas Job first only wanted to have his case heard, now, Buber suggests, Job is moved to a more profound desire no longer to be heard and to hear, but to simply 'see' God and re-experience God's presence.

> He can only ask to be confronted with God. 'Oh that one would hear me!' (31.35)... As his motive he declares that he wants to reason with the deity (13.3); he knows he will carry his point (v.18). In the last instance, however, he merely means by this that God will again become present to him. 'Oh that I knew where I might find him!' (23.3)[12]

11. Buber, *Prophetic Faith*, p. 192.
12. Buber, *Prophetic Faith*, p. 193.

Thus God's 'answer' to Job does not come in resolving the intellectual contradictions and repairing the 'rent' in the world in which Job is caught. Indeed, God frustrates the intellectual question. 'Thou cannot understand the secret of anything or being in the world, how much less the secret of man's fate.'[13] The answer comes in the appearance of God to Job. When God appears to him Job compares his first youthful knowledge of God to 'hearing' and the second to 'seeing' directly. For Buber, the crucial turning point of the book of Job lies in this seeing. 'The abyss is bridged the moment [Job] 'sees' (42.6), is permitted to see again.'[14] This is why, when God appears and speaks out of the 'tempest' (38.1), Job ceases to pose his questions and 'repents in dust and ashes' (42.6). Job's answer is God's appearance and the reason for hope that it brings. 'The true answer that Job receives is God's appearance only, only this, that distance turns into nearness, that 'his eye sees Him' (42.5), that he knows Him again.'[15]

It is crucial for us to note the form in which God appears. God discloses himself out of the winds of nature and as the God of creation. God is revealed as the one 'who laid the foundations of the earth', who 'shut up the seas...made the cloud...caused the dayspring to know its place' (38.4-12). This is the God whose 'glory', as the psalmist says, is declared by the heavens and earth. God appears to Job as God of creation and nature and not God of history who 'brought Israel out of bondage in Egypt'. The God of creation does not intervene in history to repair its injustices. This God does not erase the pain and cruelty of human suffering. 'Nothing is explained, nothing adjusted; wrong has not become right, nor cruelty kindness. Nothing has happened but that man again hears God's address. The mystery has remained unsolved.'[16]

This means that the answer to Job is the answer of Job's life and the life of the natural world which still exists around him. Each living thing in its form and shape, the world as it was before Job's suffering, remains like the great seas that continually wash the shore, as Job's source of healing. Yet still Buber suggests, this God, creator and ruler of nature, is not without justice. His is not the retributive or compensating justice which Job and humans so desire but his is a 'distributive and giving' justice nevertheless. 'God, the creator, bestows upon each what

13. Buber, *Prophetic Faith*, p. 194.
14. Buber, *Prophetic Faith*, p. 194.
15. Buber, 'Dialogue between Heaven', p. 224.
16. Buber, 'Dialogue between Heaven', p. 224.

belongs to him, upon each thing and being, as far as He allows it to become entirely itself... He cuts the dimension of this thing or being out of "all", giving it its fixed measure, the limit appropriate to this gift.'[17] Thus the answer to Job's quest for human justice, to 'give everyone his due' is divine distributive justice which 'gives to everyone what he is'.

Through God's distributive justice, Buber suggests, Job is affirmed as who he is in his unique and full dimension as an *'ish tam*. What this means is that Job is affirmed by God not only in his simplicity and righteousness but in his voice of witness to his suffering and to the suffering of innocent others as well. In addition, Job is affirmed in his protest against suffering and even in his arguments and revolt against God. God justifies and vindicates not his own actions but those of Job. God condemns the friends who have failed to 'speak rightly' (42.7) about him and in the end he refers to Job as he referred to Abraham and his other true *nevi'im* (or prophets) as his *'eved'*, his servant.

Conclusions: The Epilogue and its Critics

> Thus the Lord blessed the latter years of Job's life more than the former (Job 42.12).

In conclusion it should be clear how Job, *'ish tam* and *eved Hashem* (wholehearted man and servant of God) has become servant of post-Holocaust theological reflection. Elie Wiesel has said that 'man raises himself to God by the strength of the questions he asks'.[18] And Job certainly asks the big questions which are relevant to the Holocaust. He may not supply all the answers but his questions remain our questions and we raise ourselves up by re-asking them with him. Why do the innocent suffer and the evil prosper? If God is good and powerful why does he not reward the righteous and punish evil? And if God is all powerful is he responsible for evil?

The Holocaust has shown us that despite the enlightenment and the advances of modernity the world as we know it remains as Job saw it: broken, rent and in exile. Vast discrepancies of injustice remain, the innocent suffer, the evil prosper and genocide persists. We cannot espouse the simple platitudes that good is rewarded and evil punished.

---

17. Buber, *Prophetic Faith*, p. 195.
18. Elie Wiesel, *Night* (New York: Bantam Books, 1986), p. 2.

To Holocaust survivors we cannot say, like Job's friends, that their suffering was deserved or that it was in any way 'good for them'. Job serves post-Holocaust theology because he provides an early precedent and stunning model for how to deal with vast losses that the Jewish community experienced in the Holocaust: don't be silent, give witness to it, protest, resist, even if resistance can only be verbal. In a post-Holocaust world where genocidal events continue to occur Job's activism has become a necessary model. Virtually all of the post-Holocaust theologians, including Richard Rubenstein, Emil Fackenheim, Irving Greenberg, Buber and Wiesel have come to this conclusion. We cannot passively wait and pray for God to intervene in human history to save the world. Job provides a model for us as someone who refused to accept his suffering. Going against century-long Jewish traditions of glorification of suffering and martyrdom,[19] post-Holocaust theologians have embraced Job's free protest and revolt against God and against his suffering, as well as his struggle and service for justice and for redemption of this broken world. Again, Buber's words perform a worthy summary.

> We, by that is meant all those who have not got over what happened [in the Holocaust] and will not get over it. How is it with us? Do we stand overcome before the hidden face of God like the tragic hero of the Greeks before faceless fate? No, rather even now we contend, we too, with God, even with Him, the Lord of being, whom we once, we here, chose for our Lord. We do not put up with earthly being; we struggle for its redemption, and struggling we appeal to the help of our Lord, who is again and still a hiding one.[20]

God remains, as he was a Job, 'a hiding one' whose mysterious ways we cannot divine but whose presence we perceive in the text of the Torah, in the majesty and beauty of nature, and in the continual creation of new life. For the Jewish community which stood nearly at the brink of biological extinction only 60 years ago, the recreation of Jewish lives by survivors themselves and the continual creation of new Jewish life in the diaspora and in Israel is welcome sign of hope. God still underscores our hope and sense of justice and right, but after the Holocaust we no longer seriously entertain the childish fantasy that God will fight

---

19. Emil Fackenheim, 'On Life, Death and the Transfiguration of Martyrdom', in *The Jewish Return into History* (New York: Schocken Books, 1978), pp. 234-51.

20. Buber, 'Dialogue between Heaven', p. 225.

our human battles for justice and the right. That responsibility lies with us as free and mature beings.

But if post-Holocaust theology eschews childlike fantasies of God as its protector and warrior what does it do with the epilogue and its fairytale ending of the restoration of Job's family? There is one obvious reading that interprets the victory of Zionism and the founding of the state of Israel as a contemporary restoration that parallels that of Job's second family. But most post-Holocaust theologians have rejected this view as an 'unacceptable'[21] affront and injustice to all the innocent victims who died in the Holocaust. Irving Greenberg has said 'six million murdered Jews have not been and cannot be restored'.[22] And Elie Wiesel has likewise refused the epilogue and demanded that Job not accept his new family in 'contentment' (42.17) without 'justice being done' for his first family.[23]

21. See Irving Greenberg's now classic article: 'Cloud of Smoke, Pillar of Fire: Judaism, Christianity, and Modernity after the Holocaust', in E. Fleischner (ed.), *Auschwitz: Beginning of a New Era?* (New York: Ktav, 1977). Greenberg has deemed the view that the state of Israel represents a Joban restoration of the families lost in the Holocaust as 'unacceptable' because it violates the fundamental principle which he established for post-Holocaust theology: 'No statement...should be made that would not be credible in the presence of the [1.5 million] burning children' who perished in the Holocaust (p. 23). Yet it must be said that Greenberg still sees the state of Israel as crucial for post-Holocaust theology because it represents 'the right to hope and speak of life renewed after destruction' (p. 55). Greenberg's discussion of hope affected my own thinking on the importance of hope in my concluding paragraph.

22. Greenberg, 'Cloud of Smoke', p. 34.

23. Elie Wiesel, 'Job: Our Contemporary', in *Messengers of God* (New York: Random House, 1976), p. 234. The refusal by Wiesel and Greenberg to accept the restoration of Job in the epilogue as meaningful for post-Holocaust theology follows a trend in much post-Holocaust theology, which Zachary Braiterman has called 'anti-theodicy' in his book *(God) After Auschwitz* (Princeton: Princeton University Press, 1998). My plea for an appropriation of the epilogue follows from my view that anti-theodicy is only theologically productive in relation to theodicy. Anti-theodicy has the danger of throwing us into nihilism and thereby granting Hitler and the Nazis what Emil Fackenheim has famously called a 'posthumous victory'. Both Job and God see that life and justice must finally be reaffirmed and that, to me, is the purpose of not only theodicy but of all theology. This brings me to another possible reading of the epilogue: Job knows that despite his own suffering and loss, his second set of children, if they are to live and thrive, must be provided with belief in justice, in divine goodness and in a future. This cannot be supported on anti-theodicy alone. Thus Job accepts God's restoration. Job does this

I would argue, however, that we still can and must claim the epilogue with its restoration of Job's children. But to do this we must see the epilogue, much like the prologue (in whose style it is written) as an 'unreal' mythical reality. More specifically I would suggest that we interpret the epilogue in futuristic, messianic terms. In this way the restoration of Job's family becomes that for which we hope and that for which we wait. Real historical time is the time of Job's real life before the epilogue. This time for Job and for Holocaust victims was so filled with suffering as to easily drown out hope. The Holocaust is such a massive challenge to our faith in God and in humanity that it threatens to immobilize us in fear and despair. In the face of this despair the Job of the epilogue gives us hope and the assurance that the struggle against evil and for justice will be successful. A message of hope thus emerges from Job as it does from virtually every book of the Bible. Despite all his suffering, Job's ability to persevere in protest is obviously tied to his belief that justice, God and reality will come together in the future. In a world in which innocent victims suffer, Job shows that belief and hope are not negligible commodities but are necessities which fuel the struggle for justice and the affirmation of life.

neither out of selfish desire for pleasure nor forgetfulness of his first family but out of responsibility to the living which he sees in front of his once more amazed eyes. This suggests that as post-Holocaust theology bears witness to the suffering of the Jewish dead and protests against the absence of God it also bears responsibility to the living and thus must generate a life-affirming, just, and hopeful Judaism for the Jews to live today and into tomorrow.

ZION'S CAUSE: THE PRESENTATION OF PAIN
IN THE BOOK OF LAMENTATIONS

Tod Linafelt

> The need to let suffering speak is the condition of all truth (Theodor
> Adorno).

Given the unsparing focus on destruction, pain and suffering found in
the book of Lamentations, one might expect that Adorno's dictum, cited
as the epigraph to this chapter, would be easily met by those who have
written on it. Of any biblical book, it is logical to expect that interpretations of the book of Lamentations would value the expression of pain, if
not as 'a condition of truth' then at least as a mode of discourse with
merit in and of itself. While this has been the case in the history of
interpretation of the book (and more specifically the history of Jewish
interpretation), critical readings in the modern era have almost unanimously attempted to tone down, expunge or belittle the language of
lament and anguish.[1]

The devaluing of the lament is, in my judgment, a strategy for 'surviving' Lamentations—that is, for the reader to somehow deal with the
pain and devastation represented by the book, especially as it challenges
the reader's theology or notions of how religious language should
properly sound. This reading strategy most often is manifested in the
passing over or dismissal of the most disturbing or accusatory passages
in favor of the few passages that seem to evidence hope through
penitence and a reconciliation with God. Thus the majority of modern
interpreters are eager to move quickly through chs. 1 and 2 in order to
light upon ch. 3. In chs. 1 and 2 of the book of Lamentations, Zion is
personified as a widow and a mother lamenting her suffering and

1. For an extended treatment of the history of Jewish interpretation of the book
of Lamentations, focused around the figure of Zion, see Tod Linafelt, *Surviving
Lamentations: Catastrophe, Lament, and Protest in the Afterlife of a Biblical Book*
(Chicago: University of Chicago Press, 2000).

perishing children. Her rhetoric is acutely urgent, in particular as it addresses God, from whom Zion demands a response on behalf of her children. In contrast to Zion, the suffering man of ch. 3 presents a decidedly less tenacious figure, one that seems to exhibit a more submissive posture toward suffering and a reticence to demand anything from God. Modern scholars have almost universally proclaimed ch. 3 as the 'high point'[2] or the 'ideological core'[3] of the book. By so doing, they evade the question of how the figure of Zion might challenge and/or enrich modern interpretive and theological discourse.

In other words, biblical scholars have focused on the *interpretation* of pain, and they have done so primarily by explaining pain and suffering as resulting from the guilt of the sufferer. Taking a clue, however, from modern literature of survival—that is, literature arising out of experiences of atrocity and mass murder such as the Holocaust—I want to explore what happens when we refocus interpretation of chs. 1 and 2 around the *presentation* of pain, thereby balancing the penchant of biblical scholars to seek explanation for suffering and instead offering a fuller and more nuanced reading of these chapters. Claims that suffering is a punishment for sin or that a submissive spirit is more important than the voicing of pain have become, at the end of the twentieth century (a century that Elizabeth Bishop has famously called 'our worst yet') increasingly untenable, if not patently indefensible. It is my conviction that the figure of Zion, by valorizing the presentation of pain over its interpretation, offers a powerful alternative model of biblical theology to the 'patient sufferer' of Lamentations 3.

The Figure of the 'Suffering Man' as a Model for Theological Interpretation

The focus of nineteenth- and twentieth-century Lamentations scholarship on the suffering man of ch. 3 is variously motivated. There are at least three perceivable biases at play in such a focus: (1) a male bias toward the male figure of ch. 3; (2) a Christian bias toward the suffering man based on a perceived similarity to the figure of Christ; and (3) a broader emphasis on reconciliation with God rather than confrontation.

Chapter 3 of Lamentations begins with the statement, 'I am the man.'

2. Delbert Hillers, *Lamentations* (AB; Garden City, NY: Doubleday, 2nd edn, 1992), p. 122.
3. Jeffrey Tigay, 'Lamentations', *EncJud*, p. 1375.

It is a phrase that could just as easily begin virtually every modern commentary on the book of Lamentations. Until the last decade or so, one could search in vain for citations in the scholarly literature of commentaries on the book written by women.[4] It is difficult to assess precisely how much the gender of an interpreter affects the nature of the interpretation, yet it seems clear that the maleness of the figure in ch. 3 has exerted an influence on the evaluations of male interpreters.[5] The field of modern critical scholarship has been dominated not only by men, but more specifically by Christian men, thus adding another bias in favor of Lamentations 3. Modern interpreters have not so much claimed that Lamentations actually refers knowingly to Jesus—as for example Justin Martyr did with Lam. 4.20 in his first apology, which he read from the Greek of the Septuagint as 'The breath of our life is Jesus Christ'[6]—rather they have associated the *type* of suffering and the sub-

4.   A notable exception is Hedwig Jahnow's monograph *Das hebräische Leichenlied im Rahmen der Völkerdichtung* (Giessen: Verlag von Alfred Töpelmann, 1923), which because of its forceful argument for the connection between the book of Lamentations and the *gattung* of the funeral dirge is ubiquitous in the literature.

5.   See for example the following representative statement by Delbert Hillers, *Lamentations*, p. 6: 'The book offers, in its central chapter, the example of an unnamed man who has suffered under the hand of God. To sketch this typical sufferer, this "Everyman," it draws on the language and ideas of the psalms of individual lament, a tradition quite separate from the national history. From near despair this man wins through to confidence that God's mercy is not at an end, and that his final, inmost will for man is not suffering. From this beginning in hope the individual turns to call the nation to penitent waiting for God's mercy.'

Were this the 1972 edition of Hillers's commentary one might more easily dismiss the gender-specific language as time-bound. Indeed, I think that it is clear by his reference to God's 'inmost will for *man*' that he has 'humanity' in mind as those to whom the strongman is held out as a model. However, it is also clear that in choosing the concept of an 'Everyman' to express what he considers to be the central message of the book, Hillers has effectively ruled out the possibility of using the figure of Zion to express such a message. One could debate whether his concept of an Everyman led him to see ch. 3 as the 'high point' of the book or that his valuing of ch. 3 came first and found expression in the concept of an Everyman. In either case, the results are the same: while an Everyman figure can be taken as a model for all 'humanity', the female figure of Zion cannot be construed as an Everyman.

6.   Justin then takes this reference to breath to refer to the human nostrils, which take the shape of a cross when one looks to the sky. My thanks to Tim S.F. Horner for the Justin comment.

missive response that they find in ch. 3 with what is perceived as a similar type of suffering and response in the passion narratives of the gospels.[7]

While it is clear in my judgment that both male and Christian biases have played a part in the ubiquitous preference for ch. 3 in modern readings of Lamentations, for the purposes of this article I am more concerned with another bias, which is shared by nearly all modern biblical interpreters, both male and female, Jewish and Christian. This third and more pervasive factor is the preference for submission and reconciliation vis-à-vis God. This preference is most characteristically expressed by a dual focus on the theological categories of guilt and hope. Robert Gordis writes: 'The poet shares a conviction in the righteousness and power of God, a trust in the saving virtue of repentance, and a faith that God's love will bring forgiveness and restoration.'[8] This statement serves as a good representative example of the dual focus on guilt and hope, inasmuch as it makes clear the connection between the

---

7. Consider the comments of W.P. Merrill in his commentary concerning the question of suffering addressed in Lamentations: 'Christian men and women, of course, have an answer which far surpasses any other, in that their leader, their Lord, their object of faith, is one who suffered so terribly that he cried out, "My God, My God...?"' (*IB*, p. 7).

It is little wonder that Merrill, like so many other interpreters, opines that only in ch. 3 do 'we sound the depth and approach the climax of this little book'. Merrill is writing, it should be pointed out, for an explicitly Christian audience, and thus perhaps one should not make too much of the connections suggested to Jesus Christ. But the fact that this Christian bias seeps subtly into what is normally thought of as more objective, critical scholarship can be seen in the important commentary of Hans-Joachim Kraus, *Klagelieder* (Neukirchen–Vliyn: Neukirchener Verlag, 2nd edn, 1962). Like so many others, Kraus deems ch. 3 to be 'the true highpoint of Lamentations'. In particular, Kraus is drawn toward the two 'individual laments' in vv. 1-33 and 52-66, which are not merely personal but archetypal in nature. Chapter 3 serves as a 'model' of suffering that goes beyond its original utterance to include the suffering of the larger community, represented for example in the first person plural voice of 3.40-47. Kraus explicitly relates the weaving together of collective and individual complaint in Lam. 3 to the way in which the Christian community's triumph over sorrow is inspired by and joined with the triumph achieved by Jesus' passion and death. The 'good news' that the Christian reader can expect to find in Lamentations comes on the heels of the 'rejection of grumbling' in favor of accepting the 'message of salvation' found in the overcoming of suffering.

8. Robert Gordis, *The Song of Songs and Lamentations: A Study, Modern Translation and Commentary* (New York: Ktav, 1974), p. 126.

two: there can be no hope without a recognition of guilt. So Renate Brandscheidt states in no uncertain terms: 'Before there can be a favorable response to the lament, one thing must be clear to the people: that YHWH has ordained the punishment on account of the sins of the people.'[9]

The utilization of the concept of guilt functions for interpreters as a way of retaining God as the *author* of the destruction—something that can scarcely be avoided when reading Lam. 1.12-15 and 2.1-9—while nevertheless relieving God of any ultimate *responsibility* for the disturbing results of the destruction: 'He is declared righteous in His judgment.'[10] Indeed, with the focus on guilt the destruction itself falls away nearly altogether. 'The lament does not concern pain as such; rather, pain is the backdrop for the recognition of guilt, which is the real issue of a lament.'[11] In such a strategy for reading there is no place for either the extensive descriptions of pain and destruction or the accusations of Zion toward God, both of which the reader encounters in chs. 1 and 2. The effect of this strategy can be seen in a recent study by Paul Ferris. Though admitting that the two main motivational elements for God to respond to the laments voiced by Zion are 'the tragic reversal of the glory of Zion' and 'Jerusalem's repentance', he elaborates only on the second of these and avers that 'the admission of guilt and acceptance of responsibility for the calamity appears quite frequently'. This claim is made despite the fact that the Zion figure mentions 'sin' or 'guilt' only twice (1.18, 22) and that her only statement of 'repentance' (1.20) is textually very uncertain. But on the basis of this evidence, Ferris goes on to declare that Zion's 'misbehavior' and 'mishandling of her heritage' is the main point of the laments in chs. 1 and 2, thus effectively bracketing out the much more pervasive descriptions of pain and destruction.[12] If admission of guilt represents a capitulation to God concerning responsibility for the destruction and the suffering it causes, then hope represents the reconciliation with God that follows on the heels of capitulation.

The desire for an admission of guilt and the need for hope in the

9. This is my translation from Renate Brandscheidt, *Gotteszorn und Menschenleid* (Trier: Paulinus-Verlag, 1983), p. 212.

10. Paul Wayne Ferris, Jr, *The Genre of Communal Lament in the Bible and the Ancient Near East* (Atlanta: Scholars Press, 1992), p. 146.

11. My translation from Brandscheidt, *Gotteszorn und Menschenleid*, p. 231.

12. Ferris, *Genre of Communal Lament*, pp. 145-46.

midst of even the most intense suffering come together in the emphasis on an attitude of submission, of an acceptance of pain as either deserved or somehow beneficial, which then is presented as a model of behavior for readers both ancient and modern. Commenting on the transition from the first person singular of the suffering man in the opening of ch. 3 to the first person plural in 3.40, Alan Mintz writes that 'the appearance of the "we" at this point implies that the recovery of the solidarity of community is contingent upon an awareness of sin and a commitment to a turning back to God'.[13] Thus the behavior of the suffering man becomes the model for a recovered communal voice. Likewise, Delbert Hillers's 'Everyman' of ch. 3 is portrayed as a paragon of 'patient faith and penitence, thus becoming a model for the nation'.[14] For Brandscheidt, the model of the suffering man shows that lament is 'a stance unbecoming for the truly pious'.[15] Ewald, cited approvingly by Hillers, extols the virtues of the male figure insofar as he is able to 'come to a proper recognition of his own sins and the necessity of repentance, and thereby to believing prayer'. Ewald goes on to write:

> Who is this individual who thus laments, reflects and prays!—whose 'I' unnoticed but at exactly the right point changes to 'We'? O man, he is the image of your own self! Everyone should speak and think as he does. And so it comes about, unexpectedly, that just through this discourse which is most difficult at its beginning, for the first time pain is transformed into true prayer.[16]

More subtly, when Gottwald articulates what he calls the 'theology of hope' found in Lamentations he writes that the book 'inculcates' in its readers a 'submissive spirit'. Gottwald goes so far as to claim that 'in Lamentations we come upon the most outspoken appeals for submission to be found anywhere in the Old Testament'.[17] But all the examples he cites as support for such a far-reaching claim come solely from vv. 25-33 of ch. 3. Gottwald admits briefly that the figure of Zion does

13. Alan Mintz, *Hurban: Responses to Catastrophe in Hebrew Literature* (New York: Columbia University Press, 1984), p. 36.

14. Hillers, *Lamentations*, p. 122.

15. My translation of Brandscheidt, *Gotteszorn und Menschenleid*, p. 36: 'Damit sind die anklagenden Partien V.1-16 und 17-20 [of chapter 3] als ein für den Frommen inadaquates Verhalten erwiesen worden.'

16. Cited in Hillers, *Lamentations*, p. 123.

17. Norman Gottwald, *Studies in the Book of Lamentations* (London: SCM Press, 1954), pp. 104-105.

not quite fit this characterization, 'for she is much more concerned with the bitterness of suffering and the pangs of sin', but in the same paragraph he nevertheless asserts that 'an intimation of *suffering that is purposeful is the central teaching* of Lamentations, the axis around which all the confessing and lamenting revolves'.[18] Such a central teaching must be gleaned from ch. 3, since in chs. 1 and 2, especially in those sections attributed to the figure of Zion, the notion that suffering may have a purpose is scarcely on the horizon.

The three primary biases in modern interpretation of Lamentations identified above have worked together to ensure that readings, and especially *theological* readings, have focused on the male figure of ch. 3 to the exclusion of Zion. The Zion figure is quite obviously not male, does not dovetail easily into a typological Christian interpretation, and can hardly be characterized as modeling a submissive spirit toward suffering. Consequently, chs. 1 and 2 of Lamentations are given short-shrift, are forced into the categories of guilt and hope whether they fit or not, or are simply denigrated as inferior to ch. 3.[19]

The Figure of Zion as an Alternative Model

Evaluating the role played by pain in the literature of survival, especially that coming out of Nazi and Stalinist death camps, Terrence Des Pres writes:

> One of the strongest themes in the literature of survival is that pain is senseless; that a suffering so vast is completely without value as *suffering*. The survivor, then, is a disturber of the peace.[20]

Such an evaluation is very different from how pain and suffering are treated by biblical scholars, who seem over-eager to make the move from the fact of pain to the recognition of guilt and subsequently to repentance. I submit that viewing Lamentations 1 and 2 from the per-

---

18. Gottwald, *Studies in the Book of Lamentations*, p. 107; emphasis added.

19. There are a few notable exceptions to this tendency to focus on the suffering man among recent interpreters. See for example the work of Claus Westermann (considered more fully below), as well as F.W. Dobbs-Allsopp, *Weep O Daughter of Zion: A Study of the City-Lament Genre in the Hebrew Bible* (Rome: Editrice Pontificio Instituto Biblico, 1993), and Iain Provan, *Lamentations* (New Century Biblical Commentary; Grand Rapids: Eerdmans, 1991).

20. Terrence Des Pres, *The Survivor: An Anatomy of Life in the Death Camps*, (Oxford: Oxford University Press, 1976), p. 42.

spective of the literature of survival enables one to perceive aspects of the presentation of suffering in Lamentations that have been obscured by the theological presuppositions of biblical scholars.

The survivor's desire to witness to pain rather than to find meaning in it can be seen clearly in the speeches of Zion in chs. 1 and 2. Especially striking in this regard are the two initial interruptive statements by which personified Zion enters the poetry as a speaking subject.

> See, O LORD, my suffering—
>   how the enemy triumphs (1.9c).
> See, O LORD, and pay attention—
>   how abject I have become (1.12c)[21]

These imperatives to YHWH represent the beginning of a strong move in Lamentations away from the death represented by the genre of the funeral song (which has held sway in the poetry up to this point) and toward the drive for life represented by the genre of lament (which dominates the poetry from this point on). Such a move, however, is not easy or automatic, but proceeds through the survivor's acute experience of suffering. Such suffering must be 'seen', in the words of Zion. The lament requires that the experience of the one lamenting be looked at and acknowledged.

The importance of this requirement that suffering and pain be acknowledged is demonstrated by the compounding of imperatives in the beginning of Zion's first speech in Lamentations 1. The single imperative in 1.9c for YHWH to 'see' (ראה) becomes the double imperative in 1.11c for YHWH to 'see and pay attention' (ראה והביטה). This double imperative is then immediately repeated (in an inverted form) to the passers-by in 1.12:

> Pay attention and see![22]
> Is there any pain like my pain,
>   like my continual suffering?

---

21. Unless otherwise indicated, all translations from the Hebrew of the biblical text are my own.

22. I leave out the initial Hebrew phrase of the verse, לוֹא אליכם, though I admit this is not a completely satisfactory solution to the perennial problem it has presented translators. Nevertheless, the words do represent an anacrusis, falling outside the 3:2 meter of the rest of the verse. Obviously they are an interjection, though whether originally directed by Zion to the passers-by (and thus original to the text) or by an editor to the reader (and thus a gloss that has made its way into the text) seems finally undecidable.

Which the LORD inflicted on me,
on the day of his wrath? (1.12)

The five imperatives in a row, combined with the double repetition of 'pain' and the use of the harsh verbs 'suffering' and 'inflict', lend a rhetorical significance to Zion's presentation of pain *as pain*, rather than as the raw material for ruminations on guilt. As long as the voice of the poet holds the reader's attention in the opening verses of ch. 1, the pain of Zion has been kept at arm's length. Not only is her suffering described in the third person, but the poet is wont to make sense of Zion's suffering with reference to her sins (1.8), rebelliousness (1.5) or impurity (1.9). The irruption of first-person misery into the poem via the voice of Zion, however, defers all such sense-making. Zion is, to use Des Pres's phrase, a 'disturber of the peace' in that she will not let the subject of her suffering be settled so easily. Unlike the poet in 1.1-11, Zion makes little correlation between her sins and her suffering. Zion's first speech in 1.12-16, outside of one textually very uncertain phrase in 1.14,[23] contains no reference to sin whatsoever. In other words, there is no attempt here to interpret or explain suffering.

Instead of explanations for suffering, one finds in the Zion's speech an accusation against God combined with a terrifying description of misery. The command to 'see' gives way in 1.13-15 to the description of what may be seen, as the character of Zion gives concrete detail to fill out her general statement in v. 12 that YHWH has afflicted her. While the poet tended to focus in vv. 1-11 on the human agents of destruction—referring repeatedly to foes, enemies, betrayers, despisers, invaders in the temple, and exile among the nations, but only once naming YHWH as the subject of affliction—Zion repeatedly names YHWH as the one who afflicts and she repeatedly attributes active verbs of violence to YHWH.

In this section one begins to feel more keenly the import of the author's use of the poetic technique of personification to convey the destruction of a city, as the language of actual physical pain that can be

---

23. The Masoretic Text's *niśqad `ōl p^eśā`ay* has proven very perplexing for commentators throughout the centuries. Hillers, *Lamentations*, p. 73, proposes emending the phrase slightly to read *niśqad `ōl p^eśā`ay*, resulting in the statement that 'watch is kept over my steps'. The emendation makes good sense in the context of v. 14, though the evidence he marshals for it is by no means definitive. It nevertheless points to the difficulty of reading the text as it stands.

experienced only by living beings pervades the accusation against God. Thus, in 1.13 Zion portrays herself as being attacked by YHWH the warrior, who catches her feet in a net and hurls her backwards. Fire, no doubt a vivid image in reference to the destruction of cities, is said in this verse to penetrate to the very bones of Zion. At the same time as the personification allows for the presentation of the pain of the city itself, it also allows one to continue to speak of the suffering of the inhabitants of the city, who are portrayed as the children of personified Zion (בחורי, v. 15; בני, v. 16). The first speech of Zion presents to the reader the sheer fact of pain, told from the perspective of a figure who has survived that pain. It leads to a climax in v. 16:

> For these things I weep... My eyes, my eyes!
>> They stream with tears.
> How far from me is one to comfort,
>> one to restore my life.
> My children are ravaged,
>> for the enemy has triumphed.

Zion's lament is that of a survivor—one who has lived through death and destruction—culminating with a mother's wailing over the loss of her children.

It is important to note that the character of Zion, for all her challenging of YHWH, never claims complete innocence. Zion's lament in 1.18-22, following the brief interruption of the poet in 1.17, begins by acknowledging that 'YHWH is in the right' and that she has been 'rebellious'. And at the end of her speech in 1.22 she admits that YHWH afflicted her (עלל) because of her rebelliousness; though it must be noted that the admission is in the context of a call for a similar affliction on her enemies. Zion is, of course, not a completely autonomous figure divorced from the culture of lament characteristic of the ancient Near East in which the book of Lamentations was written. Zion is rather a literary persona created by an author who participated in that common culture, which included the notion of divine punishment on the basis of human misbehavior or disloyalty. While participating in these cultural and theological presuppositions, the author nevertheless saw fit to shift the focus of these poems away from the issue of guilt and toward the experience of pain and suffering, regardless of guilt. Even, for example, in 1.18-22 where the figure of Zion refers to sin and rebelliousness, the rhetoric continues to shift to the experience and extent of pain. Immediately on the heels of the admission of YHWH's 'righteousness' (or perhaps 'victory') in 1.18a come echoes of her earlier imperatives to the bystanders:

> Listen all you peoples,
>> notice my pain.
> My young women and my young men alike
>> have gone into captivity.

Also repeated from her earlier description of pain is the desertion of allies and the hunger of the city's inhabitants (1.19). The imperative for YHWH to see her distress is repeated in v. 20, as is the leitmotif 'there was no one to comfort me' in v. 21. Brief allusions to guilt in Zion's second speech thus give way to extended expressions of misery and desolation.

I do not mean to claim that the notion of guilt in the book of Lamentations or the ancient Near Eastern genre of lament is the same as that in twentieth-century literature of survival. I admit the very real differences between the two, even as I suggest that one might nevertheless learn something about Lamentations by reading it alongside twentieth-century survival literature. A brief comparison is thus in order. Des Pres writes:

> With very few exceptions, the testimony of survivors does not concern itself with guilt of any sort. Their books neither admonish nor condemn nor beg forgiveness; not because survivors are drained of their humanity, but because their attention lies wholly elsewhere.[24]

Compare this with the judgment of Westermann concerning Zion's admission of sin in v. 18.

> Just how important the acknowledgment of guilt is for Lam. 1 has already been shown (with ref. to vv. 5 and 9). Here, at the high point of the whole song, this motif is brought into conjunction with an acknowledgment of the justice of God's ways such that the whole preceding lament is set off: God *must* act in this way, because we have transgressed against his word.[25]

Des Pres is arguing against the prevalent concept of 'survivor guilt', the notion that those who have lived through atrocities such as mass murder are plagued by a sense of guilt over the fact that while so many others died, they somehow escaped alive. Des Pres does not claim that such

---

24. Des Pres, *The Survivor*, p. 44.
25. Westermann, *Lamentations*, pp. 135-36 (emphasis original).

guilt is non-existent, but rather that it is not the primary drive of survivor testimony, which is chiefly devoted to conveying the experience
of atrocity and survival. What Des Pres is arguing *against* in the reading of twentieth-century survival literature—the elevating of the single
theme of guilt to the status of an interpretive key—is precisely what
Westermann is *demonstrating* in his readings of the biblical laments.
Westermann has taken the element of guilt, which is undeniably present, and made it the lens through which all else is read. This element
becomes the 'highpoint' of the chapter and sets off 'the whole preced-
ing lament'.

Both Des Pres and Westermann likely overstate their cases. In the
current debate over the nature and extent of survivor guilt, Des Pres's
statement would no doubt need to be nuanced. As a biblical scholar,
however, I find that it offers a helpful corrective to the statement of
Westermann. The persona of Zion does indeed admit her sins or dis-
obedience. Such an admission is a genre convention of the lament, and
Lamentations 1 and 2 does not excise it. Yet rather than making her sins
the primary concern of her speeches, she admits them flatly and not
altogether wholeheartedly. Westermann's celebration of guilt as the
hermeneutical key to the entire chapter is unwarranted. Using Des
Pres's analysis to nuance Westermann's, it is clear that Zion, as a survivor, does not 'beg forgiveness'.

The insistence on the sheer fact of suffering, with little reference to
its deservedness or merits, becomes even more apparent in ch. 2 of
Lamentations. On the heels of Zion's utterances, which are densely
packed with the presentation of pain, the poet's language changes
significantly, leaving behind the interpretation of suffering in terms of
guilt and placing the focus on the presentation of divine wrath and
Zion's pain. In a stance similar to that of Zion, who in ch. 1 emphatically identified YHWH as the source of destruction, the poet (who has
inscribed himself into the poem almost as a character) now portrays
God as an enemy warrior in line after line. Verses 1-4, for example, are
a poetic whirlwind of fire and wrath. Verse 1: YHWH in 'his wrath'
(אפו) has shamed Zion, and has forgotten his footstool on 'the day of
his wrath' (אפו ביום). Verse 2: 'In his fury' (בעברתו) YHWH has razed
Judah's defenses. Verse 3: YHWH has cut down 'in blazing wrath'
(בחרי־אף) the horn of Israel, and has 'burned (יבער) against Israel like a
blazing fire (כאש להבה), consuming on all sides'. Verse 4: YHWH pours
out against Zion 'his wrath like fire (כאש חמתו)'. The English language

is exhausted in an attempt to describe the destructive inferno unleashed by the Lord's anger.

With its double use of 'swallowed up' (בלע),v. 5 serves as an introduction to the systematic dismantling of the city that follows. First, YHWH eradicates the public institutions in vv. 6-7, eliminating all public modes of access to God: YHWH's 'booth' and '(tent of) meeting' are destroyed, festivals and sabbaths are ended, the altar and sanctuary are rejected, and the temple desecrated. Secondly, YHWH demolishes the actual physical structures of the city in vv. 8-9a: walls and ramparts languish, gates are sunk into the ground with their bars smashed to bits. Thirdly, the conquered state of the inhabitants of the city are described in their abandonment by YHWH in vv. 9b-10: the king and the princes are exiled, the teachers of Torah are no more, the prophets receive no vision, the elders sit about in mourning, and the young women lower their heads to the ground. So while the opening speeches by the poet in both chs. 1 and 2 are similar in their description of misery, destruction, and death, there is a noticeable change in the poet's voice. Not only does the poet attribute the destruction to YHWH in ch. 2, but any reference to the sin of Zion drops away. This change in the persona of the poet, as he begins to conform more and more to the speech of Zion, leads into another element of the literature of survival that is manifested in Lamentations: the desire to *persuade* rather than simply to *report*. This aim of persuasion, while related to the present topic of the presentation of pain, warrants a treatment of its own and must be left for another time.

What emerges, then, as a result of re-reading Lamentations in terms of contemporary survival literature is an ancient text that, contrary to the consensus of biblical scholars, is more about the *expression* of suffering than the meaning behind it, more about the vicissitudes of *survival* than the abstractions of sin and guilt, more about *protest* as a religious posture than capitulation or confession. In the end this ancient text seems uncannily relevant to contemporary discourse on atrocity and those who survive it.

DEATH AS THE BEGINNING OF LIFE
IN THE BOOK OF ECCLESIASTES

Mark K. George

> No statement, theological or otherwise, should be made that would not
> be credible in the presence of the burning children.[1]

Scholars of the biblical wisdom literature have argued that the theological foundation upon which the wisdom literature rests is creation theology.[2] Perhaps most representative of this argument is Leo G. Perdue's *Wisdom and Creation*.[3] Perdue argues that the idea of creation theology and the corresponding notion of providence are at the center of the sages' ideas about God, humanity and the world.[4] By 'creation theology' Perdue has in mind the idea that the cosmos and humanity exist as a result of creation and that there is an order within the cosmos. God has given all of humanity the ability to become wise and to live a good, long life by using their perception and understanding of the cosmos to discern this order within creation. Creation, therefore, is the 'center' of wisdom theology, insofar as 'creation integrates all other dimensions of God-talk as well as anthropology, community, ethics, epistemology (both reason and revelation), and society'.[5]

For books such as Proverbs and Job, Perdue's arguments about the importance (even if not necessarily 'the center') of creation theology

1. Irving Greenberg, 'Cloud of Smoke, Pillar of Fire: Judaism, Christianity, and Modernity after the Holocaust', in Eva Fleischner (ed.), *Auschwitz: Beginning of a New Era?* (New York: Ktav, 1977), p. 23.

2. Israelite wisdom literature includes the canonical books of Proverbs, Job, and Ecclesiastes, as well as the apocryphal books of Sirach and Wisdom of Solomon.

3. L.G. Perdue, *Wisdom and Creation: The Theology of Wisdom Literature* (Nashville: Abingdon Press, 1994).

4. Perdue, *Wisdom and Creation*, p. 20.

5. Perdue, *Wisdom and Creation*, p. 35.

are appropriate. Proverbs is quite concerned with how a person, particularly a man, is to live, so that the person's life might be good, long and happy.[6] As such, creation theology, as that is conveyed in wisdom, functions in a positive sense and implies a positive outlook on life: there is an order to the world, one can discern it and, having discerned that order, one's life can be made better. The person who discerns the order in creation and then lives a life in accordance with that order is wise, while the person who does not discern that order, or who fails to live by it, is foolish. Creation also plays a significant role in the book of Job, for Job's complaints and accusations against God stem from Job's assumption of an order to the cosmos and the related idea that, because of that order within creation, there also is a system of justice in creation, with those who observe the order being blessed, while those who disregard or violate the order are cursed. Job questions the viability of that order and justice, but still assumes its existence (if not its validity). Thus, in both Proverbs and Job, creation theology is an important assumption, an assumption that is positive in its orientation toward life and the possibility of living life well.

In the book of Ecclesiastes, however, the idea that there is an order to creation, or at least that humans can discern an order and live their lives in accordance with it, is rejected. For Qohelet (the book's Hebrew title and the name of the speaker in the book; Eccl. 1.1), there *is* a general sense of order in creation (Eccl. 1.4-11; 3.1-8), but this is not to say one can live by this 'order', much less claim there is a predictable system of justice that rests on that order.[7] In fact, the only thing one can discern from this order is that one will die, for death comes to all, the wise and the foolish alike (Eccl. 2.14, 16). 'Vanity of vanities! All is vanity' (Eccl. 1.2).[8]

The rejection of the idea that there is an order in creation by which humans can live is an important reason why so many scholars have described Ecclesiastes as a skeptical wisdom book. When they approach the book of Ecclesiastes, scholars assume that Qohelet's views on life

6. On the male orientation of wisdom, see, for example, Carol Newsom, 'Woman and the Discourse of Patriarchal Wisdom: A Study of Proverbs 1–9', in P.L. Day (ed.), *Gender and Difference in Ancient Israel* (Minneapolis: Fortress Press, 1989), pp. 142-60.

7. The Hebrew word 'Qohelet' (or 'Qoheleth') is often rendered as 'Teacher' or 'Preacher' in English translations of this book.

8. All biblical quotations are from the NRSV unless otherwise noted.

and the world are, like the books of Proverbs and Job, grounded in creation theology and the corresponding positive idea that seeking wisdom and learning about creation enables people to better their lives and to live longer.[9] But this assumption is at odds with what Qohelet says in the book of Ecclesiastes. Qohelet's view is not that life is lived out as part of the order of creation, as part of a larger theological and philosophical system based on creation and the hopefulness that comes from discerning that order. Rather, Qohelet's views are predicated on the fundamental reality of death and the idea that, wise or foolish, death comes to all, and therefore life must begin from an awareness and acceptance of that reality. Death is the beginning of life in Qohelet, and it is death, not creation or providence, that frames and founds reality. I will argue, therefore, that Qohelet is not a skeptic. On the contrary, Qohelet is a realist whose understanding of life begins with the reality of death, finitude and the not-knowing that is death. Life must be enjoyed while one lives, because death comes to everyone, a reality of which the living are always aware (Eccl. 9.5). And it is this realistic awareness of the reality of death that makes the book of Ecclesiastes an appropriate book for a post-Holocaust age, a book that is, perhaps, 'credible in the presence of the burning children'.

Traditional Wisdom[10]

In the books of Proverbs and Job, to learn wisdom is to learn about the world and how the world is organized and ordered. Proverbs states that wisdom (in the form of Woman Wisdom) was created at the beginning of God's work, the first act of God (Prov. 8.22), and that wisdom was present with God when God created the heavens and earth (Prov. 8.27-31; cf. 3.19-20). According to Proverbs, therefore, wisdom is not just a

---

9.   The scholarly assumption about biblical wisdom literature being based on creation theology reveals another assumption, namely, that the use of creation theology results in a positive outlook on life (Perdue's 'correlative affirmation, providence'; *Wisdom and Creation*, p. 20). This second assumption betrays what I would call a type of Christian eschatological hope, the hope that life will, ultimately, triumph over death, and that this life will be one of blessings and goodness.

10.   The original impetus for my reading of Ecclesiastes came from a series of conversations I had with Dr G. Pemberton during his doctoral work. I wish to thank him for those conversations and for his suggestions on this essay after those conversations took this form.

part of creation but integral to it, and thus to learn wisdom is to learn about creation. The benefits of learning wisdom include such things as long life (Prov. 3.2, 16), dwelling in the land (always a concern in Israelite theology; Prov. 2.21), wealth and abundance (Prov. 3.10, 16; 22.4), honor (Prov. 8.18), and the ability to pass on one's wealth and inheritance to one's own (Prov. 5.10). Wisdom is to be sought as a means of avoiding strife (Prov. 1.26-27), poverty (Prov. 6.11), a loss of honor (Prov. 5.9), and a premature death (Prov. 2.18-19; 10.21; 11.19). In short, the book of Proverbs portrays wisdom as positive and beneficial for the wise because they have better, longer lives. Furthermore, death, or at least premature death, is avoided (if not warded off) by seeking wisdom and becoming wise.

A similar view of wisdom can be found in the book of Job. Job protests his treatment at the hands of God because he knows this treatment violates the system of justice God established in creation. This system is arranged so that a person who practices righteousness will receive blessings, while the person who practices wickedness will receive curses. In the midst of his suffering, Job protests the innocence of his own actions, that he is a righteous person, and therefore that his suffering is unjust. It is on the basis of his righteousness and innocence that he demands a trial of God (Job 13.3). Thus, although Job protests that the system of justice is not working for him, he nevertheless continues to believe in that system and trust its workings, otherwise he would not demand a trial with God. Being wise, practicing righteousness, and fearing God *should* bring a person blessings, even if that is not the case for Job himself in the midst of his suffering.

In a post-Holocaust age, the positivism of Proverbs and Job, at least to the extent that their use of creation theology leads interpreters to an unambiguous positivism about life and the world, is problematic, because it minimizes, if not ignores, the burning children of the Holocaust. Certainly post-Holocaust interpreters have found comfort in Job and the ambiguity of the book, but perhaps it is time to question the underlying positivism of creation theology in that book, and to acknowledge how problematic an ontology and epistemology based on creation theology can be in light of the Holocaust. Can such a fundamentally positive outlook on the world persist in a post-Holocaust age? This is where Qohelet's views on life, death and creation can be quite profound.

The Failure of Traditional Wisdom for Qohelet

Qohelet's belief in the impossibility of finding an order in creation by which a person can live is stated from the beginning of the book. The goal of wisdom—to discern how the world works—is pointless (it is 'vanity and a chasing after wind', Eccl. 1.14). Qohelet comes to this conclusion because he has actively sought out wisdom. Qohelet 'applied [his] mind to seek and to search out by wisdom all that is done under heaven' (Eccl. 1.13).[11] He observed the deeds done on the earth (Eccl. 1.14). He became exceptionally wise (Eccl. 1.16), not only pursuing wisdom, but also madness and folly (things a wise person would avoid; Eccl. 1.17). Being guided by wisdom (Eccl. 2.3), he indulged in every type of pleasure he could imagine (effectively engaging in hedonism; Eccl. 2.1-10). On the basis of his searching out wisdom, folly, madness and pleasure, Qohelet comes to the conclusion that all such endeavors are pointless: 'all is vanity and a chasing after wind' (Eccl. 1.14, 17; 2.11, 17). The search for wisdom is, Qohelet concludes, 'an unhappy business that God has given to human beings to be busy with' (Eccl. 1.13).

Even though Qohelet's judgment on wisdom is that it is vanity and a chasing after wind, there are several other places in Ecclesiastes where Qohelet appears to view wisdom as more positive.[12] For example, in Eccl. 2.13-14, Qohelet says, 'Then I saw that wisdom excels folly as light excels darkness. The wise have eyes in their head, but fools walk in darkness' (cf. also Eccl. 4.13; 7.5, 11, 12, 19; 8.1, 5; 9.15, 16, 17, 18; 10.2, 10, 12; 12.11). These 'positive' comments appear to suggest Qohelet is not in total disagreement with traditional wisdom. But appearances are deceiving, for these positive comments are drawn from traditional wisdom, and Qohelet cites traditional wisdom only to refute it (cf. Eccl. 2.14b, 26; 4.16; 7.14, 23-24; 8.7-9; 9.15b, 16b; 11.5; 12.1-

---

11. The scope of the fictional royal autobiography is disputed, but I agree with Seow's conclusions about where it ends (Eccl. 2.26), and thus follow him on this point (C.L. Seow, *Ecclesiastes* [AB, 18C; New York: Doubleday, 1998], pp. 117-58). For a fuller discussion of the genre of the fictional royal autobiography and Qohelet's use of it here, see Seow, *Ecclesiastes*, pp. 144-45. In general, I find Seow's comments on death in Qohelet to be supportive of my argument, although he does not see death as having the same central role in the book of Ecclesiastes.

12. On these and other contradictions in Qohelet, see Michael V. Fox, *Qohelet and his Contradictions* (JSOTSup, 71; Bible and Literature Series, 18; Sheffield: Almond Press, 1989).

8).[13] Traditional wisdom fails because of the reality of death, as I shall argue below. Thus, the wise may have eyes and the fools walk in darkness, but, 'I perceived that the same fate befalls all of them' (Eccl. 2.14b). Both wisdom and folly can lead to destruction and death (Eccl. 7.16-17). To the traditional wisdom claim that the wise will be blessed while the foolish will be cursed, Qohelet states there is no benefit to either the wise or the foolish, since they both die.

In terms of the biblical wisdom tradition, Qohelet is like the little child in the Hans Christian Andersen fairy tale 'The Emperor's New Clothes' who says what no one else is willing to say: 'The Emperor has no clothes!' Qohelet has joined the crowd to admire the emperor's new clothes; he has pursued wisdom and used wisdom to investigate everything 'under the heaven'. Having made his investigation, Qohelet boldly announces not only that he doesn't get it, but that there is nothing to get! The pursuit of wisdom is futile; it is 'vanity and a chasing after wind'.

Why Traditional Wisdom Fails

Qohelet gives three main reasons why he rejects wisdom as it is expressed in traditional wisdom. The first reason is that there is no order in creation by which one can live one's life. There *is* an order in the world, but it is not something by which people can live their lives. Generations go and come, but the earth remains (Eccl. 1.4). What Qohelet implies in this statement is that, if people could change the outcome of their lives by seeking wisdom, creation itself would change. But creation itself testifies that such is not the case: the sun continues on its course; the winds blow where they will; the waters from streams flow into the sea without filling it up; and neither the eye nor the ear are filled up (Eccl. 1.5-8). Nothing in creation is affected by humanity or wisdom: 'What has been is what will be, and what has been done is what will be done; there is nothing new under the sun' (Eccl. 1.9).[14] Qohelet cites a proverb to drive home his point that wisdom is of no use to human beings: 'What is crooked cannot be made straight, and what is lacking cannot be counted' (Eccl. 1.15). There is no value in seeking out wisdom and the order of creation because the 'order' of creation is a crooked one, and thus discerning that 'order' does not make any differ-

---

13. Seow, *Ecclesiastes*, pp. 153-54, also interprets these sayings as quotations by Qohelet.

14. See also Seow, *Ecclesiastes*, pp. 100-17, on this passage.

ence in one's life.[15] Likewise, Qohelet says, 'When I applied my mind
to know wisdom, and to see the business that is done on earth, how
one's eyes see sleep neither day nor night, then I saw all the work of
God, that no one can find out what is happening under the sun. However much they may toil in seeking, they will not find it out; even
though those who are wise claim to know, they cannot find it out' (Eccl.
8.16-17). God's ways and work cannot be discerned by seeking wisdom
(cf. Eccl. 7.24). There is, therefore, no way one can become wise, and
the pursuit of wisdom is doomed to failure.

The second reason Qohelet rejects wisdom is because it does not
deliver on its promises. Traditional wisdom asserts people are supposed
to shape or influence their futures by, among other things, leaving an
inheritance for their heirs (Prov. 5.10). Qohelet states this is impossible,
because people cannot control what happens after they are gone. 'I
turned to let my heart despair about all the toil that I toiled under the
sun, for there are people whose toil is for wisdom, knowledge, and
achievement, but to those who did not toil for it they give it as their
portion. This also is vanity and a great tragedy' (Eccl. 2.20-21).[16]
Despite people's best laid plans and attempts to control how their
estates and possessions are to be handled and divided, once they die,
their estates and possessions can and do end up in the 'wrong' hands
(i.e., in the hands of those who do not deserve these things). According
to traditional wisdom, such a thing is not supposed to happen, yet
Qohelet states that it does. When people die they leave everything
behind, including the ability to determine what happens to their possessions. 'As they came from their mother's womb, so they shall go again,
naked as they came; they shall take nothing for their toil, which they
may carry away with their hands. This also is a grievous ill: just as they
came, so shall they go; and what gain do they have from toiling for the
wind?' (Eccl. 5.15-16 [Heb. 5.14-15]). The world continues on the
same as before, unaffected by the presence of these generations and 'all
the toil at which they toil under the sun' (Eccl. 1.3; cf. also 3.22; 6.12;
7.14, 24; 8.7; 10.14).

Not only does wisdom fail to affect what happens after one dies, it
fails to help people even *before* they die. Traditional wisdom asserts

15. Cf. also Seow, *Ecclesiastes*, pp. 146-48, on Qohelet's use of this saying.
This saying may have been used in other contexts to comment on human beings,
but Qohelet uses it for his own purposes here.

16. Seow's translation (*Ecclesiastes*, p. 118).

that, if one seeks wisdom and becomes wise, then one will gain riches, which one will be able to leave as provision for one's children. Qohelet responds to this assertion by describing people who, though rich, lose their riches in 'bad venture[s]'. Even though these people have children for whom they should (or want) to provide after their deaths, they are unable to do so (Eccl. 5.13-14 [Heb. 5.12-13]). There is no possibility of shaping one's future or doing something new in the world, because 'It has already been, in the ages before us' (Eccl. 1.10). Wisdom is incapable of affecting life in the world or improving the life of the wise.

Death

The most important reason why wisdom is futile in Qohelet's view is the reality of death. Death frames the book of Ecclesiastes: at the beginning of the book, Qohelet states that generations go and come (that is, they die; Eccl. 1.4), while at the end of the book, Qohelet states that 'the dust returns to the earth as it was, and the breath returns to God who gave it' (Eccl. 12.7). Death is the great leveler of humanity. No matter who one is and what one does during one's life, everyone dies. '[T]he same fate comes to all, to the righteous and the wicked, to the good and the evil, to the clean and the unclean, to those who sacrifice and those who do not sacrifice. As are the good, so are the sinners; those who swear are like those who shun an oath. This is an evil in all that happens under the sun, that the same fate comes to everyone' (Eccl. 9.2-3; cf. 2.14). Regardless of who or what one is—wise, foolish, good, evil, clean, unclean, sacrificer, non-sacrificer, oath takers, non-oath takers—death comes to all, for death is not prejudiced in whom it will accept.[17] All are going to Sheol, the place of the dead (Eccl. 9.10). All are going to their 'eternal home' or grave (Eccl. 12.5).[18]

The reality of death and the fact that all die leads Qohelet to question why he is so very wise if in the end he will die, just as the fool dies (Eccl. 2.15). If wisdom enables one to live better, because one lives in accordance with the order of the world and creation, and if wisdom therefore enables one to shape and influence one's future (by living wisely), then why do the wise die just like the foolish? 'How can the wise die just like fools?' (Eccl. 2.16). Death renders wisdom futile.

17. Cf. Seow, *Ecclesiastes*, pp. 302-303.
18. On the translation of 'eternal home' as grave, see Seow, *Ecclesiastes*, pp. 364, 380.

Qohelet concludes that life for humans is nothing but a test by God, a test in which God demonstrates (convincingly?) to humans that they are nothing but animals (Eccl. 3.18). 'For the fate of humans and the fate of animals is the same; as one dies, so dies the other. They all have the same breath, and humans have no advantage over the animals; for all is vanity. All go to one place; all are from the dust, and all turn to dust again' (Eccl. 3.19-20). The supposed value of wisdom is ephemeral; in Qohelet's words, it is vanity, *hebel* (Eccl. 3.19). In the end, not only are people unable to change their lives or futures, they are unable to distinguish themselves from animals. Like animals, humans die, and both return to the dust from which they were formed. Once they are dead, no one knows whether or not the animating spirit within humans and animals goes to the same or to different places (Eccl. 3.21). What gain, therefore, is there in wisdom? The unborn and stillborn are better off than the living (Eccl. 4.1-3), because they do not have to see 'all the oppressions that are practiced under the sun' (Eccl. 4.1).

The Importance of Death for Qohelet

Qohelet's awareness and acceptance of the reality of death does not drive him to despair nor to consider life as not worth living. Death has a positive value for Qohelet, in a way not found in the books of Proverbs and Job. Qohelet does not believe the search for traditional wisdom will improve life, enable one to shape the future to some degree, and thus to postpone death. The only thing Qohelet knows for sure *is* death, and it is because of this certainty that death becomes the foundation for Qohelet's ontology and epistemology. Qohelet takes death very seriously as he thinks about life. Death is not something to be avoided or postponed, nor can it be, as traditional wisdom claims. Instead, death is something to be recognized, acknowledged and accepted, and life must be lived in light of death. Thus, Qohelet's statement that 'It is better to go to the house of mourning than to go to the house of feasting; for this is the end of everyone, and the living will lay it to heart' (Eccl. 7.2), reflects the centrality of death and its relationship to life in Qohelet's thinking. The house of mourning is, indeed, the end of everyone, for everyone dies and ends up in such a house. Likewise, the day of death is to be preferred to the day of birth (Eccl. 7.1), and the end of something preferred to its beginning (Eccl. 7.8), because, once death is accepted, then one can begin to live genuinely, without delusions about what can and cannot be done in one's life and lifetime.

Despite accepting the reality of death, Qohelet neither calls for or celebrates death, nor is Qohelet a nihilist. To recognize the reality of death and acknowledge one will die is different from seeking death or suggesting everyone commit suicide, as Qohelet himself makes clear: 'The living know that they will die, but the dead know nothing; they have no more reward, and even the memory of them is lost. Their love and their hate and their envy have already perished; never again will they have any share in all that happens under the sun' (Eccl. 9.5-6). It is one thing to know one will die, that death is coming, but it is another thing to be dead. There is nothing in death except death, the absence and end of knowing, and thus death is not to be rushed or desired over life.

Why, then, should people choose to live? Because, once one accepts the reality of death, one is free to live the life one has been given, and everyone is responsible for the life they have been given. One way Qohelet expresses this idea of freedom and responsibility is by the term 'portion', *ḥēleq*. 'Portion' occurs seven times in the book of Ecclesiastes (Eccl. 2.10, 21; 3.22; 5.18, 19 [Heb. 5.17, 18]; 9.6, 9), each time in the context of Qohelet's having declared the futility of wisdom (Eccl. 2.10-11, 21; 3.18-22; 5.13-17 [Heb. 5.12-16]; 9.1-10). 'Portion' conveys both the time and space each person has in life as well as the characteristics of that time and space. When he describes his pursuit of pleasure in Eccl. 2.1-11, Qohelet states that his heart 'found pleasure from all my toil. This was my portion for all my toil.'[19] Qohelet enjoys the pleasure in which he indulges, even if, in the end, it is not satisfying (he calls it a 'vanity and a chasing after wind'; Eccl. 2.11). 'Portion' also describes the space and time God gives to each person for life and work (Eccl. 5.18 [Heb. 5.17]; cf. also 2.21; 3.22; 9.6, 9). Some receive wealth and prosperity (Eccl. 5.19), while others receive hardship (Eccl. 2.26), but everyone should accept and enjoy that which they have received (Eccl. 3.22). Life, work (or toil), wealth, possessions, enjoyment; all these things are portions given by God. Qohelet says everyone must accept that portion of life and work that they have been given by God, without trying to manipulate what they have received. Having been given their portion by God, everyone is free to enjoy it (cf. Eccl. 2.24; 5.18, 19, 20; 7.14; 8.15; 9.7; 12.7), but they also are responsible to God for what they have been given: 'For God will bring every deed into

---

19. Author's translation.

judgment, including every secret thing, whether good or evil' (Eccl. 12.14). Beginning from the reality of death, then, Qohelet counsels the enjoyment of life:

> Go, eat your bread with enjoyment, and drink your wine with a merry heart; for God has long ago approved what you do. Let your garments always be white; do not let oil be lacking on your head. Enjoy life with the wife whom you love, all the days of your vain life that are given you under the sun, because that is your portion in life and in your toil at which you toil under the sun. Whatever your hand finds to do, do with your might; for there is no work or thought or knowledge or wisdom in Sheol, to which you are going. Again I saw that under the sun the race is not to the swift, nor the battle to the strong, nor bread to the wise, nor riches to the intelligent, nor favor to the skillful; but time and chance happen to them all. For no one can anticipate the time of disaster. Like fish taken in a cruel net, and like birds caught in a snare, so mortals are snared at a time of calamity, when it suddenly falls upon them (Eccl. 9.7-12).

Death as the Beginning of Life

In his book *The Gift of Death*, the philosopher Jacques Derrida discusses the question of responsibility.[20] Responsibility requires that a unique person, a subject who is finite and irreplaceable, act.[21] Derrida argues that, in a technological civilization (such as modern Western civilization), responsibility is difficult, if not impossible, to find because technological civilization has lost the idea of the unique self. 'The individualism of technological civilization relies precisely on a misunderstanding of the unique self. It is an individualism relating to a *role* and not a *person*.'[22] The problem with a civilization based on roles rather than persons is that roles do not act responsibly; it is persons (individuals as subjects) who, in the process of performing specific roles and functions, act responsibly. Given that responsibility requires a unique person to act, it would appear responsibility is impossible in a technological civilization. Derrida, however, argues that the construction of a unique person *is* possible in a technological civilization because of the reality of death.[23] It is the fact of each person's death that

20. J. Derrida, *The Gift of Death* (trans. D. Wills; Chicago: University of Chicago Press, 1995).

21. Derrida's discussion of responsibility clearly draws on the work of other philosophers, including M. Heidegger (see ch. 2 of *The Gift of Death*).

22. Derrida, *The Gift of Death*, p. 36 (italics original).

23. Derrida draws heavily on Heidegger's *Being and Time* at this point to make his argument (*The Gift of Death*, pp. 39-46).

makes possible a unique self. Each person dies, and each person's death is, therefore, unique. No one else can die in place of a person, in the sense that, by dying for that person, the person can become immortal.[24] Death is a singular act, something that can be experienced only by oneself, and thus death forms the basis of a unique self. It is the mortality and finitude of each person (both of which are made realities because of each person's death) that make possible unique individuals.[25]

The creation of unique selves, however, requires that each person accept the reality of death. By recognizing and accepting the reality and uniqueness of one's own death, as a death that is absolutely one's own, one takes one's own death upon oneself and is responsible for that event which no one else can experience. Taking one's death upon oneself, giving oneself the gift of death and living in relation to that reality, is what creates a unique self. Taking one's death upon oneself also is a responsible act; indeed, it is the original responsible act. This is because, in so doing, one has accepted that which no one else can experience.[26]

Derrida's discussion of death and responsibility provides one way of understanding why Qohelet begins with death and views death as the beginning of life. In Derrida's argument, to recognize, accept and take one's death upon oneself is to acknowledge that one's finitude and mortality are uniquely one's own; they are realities of a person's life that cannot be given or taken by another and therefore make each person unique. '[O]nly death or rather the apprehension of death can give this irreplaceability, and it is only on the basis of it that one can speak of a responsible subject, of the soul as conscience of self, of myself, etc.'[27] Furthermore, acknowledging the reality of death is not to call for one's suicide, since suicide is not necessary for establishing one's uniqueness and irreplaceability. One must live in relation to one's own death, that is, live one's life having recognized and accepted the reality of one's own, unique death, to live a responsible life.

Derrida's arguments about living in relation to one's own death echo those of Qohelet, who also, as I demonstrated above, calls for recognizing and accepting the reality of death, without calling for people to commit suicide; there is a time for everything, and no one has power

24. See ch. 3 of *The Gift of Death* for Derrida's discussion of sacrifice (a dying for, in the sense of 'in place of', another).
25. Derrida, *The Gift of Death*, pp. 41-42.
26. Derrida, *The Gift of Death*, pp. 43-45.
27. Derrida, *The Gift of Death*, p. 51.

over the day of death (Eccl. 3.2; 8.8; cf. also 9.5-6). Once one accepts the reality of one's death, then one can accept one's portion in life and enjoy it (Eccl. 9.1-10). By accepting one's portion in life, one finds freedom and responsibility. One is free to enjoy one's life and not worry about seeking wisdom, for such pursuits are futile. Likewise, accepting one's death makes one responsible for the portion of life one has been given by God (Eccl. 9.7-10).

Nevertheless, in a post-Holocaust age, Derrida's work does not go far enough. No longer can one simply recognize, acknowledge and accept the reality of one's *own* death and leave it at that. Determining subjectivity in terms of the self alone, without regard for another, for the Other, that one who is absolutely different from oneself, is what made the Holocaust possible. In a post-Holocaust age, therefore, the creation of a unique self cannot stop with one's own death, but must also take into account the Other.

The work of Emmanuel Levinas suggests one way in which the reality of the Other can be understood in the creation of a unique self.[28] Levinas argues that subjectivity arises in the encounter with the Other, that being who is absolutely other than oneself, whose reality and subjectivity is other than one's own.[29] Thus, individuals do not exist alone; they exist in relation to the Other, for it is in that relation with the Other that the distinction of the Self becomes possible.[30] Furthermore, in the encounter with the Other one not only becomes a distinct subject, one also experiences responsibility, specifically as responsibility for the Other. Ethics, therefore, is created in the encounter with the Other, for in encountering the Other one is put under an obligation to respond to that Other.[31]

Levinas's ideas about the relationship of the self to the Other are suggestive for how to read Qohelet in a post-Holocaust age. How is life possible after the Holocaust, given the reality of so many who died in it? By constructing one's identity through the recognition, acceptance, and taking upon oneself not only the reality of one's own death, but

28. Derrida also provides a response to this question; see chs. 3 and 4 of *The Gift of Death*.

29. Emmanuel Levinas, *Totality and Infinity: An Essay on Exteriority* (trans. A. Lingis; Pittsburgh: Duquesne University Press, 1969).

30. Levinas, *Totality and Infinity*, p. 26.

31. See Levinas, *Totality and Infinity*, for a fuller discussion of his ideas about this aspect of his work.

also the reality of the deaths of all those who died in the Holocaust. It no longer is possible (if it ever was possible) to create subjectivity on the basis of oneself alone, for such constructions lead to sharp distinctions between 'Self' and 'Other', to what separates me from you, and ignore the fact that 'I' only exist in relation to 'you'. If who and what one is, one's subjectivity, is understood as dependent on another, on the Other, then the ability to construct one's identity independently of the Other is removed. What affects the Other affects oneself. Thus, it is not only one's own death one must take upon oneself, but also the death of the Other, for the death of the Other is the death of oneself. Similarly, responsibility and ethics are made possible when one takes upon oneself both one's own death *and* the death of the Other.

Given this understanding of subjectivity, the death that Qohelet calls one to acknowledge is not simply one's own death, but the death of all, for wise and foolish alike die (Eccl. 2.16; 9.3). Death is an all-inclusive phenomenon. Thus, the death one must acknowledge and accept is not only one's own, but the deaths of everyone, including (in a post-Holocaust age) those who died in the Holocaust. This means, therefore, that the freedom and responsibility one has as a result of accepting death are not simply a freedom and responsibility for oneself, but a freedom and responsibility for all. The freedom each individual has to enjoy life is a freedom derived from taking on the deaths of all those who died. Likewise, the responsibility one has for one's portion of life and work is a responsibility not only to oneself or to God, but also to all those who died in the Holocaust. In a post-Holocaust age, Qohelet's argument that death is the beginning of life leads to the awareness that death includes not only one's own death, but also the deaths of all those who died in the Holocaust. Life in a post-Holocaust age is not only lived for oneself, but also for the Other, as life lived in relation to the Other.

SUGGESTIONS FOR FURTHER READING

The following short bibliography includes only books or articles that raise *explicitly* the issue of how the Holocaust might affect biblical interpretation. Thus, many worthy treatments of more general religious or theological themes in relation to the Holocaust are not included. Concerning the latter, a good starting point is the volume *Holocaust: Religious and Philosophical Implications* (ed. John K. Roth and Michael Berenbaum; New York: Paragon House, 1989).

Books

Beal, Timothy K., The Book of Hiding: Gender, Ethnicity, Annihilation and Esther (London: Routledge, 1997).

Blumenthal, David R., *Facing the Abusing God: A Theology of Protest* (Louisville: Westminster/John Knox Press, 1993). See especially the section entitled 'Text-ing', pp. 55-189.

Fackenheim, Emil, *The Jewish Bible after the Holocaust: A Re-reading* (Bloomington: Indiana University Press, 1990).

Linafelt, Tod., *Surviving Lamentations: Catastrophe, Lament, and Protest in the Afterlife of a Biblical Book* (Chicago: University of Chicago Press, 2000).

Neher, André, *The Exile of the Word: From the Silence of the Bible to the Silence of Auschwitz* (Philadelphia: Jewish Publication Society, 1981).

Plank, Karl A., *Mother of the Wire Fence: Inside and Outside the Holocaust* (Louisville: Westminster John Knox Press, 1994). See especially ch. 2, 'Eve of the Boxcar', pp. 42-57, and ch. 3, 'Leaves from a Newer Testament', pp. 58-102.

Wiesel, Elie, *Messengers of God: Biblical Portraits and Legends* (New York: Summit, 1976).

—*Five Biblical Portraits* (Notre Dame: University of Notre Dame Press, 1981).

—*Sages and Dreamers: Biblical, Talmudic, and Hasidic Portraits and Legends* (New York: Summit, 1991).

Articles

Fackenheim, Emil, 'New Hearts and the Old Covenant: On Some Possibilities of a Fraternal Jewish-Christian Reading of the Jewish Bible Today', in James Crenshaw and Samuel Sandmel (eds.), *The Divine Helmsman: Studies on God's Control of Human Events* (New York: Ktav, 1980), pp. 191-205.

Jacobs, Steven L., 'Wrestling with Biblical Texts after the Shoah', *Shofar* 15.1 (1996), pp. 80-94.

Knight, Henry F., 'Wrestling with Two Texts: A Post-Shoah Encounter', *Shofar* 15.1 (1996), pp. 54-79.

Linafelt, Tod, 'Damages Due to Fire: Levinas, the Bible, and the Holocaust, *Semeia* (2000).

—The Impossibility of Mourning: Lamentations after the Holocaust', in Tod Linafelt and Timothy K. Beal (eds.), *God in the Fray: A Tribute to Walter Brueggemann* (Minneapolis: Fortress Press, 1998), pp. 279-89.

—'Mad Midrash and the Negative Dialectics of Post-Holocaust Biblical Interpretation', in Gerhard Bodendorfer and Matthias Millard (eds.), *Bibel und Midrasch* (Tübingen: Mohr Siebeck, 1998), pp. 263-74.

Moore, James F., 'Thinking the Tradition Anew: A New Reading of Genesis 32 and Matthew 26 in Light of the Shoah and Dialogue', *Shofar* 15.1 (1996), pp. 13-37.

Rubenstein, Richard L., 'The Meaning of Torah in Contemporary Jewish Theology: An Existentialist Philosophy of Judaism', in *After Auschwitz: History, Theology, and Contemporary Judaism* (Baltimore: The Johns Hopkins University Press, 2nd edn, 1992), pp. 113-29.

Sweeney, Marvin A. 'Reconceiving the Paradigms of Old Testament Theology in the Post-Shoah Period', *BibInt* 6.2 (1998), pp. 142-61.

INDEXES

INDEX OF REFERENCES

OLD TESTAMENT

Genesis		20.1-17	198	4.27-35	155
1	113	20.13	113	4.31	155
1.2	222	21–23	55	4.35	155
2	113	21.37	216	6.16-18	155
4.10	161, 167	22.28-29	149, 150,	6.17	155
9.8-17	198		159	7.6	155
17.1-7	198	33	219	7.7	155
17.15-16	198	33.23	114	7.8-9	155
17.18	122			7.14-18	155
18	219	Leviticus		7.23	155
18.16-33	141	1–7	146, 154,	7.26	155
18.20	141		156-60	7.31-36	155
18.22	141	1.1-17	154	9.24	15
18.25	143	1.5	154	10	15, 18, 23
18.33	144	1.9	155	10.1-2	15
19	139, 144	1.10	154	10.3	16, 17
22	23, 146-	1.12	154	16	212
	51, 158,	1.13	155		
	159	1.14	154	Numbers	
22.1-14	147	1.15	154	14	219
22.1	114, 147	1.17	155	21.4-9	198
22.2	147, 148,	2.1-6	155		
	159	3	155	Deuteronomy	
22.6	148	3.3-4	155	4	169
22.7	148	3.9-10	155	4.9	161, 166,
22.12	147, 148	3.14-15	155		167, 170
22.13	147	3.16-17	155	4.10	169
22.15-18	148	4.3-12	155	4.12	169
22.16	148	4.10	155	5.17	113
22.18	149	4.12	155	11	258
22.19	147, 148	4.13-21	155	27.19	114
		4.20	155	30	170
Exodus		4.21	155	30.15-18	170
3	114	4.22-26	155	30.19	161, 167,
4	114	4.26	155		170, 171

Judges
19–21   178, 181,
                183, 186,
                187, 191
19.2   179
19.22   178
19.25-26   179
19.29   185
20.5   184
21.16   186
21.20-23   186

1 Samuel
4.4   212

2 Samuel
6.2   212
7   197, 200
7.1-11   197
7.16   197
12.1-15   212

1 Kings
3.16-28   212
5.12   229

2 Kings
16   214
19.15   212

1 Chronicles
13.6   212

Job
1.6-22   255
1.8   254
1.10   255
1.11   254
1.21   236, 254
1.25   254
2.1-10   255
2.4-5   237
2.8   31
2.9   257
3–41   255, 256
3.1-24   256
6.4   259
6.8   257

6.22-23   238
6.24   238
7.5   257
7.11   256
7.13-15   237
9.2   260
9.22-24   239
10.1   257
10.15   258
11.3   258
12.2   258
13.3   259, 261,
                283
13.4   257
13.15   260
13.18   261
16.2   257
16.18   252
16.20   258
18.4   257
19.17   258
23.3   261
23.6   259
24.1-17   259
27.1-9   260
27.5-6   258
27.12   261
27.13   261
27.17   261
28.12   261
29.2   261
29.3   261
29.9   258
29.21   258
30.9   258
30.15   258
30.18   257
30.20   259
30.21   259
31   219, 259
31.35   261
34.11   258
38.1   262
38.4-12   262
39.4-5   241
42   256
42.2-6   33, 241
42.5   262

42.6   262
42.7   31, 263
42.12   263
42.17   33, 265

Psalms
29   196
89   66, 67, 72
89.1-38   66
89.2   66
89.3   66
89.6   66
89.9   66
89.25   66
89.29   66
89.34   66
89.38   72
89.39-52   66
89.39   72
89.53   66, 72
99.1   212
132.7   212
137   32

Proverbs
1.26-27   283
2.18-19   283
2.21   283
3.2   283
3.10   283
3.16   283
3.19-20   282
5.9   283
5.10   283, 286
6.11   283
8.18   283
8.22   282
8.27-31   282
10.21   283
11.19   283
22.4   283
25.1   229

Ecclesiastes
1.1   281
1.2   281
1.3   286
1.4-11   281

Ecclesiastes (cont.)

Ref	Page
1.4	285, 287
1.5-8	285
1.9	285
1.10	287
1.13	284
1.14	284
1.15	285
1.16	284
1.17	284
2.1-11	289
2.1-10	284
2.3	284
2.10-11	289
2.10	289
2.11	284, 289
2.13-14	284
2.14	281, 284, 285, 287
2.15	287
2.16	281, 287, 293
2.17	284
2.20-21	286
2.21	289
2.24	289
2.26	284, 289
3.1-8	281
3.2	292
3.18-22	289
3.18	288
3.19-20	288
3.19	288
3.21	288
3.22	286, 289
4.1-3	288
4.1	288
4.13	284
4.16	284
5.13-17	289
5.13-14	287
5.15-16	286
5.18	289
5.19	289
5.20	289
6.12	286
7.1	288
7.2	288
7.5	284
7.8	288
7.11	284
7.12	284
7.14	284, 286, 289
7.16-17	285
7.19	284
7.23-24	284
7.24	286
8.1	284
8.5	284
8.7-9	284
8.7	286
8.8	292
8.15	289
8.16-17	286
9.1-10	292
9.2-3	287
9.3	293
9.5-6	289, 292
9.5	282
9.6	289
9.7-12	290
9.7-10	292
9.7	289
9.9	289
9.10	287
9.15	284
9.16	284
9.17	284
9.18	284
10.2	284
10.10	284
10.12	284
10.14	286
11.5	284
12.1-8	284
12.5	287
12.7	287, 289
12.11	284
12.14	290

Isaiah

Ref	Page
1–39	211
1–33	212
1.10-17	213
2.1-5	198
2.2-4	211
2.22	221
5.14	226
6.8	114
6.9-10	231
7	213
7.10-16	198
7.14	199
8.7-8	231
8.19	227, 228
11.1-10	198
13–23	211
21.2	211
28.2	231
28.8	231
28.10-13	232
28.11	231
28.13	231, 232
28.14-15	226
28.15	220
28.17	230
28.18	230, 231
28.22	232
35.1-10	198
36–39	215
36–37	214, 215
37.16	212
38	215
39	215
40–55	209, 211
40	197
40.1-11	196
40.1-2	216
43	86, 87, 97, 102
43.1-3	86
43.2	105
43.10	161, 164, 167, 168
44–45	211
44.9	102
45.1-3	210
46	211
49–55	204
50.4-9	198
51	210
53	177
55	216

55.3-5	216	1.4	278	3.52-66	270
56–66	211, 216	1.5	275, 277, 279	4.20	269
60–62	211, 216			5.1-16	272
61	197, 199, 200	1.6-7	279		
		1.8-9	279	*Ezekiel*	
61.1-4	197	1.8	275	20	146, 150, 151
61.8-11	197	1.9-10	279		
63.7–64.12	195	1.9	274, 275, 277	20.3	149
63.7-9	195			20.4-26	149
63.10-14	195	1.11	274	20.25-26	149, 159
63.10-11	196	1.12-16	275		
63.15-19	195	1.12-15	271	*Amos*	
64	197	1.12	274, 275	3.12–4.13	75
64.1-9	195, 199	1.13-15	275	3.12	72, 75
64.6	196	1.13	276	3.13-15	75
65.1	217	1.14	275	4.1-5	75
66.1	212	1.15	276	4.6-11	75
66.24	217	1.16	276	4.12	75
		1.17	276	4.13	75
Jeremiah		1.18-22	276	7.1-3	219
4.23-31	74	1.18	271, 277	7.4-6	219
4.27	74	1.19	277		
5.10	74	1.20	271, 277	*Micah*	
22.3	114	1.21	277	5.2-5	198
31.31-34	198	1.22	271, 276		
33.14-16	198	2	267, 268, 271, 273, 274, 278, 279	*Nahum*	
				1.2-8	196
Lamentations					
1	267, 268, 271, 273, 274, 278, 279	2.1-9	271	*Habakkuk*	
		3	267-70, 272, 273	3.1-5	196
1.1-11	275	3.1-33	270	*Zephaniah*	
1.1-4	278	3.17-20	272	3.14-20	198
1.1	278	3.25-33	272		
1.2	278	3.40-47	270	*Malachi*	
1.3	278	3.40	272	3.1-4	198

NEW TESTAMENT

Mark		*Luke*		*John*	
1	200	1	200	1.6-8	197
1.1-8	196	1.26-38	197	1.19-28	197
13.24-37	196	4.18-19	197		

Romans
5.18   234

1 Corinthians
1.3-9   196

Galatians
2.19-20   171

James
1.17   71

b. Qid.
39b   239

b. Šab.
55a   234

Talmuds
b. B. Bat.
14b   208
15a   238

Other Ancient References
Midrash
Gen. R.
49.7   141

Christian Authors
Justin
Dial.
51.220-21   203
79   203
123.261   203
142   203

Index of Authors

Abuyah, E. ben 144
Ackroyd, P. 214, 215
Adorno, T.W. 18, 34, 62, 75, 267
Allen, M. 157
Andersen, H.C. 285
Arendt, H. 146, 156, 157, 248, 249

Bag, B.B. 58, 60
Bakan, D. 235, 236, 238
Bar-On, D. 104
Barthel, J. 227, 230, 232
Bauer, Y. 144, 145
Bauman, Z. 87, 99, 105
Beal, T.K. 22
Beckett, S. 220
Bennington, G. 48
Berenbaum, M. 62, 87, 88, 139, 162, 163, 181
Bergen, D.L. 104
Berger, R. 157
Berkovitz, E. 88, 218
Bernasconi, R. 117, 188
Beuken, W. 231
Bishop, E. 268
Blanchot, M. 222, 232
Bluhm, H.O. 246
Blumenthal, D.R. 36, 88, 219
Bodendorfer, G. 36
Boer, R. 153, 160
Borowsky, I.J. 192, 199
Boutel, D. 130
Braiterman, Z. 88, 265
Brandscheidt, R. 271, 272
Brenner, A. 180
Briant, P. 210, 217
Bright, J. 193

Brockway, A. 77
Brueggemann, W. 65, 66, 199
Buber, M. 37, 39, 45, 252, 253, 255-57, 260-64
Budick, S. 69, 224
Bultmann, R. 77-79
Bumiller, E. 184

Calvin, J. 199, 203
Carter, W. 196
Celan, P. 220, 222-25
Charry, E.Z. 88
Christ, C. 99
Cixous, H. 222
Clements, R. 193
Clines, D.J.A. 227
Cochran, S. 195
Cohen, A.A. 88, 142, 232
Cohen, E. 242-44
Cohen, M. 130
Condillac, E.B. de 41, 42, 44
Crüsemann, F. 85

Dan, J. 69
Daniélou, J. 242
Davies, C. 189
Day, P.L. 281
Derrida, J. 37-47, 50, 70, 71, 221, 224, 225, 290-92
Dewey, A. 199, 200
Dietrich, D.J. 88
Dobbs-Allsopp, F.W. 273
Dohmen, C. 82, 83
Donaldson, J. 202
Dostoevsky, F. 240
Dozeman, T. 199

Elias, R. 182
Elieli, R. 162, 174
Ellis, M.H. 88
Eluard, P. 128
Erikson, E. 238, 246
Exum, J.C. 227, 229, 231
Ezra, A. Ibn 55

Fackenheim, E.L. 18, 36-41, 43-45, 47-
    51, 65, 70, 88, 119, 136, 137, 264,
    265
Faurisson, R. 144
Felstiner, J. 223
Fenichel, O. 237
Ferris, P.W., Jr 271
Fishbane, M. 68, 72, 205
Flax, J. 71
Fleischner, E. 88, 265, 280
Fowl, S.E. 65, 67, 71
Fox, E. 141, 142
Fox, M.V. 284
Frankl, V. 243
Freud, A. 245
Freud, S. 69-71, 158, 235, 245
Friedlander, A. 177
Friedman, M. 235
Fuchs, E. 182
Fuchs-Kreimer, N. 203

Garber, Z. 137
Gastfriend, E. 92
Gese, H. 230
Gibbs, R. 116
Giordano, R. 104
Glatzer, N.N. 242, 255
Goldhagen, D.J. 248, 249
Gordis, R. 270
Görg, M. 89, 90, 93, 96-102, 104
Gottwald, N. 272, 273
Gourevitch, P. 163, 168
Greenberg, I. 36, 62, 65, 88, 139, 264,
    265, 280
Grüber, D. 176
Gunn, D.M. 227
Gunneweg, A.H.J. 79

Haas, P. 248
Hahn, F. 93-95, 97, 99

Halpern, B. 228
Hand, S. 114
Handelman, S.A. 68-70
Hanson, P. 217
Hartley, J. 155
Hartman, G.H. 69, 224
Hauser, A.J. 227
Haynes, S. 205
Haynes, S.R. 88
Hays, R.B. 67, 204
Hegel, M. 220
Heidegger, M. 221, 224, 225, 229, 290
Heimannsberg, B. 104
Helmreich, W. 186
Hertz, J.H. 142, 143
Hilberg, R. 249
Hillers, D. 268, 269, 272, 275
Hirsch, E. 77, 78
Hirsch, S.R. 142
Holtschneider, K. 90
Horner, T.S.F. 269
Höss, R. 102, 103, 105

Inbody, T. 177
Irving, D. 144
Irwin, W.H. 227

Jabès, E. 121-34
Jacob, M. 128-33
Jacobs, S.L. 139
Jahnow, H. 269
Jameson, F. 148
Jones-Warsaw, K. 180, 186, 190
Jüngst, B. 88-90

Kaes, A. 87
Kaiser, O. 78, 79
Kant, I. 146, 149-53, 157
Kaplan, M. 182
Katz, S. 63, 88
Kee, H.C. 192, 199
Keefe, A. 179
Kellenbach, K. von 48, 49, 180, 182
Kierkegaard, S. 234
Kimhi, D. 55
Klein, C. 105
Klein, J. 210
Knight, H. 137

Kohn, J. 90
Koyré, A. 126
Kraus, H.-J. 270
Krell, D. 225
Kristeva, J. 220, 221, 226, 228
Krondorfer, B. 91, 92, 104

Lacan, J. 146, 151-54, 160, 226
Landau, D. 176
Langer, L. 181, 182, 186, 187
Langer, M. 89, 90, 93, 104
Levenson, J.D. 65, 147, 208
Levi, P. 243-45
Levinas, E. 29, 50, 106-20, 188-91, 292
Linafelt, T. 36, 37, 267
Littell, F. 137
Locke, H. 137
Lohfink, N. 83

MacCannell, J.F. 157
Manuel, F. 203
Marcus, J. 59
Marquardt, F.-W. 90
Maybaum, I. 178
McKenzie, S. 205
Melugin, R.F. 208
Merrill, W.P. 270
Metz, J.B. 90
Milgrom, J. 154
Millard, M. 36
Miller, A. 157
Miller, P.D. 66
Milton, J. 31
Minnow, M. 191
Mintz, A. 272
Miscall, P. 227
Mitchell, S. 147
Moltmann, J. 89, 90, 104
Moor, J.C. de 231
Moore, J. 137
Mouffe, C. 47, 49
Muilenburg, J. 69
Müllner, I. 180, 181
Mussner, F. 82, 83

Neher, A. 139
Neuman, G. 230
Neusner, J. 117

Newman, J.S. 87
Newsom, C. 281
Noth, M. 156
Novick, P. 172, 173

Oldenhage, T. 90
Osten Sacken, P. von der 90, 103

Panzani, A. 130
Patte, D. 200-202, 204
Pawlikowski, J. 192, 198
Penchansky, D. 65
Perdue, L.G. 280, 282
Perechodnik, C. 178, 183-86, 191
Plaut, W.G. 142, 143
Pope, M.H. 236, 237
Pres, T. des 257, 273, 275, 277, 278
Pritchard, J.B. 210
Proust, M. 24
Provan, I. 273

Read, D.H.C. 199
Reck, N. 89, 90, 100, 101, 104
Reinhard, K. 151
Rendtorff, R. 82, 83, 90
Ringelheim, J. 182
Rittner, C. 182
Roberts, A. 202
Rohls, J. 72
Rosenthal, G. 104
Roth, J.K. 62, 87, 88, 181, 182
Rubenstein, R.L. 51, 74, 88, 176, 218, 234, 247, 249, 251, 254, 264

Sandbank, S. 223, 224
Sanders, J.A. 208
Sarna, N.M. 142, 143
Schecter, S. 64
Schmidt, C.J. 104
Schottroff, L. 181
Schüssler-Fiorenza, E. 87
Seitz, C.R. 215
Seow, C.L. 284-87
Shakespeare, W. 220
Smith, R. 160
Söding, T. 82
Sölle, D. 90
Solotorevshy, M. 69

Spacks, P.M. 156
Spieckermann, H. 79
Stanton, G.N. 202
Stemberger, G. 82
Stern, E. 204
Stöhr, M. 90
Sweeney, M.A. 208, 211-13

Taylor, M.C. 225
Theissmann, U. 85
Thoma, C. 90
Tigay, J. 268
Toorn, K. van der 228
Tracy, D. 87
Trible, P. 178-80, 185

Vischer, W. 78

Wacker, M.-T. 181
Weinberg, J. 162, 163, 174
Weiss, M. 256

Wellhausen, J. 146, 203
Westermann, C. 66, 78, 147, 273, 277, 278
Whybray, R.N. 210
Wiesel, E. 22, 36, 59, 87, 173, 177, 234, 235, 241, 242, 246, 252, 253, 263-65
Wildberger, H. 214, 226-28
Williams, J.G. 230
Winnicott, D.W. 221, 226
Wood, D. 117, 188
Wyschogrod, E. 221, 225, 232

Young, J.E. 163

Zenger, E. 82, 83
Zimmerli, W. 149
Žižek, S. 149, 150, 153
Zuckerman, B. 148
Zundel, E. 144
Zupancic, A. 150